LABOR RELATIONS
IN THE PUBLIC SECTOR

LABOR RELATIONS IN THE PUBLIC SECTOR

Readings, Cases, and Experiential Exercises

Marvin J. Levine
Eugene C. Hagburg
University of Maryland

BRIGHTON PUBLISHING COMPANY
3163 Highland Drive • P.O. Box 6235
Salt Lake City, Utah 84106

196816

This book is dedicated to
the new scholars in labor relations.

CONTENTS

PART I:
THE EVOLUTION OF
PUBLIC SECTOR LABOR RELATIONS   1

PART II:
COLLECTIVE BARGAINING—STRUCTURE AND
PROCESS   159

PART III:
DISPUTE SETTLEMENT AND CONTRACT
ADMINISTRATION

CHAPTER 8. STRIKES AND THE JUDICIAL RESPONSE

CHAPTER 9. TYPES OF THIRD-PARTY INTERVENTION

CHAPTER 10. ADMINISTERING THE CONTRACT

CHAPTER 11. GRIEVANCE AND ARBITRATION MACHINERY

PREFACE

The purpose of this book is to provide stimulating contemporary ideas as expressed by a number of scholars in the field of labor relations. This collection of readings, cases, and experiential exercises may be used as a companion volume to our text *Public Sector Labor Relations*, West Publishing Company, 1979. Or it may be used alone if the teacher wishes to use it primarily with a discussion format. In order to facilitate the use of this book with our basic text, we have keyed it to our Labor Relations Model which focuses on three main phases in the process:

- Selecting the bargaining representative
- Negotiating the contract and disputes settlement
- Administering the contract

The teacher may extend the learning experience by assigning the readings which express various ideas, by analyzing the cases with the students, and by structuring a real-life learning environment with the experiential exercises.

We are indebted to the authors, researchers, and publishers who granted us permission to reprint the articles and ideas in this collection. Specific acknowledgment is accorded the authors in the introduction to each part of the book. We are grateful to these scholars for allowing us to use their views in this attempt to establish broader understanding of the dynamic aspects of evolving labor relations in the public sector.

Marvin J. Levine
Eugene C. Hagburg

INTRODUCTION

Public sector labor relations is becoming increasingly important in our society. The legal framework which emerges to guide it and the procedures and practices which the parties evolve are important to its success. But beyond such structures, there must be a maturity of attitudes if labor relations is to be as functional in the public domain as it has been in the private sector of our economy.

It is important to examine the ideas of a number of scholars in this field and to have these perspectives before us as we confront the daily reality so vividly communicated by the media. We may see firemen watching homes burn down as they pursue their labor relations goals, or nurses walking a picket line to achieve proper union recognition. Your local police may suddenly begin giving traffic tickets for everything as they carry out a planned slowdown, or air traffic controllers may catch the flu en masse and slow down air traffic. Sanitation workers might leave your garbage to pile up in your driveway, or the guards at a correctional facility might decide to withhold their services. It may be the postal employees who become reluctant to handle your mail unless collective bargaining works for them, or the teachers who carry out a strike action to effect an increase. There are a dozen other examples of the criticality of labor relations in the public sector. One conclusion is simple for all of us to arrive at: labor relations must work in the public sector or ours will become a disadvantaged society.

What now becomes important is the design of appropriate legal guidelines and administrative procedures, combined with a compatible attitudinal perspective to give labor relations a chance to serve us and reduce conflict among us.

This book looks at the broader options and is designed to facilitate understanding of the elements which may contribute to a more effective approach. The book contains:

> *Readings* intended to share a wide example of views on labor relations. They may discuss the relevance of a strike or quasi-strike or focus on alternative methods for disputes settlement.

Cases which focus on specific labor relations situations in a geographic area or in a particular organization. These cases may be used to better understand how the concepts of labor relations work or don't work in a given situation.

Experiential exercises which describe the emergence of a specific conflict situation in the labor relations context. It is a contemporary happening in the world of work when the interests of an employee, or group of employees, and management clash. These experiential exercises may be used as a basis for discussing the real world of labor relations. They will serve as a vehicle for the students' creativity.

In addition, we have provided our Labor Relations Model (Fig. 1) as a frame of reference for the many ideas which you will be trying to place in some systematic order as you read and discuss them. The model structurally represents the primary elements of the collective bargaining process which has evolved in the private sector of our economy. As public sector labor relations develops, it tends to adopt these elements piece by piece. The public sector appears to be reluctant to simply adopt the entire system as reflected in the model. This will become quite evident as you read the various articles and cases in this book.

FIGURE 1. THE LABOR RELATIONS MODEL

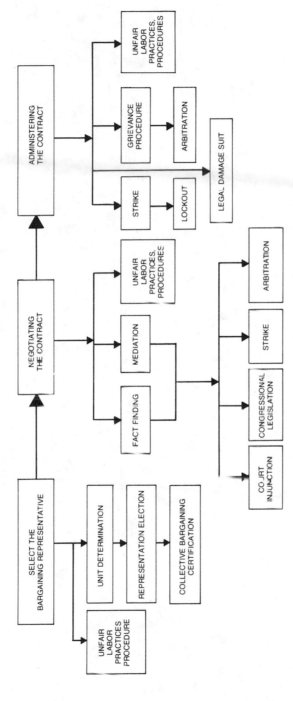

This model structurally represents the basic procedures available to the parties in a collective bargaining relationship. Such basic procedures have evolved out of labor-management conflict to facilitate the management of such conflict within society.

PART I

THE EVOLUTION OF PUBLIC SECTOR LABOR RELATIONS

PART I
THE EVOLUTION OF PUBLIC SECTOR LABOR RELATIONS

A common characteristic of our society is that institutions and individuals are resistant to rapid changes in existing organizational structures and interpersonal relationships. Friction and instability often are the products of such changes and persist until rational accomodations can be developed. Consequently, the almost kaleidoscopic sequence of events in public sector labor relations, particularly during the past decade, has produced a threat to the status quo in public employment, necessitating important adjustments on the part of governmental managers, unions, employees, and the public at large.

The two readings in Chapter 1 highlight the significant problem areas that have arisen due to these rapid developments in the public sector. Charles Redenius points out the basic differences between public and private sector collective bargaining, describes the negative results caused by the inexperience of the actors, and opposes third-party intervention to resolve disputes. He also discusses the difficulties created by political considerations and suggests a more uniform legal framework, within certain constraints.

A potential for conflict develops whenever a union representing federal, state, or local employees secures exclusive recognition and seeks to expand the scope of topics subject to negotiation in the face of civil service system prohibitions. Although originally devised to eliminate political patronage in public employment decisions, with merit ostensibly the sole criterion, civil service rules and regulations now cover many personnel functions. Wages, hours, working conditions, grievances, promotions, pensions, vacations, and so on are defined as excluded from the negotiations process. In the second offering, Charles Feigenbaum describes the impact of collective bargaining upon the merit system and the attendant erosion of management control over personnel policies and practices.

In Chapter 2, Louis Imundo details comparisons between

public and private sector labor relations and predicts continued pressure by public sector unions in their quest for equalization of bargaining rights with their private sector counterparts. He delineates the growth of private sector collective bargaining in the 1930's and 1940's and indicates that similar problems have arisen during the initial stages of public sector collective action.

The fact that public managers are also officials subject to the whim of the electorate interjects the political variable, which is lacking in private sector labor relations. In the opening selection in Chapter 3, Robert Helsby explains why and how unionized public employees take advantage of the political environment while other interest groups are only able to utilize the conventional lobbying approach to achieve their objectives.

Michael Mass and Anita Gottlieb next analyze the end product of the political process—legislation. They contend that the hodgepodge of state labor relations laws impedes rather than facilitates rational labor-management relations in the public sector and that uniform federal legislation would eliminate many of the negative results of the present legal framework.

Executive Order 10988, promulgated in 1962 during the administration of President John F. Kennedy, established a program of labor-management relations in the Federal government and is often credited as providing the stimulus for the rapid growth of unionism and collective bargaining at the state and local level. Milden Fox and Huntly Shelton conclude the third chapter by tracing the evolution of collective action in the federal service via a comparison of E O 10988 and its successor, E O 11491.

One group of public employees notable for their militancy has been public school teachers. Along with a desire for improved compensation and working conditions, they have exhibited increased dissatisfaction with their role in formulating educational policies and consider their status as professionals to be diminished by unilateral management decisions. Lester Vander Werf addresses these problems in the leadoff three-part reading in Chapter 5. Sol Elkin continues by supporting the premise that professionalism and unionization of teachers are not necessarily incompatible, and can assure the public of higher educational standards. John Maguire then describes the pattern of state professional negotiation statutes in an appeal for uniform federal legislation.

Recent strikes by police in several urban centers have pointed up the threat to the public safety which results from work stoppages by uniformed personnel. Hervey Juris discusses the chronological growth of police unionism and the social issues posed by the increasing militancy of these highly visible public employees.

Work stoppages by firemen have also increased sharply in recent years. Many fire fighters belong to the oldest national union at the state and local level, the International Association of Fire Fighters (IAFF), which affiliated with the AF of L in 1918. James Craft presents a succinct treatment of the range of bargaining strategies used by organized fire fighters in wage negotiations ranging from conciliation to coercion. He describes the influence of bargaining gains achieved by police upon fire fighter tactics and the evolution of fire fighter bargaining strategy over nearly half a century.

The first of the case studies in Part I is authored by I. B. Helburn, who indicates that de facto bargaining is practiced by municipal employees in Texas, a state where stringent legal barriers have been erected against public employee unionism and collective bargaining activities. However, his prediction that permissive legislation would be passed has not been borne out by subsequent events. A 1973 statute does grant police and fire personnel in local jurisdictions exclusive recognition and bargaining rights, prohibits strikes, and permits binding arbitration of bargaining impasses. However, each municipality must vote by public referendum to be covered by the law. All other employees are denied recognition, negotiations are prohibited and contracts are considered null and void. Yet some collective action has occurred in the face of these legal impediments.

In Case #2, John Schmidman describes the development of Pennsylvania's comprehensive public employee statute, which in 1970 became one of the first laws granting government workers a "limited" right to strike. His discussion centers upon the impact of the statute on the Pennsylvania Nurses Association and its membership. Initially viewed as a panacea, it turns out that the enactment, in its first year of operation, created far more problems than it solved for the state's nurses.

The final selection in Part I is an experiential exercise involving an actual nurses' strike at a hospital in a large metropolitan area which took place during the summer of 1978. Only the names of the city, the hospital, and the nurses' union remain confidential as a labor dispute in the health care industry is chronicled.

CHAPTER 1.
PROBLEMS AND PROSPECTS

Public Employees:
A Survey of Some Critical Problems on the Frontier of Collective Bargaining
Charles Redenius

The decade of the sixties saw the beginning of the shift in the thrust of the organization of labor from the private sector of the economy to the public sector. The seventies have seen an acceleration of that trend. The growth of public employee organization is even more dramatic when we contrast that growth with trends in union membership in the total labor force. Since 1960, membership in public employee organizations has more than doubled to almost five million. As of 1975, about one third of the public employee work force was organized.[1] By contrast, union membership as a proportion of the labor force has undergone a decline since 1953, falling from a little more than one fourth to a little over one one fifth.[2]

Given the prospect of the continued growth of public employee collective bargaining, the public sector will soon provide more than enough newly organized workers to offset and even reverse the decline in union membership. Unless the organization of service workers in the private sector accelerates rapidly, and there is little evidence indicating the likelihood of such a development, this trend of rapid public employee organization will continue to be the frontier of collective bargaining.

Reproduced from the September, 1976 issue of the LABOR LAW JOURNAL, published and copyrighted (1976) by Commerce Clearing House, Inc., 4025 W. Peterson Avenue, Chicago, Illinois, 60646. Reprinted by permission of the author and Commerce Clearing House, Inc.

Charles Redenius is Associate Professor of Political Science, The Behrend College of the Pennsylvania State University.

Public employee bargaining has become so pervasive that hardly a week passes that we do not hear of, or read of, public employees engaging in collective bargaining or resorting to strike action when negotiations fail to produce a contract. Public employee unions range across the entire spectrum of governmental activities.[3] Whether we speak of the national government, state governments, local government, or special districts, especially school districts, the impact of public employee unionism is apparent even to the most casual observer. We can safely state that the continued growth of the public sector will be more than matched by the continued growth of public employee unions.

KEY DIFFERENCES

This continued growth will bring into sharper focus some of the key differences between collective bargaining patterns in the public sector as opposed to those in the private sector.[4] Let us briefly review a few of these differences. First, public employee bargaining differs from the private sector in that public employees work for governmental units that almost always have a monopoly or near monopoly of the services in a community. The importance of this difference can readily be seen when we examine the effects of work stoppages by public employees on a community.

Let us cite some examples: governmental units provide, usually on an exclusive basis or nearly so, postal service, water and sewage disposal, elementary and secondary education, sanitation services, police and fire protection. The disruption of these services is felt by every part of the service area. A coordinated work stoppage, although never attempted and highly unlikely, given the lack of public employee union integration, could quickly bring a community to its knees. Thus, the impact of a public employee strike is immeasurably heightened by the fact that there are usually no readily available and adequate alternatives to governmental services.

Secondly, certain governmental services are deemed "essential" to the well-being of the community. Fire and police protection, garbage collection, health care, and perhaps education are services that cannot be disrupted without severe consequences for the community as a whole. The more extreme opponents of public employee collective bargaining, and the strike action taken when such bargaining is unsuccessful, see a society on the brink of anarchy. Although it is dated, Calvin Coolidge's statement about the 1919 Boston police strike (while he was governor)

"There is no right to strike against the public safety by anybody, anywhere, anytime," still commands wide support among legislators and judges. Indeed, thirty-seven states prohibit public employee strikes by statute and/or case law.[5] It is difficult to argue that a strike in the private sector would have such disruptive consequences or provoke such a strong reaction by legislators and judges.

Thirdly, most bargaining conflicts in the private sector are resolved without recourse to litigation and judicial intervention. This is often not the case with work stoppages by public employees. Most states, as noted above, have laws expressly denying public employees the right to strike. Such laws, of course, do not prevent strikes. When such strikes do occur, governmental officials in these states are tempted to resort to litigation rather than tackle the difficult process of negotiating a contract.

It is interesting to note that in certain respects the seeking of judicial intervention by public officials is a repetition of the early experiences of collective bargaining in the private sector. The end result is a dragging out of the collective bargaining process because judicial intervention can not come to grips with the issues in dispute nor can it produce a contract.[6] The most that can be hoped for by litigation is that public employees will be forced back to work. It will come as no surprise that public employees bitterly resent the issuance of an injunction just as an earlier generation of employees in the private sector resented such action.

There are still other characteristics shaping the environment of public employee collective bargaining that should be mentioned at this point. An important characteristic that is almost always ignored, or commented upon casually, is that public employees can best be characterized as service workers. In terms of labor force participation rates, public employees make up a negligible fraction of workers engaged in agriculture, commerce, and manufacturing.

The importance of this characteristic lies in the fact that the organization of public employees has been vastly more successful than the organization of service workers in the private sector. This fact has dual implications: Public employes are, as noted earlier, at the frontier of collective bargaining, and consequently the private sector will be emulating, in certain respects, the experience of public employees in their collective bargaining experiences, strategies, and outcomes rather than the other way around as it has been up till now. This seems especially important when we note another characteristic of bargaining in the public sector.

Both service sectors, the public and the private, are highly heterogeneous. Public employees, concentrating only on those already organized, have made their presence felt in virtually every area of governmental activity. This means there exist organizations at the federal level and the state and local levels covering virtually every type of public employee. Organizers of service workers in the private sector should be able to profit from examining the successes of these groups. The surface heterogeneity of the service sectors may be underlaid by some commonalities that would be revealed after a careful scrutiny of the experiences of successful organizations in both sectors.

A final characteristic of the public employee collective bargaining setting is the complexity of the legal environment. Employees and employers in the private sector, whether in agriculture, commerce, manufacturing, or service, and whether competing in a local, regional, or national market, come within the jurisdiction of either the National Labor Relations Act (Wagner Act) or the Railway Labor Act. Their legal environment, although it may be tedious in some respects and complex in still others, is a model of clarity and simplicity when we compare it with the multiplicity of laws confronting public officials and their employees who want to organize and bargain collectively.

Nor is this legal environment a fixed and unchanging one. In 1975, seventeen of twenty state laws on labor relations dealt with the collective bargaining rights of public employees.[7] Thus, whereas the bargaining setting in the private sector is characterized by its relative simplicity, clarity, and stability, the bargaining environment of the public sector is characterized by complexity, lack of clarity, and change.

But even this does not fully state the case. In twenty-three of the states, public employee organizations operate either wholly or partially in the absence of protective legislation.[8] Without the benefit of such legislation or case law, public labor unions are at a severe disadvantage when compared with public employee organizations in states with public labor relations laws. Public officials cannot be legally compelled to bargain in good faith; a union cannot legally be designated as the exclusive representative of the employees for bargaining purposes; and the legal status of a collective bargaining agreement is even questionable. These are only some of the most important disadvantages. Yet bargain they must, and the absence of a fixed legal environment coupled with their inexperience with collective bargaining are two of the most difficult obstacles that must be overcome.

THE CONSEQUENCES OF INEXPERIENCE

The rapid growth of collective bargaining in the public sector has brought to light the inexperience of both public officials and public employees in grappling with the problems of negotiating a contract, establishing a grievance procedure, and defining the new employer-employee relationship. Many public officials now expected to act as "management" have had little or no training in dealing with labor organizations. In the past they have been able to rely on civil service commissions,[9] personnel offices, or school administrators, to handle most employer-employee matters. That is no longer the case in many instances.

The same is true for public employees. Until the last decade and a half, public employees were likely to be passive and docile employees. Exerting their influence through labor organizations is new to them, and they have not yet learned to identify those situations when it would better serve their interests to temper their emerging militance. Instead of dealing with their immediate supervisor, they are expected to bargain directly with public officials who are now seen as merely their employers.

Thus, collective bargaining has introduced some of the features of an adversial relationship into a setting which heretofore had been, or could be, characterized as paternalistic or collegial. Indeed, in the field of higher education, one of the major objections to collective bargaining, pointed out by faculty and administration alike, is that it will destroy the collegial relationship and replace it with an adversial one. There is no doubt collective bargaining is seen as an almost wholly negative development by advocates of this position. Despite this widely held view, sixty institutions of higher education opted for collective bargaining in the last year alone, bringing the total to four hundred and sixty-one.[10] The implication seems to be that one can champion the adversial system in the courtroom but be quick to decry its supposedly corrosive effects elsewhere.

However, if we examine the collective bargaining situation more carefully, we might find that the higher level of tension between public officials and public employees could be traced to the inexperience of both parties, and the difficulties in adjusting to new relationships with one another. Such a dramatic change as the adoption of collective bargaining is certain to have an impact on behavior patterns and that impact may initially be an adverse one. But as the parties gain experience in negotiating contracts and resolving grievances, and in adjusting to their new

relationships, most of the deleterious side effects initially attributed to the adversial nature of collective bargaining may be
considerably alleviated or disappear altogether.

That has certainly been the experience of collective bargaining in the private sector. The level of violence and abrasiveness
which occurred during the early days of the organization of the
automobile industry, for example, is not apparent today. Since
that level has not been and is unlikely to be matched by public
employee bargaining, the long term diminution of the initial adverse experiences will be less dramatic but nonetheless markedly
perceptible.

As the parties gain confidence in their abilities to negotiate
contracts and resolve grievances we are also quite likely to see a
reduction in the number of disputes brought into the courts.
Judicial intervention in public employee bargaining disputes can
be viewed as an indicator of inexperience with collective bargaining and/or a lack of confidence in one's abilities to resolve disputes without outside assistance. Those who have had experience
with judicial intervention quickly learn that such intervention
will not resolve the dispute, produce a contract, or even, in some
instances, avert a work stoppage. Again the experience of the
private sector is instructive. Most bargaining disputes are resolved without judicial intervention, or outside mediation of any
kind. Indeed, the parties to such disputes resist outside assistance, preferring to resolve their disputes in their own way.

Perhaps we ought not to recapitulate in the public sector the
experiences of the private sector. Instead of gaining experience in
a trial-by-error fashion, public employers and public employees
could be taught the skills necessary to negotiate contracts and
establish grievance procedures. The mere fact that we have such a
broad range of disciplines dealing with labor relations in our
schools and colleges indicates we believe such skills can be
taught. The learning which would occur could only be put to the
test in a real bargaining situation. If successful, the teaching of
these skills would produce a healthier bargaining climate. The
division of interest between employer and employee would be just
as real and just as formidable, but the skills necessary to reconcile
differences would reduce the amount of wasted energy and concentrate it on the issues in dispute.

An alternative to the academic teaching of these skills would
be to institute training programs in collective bargaining.[11] At the
state level, these programs could be coordinated by a public labor
relations agency and should be open to state and local officials

and public labor organization representatives. This type of program would have a dual benefit. It would equip both public officials and employee representatives with the skills necessary for collective bargaining. It would also, as a result of "management" and "labor" participation, create a greater awareness of the perspectives and problems each brings to the bargaining table. To restrict a training program to only public officials would seriously impair, if not defeat, the effectiveness of such an effort. Indeed, there do not seem to be sound reasons for excluding labor representatives from a training program of this nature.

THE INEFFICACY OF THIRD PARTY INTERVENTION

However, before programs of this type can be implemented successfully, the state legislatures must be educated to write public employee bargaining laws that place strong incentives on voluntarism in collective bargaining and strong disincentives on reliance on involuntary third party intervention. The process of negotiating a labor contract is a difficult and complex one. If state legislatures enact statutes that obviate facing this difficult task directly, then we can expect employers and employees alike to seek an easy way out. Ultimately, however, a labor contract satisfactory to both parties can come about only through the willingness of those parties to engage in the give and take that is an inherent characteristic of the collective bargaining process. Intervention by a third party that thwarts, or even by its presence diminishes, this willingness can only prolong the process.

   None of this is meant to imply that mediation, fact finding, and non-binding recommendations are to be ruled out. Quite the contrary is the case. All these "tools" are useful in facilitating the collective bargaining process. Note: they facilitate. They cannot be substituted for that process.

   Mediation can perform an invaluable service in certain instances where rancor between the parties or a breakdown in communication has either emotionally overheated or stalemated the bargaining process. In instances like these, mediation can bring *willing* parties together by *facilitating* the give and take which must occur. Fact finding can insure that both parties share a basic understanding of the issues in dispute. It can create channels of communication by establishing a common framework. As a result, fact finding can, in those instances, expedite the bargaining process.

   Non-binding recommendations can also play an invaluable

role in bringing the parties in dispute together. The recommendations reveal how a third party would reconcile the differences. This gives the parties an opportunity to reassess their bargaining positions. Involuntary third party intervention, however, which attempts to *control* the bargaining process, by endeavoring to define the issues and then resolve them, can only result in an involuntary agreement which is unlikely to gain the support of either party if indeed the third party can force acceptance upon the disputants.

The involuntary impasse procedures which must be eschewed are binding arbitration and judicial intervention.[12] Let us examine each of them in turn. Compulsory arbitration is often advocated as the "solution" to bargaining impasses. However even in states where compulsory arbitration is mandatory when bargaining breaks down, it is difficult to evaluate the results of arbitration.[13] Most statutory provisions are concerned more with preventing or ending work stoppages than they are with encouraging voluntarism in the bargaining process by the threat of an involuntary technique.

Thus, these procedures are likely to have an adverse effect rather than a positive one on the willingness of public officials to bargain in good faith. They realize, as well as the unions, that the strike weapon's effectiveness is considerably diminished when mandatory arbitration procedures can be invoked. On the other hand, a weak union can increase its bargaining leverage significantly if it can invoke arbitration.

The weakness, then, of binding arbitration is twofold. One, it is difficult to write a statutory procedure that does not affect the bargaining leverage which can be exerted by one or the other of the parties. The result is that such a procedure benefits one party and penalizes the other. Second, it often inhibits the bargaining process by diminishing incentives for voluntary negotiation in favor of reliance on a third party to issue a formal award. If access to arbitration is not strictly limited, voluntary agreements will undergo a marked decline.

Judicial intervention has been tried and found wanting in both private sector and public sector collective bargaining. The history of the private sector, with judicial intervention especially in the early days of collective bargaining, provides experiential evidence in support of this statement. Although certain segments of management might deny it, most would agree that the efficacy and efficiency of collective bargaining has gained as the result of the passage of the Norris-LaGuardia Act and the Wagner Act. The fact that labor and management in the private sector negotiate most of their collective bargaining contracts without the use of involuntary impasse resolution techniques indicates in a very important way their understanding of the best method of reaching agreement.

Even the federal executive branch recognizes the inefficacy of judicial intervention. The injunctive relief available under Taft-Hartley in private sector "national emergency" disputes is sought only when all else fails, including the threat to invoke its provisions. Binding arbitration and other involuntary impasse resolution techniques are used only as a last resort. Thus, when involuntary techniques are utilized, it means failure in some respect.

MEAGER SUCCESS

Likewise, the limited history of bargaining in the public sector also supports the nonutility of judicial intervention. It can force public employees back to work in most instances, but judicial intervention has had meager success in producing any other positive results. This can be traced not only to its inappropriateness in the bargaining situation but also to the character of the instruments which the judiciary can wield. The injunction can stop a strike but it does so at the expense of fostering bitterness on the part of employees who are forced to work without a contract. Nor does the injunction compel the public employer to bargain in good faith. With the employees back on the job, the pressure to negotiate is considerably diminished if not altogether absent.

If public employees resist a back to work order, the judge can punish such resistance summarily by use of the contempt power. Normally this takes the form of heavy fines for the union, and possible imprisonment of union leaders. Since union leaders and their attorneys rarely seek injunctions, nor do statutes usually provide for such a step by public employees, judicial intervention is weighted in favor of public employers. Seldom, if ever, is an injunction issued against a public employer. Consequently, they are not often, if ever, faced with the threat of fines and/or imprisonment.

The widespread disaffection among labor and management in both the public and private sectors with involuntary techniques for resolving collective bargaining disputes indicates that such techniques do not enjoy a preferred position in their hierarchy of values. Thus, a general rule against involuntary third party intervention either in the form of binding arbitration or judicial intervention can be persuasively argued. It cannot force unwilling parties to bargain. It cannot remove either the difficulty or complexity inherent in the bargaining process. It cannot resolve the issues in dispute. It cannot effectively forge an agreement which will receive the support of the parties to the dispute.

The use of involuntary procedures, then, appeals not to the parties to bargaining disputes but rather to legislators, judges, and labor relations scholars.[14] State legislators in particular seem to be attracted to involuntary impasse resolution techniques when writing public labor relations laws. These techniques are often coupled with a ban on strikes by public employees.[15] When we contrast such laws with laws governing collective bargaining in the private sector the difference is glaring.

The theoretical grounds for the differences between labor laws governing the public sector versus labor laws governing the private sector are usually attributed to the character of public employment.[16] However, the actual differences between bargaining in the private sector versus bargaining in the public sector are very often more differences in degree than differences in kind.

The differences are great enough to justify separate labor laws, but both should be characterized by voluntarism and any departure from that norm should be subjected to careful analysis. With the exception of "essential" services, there do not seem to be adequate grounds for discriminating against public employees by insisting on involuntary procedures not imposed on private sector collective bargaining.

Thus, a necessary element in the improvement of the environment for public emoployee bargaining must be laws that rule out involuntary third party intervention in bargaining disputes except when "essential" services have been disrupted by a work stoppage. The definition of "essential" services and what would constitute an acceptable minimum level of such services should be carefully spelled out to insure the integrity of such laws. To insure their evenhandedness, these laws should attempt to create a comprehensive framework for public employee bargaining, one that matches, insofar as possible, the voluntarism of the bargaining framework estabished for the private sector.

IMPACT OF POLITICAL CONSIDERATIONS

Public labor laws are written in an environment quite different from that for labor laws governing the private sector. State legislators are responding to a different set of pressures and the "clients" of such laws are employees of the state. This means decision making in regard to public labor laws is more likely to be dominated by political considerations than economic considerations or questions concerning the nature of collective bargaining.[17] Since legislators always have one eye on the next election, they will be slow to write laws which they think might jeopardize their chances of reelection. Permitting public employees to strike, or more accurately not placing a prohibition on work stoppages, would seem to imply that legislators were condoning the disruption of governmental services.

Let us cite just one example. Education is a core value to most middle class Americans. If legislators do not ban teacher strikes they might be perceived as allowing teachers to do great damage to the education of our children by disrupting the learning process. It is not surprising to learn that many states ban teacher strikes. As noted earlier, the trouble with such bans is they do not prevent strikes and they usually encourage school boards to seek judicial intervention which cannot resolve bargaining disputes. However, the real damage done in these instances is that such bans encourage disrespect for the law. The other impasse resolution route, requiring arbitration in teacher disputes, has nearly as many pitfalls for school boards and teacher alike. Indeed, school boards are as likely to reject arbitration as unions.

The appeal of judicial intervention or binding arbitration, in public employee disputes, then, is more clearly due to political considerations than it is to economic factors, or to the insufficiencies and/or inadequacies of collective bargaining. Until such time as public employee unions are able to effectively counter such political considerations with pressure of their own, state legislators will continue to respond to what they perceive as most threatening to their continuance in office.

Public officials must bargain not only in the context of this politicized legal environment but also within the constraints of allowable budgets and tax revenues.[18] These constraints are much more severe at the state and local level given the nature of the property tax, sales tax, and the narrow limits of the income tax. By contrast, the federal sector has access to revenues which are much more elastic. In fact, if the federal government did not return a large fraction of the revenue it collects to the states, state governments would be unable to function without some drastic modifications in their access to resouces.[19]

The impact on state programs of these constraints is also immediate. Given limited resources, what is allocated to wage increases, cannot be allocated for implementing or expanding programs. This is particularly the case in education. In an era of scarce resources, increases in teacher salaries will have an impact on the curriculum. That impact, unfortunately, will largely be a negative one. Special services such as counseling, individual tutoring, and secretarial assistance will be cut back. Special enrichment programs including music appreciation, the arts, and extracurricular activities are also likely to suffer. It is easy to appreciate the manifold problems faced by school boards in their collective bargaining efforts. Perhaps the most disturbing fact about these problems is that they lie outside the decision-making capacity of the public officials most directly affected.

The collective bargaining setting for public employees is thus hedged with difficulties from a number of directions. Public labor relations laws which are the result of political considerations, economic constraints which are largely outside the control of public officials, and increasing taxpayer resistance are just some of the more important problems. The private sector is not confronted by these types of difficulties. They may argue that their problems are just as formidable, but surely the problems they face are different in kind. In coming to grips with these difficulties, the experiences of the private sector will be of little utility. Once again we see the meaning of being on the frontier of collective bargaining.

Without the experience of the private sector to rely on, the short range future is unlikely to be an unclouded one. Public employee collective bargaining will be breaking new ground and that experience will shape the bargaining process and its outcomes as surely as the industrial union experience was different from the craft union experience. Each type of union shaped the bargaining process in its own way, and each process led to different outcomes.

To improve the bargaining process for public employees will require further modifications in the legal environment, perhaps greater local control over economic constraints, and tax revenues derived from greater reliance on income rather than property or sales. This last will distribute the tax more equitably.

CONCLUSION

The continuing growth of the public sector and the accompanying surge of public employee organization increases the need for a comprehensive effort to reconcile the rights of public employees to bargain collectively with the safeguarding of the public well-being. Since the American political system at both the federal and state levels responds to problems with incremental adjustments, we can expect this task to occupy legislators for some time to come. Most state public labor laws now on the books have nearly all of the features—secret elections, provisions for exclusive representation, enumeration of unfair labor practices, impasse resolution techniques quite often coupled with a ban on strikes, and labor relations agencies—which have been touted as necessary to the collective bargaining environment.

Despite these laws, public employee bargaining still suffers from some major deficiencies. The absence of public labor relations laws in other states represents an opportunity to write laws that would correct these deficiencies. However, what is needed is a comprehensive national framework for public employee collective bargaining to parallel the Wagner Act and the Railway Labor Act. Such a federal law would insure some minimal level of uniformity rather than the existing patchwork of state laws.

This development, unfortunately, is unlikely given the recent Supreme Court decision in *National League of Cities v. Usery*,[20] which invalidated federal wage-and-hour regulations for state employees. This decision would seem to virtually rule out a federal law granting collective bargaining rights to all public employees at the state and local levels regardless of whether there was pertinent state law or not. Thus the effort to overcome the deficiencies of the public employee collective bargaining environment must be concentrated on the state level, especially in those states without public labor relations laws.

These laws must more carefully take into account the key differences between bargaining in the public sector versus bargaining in the private sector. The accomodation of these differences is essential to the definition of the collective bargaining rights of public employees. In this way these rights can be reconciled with the safeguarding of the community's well-being.

Secondly, state laws should include provisions for instituting training programs in collective bargaining practices which would be open to both public "managers" and public labor representatives. These workshop programs would temper the inexperience of both managers and union officials while at the same time acquainting them with each other's perspective.

Next, public labor relations laws should foster voluntarism in collective bargaining insofar as possible. Public employees must be able to perceive themselves as being on an equal footing with their counterparts in the private sector. This means that utilization of involuntary impasse resolution techniques must be ruled out except under carefully prescribed conditions such as the failure to maintain a clearly defined minimum level of an "essential" service.

Finally, legislators and the public alike have to begin to recognize the legitimate claims of public employees. This would seem to be the only way legislaors will be able to write public labor relations laws which are not largely the result of political considerations. Legislators may be unwilling to take such political risks and the public is certainly averse to higher taxes. But unless these steps are taken, public employees will continue to be treated inequitably.

If the states can avail themselves of this opportunity to take a comprehensive look at public employee collective bargaining, they will demonstrate the vitality of the federal system as a laboratory for the resolution of social problems of the first order.

NOTES

1. U. S. Department of Labor, Labor-Management Services Administration, *Summary of State Policy Regulations for Public Sector Labor Relations*, (Washington, D. C.: U. S. Government Printing Office, 1975), p. i, Hereafter cited as *Summary of State Policy.*

2. U. S. Department of Labor, Bureau of Labor Statistics, *Handbook of Labor Statistics 1975–Reference Edition* (Washington, D. C.: U. S. Government Printing Office, 1975), p. 389 Table 158. The one fifth figure is for 1972, the last year reported.

3. For Federal Employee Unions see: U. S. Department of Labor, Labor-Management Services Administration, *Register of Federal Employee Unions* (Washington, D. C.: United States Government Printing Office, 1975). For State Employee Unions see: U. S. Department of Labor, Labor-Management Services Administration, *A Directory of Public Employee Organizations* (Washington, D. C.: U. S. Government Printing Office, 1974).

4. The following sources provide some different perspectives on this subject: W. H. Holley, Jr., "Unique Complexities of Public Sector Labor Relations." 55 *Personnel Journal* 72-5 (February 1976): Louis V. Imundo, Jr., "Some Comparisons Between Public Sector and Private Sector Collective Bargaining," 24 LABOR LAW JOURNAL 810-817 (December 1973); Lee C. Shaw and R. Theodore Clark, Jr., "The Practical Differences Between Public and Private Sector Collective Bargaining," 19 *UCLA Law Review 867-86* (August 1972).

5. *Summary of State Policy,* cited at note 1. See the heading "Strike Policy" under each state for particulars.

6. The Wisconsin experience with judicial intervention is instructive. See my "Participant Attitudes Toward a Judicial Role in Public Employee Collective Bargaining" 25 LABOR LAW JOURNAL 94-113 (February 1974).

7. Deborah T. Bond, "State Labor Legislation Enacted in 1975," 99 *Monthly Labor Review* 18 (January 1976).

8. *Summary of State Policy,* cited at note 1. See the headings, "Coverage," and "Authority and Date," under each state for particulars.

9. The relationship between civil service and public employee bargaining is explored in: Charles Feigenbaum, "Civil Service and Collective Bargaining: Conflict or Compatibility," 3 *Public Personnel Management* 244-52 (May 1974).

10. Philip W. Semas, "Faculty Unions Add 60 Campuses in 1975-76 Academic Year," 12 *Chronicle of Higher Education* 5 (May 31, 1976).

11. Such a program has been advocated for state and local public managers. See William D. Torrence, "Collective Bargaining and Labor Relations Training of State-Level Management," 2 *Public Personnel Management* 256-60 (July 1973). The national government operates a Labor Relations Training Center to meet this need at the federal level.

12. For other views on impasse procedures see, Thomas P. Gilroy and Anthony V. Simicropi, "Impasse Resolution in Public Employment. A Current Assessment," 25 *Industrial and Labor Relations Review* 496-511 (July 1972): Joseph R. Grodin, "Arbitration of Public Sector Labor Disputes: The Nevada Experiment," 28 *Industrial and Labor Relations Review* 89-102 (October 1974); Richard P. McLaughlin, "Collective Bargaining Suggestions for the Public Sector," 20 LABOR LAW JOURNAL 131-37 (March 1969); Paul D. Staudohar, "Some Implications of Mediation for Resolution of Bargaining Impasses in Public Employment" 2 *Public Personnel Management* 299-304 (July 1973); William R. Word, "Toward More Negotiations in the Public Sector," 2 *Public Personnel Management* 345-50 (September 1973).

13. Grodin, cited at note 12, pp. 92-94.

14. The literature on involuntary impasse procedures far outweighs that of articles concerned with voluntary collective bargaining models. The materials cited in footnote twelve could easily be doubled or tripled. There is a surprising paucity of research exploring collective bargaining models given the norm of voluntarism that characterizes labor relations in both the public and private sectors.

15. The Connecticut public labor relations law is a good example.

16. One of the theoretical grounds for differentiating public employment from private employment is the concept of state sovereignty. For an elucidation of the ramifications of this concept see: Abraham L. Gitlow, "Public Employee Unionism in the United States: Growth and Outlook," 21 LABOR LAW JOURNAL 766-778 (December 1970) and Anne M. Ross, "Public Employee Unions and the Right to Strike," 92 *Monthly Labor Review* 14-18 (March 1969).

17. For two different perspectives on the impact of political considerations see: Thomas M. Love, and George T. Sulzer, "Political Implications of Public Employee Bargaining" 11 *Industrial Relations* 18-33 (February 1972) and Clyde W. Summers, "Public Employee Bargaining: A Political Perspective," 83 *Yale Law Journal* 1156-2000 (May, 1974).

18. For a case study see: Milton Derber, Ken Jennings, Ian McAndrew, and Martin Wagner, "Bargaining and Budget Making in Illinois Public Institutions," 27 *Industrial and Labor Relations Review* 49-62 (October 1973).

19. The fraction for 1973-74 was 17.5%. See U. S. Department of Commerce, Bureau of the Census, "Governmental Finances and Employment at a Glance," (Washington, D.C.: Subscriber Services Section (Publications), January 1976), p. 1.

20. 44 *U. S. Law Week* 4974 (June 22, 1976): (S Ct 1976) 12 EPD Sec. 10,996.

Civil Service
and Collective Bargaining:
Conflict or Compatibility?

Charles Feigenbaum

INTRODUCTION

Civil service in the United States began its career as a reform movement in reaction to the abuses of the spoils systems. Since the time of Andrew Jackson (1829-37), "spoils" had flourished as the nation's system for public personnel administration.[1]

Rotation-in-office is a more dignified synonym for spoils, and it has a rationale to support it. One article of Jacksonian democratic faith was that ordinary men of intelligence could readily be

---

Reprinted by permission of PUBLIC PERSONNEL MANAGEMENT from PUBLIC PERSONNEL MANAGEMENT, Vol. 3, May-June, 1974, pp. 244-252.

Charles Feigenbaum is a supervisory labor management relations specialist with the U.S. Internal Revenue Service, Washington, D.C. He was a Fellow of the National Institute for Public Affairs (1969-70) and holds an M.A. in government from American University, an M.S. in industrial and labor relations from Cornell University, and teaches labor relations at the University of Maryland. The views expressed in this article do not purport to reflect the position of the Internal Revenue Service.

qualified for public office. Also, a new administration needs
people in public positions who can be counted on to faithfully
administer its policies. Rotation-in-office follows naturally.

While the spoils system can be defended in terms of democratic theory, its practice became indefensible. Partisan political activity became the crucial test for public office. The rapid rotation-
in-office of unqualified men guaranteed a certain degree of ineffi-
ciency, and set up hothouse conditions for dishonesty and
sinecurism. The assassination of President James A. Garfield in
1881 by a disappointed office seeker gave the reform movement
the impetus it needed to achieve its key success: the passage in
1883 of the Civil Service Act. Since that time, civil service systems
have been adopted by an increasing number of jurisdictions. As of
1961, 27 of the states had general merit systems, and 95 percent
of the cities with populations of 100,000 or more, had some civil
service coverage.[2]

Because of its history, civil service is more than a system of
public personnel administration. Its roots are moral and political.
Civil service reform was seen as the indispensable reform needed
". . . for the success and perpetuation of our republican institutions."[3]

The present time finds us in the middle of another deeply
significant public personnel movement. This movement, the
growth of collective bargaining in the public service, is more
pragmatic and economic, but it too, has its political and moral
roots. One school of thought sees civil service and collective bargaining as two incompatible systems. "They employ different
principles, and they have different concerns. We can no longer
believe that we can be half collective bargaining and half merit
system."[4]

DEFINITIONS

Collective Bargaining
In considering the relationship of collective bargaining and civil
service, some definitions are in order. Collective bargaining, as
used in this paper, means the right of self-organization, with no
interference, coercion or domination by management; exclusive
representation by the labor organization with majority status in
the unit to be represented; a significant range of issues to be
negotiated; agreements reduced to writing and regarded as essentially binding, whatever their technical legal status; and proce-

dures for resolving impasse and grievance disputes which are not subject to the unilateral control or influence of one of the parties. In short, a system of bilateral determination of important personnel and working conditions.

This definition does not require that pay, or any other specific issue, be subject to negotiations. Nor does it require the right to strike. Obviously, the more issues to be determined bilaterally, and the more power available to the labor organization, the greater will be the impact of collective bargaining.

Civil Service

Next, what do we mean when we speak of civil service? This paper considers three aspects of civil service: substantive, representational, and structural.

Substantive. The substance of a civil service system is the merit system. Originally, a merit system was one which was based on (1) competitive examinations, (2) relative security of tenure, and (3) political neutrality.[5] This original meaning has been broadened considerably. A leading text on public personnel administration defines the merit system as ". . . *a personnel system in which competitive merit or achievement governs each individual's selection and progress in the service and in which the conditions and rewards of performance contribute to the competency and continuity of the service.*"[6] There is nothing unique to the public service in that definition; it would apply equally to any rational and progressive personnel system, public or private.

Representational. Civil service has traditionally been concerned with protecting the rights of employees, as well as improving the efficiency of the service. There is the connotation of an impartial system which represents the interests of employees, management, and the public.

Structural. At the state and federal levels, civil service typically means a centralized personnel agency, usually a board or commission, with responsibility for setting some or all of the personnel rules for the jurisdiction, and for acting as the watchdog of the merit system.

The purpose of this paper is to explore what impact a bilateral system for determining important personnel and working conditions will have on the merit system, the concept of impartiality, and centralized personnel agencies.

COLLECTIVE BARGAINING AND THE MERIT SYSTEM

Politics

The merit system has as its historical foundation freedom from partisan politics. Will collective bargaining undermine that foundation? On one level, the answer is clearly "no." Employees and their unions are interested in job security. They also want employees treated in accordance with relatively predictable and objective standards and procedures.

An alliance with incumbent politicians to secure special favors implies opposition to rival politicians. And what if the latter are elected? The self-interest of public employees and their unions lies in the direction of a sharp cleavage between the public personnel system and partisan politics. In fact, one would expect unions to insist on contractual safeguards in jurisdictions where there is no merit system, or where it is too weak to offer adequate safeguards. Such safeguards need not specifically speak to the question of political influence, but to the extent that they protect employees from arbitrary and non-work connected dismissals, they can be said to strengthen the merit system.

But this is not enough to dispose of the troublesome issue of politics. Collective bargaining is a power process, and in the public sector, the power ultimately resides with political officials. Public employee unions represent people who are both employees and citizens. Strong unions may exert enough influence to get settlements beyond their due. And indeed, they may join with a particular party or individual politicians to gain benefits which they could not gain at the bargaining table,[7] while at the same time safeguarding their members' employment against a return to patronage politics.

There are no clear solutions to this problem, but some observations are possible. First, who knows, with any precision, what is "beyond their due?" Second, we are now discussing the exercise of political power by a special interest group, and the relationship of that exercise to "the general good" or "the public interest." This is one of the perennial concerns of the political scientist. Public employee unionism may complicate the issue, but it did not create it. Third, this problem is related to employee organization, not the institution of collective bargaining. The history of postal unions before Executive Order 10988 instructs us that significant political influence may exist without collective bargaining. Fourth, it is the political process which is often pointed to as an effective substitute for the right to strike.[8] And finally, we should consider where and when unions exert political pressure to achieve negotiating ends.

One commentator states that unions tend to use politics in states which do not clearly provide for collective bargaining for public employees and in cities with a "machine" style of politics.[9] (The implication of the latter point is that in such cities, the merit system is weak, if it exists at all.) Further, we are told that unions will rely on politics when it appears to be a more fruitful approach than formal negotiations would be. Such an assessment would include at least two factors, the responsiveness of the public employer (including the power to be able to respond), and the accessibility of political officials.

In summary, public employee unions are political organisms living in a world of political power. They will use politics as an adjunct to negotiations to the extent that they think they must, or that it will be fruitful, or both. At the same time, where an effective merit system exists, the self-interest of their members makes them hostile to patronage and strongly attached to the merit tenet of job security independent of the vicissitudes of partisan politics.

Compulsory Union Membership or Support

First, a stipulation: the unions to be discussed in this context are open, non-discriminatory unions that accept all to membership who come within their jurisdiction. Thus, if through collective bargaining an employee is obliged to join, or at least support, a union, there is no bar to full membership in that union.

As a practical matter, the subject of compulsory union membership (union shop) or support (agency shop), is of little consequence where these arrangements are illegal; e.g., the federal service and New York State. Still, they are topics of lively interest whenever collective bargaining in the public service is discussed. And for good reason, for they illustrate the three-way tension between the labor organization's need for institutional security, the individual's desire to protect his right of non-association, and the merit system's insistence that employment be based on merit, not affiliation.

The reasoning that sees the union or agency shop as a significant threat to the merit system goes something like this:

1. Someone who does not want to join or support a union will not apply for a position in the system.
2. Because of this, there will be less competition for places in the system, and those selected may be less meritorious than would have been the case had there been greater competition.

3. Employees who drop out of the union must be dismissed, no matter how competent they are.[10]

There is nothing untrue about this formulation, but its practical importance is questionable. There is little to indicate that significant numbers of otherwise qualified employees would shy away from suitable employment in a public jurisdiction because of a requirement that they join or support a union. More likely they must simply accept such a requirement as a condition of employment. Certainly, problems may occur at the margin: unionism may be regarded as distasteful in some places and among some occupational groups. Where this is true unions are unlikely to have the strength to demand such arrangements, and would probably be unwise to press the issue even if they could. Finally, of course, management need not agree to the union or agency shop. No matter how few these situations may be, one may argue that the theory of the merit system demands that no one be turned away for non-merit reasons.

Whatever the theory of the merit system, the fact is that non-merit bars to employment exist and abound in the public service. Many civil service systems are restricted to U.S. citizens except for the rare cases where qualified U.S. citizens are not available.[11] Many jurisdictions have residence requirements.[12] Such requirements are generally not too onerous where all that is needed is a move into the particular geographic area. But some residence requirements specify one or two years' residence before employment. (The geographical equivalent of the closed shop?)

More serious is veteran preference as it exists on the federal scene and in some states. A veteran who attains a passing score gets 5 points added to his score. A disabled veteran gets 10 points and is added to the top of the eligible list for certain positions, even if others have higher scores.[13] The connection between merit and veteran preference is tenuous, if it exists at all. More important, the employee has little choice about his veteran's status. Other people decided whether or not to draft him, or to accept him if he volunteered. Veteran preference discriminates against women, and all others who did not serve in the armed forces during specified periods, whatever the reasons.

The final objection to the agency or union shop is that it improperly limits the employee's right of non-association. The old answer to that, to paraphrase Justice Holmes, was that while a person has a right not to join an organization, he does not have a right to a government job. There may be a new answer emerging, but that takes us beyond the scope of this paper. It is sufficient to say that the agency or union shop may raise a serious question of constitutional rights, and that it will eventually have to be reconciled with the strivings of public employee unions for greater institutional security. The suggestion of one commentator—a modified agency shop—might be the acceptable compromise.[124] Under this plan, employees would be required to join the union, or, if they prefer, to pay a fee to the union which would be a pro-rated share of the expense of negotiation and administration of the contract.

The foregoing is not an endorsement of the agency or union shop. Those arrangements pose serious questions of public policy, aside from those of merit. My point has simply been to show that the union or agency shop, if adopted in the public service, would be no more a deviation from merit than what already exists in many jurisdictions.

Seniority

A prime concern of a rational management is that its work force shall be as efficient as possible. Those who fall below a certain standard are let go, with those remaining given salaries, promotions, and other rewards, according to their merits. One might not have too difficult a job convincing a union of the theoretical soundness of this position. The difficulty lies with the practice. The criteria for making these decisions are intangible and subjective. Even worse, they are often unarticulated. The criterion much preferred by the unions is seniority whose two great virtues are that it is objective and it can be counted. The question of the appropriateness of the use of seniority is of equal concern in the public and private sectors. It is, therefore, instructive to review private sector practice.[15]

Seniority means the giving of weight to length of service in connection with various personnel actions and benefits. In private industry, seniority is used for such diverse considerations as layoffs and recalls, promotions, transfers, job or work assignments, shift preference, selection of days off, overtime distribution, as well as extent of benefits; *e.g.*, how many days of vacation, severance pay, etc. But how seniority is counted and how much weight it is given, may vary with the kind of action or benefit involved.

The rule for vacations may be that employees with less than five years of service get one week of vacation, while those with more than five years get two weeks off. Here, the seniority counted would be length of service with the company, and it would be the absolute determinant. No other factor would influence how much vacation an employee gets. The seniority rule for promotions, on the other hand, might count only length of service in a particular department, or on a particular job, and might be considered in relation to such other factors as ability, attendance record, cooperativeness and versatility.

The use of seniority to determine off-the-job benefits such as amount of vacation time poses no threat to merit principles. But there may very well be a conflict between the use of seniority and the merit system when a promotion is being considered. It is established practice in unionized companies that, as a minimum, seniority will govern *where ability is relatively equal.* This practice is accepted as compatible with merit,[16] but even where seniority carries greater weight as a promotion factor, this does not necessarily compromise merit principles. Seniority is a more appropriate consideration for some jobs than it is for others. "The point is. . . that there are various types of duties and that length of service affects their performance differently. In promoting from one routine position to a comparable one, it may justifiably be given considerable weight."[17] Of extreme importance is how seniority is applied.

In the federal service, "length of service and length of experience may be used as evaluation criteria only when they are clearly related to quality of performance. They may be used. . . to resolve ties between candidates."[18] In Massachusetts, the person selected for promotion must be one of the three oldest qualified employees in length of service.

The federal and Massachusetts provisions are not the products of collective bargaining, but the differing weights accorded seniority can also be seen in negotiated agreements. One county in Wisconsin negotiated this provision:

> Whenever any vacancy occurs on a job performed by a full-time employee, it shall be given to the employee with the greatest seniority. . . . subject to the right of the Employer to determine whether the employee . . . is qualified to perform the job."[20] Another Wisconsin county negotiated an entirely different seniority provision: "The County shall determine the qualifications of the applicants and in the event that qualifications as determined by the County are relatively equal, the applicant with the greater seniority shall be selected. . . ."[21]

But it is not enough to say that seniority can be found where no collective bargaining takes place, and that seniority may be usefully and intelligently applied. The concern is that collective bargaining will so intensify the pressures toward dependence on seniority that public employers will allow it to be substituted for judgment, to the eventual detriment of the merit system.

The experience of private industry is interesting, but not conclusive. Seniority has progressively become more important over the years. Whether management has given in to pressure, or become convinced of the utility of seniority, is unknown. There is little evidence that the efficiency of private industry has been harmed. "Many managements are of the view that whatever loss in individual efficiency has occurred is offset by the gain in morale among employees."[22] In spite of this generally favorable assessment, there is concern that management has allowed seniority rules to impair needed flexibility with regard to promotions and work assignments. In some cases showdowns with the unions become necessary.[23]

There are two further points to be considered. First, management has a say in what it agrees to. Second, the need for seniority is most persuasive where discrimination and favoritism occur, or where the exercise of management judgment appears arbitrary or ill-founded. The best insulation against unreasonable demands for seniority would be the development of criteria for promotions, layoffs, etc. which are intelligently and fairly related to the job situation and the action to be taken.

Pay Structure
Another concern is the impact of collective bargaining on the internal consistency of job classification and pay plans.

> . . . [T]he position classification program is the fundamental element required for maintaining the merit philosophy. As the cornerstone of the merit system, it cannot be subject to a labor agreement without risking the destruction of the entire merit service. The allocation of positions does not provide opportunity for collective negotiation in that there is no room for compromise or bargaining if positions are to be properly classified.[24]

The principle being defended is that of "equal pay for equal work"—and of course, its corollary, pay distinctions for unequal work. Equal pay for equal work is a simple concept when applied to such concrete situations as the same duties and responsibilities being performed by a Republican and a Democrat, a man and a woman, a white and a black. But the concept goes beyond that. It means equal pay for *equal levels* of work, and thus cuts through a large number of varied positions. An equal level of work could include, among others, a senior secretary, a fledgling per-

sonnel specialist right out of college, and the supervisor of a key
punching unit. Under those circumstances, a good deal of subjec-
tivity and value judgments go into deciding what is equal and
unequal, and by how much. Those decisions are developed
through meetings, discussions and even controversies within the
personnel and general management structure to decide what the
proper relationship between particular jobs should be. There are
often sound arguments which point in more than one direction.
Different parts of management hold differing views on the relative
worth of jobs, occupations and hierarchical levels. A negotiation
of sorts occurs in developing a plan which is reasonably satisfactory to those who can influence the decision.

This is not to say that the appearance of the collective bargaining process does not present real problems. New headaches
are introduced when a management which is concerned with a
broad range of jobs must deal with a union concerned only with
one or a few functions or occupations. The basic structure of the
bargaining unit is the problem here, and management should
attempt to deal with a union or a council of unions whose scope of
responsibility is as broad as its own.

Use of the market as the standard for comparison will also
ease the problem considerably. This approach does not end the
problem of pay consistency, but it does furnish a rational and
understood yardstick for comparison. The use of prevailing rates
is widespread for blue-collar (with significant union participation
in determining the companies to be surveyed and how the data is
to be interpreted[25]) but not white collar jobs. A notable exception
to this is the Tennessee Valley Authority which negotiates white-
collar salaries based on a plan which considers among other
things, comparable rates in the area.[26]

Summary
In summary, I would make the following points:
1. There are certain elements of conflict between collective bargaining and the merit system, but there is no reason to believe
   that the conflicts are crucial or irreconcilable.[27]
2. A generalized reaction to such matters as the agency shop, or
   seniority, fails to consider that these are not simple concepts
   that mean the same things at all times and places.
3. Similarly there is no one "merit system." There are a number
   of personnel systems which can fit comfortably under that
   umbrella because, by and large, employees are free from politi-

cal interference and are otherwise generally treated in accordance with their merits *as employees.*

4. Many merit tenets are not absolute. They are arrived at, and applied, through a negotiation-type process where compromises are made, and points of agreement and disagreement are traded off.

5. There are flaws in present merit systems which are as bad as, or worse than, some of the union demands, e.g., veteran preference and residence requirements. Yet we live with them.

6. Collective bargaining will undoubtedly require changes in the public personnel process. There is no necessity that those changes be for the worse. Alert and responsive management can develop better systems in the attempt to meet legitimate union complaints and avoid short-sighted union solutions. An attempt to solve problems can avoid showdowns in such situations where both sides may be wrong and a victory for either party will be a loss for both.

COLLECTIVE BARGAINING AND
THE "IMPARTIAL" ROLE OF CIVIL SERVICE

According to the Michigan State Personnel Director, the Civil Service Commission of that state feels that ". . . it has a third party responsibility to provide the employee with his just due, while at the same time protecting the public interest."[28] The negative to that proposition was rather forcefully stated by Jerry Wurf, the president of AFSCME:

> In my view, civil service is nothing more—and not much less than management's personnel system. Viewed as such, it fills an impor tant role in government—as a tool of management. . . ,
> The employee's rights and benefits are best protected through some form or other of negotiation and collective bargaining between his representative agency—preferably a trade union—on the one hand, and the representative of governmental management, which is often called Civil Service, on the other hand.[29]

If there is an area where it can be said that there is a definite conflict between civil service and collective bargaining, it is on the question of who shall represent the employee. The omens are reasonably clear that the unions shall. The growth of public unionism in itself tells us who the employees are voting for. And the process of collective bargaining requires a changed role for civil service.

The New York State Public Employment Board has taken the position that:

> Historically, civil service came into being to overcome the evils of the spoils system, and in such role, it has been the chief administrator of a centralized personnel system. In that function, it has been an arbiter in many matters relating to terms and conditions of employment. In the light of the statutory grant of collective negotiations rights to public employees, this role of civil service must be modified. The fact that State employees have the right to negotiate with respect to terms and conditions of their employment should result in the role of the Civil Service Department becoming more of an advisor to the Governor than an adjudicator.[30]

While the function of the civil service system will move increasingly in the direction of becoming management's personnel advisor, it will continue to consider employee needs and problems. The most important resources available to management is its employees; inevitably, management's personnel advisor must consider employee desires and reactions. But it will be done in the framework of management's thinking and management's needs.

COLLECTIVE BARGAINING AND
THE CENTRALIZED PERSONNEL AGENCY

Public jurisdictions vary greatly in size, variety of occupations contained in the public service, and complexity of the problems of personnel administration. They also vary greatly in the distribution of personnel responsibilities between the centralized civil service commissions and department managements.

   Generalizations regarding the impact of collective bargaining on such a diversity of personnel structures must be very general indeed. Ignoring structural advantages and disadvantages based on tactical considerations, we can see that there will be forces pressing to see that structure is influenced as follows:

1. The unions will want to bargain with the party with the power to make the decision.
2. All parties will feel the need for central control of certain issues, pensions, for example. They will probably desire a certain coherence and coordination of general personnel policies, with marked disagreements about whether or not there should be a policy about issue X, and if so, how general it should be.
3. The parties will also probably agree that a certain degree of decentralized authority to the departments and agencies is

needed. Once again, we can expect disagreements about scope and extent of decentralization.

4. Thus, a system for jurisdiction-wide bargaining for broad issues and local bargaining for local issues will emerge. Such arrangements are found now in large, multi-plant, private firms.[31]

When you consider that civil service systems exist in cities with a total population of 10,000 up through the federal government with an employee population numbering in the millions, it can be seen that the force and logic of these pressures will vary.

It seems clear that the impact of collective bargaining on the traditional civil service commission will be to narrow its scope. A study conducted by the California State Personnel Board indicated that ". . . the independent civil service commission in a majority of the jurisdictions has no role or responsibility in the collective bargaining process."[32]

The civil service commission will retain its role as the watchdog of the merit system, as the developer of general personel policies, and as the prime mover in recruitment and examining. These processes relate to people before they become employees, and typically unions have been perfectly willing to leave pre-employment matters to management. Indeed, in Montreal, the unions are credited with being instrumental in the creation of a civil service commission to handle these functions.[33]

SUMMARY

Collective bargaining and the merit system are compatible. Changes induced by collective bargaining may be for the better, but certainly there is no inevitability that they be for the worse. Management can exercise some control here.

Collective bargaining and the concept of civil service as the employee's protector are in conflict. That role of civil service is on the way out. Collective bargaining will induce changes in the structure of civil service, and it should rationalize and define the distribution of power.

NOTES

1. On the historical background to civil service, see O. Glenn Stahl, *Public Personnel Administration* (5th ed. 1962), pp. 26-48.

2. Stahl, *op. cit.*, pp. 44-47. The counties present a different picture. Stahl refers to them as a "dark continent," on page 46.

3. Paul P. Van Riper, *History of the U.S. Civil Service* (1958), p. 83.

4. Muriel M. Morse, "Shall We Bargain Away the Merit System?" in Kenneth O. Warner (ed.), *Developments in Public Employee Relations* (1965), pp. 154-160.

5. Van Riper, *op. cit.*, p. 100.

6. Stahl, *op. cit.*, p. 28.

7. Hildebrand, "The Public Sector," Dunlop and Chamberlain, *Frontiers of Collective Bargaining* (1967), pp. 125, 131-133.

8. Sterling Spero, "Collective Bargaining in Public Employment," *Public Administration Review*, vol. 22 (1962), pp. 1,5.

9. Paul F. Gerhart, "The Scope of Bargaining in Local Government Labor Negotiations," *Labor Law Journal*, vol. 20 (August 1969), p. 545.

10. Felix A. Nigro, *Management-Employee Relations in the Public Service* (1969), p. 94.

11. Stahl, *op. cit.*, pp. 57-58.

12. *Ibid.*, p. 58.

13. *Ibid.*, pp. 90-96.

14. Walter E. Oberer, "The Future of Collective Bargaining in Public Employment," *Labor Law Journal*, vol. 20 (December 1969), p. 777.

15. Slichter, Healy, and Livernash, *The Impact of Collective Bargaining on Management* (1960), pp. 104-141.

16. Stahl, *op. cit.*, p. 116.

17. *Ibid.*, p. 120.

18. The Bureau of National Affairs, *Government Employee Relations Report*, No. 259 (August 26, 1968), p. A-5.

19. The League of Women Voters of Massachusetts, *The Merit System in Massachusetts* (1961), p. 63.

20. BNA, *GERR*, No. 299 (June 2, 1969), p. B-4.

21. BNA, *GERR*, No. 291 (April 7, 1969), p. B-1.

22. Slichter, Healy, and Livernash, *op. cit.*, p. 140.

23. *Ibid.*

24. Norman Schwab, "Pay Consistency and Collective Bargaining," *Public Personnel Review*, vol. 30 (1969), p. 181.

25. Charles B. Craver, "Bargaining in the Federal Sector," *Labor Law Journal*, vol. 19 (September 1968), pp. 596-576.

26. Case, *Personnel Policy in a Public Agency* (1955), pp. 78-79.

27. Anderson, "The U.S. Experience in Collective Bargaining in Public Employment—Part III," *Practicing Law*, vol. 14 (1968), pp. 83, 88.

28. BNA, *GERR*, No. 237 (March 25, 1968), p. D-2.

29. Address by Jerry Wurf, Federal Bar Association, March 28, 1968.

30. In the matter of State of New York 2PERB3335, 3337 (1969).

31. Kenneth O. Warner and Mary L. Hennessy, *Public Management at the Bargaining Table* (1967), p. 299.

32. BNA, *GERR*, No. 303 (June 30, 1969), p. D-1.

33. Sullivan, "Canada: 20 Years of Public Employee Collective Bargaining," 10 N.H.B.J., 144.

CHAPTER 2.
THE PRIVATE
SECTOR INFLUENCE

Some Comparisons
Between Public Sector and Private Sector
Collective Bargaining

Louis V. Imundo, Jr.

The author views current activities in the public sector as roughly analogous to experience in the private sector during the 1930's and 40's. The doctrine of sovereignty and the political pressures exerted in the public sector are noted as particular obstacles to fruitful collective bargaining. Dr. Imundo concludes that government unions will continue to work for equalization of the bargaining relationship between labor and management in the public area. Dr. Imundo is an Assistant Professor of Management at Wright State University, Dayton, Ohio.

In the complex field of public sector labor-management relations many authors have made the point that government labor-management relationships are unique when compared to the relationship between labor and management in the private sector.[1] Others have maintained that no real differences exist between labor-management relations in the public sector and labor-management relations in the private sector.

Examination of federal executive orders and state statutes show that in certain respects meaningful comparisons with the private sector can be developed. In other respects the relationships are unique to the point where meaningful comparisons

Reproduced from the December, 1973 issue of the LABOR LAW JOURNAL, published and copyrighted (1973) by Commerce Clearing House, Inc., 4025 W. Peterson Avenue, Chicago, Illinois, 60646. Reprinted by permission of Dr. Louis V. Imundo, Associate Professor of Management, Wright State University and President of Management Perspectives Organizational Development Consultants, and Commerce Clearing House, Inc.

cannot be developed. In the areas where comparisons can be developed, the present state of collective bargaining in the public sector is comparable to private sector collective bargaining during the 1930's and 40's. Many of the private sector collective bargaining relationship problems of the 1930's and 40's which precipitated bitter conflicts have been settled only to arise again to restrict public sector collective bargaining.

During the 1930's and 40's, bitter conflicts between private sector labor and management erupted over labor's right to organize and the scope of negotiable issues. Until the Wagner Act guaranteed labor the right to organize and collectively bargain with their employer, many managements refused to recognize or negotiate with unions. Once organized labor secured the right to organize and negotiate agreements, managements, in the name of "managements' rights" attempted to limit the scope of negotiable issues. Changes in the law, NLRB and court interpretations of the law, increased union power and a maturing of management and labor were all factors that brought about an eventual broadening of the scope of negotiable issues. When the scope of negotiable issues in the private sector was compared with the scope of negotiable issues in the public sector, significant differences were found to exist. The scope of negotiable issues in the private sector is generally broader than the scope of negotiable issues in the public sector.

THE PROBLEM OF SOVEREIGNTY

In the private sector the law is structured to make the bargaining parties equals. In the public sector, the sovereignty doctrine makes it impossible for labor and management to bargain as equals. Two states, Alabama and North Carolina, have statutes that forbid public employees to join unions for the purposes of collective bargaining. At the end of 1970, eight states had not accorded their employees legal protection for collective bargaining. A number of states that have enacted legislation have stipulated that management's only obligation is to "meet and confer" with public employee unions. There is no mention about "collective bargaining in good faith."[2] In effect, a number of states have labor-management relations policies comparable to conditions in the private sector during the 1930's.

The sovereignty doctrine, i.e. the rights of the state, is at the forefront of many of the problems in public sector labor-management relations. In certain respects the sovereignty doctrine is comparable to the issue of management's rights in the private sector. In other respects the doctrine is a broader concept and meaningful comparisons are difficult to develop. The concept of sovereignty is inherent in the supreme power of a political state. Any state that possesses and maintains supreme power can determine whether or not an individual or a group of individuals can initiate a claim against the state. Sovereignty may be exercised by an individual, as in the form of an absolute monarchy, or by a body politic as is the case in contemporary society.[3]

The concept of sovereignty is difficult to understand and over time this inherent difficulty has caused considerable misunderstanding in the area of government labor-management relations. The difficulty of the concept lies in the fact that sovereignty conveys two ideas: legal sovereignty and political sovereignty. In the legal sense, sovereignty means that a governmental source of law must exist which is final and definitive.[4]

With regard to government's relationship with its employees, the theoretical application of the sovereignty doctrine permits only the government employer to establish the terms and conditions of employment. Any system of collective bargaining under which unions and government jointly determine the terms and conditions of employment is incompatible with this doctrine.[5]

The theoretical interpetation of the sovereignty doctrine as applied to government employees has been advanced for nearly one hundred years by government officials at all levels who believed that there could be no questioning of the decisions made by the state. Their logic was based upon the belief that; "Government service is public in character, belonging to and responsible to the people of our country."[6]

In the area of labor-management relations, state statutes and federal executive orders have been carefully shaped around preserving the sovereignty doctrine. Even the most recent change in the federal government's labor-management relations policies, Executive Order 11616, August 26, 1971, is carefully worded to protect federal government sovereignty. Section 12 of the order carefully delineates management's rights in unilateral decision making. In addition, federal government employees are denied the right to strike and the subject areas of wages, fringe benefits, and hours normally covered within the scope of collective bargaining in the private sector are still nonnegotiable because they are covered by statute and U. S. Civil Service Commission regulations. Section 13 of the order limits the use of the negotiable grievance procedure to the interpretation and application of the negotiated agreement. Many of the state and local laws reflect the tone of the federal executive order.[7]

THE POLITICAL FACTION

A paradox exists when we consider that the government employee lives in a democratic society. However, when he is in the employ of the same government which guarantees and maintains his democratic rights, he finds that his rights as an employee are severely limited. Aside from the argument that the government has a sovereign status, another rationale is used to justify this paradox. This other rationale is that the government employee's share in the control of his working life should be exercised through his capacity as a voting citizen of the state rather than as an employee of the state. The government employee through the use of his vote can exert political pressure upon the legislative and executive branches of government which estabish the conditions of employment.[8] This argument is fallacious in that the political activities of government employees are often limited by statute.[9] In effect statutes make it illegal for government employees to be active in any real sense in political affairs.

Another problem arises when we examine labor-management relationships with regard to political sovereignty. Political sovereignty is the exercising of sovereignty in an independent government system. The operation of government is organized around a system of checks and balances that delimit the exercise of power by an individual or group. The check and balance system exists because of separation of powers, elections, and constitutions. Employment and personnel policies are shared by legislatures, governors, departments, independent agencies, commissions, and even political parties.[10]

Decentralization of authority causes a limiting of the negotiable subjects because one branch of government cannot make decisions regarding public employees when another branch of government may hold the power of determination.[11] This viewpoint is supported by the fact that in the federal government the President may recommend pay increases for federal government employees but the Congress must grant the pay increases. Similar situations exist in many of the states.

In the same vein, decentralization of authority limits the bargaining authority of local management. Many subject areas covered under collective bargaining agreements in the private sector are also covered by statutes, executive orders, civil service regulations, and agency policies and regulations thus, management representatives often find themselves in the position where they "cannot", rather than they "will not" negotiate with the unions.

Because a locus of authority to conclude an agreement often does not exist, public employee unions are all too often shunted around among the conflicting or overlapping authorities of particular agencies, public officials, and commissions.

Although this condition often presents a constraint on collective bargaining, unions have used it to their advantage. The unions will often circumvent managements and apply political pressure to elected officials to secure their needs. Continuance of this sytem of circumvention will not facilitate meaningful collective bargaining at the local levels where agreements must be implemented.

The lack of authority on the part of local management to conclude an agreement is analogous to private sector labor-management conditions in the 1930's. In the 30's the union negotiators often had great difficulty in locating the seat of corporate authority. Today this problem rarely exists in the private sector.

The government employee is again limited in his attempts to collectively bargain with his employer, considering the fact that in the final analysis government employees' salaries come from taxes. The Government's position is a function of the specific power and personnel relationships between individuals and groups at any one time. Many organized pressure groups outside of government have as their main objective the reduction of taxes. In effect the reduction of taxes means either a reduction in the number of government employees or the reduction of salary levels.[12] The organized government employee is but one of many interest groups attempting to exert pressure upon government. Governments are generally reluctant to raise taxes bcause of the political infeasibility. For this reason the wages and fringe benefits of government employees, especially at the state and local levels, have generally lagged behind their counterparts in the private sector.[13]

In the private sector the situation is different. While government must cover increased labor costs primarily by eventual increases in taxes, firms in the private sector can meet rising labor costs in a number of ways. One, they can raise prices, which is analogous to government's raising taxes. Two, they can increase efficiency. Generally, it is easier for firms producing goods to increase efficiency than firms producing services. The product of government is service. Therefore it is often difficult for government to increase efficiency. Last, firms in the private sector can absorb increased costs by reducing profits. Government cannot absorb increased costs by reducing profits because government does not produce profit as defined by accountancy practices.

Civil service commissions or their counterparts have had the responsibility for administering and implementing government personnel policies and programs. These policies and programs are designed to protect the rights and benefits of government employees. In implementing and administering these policies and programs, the civil service commissions interpret their language, promulgate guidelines for personnel management, and, to varying degrees, the guidelines for labor-management relations. In addition, the civil service commissions are the guardians of the older merit system principles . . . open and equal competition and equal pay for equal work.[14]

Public employee unions do not view the civil service commissions as the protectors of the employees' rights but rather as an extension of management. Jerry Wurf, President of the American Federation of State, County, and Municipal Employees and John Griner, past president of the American Federation of Government Employees have both argued that in their experience Civil Service Commissions have been extensions of management.[15] Underlying their statements is the belief that administration of government personnel by Civil Service Commissions is incompatible with collective bargaining. This incompatibility is based on government sovereignty as reflected in management paternalism and the individualism of the merit system.[16] Merit systems at the federal and state levels have deep historical roots and have been slow to change.

This condition is analogous to labor-management relations in the private sector during the 1930's. In the past, management rights in developing and administering personnel policies and procedures were unquestioned. Today, largely due to changes in the law and union power, private sector managements are more careful, more responsible, and more responsive in personnel matters. As unions in the public sector develop more power and continue to bring about changes in the law, the merit system and role of the commissions will also change. Government management will also be more careful, more responsible, and more responsive in personnel matters.

THE USE OF THE STRIKE

A major problem in public sector collective bargaining is the use of the strike. Although the use of the strike in the private sector as a means of compelling disputing parties to reach an agreement has in recent years become increasingly controversial, its use as a bargaining tactic is still widespread. In accord with the sovereignty doctrine, federal, state, and local governments have by statute and executive order denied employees and their unions the right to participate in a strike against the government.[17] The right to strike as a social and economic weapon in private sector labor-management relations has been legally accorded workers and their unions since 1935.[18] Without the right to strike, unions in the public sector are limited in their ability to effectively negotiate with management. In lieu of the right to strike, government unions have used political pressure to meet their objectives. The limitation of political pressure is that it does not bring about results as quickly as striking.

The logic underlying the government's position prohibiting use of the strike consists of two points:

1. Strikes against the government cannot be tolerated since the government is sovereign and cannot share its sovereign authority with its employees or their unions. Any strike against the government is an attack upon the state and a challenge to the government's authority.

2. In the private sector, the use of the strike by labor and the lockout by management are economic and social weapons used for testing the strengths and weaknesses of the bargaining parties when impasses occur. Governments do not use the politically infeasible lockout because the government provides essential services to society. Any disruption of these essential services by a strike would repudiate the function of government. Therefore, the strike is not an appropriate means for settling collective bargaining impasses in the government. Even if some government services are not essential it is impossible or infeasible to attempt to differentiate between nonessential and essential services permitting strikes in the former but not in the latter.[20]

In recent years, a number of writers have expressed the view that the sovereignty doctrine and the prohibition of the right to strike limits meaningful collective bargaining in the public sector. Although the government continues to assert its sovereignty by imposing severe penalties on individuals and groups who strike the government, there is some doubt as to whether the strike ban is enforceable. Statistics on strike data for the period 1958 through 1968 show that the number of government employee strikes per year rose from 15 to 254. The number of workers involved rose from 1700 to 202,000. Man-days lost increased from 7500 to 2.5 millions.[21]

During this same period, strikes in the private sector increased, but at a lower rate than those in government. In 1958 government employee strikes constituted four-tenths of 1 per cent of all strikes, eight one-hundredths of a per cent of total idleness. By 1968 these ratios had risen to 5.0 per cent, 7.6 per cent, and 5.2 per cent respectively.[22]

Essentiality of service means that the consumers' demand for the service is inelastic. Except for some limited functions, such as the armed forces, there is no empirical evidence demonstrating differences in elasticity of demand between private sector services and government services.[23] Government services are expanding in scope and increasingly the services provided are similar to those available from private industry. As far as the public is concerned, a strike is the same whether it is in a privately operated hospital or a government operated hospital, in a transportation system privately operated or government operated.[24]

Government's denial of strike rights to any of its employees in any of its services makes no distinction between the essentiality of nonessentiality of the service. John F. Burton's analysis of Bureau of Labor Statistics strike data for 1965-68 showed that some state and local governments differentiate between a strike in an essential service and a strike in an nonessential service by their use of countersanctions.[25] A few states now permit some, but not all of their employees the right to strike. Pennsylvania permits its public employees (certain employees groups are specifically prohibited) to strike or refuse to cross a picket line after the statutory impasses have been exhausted. "This action will not be prohibited unless it creates 'a clear and present danger to the health, safety, or welfare of the public'."[26]

In an attempt to make collective bargaining more meaningful while maintaining its sovereignty, government at the federal and many state and local levels have established provisions for third-party fact-finding or arbitration to settle collective bargaining impasses. The pros and cons of third party intervention in settling labor-management impasses have been debated both publicly and privately for a number of years. The use of fact finding does not mean that the disputing parties are compelled to abide by the fact finders' recommendations. Agreement to the recommendations of fact finders implies that both parties have developed bargaining maturity or that other circumstances such as threats of illegal strikes or adverse publicity have compelled the parties to agree.

Some writers believe that compulsory arbitration in lieu of the right to strike spells an end to collective bargaining. Their logic is based on the belief that the negotiating parties will prepare for the arbitration procedure instead of for the give and take environment of private agreement. In arbitration proceedings the payoff is greatest to those willing to take extreme positions.[27]

CONCLUSION

Compared to labor-management relations in the private sector, labor-management relations in the public sector is a recent development. Some governments, notably the federal government and New York, Wisconsin, and Minnesota state governments, have enacted comprehensive legislation that covers the total environment of labor-management relations. However, most of the state and local governments have failed to follow suit. Many of the statutes initiated at the state and local levels have been oriented toward specific groups and are limited in scope. The failure to enact comprehensive legislation means that inconsistencies between the various laws affecting certain groups are apt to develop. This fragmentation will increase the confusion that presently exists. As confusion increases, the frequency, intensity, and duration of disputes is likely to increase.

Government's tenacious grip on the sovereignty doctrine, the concept of "meet and confer" rather than "collectively bargaining in good faith," and limitations on union security clauses, limiting the scope of negotiable issues, and the right to strike will not facilitate meaningful collective bargaining in government. Indications are that unions at all levels of government will attempt to equalize the bargaining relationships. Governments who continue to assert the traditional aspects of sovereignty and resist collective bargaining efforts can expect a repeat of the private sector experiences which occurred during the 1930's and 40's.

NOTES

1. Glenn Stahl, *Public Personnel Administration* (New York: Harper and Row, 1971). Dr. Stahl is the foremost writer in the field of public administration holding this view.

2. Joseph P. Goldberg, "Public Employee Developments in 1971," *Monthly Labor Review*, Volume 95 (January, 1972), p. 63.

3. Kenneth O. Warner and Mary L. Hennessey, *Public Management at the Bargaining Table* (Chicago: Public Personnel Association, 1967), p. 248.

4. Willem B. Vosloo, *Collective Bargaining in the United States Civil Service* (Chicago: Public Personnel Association, 1966), p. 19.

5. M. Moskow, J. Lowenberg, E. Koziaria, *Collective Bargaining in Public Employment* (New York: Random House, 1970), p. 17.

6. United States Civil Service Commission, *The Government Personnel System*, Personnel Management Series No. 4 (November, 1960).

7. Joseph Goldberg, "Labor Management Relations Laws in Public Service," *Monthly Labor Review*, Volume 9 (June, 1968). Review of the laws enacted since 1968 show the same pattern, pp. 48-55. And Joseph P. Goldberg, "Public Employee Developments in 1971," *Monthly Labor Review*, Volume 95 (January, 1972), pp. 56-66.

8. Civil Service Assembly, Committee on Employee Relations in the Public Service, Gordon R. Clapp, Chairman, *Employee Relations in the Public Service* (Chicago: C. S. A. of the U. S. and Canada, 1942), p. 47.

9. Donald R. Harvey, *The Civil Service Commission* (New York: Praeger Publishers, 1970), p. 16.

10. Kenneth O. Warner and Mary L. Hennessey, *Public Management at the Bargaining Table* (Chicago: Public Personnel Association, 1967), p. 249.

11. B. V. H. Schneider, "Collective Bargaining and the Federal Civil Service," *Industrial Relations*, Volume 3 (May, 1964), pp. 97-120.

12. Civil Service Assembly, Committee on Employee Relations in the Public Service, Gordon R. Clapp, Chairman, *op. cit.*, p. 49.

13. The objectives of the Federal Salary Reform Act of 1962, the Federal Pay Comparability Act of 1970, the Federal Coordinated Wage System of 1967, are to maintain federal government employees salaries at levels comparable to their counterparts in the private sector. The states have not enacted similar legislation.

14. Frederick Mosher, *Democracy in the Public Service* (London: Oxford University Press, 1968). p. 195.

15. Robert T. Woodworth and Richard B. Peterson (editors) *Collective Negotiations for Public and Professional Employees* (Glenview, Illinois: Scott Foresman and Company, 1969), p. 26. Article by Everett M. Kassalow, "Prospective on the Upsurge of Public Employee Unionism," citing Jerry Wurf, p. 26.

   "The Unions View of Public Management's Responsibilities in Collective Bargaining," *Public Employees Relations Library*, No. 26, citing John Griner (Chicago: Public Personnel Association, 1970), p. 5.

16. Frederick Mosher, *op. cit.*, p. 197.

17. Joseph Goldberg, *op. cit.* In the federal government Public Law 55-330 and Executive order 11616 deny government employees the right to strike.

18. The National Labor Relations Act legally accords workers in the private sector the right to strike.

19. Ann M. Ross, "Public Employee Unions and the Right to Strike," *Monthly Labor Review*, Volume 92 (March, 1969), p. 15.

20. John F. Burton, Jr., "Can Public Employees Be Given the Right to Strike?" *Labor Law Journal*, Volume 21 (August, 1970), pp. 469-70.

21. Sheila C. White, "Work Stoppages of Government Employees," *Monthly Labor Review*, Volume 92 (December, 1969), pp. 29-30.

22. *Ibid.*

23. John F. Burton, Jr., *op. cit.*, p. 475.

24. George W. Taylor, "Public Employment: Strikes or Procedures," *Industrial and Labor Relations Review*, Volume 20 (July, 1967), p. 625.

25. John F. Burton, Jr., *op. cit.*, p. 474.

26. Terrence N. Tice, ed., *Faculty Power: Collective Bargaining on Campus*. (Ann Arbor, Michigan: Institute of Continuing Legal Education, 1972), p. 181 citing Penna Stat. Ann Tit. 43, 1101.101 — 1101.2301 added by Act No. 195, effective July 23, 1970.

27. Kenneth O. Warner, editor. *Collective Bargaining in the Public Service: Theory and Practice*, "When Bargaining Fails," Jacob Finkelman (Chicago: Public Personnel Association, 1967), p. 125-26.

CHAPTER 3.
THE POLITICAL AND LEGAL FRAMEWORK

A Political System for a Political World— in Public Sector Labor Relations
Robert D. Helsby

During the past decade a substantial body of experience has evolved as public employees have sought and have obtained the right to organize and to bargain. It is not an overstatement to point out that some 38 separate experiments are underway in the various states with respect to public sector labor relations. Although the approach of each state law has some similarities, there are enough variations so that over time it may well be that experimentation will provide a means to evaluate and to choose the best of these various approaches.

However, a fundamental question raised at the beginning of the era of public sector labor relations remains unanswered. I suspect that perhaps the question has actually been answered in practice although not all participants will accept the answer which I think has emerged.

The answer also depends on how one phrases the question. The Taylor Committee, in its original report proposing the New York Law in 1966, phrased the question as follows: "How should collective negotiation in the public service be distinguished from collective bargaining in the private sector?" Others, including such distinguished practitioners as Theodore Kheel, have won-

Reproduced from the August, 1973 issue of the LABOR LAW JOURNAL, published and copyrighted (1973) by Commerce Clearing House, Inc., 4025 W. Peterson Avenue, Chicago, Illinois, 60646. Reprinted by permission of the author, the Industrial Relations Research Association, and Commerce Clearing House, Inc.

Robert D. Helsby is a member of the New York State Public Employment Relations Board.

dered whether or not collective bargaining as it has evolved in the private sector is possible or appropriate in the public sector. Certainly this, and the related questions which flow from it, are not as theoretical as was the case five or ten years ago.

In fact, I think that time and experience have provided a pretty clear answer. Whether you call it collective bargaining or collective negotiations, I submit that the process in the public sector is different.

COMPONENTS OF PUBLIC SECTOR NEGOTIATIONS

Dr. Seymour Scher, a one-time professor of political science and more recently a city manager in two of New York State's larger cities, outlines five basic components of public sector negotiations:

1. The mood, needs, and demands of the community constituency.

2. The mood, needs, and demands of the political establishment.

3. The limitations, restrictions, and requirements of constitutions, statutes, ordinances, civil service, education laws, municipal charters, etc.

4. The mood, needs, and demands of the employer.

5. The mood, needs, and demands of the employees.

Dr. Scher points out that the first three of the five elements he has listed do not exist in the private sector. Whether one agrees with his listing or not, there is certainly one major factor which differentiates the public from the private sector. The bargaining process in the public sector takes place in a political arena and the parties to the bargain—both the union and the executive—must seek political ratification of their product. The union, of course, also faces the problem of obtaining acceptance from the membership—the public employees affected. The political ratification to which I refer, however, means acceptance by the appropriate legislative body; in most situations at least the part of the agreement which costs money must have such ratification. In short, funds have to be appropriated to implement the agreement.

Let me be concrete. Two years ago in response to rising clamor about the cost of public employee pension systems in New York State, Governor Rockefeller and the Legislature appointed a pension commission. Two years later the commission made its report. The New York State Constitution precludes diminishing existing public employee pensions. Therefore, the commission recommended that public employee pensions be removed from the bargaining table and the various existing pension systems be closed and that a new system covering all state and local public employees in the State except police and firemen be created. While the details of the proposed new system are not pertinent here, I note that under the proposal the long-run cost to public employers would be reduced from 20 per cent of payroll to 10 per cent of payroll, that there would be a Social Security offset against the pension, that the system would be non-contributory, and that there would be a substantial reduction in benefits. At this point, I would not wish to venture a prediction as to the ultimate fate of these recommendations in the Legislature.

A REVIEW OF PENSION COMMISSION

I think it is instructive to review for a moment the genesis of the pension commission. Council 37, AFSCME, negotiated a pension improvement for most New York City employees which would have provided retirement at half pay after twenty years' service at age 55. Changes of this type in the various pension systems applicable to New York City employees require approval in the State Legislature. It produced substantial public outcry. Legislation to approve the agreement at the State level never got out of committee the following year. Council 37 and the Teamsters Local considered this an affront and struck. This was the famous strike during which various drawbridges were left open and untreated sewage was poured into the waters around New York City. After a day or two, the City and the affected unions negotiated what the New York Times characterized as a "face-saving agreement" which provided, in effect, that if the Legislature failed to approve the pension improvement, the City would provide alternate and equivalent benefits. Two legislative sessions have now nearly passed, and in the current climate, the Legislature seems most unlikely to approve the pension agreement between New York City and Council 37.

In this situation the State Legislature was, of course, one level removed from that of the bargaining process. The resulting strike was clearly not against the employer involved but against the State Legislature. The strike was illegal. It caused substantial disruption and inconvenience to thousands of people.

In this particular situation, the rent in the social fabric was not irreparable. The situation may, in fact, have taught a valuable lesson to all concerned. The State Legislature can, and sometimes will, repudiate a bargain between, in this instance, a subsidiary government—New York City—and a union coalition. The Legislature could reject, but so far has not, an agreement between State employee unions and the Office of Employee Relations—the negotiating arm of the Governor. And it is at least a reasonable probability that the Legislature may modify nearly every existing agreement in the State by substantially modifying the pension system for new employees.

Thus one major key to the difference between bargaining in the public sector and in the private sector is the role of the legislative body. It is not the semantic difference between collective negotiations and collective bargaining. The dynamics of the bargaining process itself are essentially similar in both the public and the private sectors. The basic fact of public sector bargaining is that a substantial part of the bargain arrived at must be ratified, directly or indirectly by the appropriate Legislature. Whatever else may be involved, the Legislature must appropriate the money to effectuate the bargain. The Legislature is composed of a group of elected people in a democracy, each with his or her own political constituency, accountability and needs for survival.

RIGHT TO STRIKE

At its meeting in May 1972, the Western Assembly in considering "collective bargaining in American government" concluded that public employees should have the right to strike. The Western Assembly also recognized that "in some instances, federal and state legislatures will be compelled to adopt legislation that supplants or supplements collective bargaining on some issues in the public sector."

At this point one has to recognize the potential of the collision course. The Western Assembly report also states "in government the basic policy-making decisions are primarily the responsibility of legislative bodies, while collective bargaining is engaged in by governmental agencies whose duty it is to effectuate these policies." Herein, it seems to me, is to be found a dilemma which so far defies solution. To phrase the question as dramatically as possible, what happens if a legislature "supplements or supplants" the bargain or, as the New York State Legislature did in the aforementioned episode, simply refuses to act? If the result is a strike, how does it get resolved?

Fortunately most situations are not this draconian. Normally the parties at the table have some realistic notion of the political parameters within which they are constrained to operate. Difficulties, of course, may arise if their respective assessments of the parameters differ. In fact, this is the normal situation encountered in public employee strikes. The parties at the table are unable or unwilling to reach a bargain. Occasionally such strikes may even be part of the political dynamics necessary to get the ultimate agreement ratified.

At this point, recognition needs to be given to the fact that the situation differs at various governmental levels. Somehow or other the situation is not exactly the same when a city manager or a mayor arrives at an agreement with a public employee union which a city council repudiates. If this does happen, the city manager is probably looking for other employment. The mayor is undoubtedly in political difficulty. The difference is even more significant in smaller governments and school districts where the employer-executive and the legislative body are essentially the same. But what if the State Legislature rejects an agreement negotiated by a Governor or his agent and unions representing state employees? Is the situation any different if Congress repudiates an agreement negotiated by presidential agents and the result is a strike?

The essential question thus becomes, what resort, if any, does a public employee union have if the applicable legislature repudiates all or part of a bargain arrived at between the executive and the union? Or, to state the question another way, if the joint political efforts of the employee union and the executive-employer fail to get the bargain implemented, what happens then?

In recent years the question of what happens when the political process yields an undesirable result from a point of view of the activists has been with us in a good many forms. Some forms of social action are obviously more tolerable than others. Rallies, peaceful demonstrations, informational picketing, vigils, etc., have been commonplace in recent years.

The question I am really asking is: After the development of a collectively negotiated agreement, why should the rights of a public employee be any greater or any less than those of any other citizen?

This is the issue, it seems to me, that those who advocate an unrestricted right for public employees to strike have simply not faced up to. What the bargaining process does in the public sector is to give public employees, through their bargaining agent, a meaningful voice in the determination of what the executive-employer proposes to the legislature with respect to terms and conditions of employment. The public sector bargain cannot be more than this. Hopefully it is not less.

Once the parties have balanced the needs of the union, the needs of the employees and the public, the resources which the executive-employer thinks he can commit, and agreed that their mutual understanding of the political parameters within which they are operating are essentially the same, both have an obligation to seek legislative approval of their joint product.

At this point the union, in seeking legislative apoproval of the agreement, has the same right as any other group of citizens to attempt to pressure the legislature to take desired action.

If, for some reason, the legislature fails to approve all or part of the bargain, it seems clear that giving public employees the right to strike at this point is giving them a right which no other citizen has. Should other groups adversely affected by legislative decisions be given the right to strike or its equivalent, whatever that is? One suspects that the answer is no in both cases.

In any event, such limited experience as we have suggests that strikes by public employees at this point would be largely futile, particularly at the state or federal level. The concept of the general strike is generally unknown and unaccepted in this country. Abroad, public employee strikes (excepting a few nationalized industries) are generally one-or two-day protest movements, usually announced in advance, rather than a fight to the finish as in the private sector in the United States.

If the economic strike against a legislature and therefore against the political process is in all probability liable to be ineffective on the one hand and intolerable on the other, and the concept of the general strike is both unknown and unacceptable, then the question arises can a strike against the executive-employer resulting from failure to reach agreement at the table be tolerated and institutionalized. This is really what those who advocate the right to strike for public employees seem to favor, at least within limits. Those public empoloyee statutes which do provide a limited right to strike mandate impasse procedures which must be exhausted before the strike becomes legal. Even then the threat to public health and safety must be assessed.

In New York State, about 3,000 contracts are negotiated annually in the public sector. Third-party assistance is required in reaching about 30 per cent of these agreements—mediation, fact-finding, or both. Strikes—illegal ones—occur in about one per cent of these situations—about 30 per year—although not all are caused by bargaining. Some result from disputes over working conditions during the term of the contract and related questions.

About 90 per cent of public employees in New York State—900,000 of some 1,000,000—presently exercise their rights under the Taylor Law. The passage of a law applicable to all state and local public employees brought about almost instant unionization. Those public employees not organized are either management-confidential employees or are employed by very small employers—less than ten. I have the impression but cannot document the fact that there have been similar developments in those states which have adopted a law, or laws, applicable to all state and local public employees.

In contrast, in the private sector in New York State, only about 30 per cent of non-farm employment is organized. While there are many factors which limit the ability of *private* sector unions to organize or to penetrate more than they have, there seems to be general agreement that the ability to organize and to bargain effectively depends in large measure on the ability and the willingness of the employees involved to strike—thus the maxim that there cannot be real collective bargaining without the right to strike.

IS THE MAXIM APPLICABLE TO THE PUBLIC SECTOR?

In 1966 and 1967 if one listened to the sound and fury of the debates in New York State, both in the Legislature and outside, out of which grew the Taylor Law, one would have to say that most of the labor leadershp thought so. At that point in time, union leadership and their allies in the Legislature contended with vim, vigor and vitality that there could be no genuine collective bargaining in the public sector without the right to strike. Within a month after the Taylor Law was passed, some 15,000 unionists gathered in Madison Square Garden to denounce the Law and establish a fund for its repeal. It was characterized as anti-union. Public management was equally vehement—strikes were intolerable and should never take plae under any circumstances.

Six years later the situation is somewhat different. This is not to say that the parties have officially reversed their 1966 and 1967 positions. Almost all union leaders still officially advocate the right to strike for public employees. I am not aware of any management representatives in New York State who have officially reversed their positions. However, I think it is fair to say that these positions have become more ritualistic than real. Certainly the noise and the din on the labor side is diminished. There has not been a repetition of the Madison Square Garden rally. Nor has management conducted any celebrations on the anniversaries of its enactment. Government has learned not to panic at the threat of a strike, or indeed in an actual strike; employees have often learned to their sorrow that a strike has not been the great pressure for equity which they had formerly envisioned.

In private discussions with both sides, one can begin to perceive the development of a reversal of position. Public management would rather continue the present system than face up to some of the alternatives. And, more particularly, at least some representatives in public management would rather legalize the strike than be faced with compulsory arbitration. On the labor side there is some private recognition that most public employees might be in a weaker position with a law which permitted strikes than at present. Both sides will generally concede, even though there are particular aspects that one or the other would like to see changed, that the present system works.

This is another way of saying that in the past six years a workable labor relations system for the public sector has gradually evolved in New York State. This evolution is, of course, still in process. It is not the traditional collective bargaining of the private sector which utilizes the bargaining-strike syndrome. Rather it is a political process which utilizes a whole new array of techniques and processes in the negotiation of an agreement. One cannot predict the ultimate direction, but I think it can safely be said that no radical changes are in the offing for the immediate future.

The basics of the system, I think, can be briefly outlined as follows. The executive-employer and the public employee union go to the table and do their thing. Seventy per cent of the time they appear to be able to agree upon the applicable political and economic parameters and to be able to reach a mutually satisfactory bargain. Where they cannot, mandated impasse procedures become applicable. At the mediation stage, settlement can generally be reached—historically in about half of the cases that go to impasse—if the parties are divided only by economic or technical issues, but not if the mix includes basic disagreement on both the economic and political parameters. Of the cases which go to fact-finding, a substantial number—historically about 40 per cent—are mediated by the fact-finder, e.g., the threat of what he might recommend is enough to bring the parties to agreement. In about a fourth of these cases, the report and recommendations become a politically and economically acceptable document which both parties can buy. In about 40 per cent of the cases which go to fact-finding, the report and recommendations provide a political and economic frame within which and upon which the parties generally manage to reach agreement. Additional third-party assistance is sometimes required. And, of course, as has already been indicated, there are occasional strikes. Approximately 20 of the 30 strikes a year result from failure of the bargaining process and impasse procedures—considerably less than one per cent of the agreements. There are about an equal number of valid strike threats. Taken together, some would say that these are necessary to lubricate the system.

Thus bargaining in the public sector has become, in New York State and I suspect in many other jurisdictions, a process for the mutual formulation of the public employee compensation package and related matters before it is dropped into the legislative-political arena to compete with other claimants for the allocation of public resources. However imperfect, this is the only process which we have to legitimately resolve such questions. It is not a particularly neat and tidy process, but neither are the tugs and hauls of public opinion which constitute the democratic system.

If the only alternative is to give public employees the right to strike, the question needs to be asked not only what effect would this have upon the continuity of public service but what effect would it have upon public employees? Would their bargaining strength be increased or weakened? For some, particularly in the large unions, their position would quite clearly be strengthened. For many others, however, the opposite would be the case. My judgment is that in New York State, for example, 60 to 70 per cent are probably better served by the present system. Oftentimes the news media refer to our PERB-appointd and financed mediators, fact-finders, and conciliators as the "public employee rescue battalion." Unless employees have the will and ability to mount a cohesive strike, the right to strike by itself becomes meaningless. In short, their circumstances are such that a strike weapon is not a viable alternative.

As experience builds in the public sector, what we really need is less ideology and more research. We need to take a hard look at what is going on in the various "experiments" which have been under way in various states for some time. To be truly objective this effort should be made by others than those who have a vested interest—in other words, not by agencies administering programs or by representatives of the parties.

Someone recently said: "Arbitration is to collective bargaining what artificial insemination is to reproduction; it takes all the fun out of it." Sometimes I think those who advocate the right to strike for public employees are taking a somewhat similar position. Somehow, they feel that without the right to strike, the whole process is less fun.

It may be fun, however, which we neither need nor can afford. When I see communities literally torn apart from a strike of teaches for example; when I see the acrimony and divisiveness caused by youngsters on picket lines, teacher pitted against boards of education, neighbor against neighbor, parents and families divided in bitter battles which leave wounds and scars which are so hard to heal; then I believe that our quest must be to find a better way.

What is really emerging is a system of employee participation in the determination of conditions of employment—a bargaining process applicable to and more appropriate for the political process.

CONCLUSION

To summarize, I believe that:

1. The political world in which public employees negotiate their conditions of employment calls for very different considerations than the predominantly economic world of the private sector.

2. Contrary to the characterization by some, this does not make a second-class citizen of the public employee. Rather, it calls for approaches which are different from, and more appropriate to the public sector.

3. The requirement for ratification by appropriate legislative bodies is one basic element of the political equation which drastically influences every aspect of public sector bargaining.

4. Out of the vast array of experimentation taking place in the various states, many techniques and systems are developing to balance the needs of government, its employees and the public interest.

5. The tenet of collective bargaining in the private sector— namely, the need for the right to strike as an inherent requirement of the process—is being seriously questioned in the public

sector. Both employers and employees are taking a long constructive look at the alternatives.

    6. A whole new system of dispute settlement is emerging
which uses the widest possible variety of mechanisms—
mediation, mediation-arbitration, fact-finding, arbitration,
etc.—with the utmost of tailormade flexibility. In short, it is a
political system which responds to the tug and haul of public
opinion in a democratic society. The Taylor Law in New York is
one such experiment. Its initial six years would indicate considerable promise for such systems.

    7. The components of this exciting new field of human rela-
tions are as complex as human nature and as dynamic as democracy itself. And the stakes for success are high indeed.

Federally Legislated Collective Bargaining for State and Local Government: A Logical Imperative

Michael A. Mass and Anita F. Gottlieb

*Federal legislation to regulate state and local government col-
lective bargaining has been proposed for a number of years. The
growing importance of state and local governments, the dramatic increase in public sector unionism and in union militancy,
and the labor-management strife which exists in many
localities are cited by the authors as indications that such legislation is an idea whose time has come. After reviewing the
present status of state collective bargaining laws, the authors
conclude that federal legislation for state and local government
employees is necessary both to provide the public sector with the
environment in which rational labor-management relations can*

(C) Executive Enterprises Publications Co., Inc., EMPLOYEE RELATIONS LAW
JOURNAL, Vol. 2., No. 3, Winter 1977. Reprinted by permission.

Michael A. Mass is assistant professor of business law at the American University,
Washington, D.C. and is in private practice.

Anita F. Gottlieb, a management consultant, formerly was assistant professor of
management at the American University.

*occur and to facilitate the transferablity—often impossible
today—from locale to locale of expertise in state and local government labor relations. They review proposed federal legislation and discuss the constitutionality of such legislation in the
wake of a recent landmark Supreme Court decision.*

On April 4, 1968, Martin Luther King, Jr., was shot and killed
in Memphis, Tennessee. He was there to support a strike by
sanitation workers to gain recognition of their union, Local 1733
of the American Federation of State, County, and Municipal
Employees (AFSCME). Local 1733 received its charter from
AFSCME in October 1964 and had attempted to be recognized by
the city since that time. In 1964, there was no law in Tennessee
regarding the rights of local government employees to have a
union as their bargaining agent; there was no law stating that
local governments could, or must, recognize an employee bargaining agent. There was still no such law in 1968, and there is as yet
no such law today. But after the sixty-five-day strike, with the
tragic and violent events that surrounded it—and with federal
intervention—Local 1733 was granted recognition as the sole
bargaining representative of the laborers and drivers of the Memphis Sanitation Department.

If the Memphis sanitation workers had been employed by a
private company which had a contract with the city to collect its
citizens' garbage, the strike would not have taken place. If the
sanitation workers had worked for the City of Milwaukee, Wisconsin, the strike would not have taken place. But in Memphis in
1968, as in hundreds of cities and counties in the United States
today, there was no mechanism to provide for the recognition of a
union as the bargaining agent of state or local government
employees.

The Memphis strike is a dramatic illustration of the increased
and widespread militancy of public employees, particularly state
and local government employees, that has been emerging over the
past decade. It is also an example of the kind of labor strife that is
likely to occur in an atmosphere of public sector employee relations anarchy when there are no legal procedures governing the
process of collective bargaining between management and labor.
Such an atmosphere exists in many states and localities today.

One solution to this lack of legal procedures is a federal law
regulating state and local government labor-management relations. Before determining whether this is the best solution, it is
necessary to understand the changes which have occurred in

state and local governments and in the unions which represent these employees.

Public Sector Employees in the American Economy

In the United States today, one of every five employed persons works for some level of government. The vast majority of these more than 15 million people do not work for the federal government. Rather, more than 12.5 million of these public employees are employed by state and local governments.[1]

This figure becomes more significant when viewed in historical perspective. Forty years ago, the federal government had 2.4 million civilian employees; today, it has 2.7 million. In this same period of time, however, state and local government employment rose from 3.5 million to its present level of more than 12.5 million. According to projections by the Bureau of Labor Statistics, the level of civilian federal employment in 1985 will actually be less than the present level, while state and local government employment will be more than 15.7 million. If these projections hold up, state and local government will show the most rapid growth of any sector in the economy in the coming decade.

The growth of state and local government employment in the past decades has been accompanied by a dramatic increase in union activity in the public sector. In 1956, only 5.1 percent of American union members were public employees. This percentage had more than doubled, to 11.8 percent, by 1972. Between 1972 and 1974, three-quarters of the increase in total U.S. union membership was among governmental employees. Between 1965 and 1975, only three unions—AFSCME, the American Federation of Teachers (AFT), and the American Federation of Government Employees—doubled their memberships.[2] These three unions organize almost exclusively in the public sector, with AFSCME and AFT doing so on the state and local level. This increase in public sector union membership is occurring in all states, both those that have collective bargaining legislation and those that do not.

The growing importance of the public sector in the field of labor relations is, therefore, obvious from examining the statistics. But even these statistics do not fully convey the effects of labor strife in the public sector on the private sector and on the lives of private citizens. No long discussion is needed here to describe the disruptive effect of labor strife in state and local governments. What is needed, however, is a discussion of the mechanisms available to cope better with management-labor relationships in these crucial areas.[3]

State Collective Bargaining Laws Today

The first bargaining law recognizing the rights of municipal employees to bargain was passed in Wisconsin in 1959.[4] Since that time, a majority of the states have enacted some type of legislation concerning the bargaining rights of state and/or local government employees.[5] At the present time, nineteen states have comprehensive laws which provide for broad collective bargaining rights for state and local government employees.[6] Mandatory, full-scope bargaining laws for local government employees exist in four states.[7] Alaska mandates full-scope bargaining for state employees, but allows local governments to bargain at their own option. Wages and fringe benefits are excluded from the scope of bargaining in laws covering state employees in Delaware and Washington. Also, Delaware has a law which allows comprehensive bargaining at the local level at the option of the local governing body. A different approach to labor-management relations exists in Kansas and Missouri, where state and local government employees are covered by legislation requiring public employers merely to "meet and confer" with employee representatives. In other states, attorney general rulings, executive orders, and court decisions provide the framework in which bargaining by state and local government employees takes place.

In addition to the laws listed above, a number of states, such as California, have laws which cover a selected group of employees in a manner different from the general state law, or have laws only for selected employees.[8]

The legal framework in which labor-management relations for state and local government employees take place varies widely from state to state and even within one state. There is no uniformity in the handling of major issues such as scope of bargaining, unit determination, bargaining rights, union security, grievance procedure, impasse procedure, strike policy,[9] representation procedure, and administrative agency. It is this maze of state laws, the increased amount of legislative activity on state and local levels in recent years, and the increased demands by public employees that make it essential to examine the possible direction of legislation governing the bargaining rights of state and local government employees.

Are State Laws Enough?

The passage of the Wagner Act in 1935 (designed specifically to promote collective bargaining) followed a long period of labor-management strife in the United States, strife exacerbated by the

Great Depression. Public employees in 1935, however, were generally uninterested in collective bargaining. They, unlike workers in the private sector at that time, had basic job security, generally good working conditions, adequate compensation, and some pension coverage. In the forty years since the passage of the Wagner Act, public sector employees often have fallen behind their private sector counterparts in compensation and benefits. The increased pressure on city and state budgets in the 1970s, resulting in numerous RIFs (reduction in force) at the state and local levels, has eliminated the feelings of job security once held by the public employees.

The changing conditions of public employment have resulted in the new militancy of public employees and their unions. This militancy, some believe, can be abated by blocking legislation which would provide collective bargaining procedures and a mechanism for union recognition; this is the equivalent of suggesting that the public sector ignore history and follow the same path that led to the violent labor-management wars of the early part of this century in the private sector.[10] The absence of legislation did not produce rational, productive, labor-management relations for the private sector then, and the absence of comprehensive national legislation is not producing rational labor-management relations in the public sector now. Almost every recognition strike, such as the 1968 Memphis sanitationmen's strike, is a strike that would not have occurred had mechanisms for union recognition existed.

States which have passed legislation prohibiting strikes and/or providing severe penalties for strikes, such as New York's Taylor Law,[11] have found that legislation alone does not prevent strikes. Fewer strikes and constructive, rational, labor-management relations result from: (1) a mechanism for the designation of workers' representatives to take part in a comprehensive mechanism for collective bargaining, including impasse procedures; and (2) "actors" in the process who are trained and who understand the "rules of the game."

Federal legislation is the only way that these conditions will be achieved for all state and local government employees in the foreseeable future. In the almost two decades since the first state law recognizing the right of municipal employees to bargain collectively was passed, less than half of the states have passed comprehensive laws covering all state and local government employees, and many of these laws are lacking in certain areas (such as impasse procedures). It is politically unrealistic to believe that many of the states which have not yet passed such legislation will do so in the near future.

The positive effect of binding arbitration procedures in Pennsylvania, Michigan, and Wisconsin was demonstrated in a 1974 study which concluded that these laws had a salutary effect on bargaining, while at the same time they greatly decreased the likelihood of strikes by those covered by the laws.[12] The stabilizing effect of such provisions should be provided to all state and local government labor-management relations, not merely to a select few.

Federal legislation is necessary to provide actors who are trained in and who understand the process of public sector collective bargaining. While numerous university programs produce actors for private sector bargaining proesses, it is almost impossible to develop a comprehensive program in public sector labor relations. The diversity of the laws and processes gives much of the training limited applicability. This also applies to experience. In an era of highly mobile public administrators, the experience gained in one locality loses much of its value when the manager moves to another locality.

In many instances, the very public managers who oppose federal legislation[13] are the ones most affected by the lack of applicable training when a new state law is passed. For example, when California provided collective bargaining rights for education employees in 1975,[14] the California Teachers Association[15] provided massive training sessions for its staff and members on the provisions of the law and on the techniques of bargaining. Many school districts, particularly small ones, had no training available for their managers These districts generally have turned to a select group of private attorneys who have made the California law their only specialty; the school districts simply excluded their own managers from this crucial role. In many states, the unions have a clear advantage because they are the actors who have the best resources for utilizing the rules of the game to their own advantage.

It seems clear that some scheme of federal legislation is needed to bring order and uniformity to an area currently in disarray. With one set of laws applicable nationwide, we would not suffer the loss of resources that now occurs when an experienced administrator moves to a new locale.

Proposed Federal Legislation

Several legislative approaches have been proposd to govern the processes of state and local collective bargaining in some states and to create uniformity between states that already have such a law.

By far, the simplest of the proposed legislative solutions is to remove[16] the National Labor Relations Act (NLRA)[17] immunity applicable to "any State or political subdivision thereof," thus bringing state and local collective bargaining within the NLRA. This would expand the jurisdiction of the National Labor Relations Board (NLRB) to include state and local bargaining.

Another proposed bill[18] would create a new federal agency to govern the special problems of state and local bargaining. This National Public Employment Relations Commission would function much like the NLRB but would be designed solely to handle the special circumstances of the public sector. Although the bill also includes several pro-union provisions, such as a union shop, a checkoff, and a very wide description of issues to be bargained, it must be acknowledged that the final content of any federal legislation passed by Congress probably would not resemble this bill in some of the details.

A third alternative would not subject state and local collective bargaining to direct federal regulation but would set up minimum standards for state statutes authorizing and reglating public sector bargaining.[19] Such a statute would condition the payment of federal funds to states upon the passage of an appropriate state collective bargaining statute. Although this alternative would end the collective bargaining anarchy in some states, it would not have the advantage of creating national uniformity that would foster the training of more highly skilled and mobile bargainers. Additionally, the question remains as to how effectively a state would administer a law forced upon it by Congress.

Although there is a great deal of variability among the proposed bills,[20] as well as a great likelihood that the political realities of the legislative process will cause the final statute to be a compromise solution, the important result is a solution that will attain some degree of national uniformity and estabish the right to bargain collectively in every state.

IS FEDERAL LEGISLATION CONSTITUTIONAL?

Serious questions as to the constitutionality of any attempt by Congress to legislate state collective bargaining procedures are raised by the recent Supreme Court decision in *National League of Cities v. Usery.*[21] This "landmark"[22] decision by a bitterly divided Court has been said to "doom"[23] pending legislation extending federal control over state collective bargaining. Careful analysis of *National League of Cities* is necessary in order to grasp the impact of this decision on proposed legislation.

The case involves a challenge by state and local governments to the 1974 amendments to the Fair Labor Standards Act.[24] These amendments extended minimum wage and maximum hour provisions to almost all employees of states and their political subdivisions. Mr. Justice Rehnquist, writing for the majority in this 5-to-4 decision, struck down the federal statute as impairing "the States' 'ability to function effectively within a federal system.' "[25] The majority, while conceding that such congressional activity is well within the authority of the Commerce Clause,[26] invented a new limitation[27] on congressional actions that "directly displace the States' freedom to structure integral operations in areas of traditional governmental functions. . . "[28] The court further concluded that the statute would "alter or displace the States' abilities to structure employer-employee relationships . . ."[29] and therefore "impermissibly interfere with the integral governmental functions of these bodies."[30]

The possible significance of this decision extends not only to proposed public sector collective bargaining legislation, but also to the constitutional relationship between federal and state governments. *National League of Cities* represents the first Court-declared limitation in forty years on the congressional power to regulate interstate commerce. It squarely overrules *Maryland v. Wirtz,*[31] which upheld the extension of the Fair Labor Standards Act to employees of state hospitals, schools, and other institutions on the theory that the states were engaged in "enterprises" not dissimilar to those in the private sector. The annihilation of the enterprise concept, coupled with the pronouncement of this new "integral governmental functions" limitation on the Commerce Clause, could well have implications of staggering proportions. Indeed, Mr. Justice Brennan, writing for the dissenters, exclaims,

> "The portent of such a sweeping holding is so ominous for our constitutional jurisprudence as to leave one incredulous."[32]

Perhaps one should be incredulous, since there are several reasons why this decision should be read narrowly, rendering its portent less ominous.

Possibly the most limiting aspect of this decision is the division of the Court. The 5-to-4 majority consisted of the Nixon appointees, Burger, Blackmun, Powell, and Rehnquist, plus Stewart, opposing Brennan, White, Marshall, and Stevens. The deciding vote apparently was cast by Justice Blackmun, who in a brief concurring opinion indicated that he was "not untroubled by certain possible implications of the Court's opinion."[33]

Blackmun's opinion limits the impact of the majority view by interpreting it as a "balancing approach."[34] Apparently, whenever Congress' powers under the Commerce Clause collide with this newfangled concept of state sovereignty, Blackmun envisions a case-by-case balancing of interests. Blackmun indicates that in his view, for example, the majority decision would not

> "outlaw federal power in areas such as environmental protection where the federal interest is demonstrably greater and where state facility compliance with imposed federal standards would be essential."[35]

Since Blackmun cast the deciding vote, his interpretation has special significance. This balancing approach is vigorously criticized by Brennan as "a thinly veiled rationalization for judicial supervision of a policy judgment that our system of government reserves to Congress."[36] However, the likelihood that future cases will be decided on the basis of policy judgment rather than on a doctrine of constitutional law dramatically limits the breadth of this decision's significance.

For example, it could be argued that *National League of Cities* would invalidate Equal Employment Opportunity (EEO) laws[37] as they apply to the states as employers; that is, EEO legislation would interfere with certain states' abilities to structure employment relationships and make "fundamental employment decisions."[38] For example, would Congress be powerless to prevent Alabama from systematically excluding blacks from state employment? It seems, in light of this balancing approach, that the Court would view federal policy as outweighing such an infringement upon state sovereignty.[39]

Further insight into the Court's application of the *National League of Cities* decision can be gleaned from the method used by the majority to distinguish *Fry v. United States.*[40] In that case, application of the Economic Stabilization Act of 1970 to the temporary wage freeze of state and local government employees was held to be constitutional. Rehnquist's opinion in *National League of Cities* distinguishes *Fry* on the grounds that the degree of intrusion on essential state functions was less severe in that it "displaced no state choices"[41] and that the freezing of wages "reduced the pressures on state budgets rather than increased them."[42]

If the Court can distinguish *Fry*, it certainly seems plausible that federal legislation creating uniform procedures for state employee collective bargaining could also be distinguished. Such legislation would not directly mandate terms of employment, but would merely provide a procedure by which the state would bargain in good faith with the employees' elected representatives. Although it is clear that the constitutionality of proposed collective bargaining legislation was considered by certain members of the majority during their deliberation in *National League of Cities*,[43] of course no direct reference to such legislation was made by the Court. It could be argued, however, that federal legislation of state public sector bargaining is less intrusive upon a state's prerogative than the mandate of minimum wages for state employees. Such legislation does not require the expenditure of additional state revenues, but merely affords to the state employee essentially the same collective bargaining rights as their private sector counterparts have had since 1935.

It seems likely, therefore, that the Court, in deciding the constitutionality of such a statute as H.R. 1488 or H.R. 77, would find at least five justices agreeing that the national objectives[44] outlined here do outweigh the state-sovereignty arguments; this would severely limit the application of *National League of Cities*.

Even if legislation creating direct federal regulation of state collective bargaining does not pass constitutional muster, similar ends may be accomplished by other means. As has been proposed,[45] Congress could condition the payment of funds upon each state's implementation of public sector collective bargaining laws that meet certain federal standards. This approach seems particularly viable, since the Court in *National League of Cities* stated:

> "We express no view as to whether different results might obtain if Congress seeks to affect integral operations of state government by exercising authority granted to it under other sections of the Constitution such as the Spending Power, Art. 1, Sec. 8, Cl. 1 or Sec. 5 of the Fourteenth Amendment."[46]

After close scrutiny, it is apparent that federal legislation of state and local collective bargaining is not necessarily constitutionally "doomed," although serious questions remain unresolved about the relationship between the state and federal governments in the aftermath of *National League of Cities*. It seems clear, however, that the benefits of such legislation and the possibility, if not probability, of its constitutionality make its passage and eventual testing in the courts a worthwhile governmental exercise.

NOTES

1. Unless otherwise indicated, all statistics as to levels of employment and union membership in the public sector have been obtained from the Bureau of Labor Statistics.

2. 98 Monthly Labor rev. 2 (1975).

3. Federal employees, while not enjoying all the rights of private sector employees, do have a procedure for bargaining-unit recognition and collective bargaining. These procedures were provided by Exec. Order No. 10988 (1962) and Exec. Order No. 11491 (1969), as amended by Exec. Order No. 11838 (1975).

4. Wisconsin Employment Relations Act, Wis. Stat. Ann. Sec. 111.70-71.

5. For a state-by-state analysis of regulations governing labor relations for state and local government employees, see U.S. Department of Labor, *Summary of State Policy Regulations for Public Sector Labor Relations: Statutes, Attorney General Opinions, and Selected Court Decisions* (1975). For yearly updates, see January issues of *Monthly Labor Review*.

6. Connecticut, Florida, Hawaii, Indiana, Iowa, Maine, Massachusetts, Minnesota, Montana, Nebraska, New Jersey, New Hampshire, New York, Oregon, Pennsylvania, Rhode Island, South Dakota, Vermont, and Wisconsin.

7. Michigan, Nevada, Oklahoma, and Washington.

8. Because of selective coverage of public employees' bargaining rights and coverage of some employees' bargaining rights by ruling of attorneys general and court dcisions, it is difficult, if not impossible, to list those states where no public employees have rights to organize or bargain.

9. A limited legal right to strike exists for some public emloyees in Alaska, Hawaii, Minnesota, Montana, Oregon, Pennsylvania, and Vermont.

10. All public employees have the right to join unions regardless of their right in a particular state to bargain collectively. The existence of this right was held by the courts in AFSCME v. Woodward, 406 F.2d 137 (1969), and in subsequent decisions.

11. Taylor Law, N.Y. Civ. Serv. Law Sec. 200 to 214 (1967).

12. Rehmus, "Legislated Interest Arbitration," Proceedings of the Twenty-Seventh Annual Winter Meetings, Industrial Research Association 307-314 (1974).

13. Federal legislation is opposed by the National Association of Profes-

sional Educators, the National School Boards Association, the National League of Cities, the U.S. Conference of Mayors, and the American Association of School Administrators, among others.

14. Educational Employment Relations Act, Ch. 10.7, div. 4, tit. 1, Cal. Educ. Code, commencing with Sec. 35-40.

15. The California Teachers Association is a state affiliate of the National Education Association.

16. H.R. 77, introduced in the Ninety-Fourth Congress.

17. 29 U.S.C. Sec. 152(2).

18. H.R. 1488, introduced in the Ninety-Fourth Congress. H.R. 1488 is similar to H.R. 8677, introduced in the Ninety-Third Congress and referred to as the Clay-Perkins bill.

19. H.R. 4293, introduced in the Ninety-Third Congress.

20. For a full discussion of the issues involved in federal collective bargaining legislation for state and local government employees, see Colosi and Rynecki, *Federal Legislation of Public Sector Collective Bargaining.* American Arbitration Association: Washington D.C. (1975).

21. National League of Cities v. Usery, _____ U.S. _____, 96 S. Ct. 2465, 49 L. Ed. 2d 245 (1976).

22. Oelsner, "High Court Frees States and Cities From U.S. Pay Law," New York Times, June 25, 1976, p. A-1.

23. See MacKenzie, "Court Backs States on Pay of Employees," Washington Post, June 25, 1976, p. A-8; Green, "Public Employee Pay Law Loses in High Court," Wall Street Journal, June 25, 1976, p. 3.

24. 29 U.S.C. Sec. 201 *et seq.* (1940 ed.)

25. Note 21 *supra* at 96 S. Ct. 2474, 49 L. Ed. 2d 257.

26. U.S. Const. art. I, Sec. 8, Cl. 3.

27. Somewhat similar limitations on the Commerce Clause have been found in other parts of the Constitution, e.g., the Sixth Amendment, United States v. Jackson, 390 U.S. 570 (1968), and due process of the Fifth Amendment, Leary v. United States, 395 U.S. 6 (1969).

28. Note 21 *supra* at 96 S. Ct. 2474, 49 L. Ed. 2d 257-258.

29. *Id.*

30. *Id.* at 96 S. Ct. 2473, 49 L. Ed. 2d 257.

31. 392 U.S. 183 (1968).

32. Note 21 *supra* at 96 S. Ct. 2485, 49 L. Ed. 2d 271.

33. *Id.* at 96 S. Ct. 2476, 49 L. Ed. 2d 260.

34. *Id.*

35. *Id.*

36. *Id.* at 96 S. Ct. 2486, 49 L. Ed. 2d 272.

37. 42 U.S.C.A. Sec. 2000e *et seq.*.

38. Note 30 *supra.*

39. This seems especially likely since Rehnquist uses affirmative action as an example of fair Labor Standards Act interference with state programs. See note 21 *supra* at 96 S. Ct. 2472, 49 L. Ed. 2d 255.

40. 421 U.S. 542 (1975).

41. Brennan, in dissent, writes, "it is sophistry to say the Economic

Stabilization Act displaces no state choices," note 21 *supra* at 96 S. Ct. 2484, 49 L. Ed. 2d 269.

42. Note 21 *supra* at 96 S. Ct. 2475, 49 L. Ed. 2d 258.

43. In reargument on March 2, 1976, Burger, Powell, and Rehnquist each asked specific questions about congressional power to legislate in the area of state employee collective bargaining. Transcript at 40, 47.

44. These objectives as described herein include labor-management peace and national uniformity of procedures.

45. See National Public Employee Merit System Act, H.R. 4293.

46. Note 21 *supra* at 96 S. Ct. 2474, 49 L. Ed. 2d 258. See also Oklahoma v. United States Civil Service, 330 U.S. 127 (1947).

The Impact of Executive Order 11491 on the Federal Labor Management Relations Program

Dr. Milden J. Fox, Jr. and Huntly E. Shelton, Jr.

President Kennedy signed Executive Order 10988 in 1962 to begin a government wide labor relations policy for Federal workers. This program worked well but needed revision as conditions changed, leading President Johnson to appoint a Review Committee. After study, a new executive order, No. 11491, was signed by President Nixon in 1969, which redirected the program toward greater conformance with private sector practices.

New Order 11491 abolished informal and formal recognition in favor of exclusive recognition, established the Federal Labor Relations Council to administer the program, the Federal Services Impasses Panel to resolve disputes, and extended use

---

Dr. M. J. Fox, Jr., is an Associate Professor of Industrial Engineering at Texas A & M University. He also serves on the Labor Arbitration Panels of the American Arbitration Association and the Federal Meditation and Conciliation Service. Dr. Fox has published a number of articles in the labor-management area. Lt. Colonel Huntly E. Shelton has been a career officer in the U.S. Signal Corps since 1955. He is currently completing his requirements for a Master of Engineering degree in Industrial Engineering at Texas A & M University.

of the Federal Mediation and Conciliation Service to the Federal program at no cost to either party.

INTRODUCTION

An executive order that made sweeping changes for improving the Federal labor-management relations program was signed by President Nixon on October 29, 1969. The order, known as Executive Order 11491, became effective January 13, 1970, and replaced the 1962 Executive Order 10988 that established the first Federal labor-management policy. The new order was designed to eliminate deficiencies that had been found to exist in the order of 1962 and to substantially strengthen the Federal labor-relations system by bringing it more into line with practices in the private sector of the economy.

Although collective bargaining had been encouraged and regulated within the private sector by the Federal Government since the Norris-LaGuardia Act was passed in 1932, no government-wide policy existed for labor relations within the Federal sector until Executive Order 10988 was promulgated on January 17, 1962, by President Kennedy. Executive order 10988 signaled the start of a new era in personnel management within the government and was the basis of the federal labor-relations program for seven and one-half years beginning July 1, 1962.

Growth of union representation in the Federal sector and changes in labor-management conditions, which the 1962 order addressed, required review of the entire Federal program in the late 1960's. President Nixon appointed the Shultz Review Committee to review both the Federal labor-relations program and the findings of a previous study group appointed by President Johnson and to make appropriate recommendations The efforts of this group, transmitted to President Nixon September 10, 1969, resulted in the currently effective Executive Order 11491. This paper provides a review of the development of Executive Order 11491 and discusses the principal adjustments it makes to the federal labor-management relations program established by Executive Order 10988. No attempt is made to digest Executive Order 11491 in its entirety.

BACKGROUND

In his memorandum of June 22, 1961, establishing the task force for Executive order 10988, President Kennedy stated his belief that:

The right of all employees of the Federal Government to join and participate in the activities of employee organizations, and to seek to improve working conditions and the resolution of grievances should be recognized by management officials at all departments and agencies. The participation of Federal employees in the formulation and implementation of employee policies and procedures affecting them contributes to the effective conduct of public business. . . . We need to improve practices which will assure the rights and obligations of employees, employee organizations and the Executive Branch in pursuing the objective of effective labor-management cooperation in the public service.[5]

This has remained the guiding principle for each review committee that addressed employee-management relations within the Federal sector in the years following 1961. Executive order 10988 proved an excellent guide that benefited both Federal agencies and Federal employees, but as time and conditions changed it was found to have weaknesses and inherent defects. Berger, an Assistant Professor at Drexel University, stated that there were three primary deficiencies in the order that contributed to slow development of collective bargaining in the Federal sector. These were:

1. failure of the order to provide the beginnings of a substitute for the strike as an inducement to agreement;
2. a lack of congruent management and union authority to bargain;
3. the nonexclusiveness of the so-called exclusive bargaining agent.[3]

Growing dissatisfaction with the functioning of executive Order 10988 in the middle 1960's by both Federal agencies and unions caused President Johnson to appoint a Review Committee for the purpose of reviewing the existing program and recommending appropriate changes. Total agreement on appropriate reform measures could not be reached by all members of the Committee. They did, however, concede in general that Order 10988 required revision in order to strengthen the Federal employee-management relationship. Consensus of opinion among the members indicated that changes in forms of recognition, scope of agreement, negotiating process, and dispute settlement were required. Other agreement centered on use of an independent agency to interpret and implement the Executive Order. A final report was never forwarded to President Johnson by the Committee.

President Nixon, faced with the same dissatisfactions in 1969 that had earlier confronted his predecessor, was forced to review the program anew. The Shultz Review Committee was appointed for this task. Its membership consisted of Melvin R. Laird, Secretary of Defense; George P. Shultz, Secretary of Labor; Robert P. Mayo, Director of the Bureau of the Budget; and Robert E. Hampton, Chairman of the Civil Service Commission. Foremost in the minds of the Shultz Committee members during their deliberations in 1969 was the fact that the public interest is paramount in all the operations of government.[4] This concept was not far removed from the guiding principle of President Kennedy's 1961 Task Force. The Shultz Committee forwarded its report to President Nixon on September 10, 1969. Contained therein was a recommendation for promulgation of a new executive order with program changes centered in six major areas. President Nixon approved the Shultz Committee report and signed Executive Order 11491 on October 29, 1969.[1]

FINDINGS OF THE SHULTZ COMMITTEE

Examination of the Shultz Review Committee Report dated September 10, 1969, reveals that from the beginning Executive Order 10988 produced outstanding results in improvement of Federal employee-management relations.[4] This finding of the Committee was substantiated by the views of a large number of organizations, union officials, agency managers, and Federal employees. It was found that both the federal employee and the Federal agency benefited alike from the excellent program that evolved from Executive Order 10988. Significant accomplishments were readily apparent, particularly in improved communications between the agencies and their respective employees and in a more democratic management of the workforce. Improved working conditions and personnel policies vividly reflected these achievements at the employee level. Reasonable harmony was maintained between labor and management throughout the period of adjustment in the early 1960's as the new era in Federal employee management, brought on by Executive Order 10988, had its beginning.[7]

Over a period of years, however, Order 10988 slowly became nonresponsive to the needs and demands of the Federal sector. Federal labor-management conditions addressed at the time Order 10988 became effective in 1962 were no longer the same in 1969. Dissatisfaction was voiced by both union and Federal agency officials at most levels by the late 1960's, and a reorientation of the program appeared necessary.

The Shultz Committee found that in the seven-year period following the promulgation of Order 10988 the number of exclusive units within the Federal sector grew considerably. Beginning with 19 units covering approximately 19,000 employees, exclusive representation grew to 2,305 units covering 1,416,073 employees. This latter figure amounted to 52 per cent of the Federal workforce which was subject to the order.[7] Provisions of Order 10988 were inadequate for union representation of this magnitude and major revisions to the program were considered necessary if it was to remain viable. The Shultz Committee determined that program changes in the following six major areas should be implemented without delay:

- A central body to administer the program and make final decisions on policy questions and disputed matters.
- Revision in the multiple forms of recognition authorized and improved criteria for appropriate units and consultation and negotiation rights.
- Clarification and improvements in the status of supervisors.
- An enlarged scope of negotiation and better rules for insuring that it is not arbitrarily or erroneously limited by management representatives.
- Third-party processes for resolving disputes on unit and election questions, for investigation and resolution of complaints under the "Standards of Conduct for Employee Organizations" and "Code of Fair Labor Practices," and for assistance in resolving negotiation impasse problems and grievances.
- Union financial reporting and disclosure.[7]

The Committee sought to change the existing program only in those areas that had been proven by experience to be deficient. It was not intended that the concepts which provided the basic foundations for Order 10988 be replaced and a totally new Federal labor-management relations program be developed and implemented. Instead, the Committee findings and recommendations dealt primarily with strengthening the existing program and attempting to better align it with the law and labor relations as practiced in the private sector.[6]

MAJOR CHANGES INTRODUCED BY EXECUTIVE ORDER 11491

Central Authority to Administer the Program

The Shultz Review Committee found that experience with the program established by Order 10988 clearly required establishment of a central authority to administer the entire Federal service labor-relations program. The 1961 Task Force recommended that authority be vested in the heads of the various Federal agencies and executive departments and that the Civil Service Commission and Department of Labor furnish only technical guidance and required assistance. It was thought that this arrangement would allow for flexibility during the developmental stages of Federal labor-management relations, better accommodate the wide diversity of labor-management situations that existed among the agencies, and encourage mutual development of meaningful labor-relations programs.[8]

In so doing, however, much of the power to decide the nature of the relationship and the ability to decide key questions was left in the hands of management. The inherent bias effect tended to build unreasonable pressure on the labor-management relationship over the years. Furthermore, since management was decentralized, uneven and confusing results were prevalent among the agencies. This unhealthy situation strengthened the demand for a central authority to administer the overall program and for third-party handling of disputed matters.

The Shultz Committee felt that a central council, having appropriate responsibility and consisting of high-level executive officials of the government, would ensure a balance of judgment that would give the program the stability and constructive direction desired for future years. The Committee further stated, however, that: "Although armed with full authority, the Council should use calculated restraint in exercising its responsibilities so as to leave the agencies and labor organizations free to work out their differences to the maximum extent possible without damaging the overall program."[8]

Section 4 of Executive Order 11491 establishes a Federal Labor Relations Council, consisting of the Chairman of the Civil Service Commission, Secretary of Labor, an Official of the Executive Office of the President, and any other officials the President may designate.[9] The Chairman of the Civil Service Commission is designated Chairman of the Council.

The Council is to administer and interpret Executive Order 11491, develop appropriate regulations, decide major policy issues and consider appeals from decisions of the Assistant Secretary of Labor for Labor-Management Relations. The latter is to decide unit and representation disputes, supervise elections and certify the results, decide complaints of alleged unfair labor practices and alleged violations of the Standards of Conduct for Labor

Organizations, and prescribe the necessary regulations needed to discharge his duties under Executive Order 11491.

Recognition

The public nature of Government business imposes on Federal officials certain obligations toward employees and other citizens that in many cases are not common to the manager-employee relationship found in the private sector. Federal officials must be prepared at any time to entertain the views of their employees. Also, it has been customary in the Federal service to seek and consider employee views when developing personnel policy. For these reasons Order 10988 was designed to accomodate a wide variation of employee organizations among the Federal departments and agencies and provided for three types of recognition— informal, formal, and exclusive.[10]

The Shultz Committee found that in the seven years following promulgation of Executive Order 10988 unionization of Federal employees was continually on a strong upswing, and by 1969 over 50 per cent of the Federal workforce was covered by exclusive representation—a quantity far greater than that found in the private sector.[11] It was concluded that in view of these conditions each type of recognition available under the 1962 Order should be examined in terms of its own merit and contribution to the Federal labor-management relations program.

Executive Order 10988 provided informal recognition as a transitional feature to preserve small union group relationships in the early phases of the program. Formal recognition was given to employee organizations having a membership of 10 per cent or more of the employees in a unit, and was designed to permit continuation of the recognition practice which prevailed prior to 1962 in the Federal sector. Exclusive recognition, virtually nonexistent in Federal agencies prior to 1962, was included to provide for the growth of a stable and meaningful employee-management relationship based upon bilateral agreements. An employee organization chosen by a majority of the employees in an appropriate unit became the only formal representative for the particular unit under the exclusive recognition system.[12]

It was concluded by the Shultz Committee that both informal and formal recognition should be abolished. Exclusive recognition should be made available without membership, authorization cards, or petition requirements and determined by use of secret ballot elections in all cases.[13] Furthermore, only one valid election should be held in a bargaining unit in a twelve-month period, and all elections should be conducted under the supervision of the Assistant Secretary for Labor-Management Relations. The Committee also recommended that the right of exclusive representation be determined by the majority voting and that the rule requiring participation of at least 60 per cent of the present and eligible voters in a representation election be deleted.[13] It was believed these changes pertaining to recognition policy would provide for development of stable labor-management relations and greatly benefit the overall Federal program.

Sections 7,8 and 10 of Executive Order 11491 reflect the changes in types of recognition proposed by the Shultz Committee.[14] Benjamin Naumoff, Regional Administrator of the U.S. Labor Department's Labor-Management Services Administration, New York City, sees this as a significant remedial step forward and states: "The Order has been fashioned and adapted to what we have become accustomed to in the private sector."[15] He further indicates that the intent is not to regulate indifference but rather to encourage individuals, using their own judgment, to exercise their given freedoms.

Resolution of Disputes and Impasses

Executive Order 10988 lacked any procedure for use in negotiations should an impasse be reached and expressly forbade the use of arbitration.[16] As such it lacked a method of inducing or enforcing an agreement. Agency administrators, given the task of implementing the Order, determined the units, conducted the elections, determined the majority representatives, and negotiated as they deemed necessary.[17] There was no appeal procedure above the agency head, and since the unions could not strike in the Federal sector, management had the ultimate say in most matters. Without the strike privilege or third-party procedures for settlement of disputes and impasses, the union was powerless. Needless to say, after Executive Order 10988 was signed and implemented, the union voiced loud demands for third-party procedures as a means to force collective bargaining in good faith.

President Kennedy's 1961 Task Force expressed concern that availability of arbitration procedures would result in escalation of minor issues to third-party involvement. This would preclude the bargaining parties from mutually working out their differences by hard and sincere negotiation.[16] The Shultz Committee shared this concern but also believed that procedures for third-party effort were necessary in order to promote good faith bargaining. The members concluded that prior to using arbitration or third-party fact finding with recommendations for impasse resolution, authorization should be obtained from governmental authority separate from the negotiating agency or union.[18]

The Committee found that mediation services had been provided on a limited basis to the Federal program by the Federal Mediation and Conciliation Service in the latter 1960's and that the services were extremely fruitful. Therefore, they recommended that the Federal Mediation and Conciliation Service be directed to assist Federal-sector parties to the fullest extent possible at no cost to either party. It was further agreed upon and recommended by the members that the parties should also have the right to retain third-party mediation other than the Federal Mediation and Conciliation Service on a cost-sharing basis if they so desired.[18]

To provide for resolution of impasses continuing to exist after application of all reasonable measures, including earnest negotiation and use of the Federal Mediation and Conciliation Service, the Committee concluded that the parties should have the right to seek assistance from a governmental body specifically appointed for that purpose. To that end it recommended establishment of a three-member Federal Service Impasses Panel whose interest should be with the public rather than with a party to the impasse. The members were to be knowledgeable in labor-management relations, public personnel administration, or the Federal Government and were to be appointed by the President.

Full assistance by the Federal Mediation and Conciliation Service to parties in negotiating agreements and settling disputes is provided by Section 16 of Executive Order 11491. Section 17 provides for use of the Federal Service Impasses Panel if Federal Mediation and Conciliation Service or other third-party mediation fails to resolve a negotiation impasse and either party so requests its services. The Federal Service Impasses Panel has the authority to settle the impasse or to recommend procedures to the parties for resolution at its discretion.[19]

Berger contends that Executive Order 11491 does not truly provide for impasse resolution by independent parties as implied.[20] The Federal Mediation and Conciliation Service, Federal Service Impasses Panel, and Assistant Secretary are not genuine independent third-parties but rather are a part of management. Thus, the employee has no vote in resolution of an impasse or other type appeal.

Financial Disclosure

The Shultz Committee determined that not all labor organizations representing Federal employees were required to make financial disclosures as was being done in the private sector. It was felt by the Committee members that labor organizations of Federal employees were of sufficient size in 1969 that all should make financial disclosures similar to those required by the Landrum-Griffin Act.[21] Accordingly, Section 18 of Executive Order 11491, Standards of Conduct for Labor Organizations, requires that labor organizations file financial reports as prescribed in regulations published by the Assistant Secretary of Labor for Labor-Management Relations.[22]

SUMMARY

President Kennedy realized early in his administration the valid need for a government-wide policy that would give direction to a viable labor-management program within the Federal sector. Consequently, he appointed a Task Force on June 22, 1961, to review and make recommendations on employee-management relations in the Federal service. The Task Force devoted approximately five months to the task and on November 30, 1961, transmitted its report to the President. The report recommended promulgation of an executive order that would establish a government-wide presidential policy acknowledging the legitimate role of labor organizations within the Federal sector and at the same time provide the necessary framework and guidance for development of a meaningful Federal employee-management relations program. On January 17, 1962, President Kennedy signed Executive Order 10988 and thus began a new era in Federal personnel practice.

Over the years the conditions that the 1962 order addressed changed considerably and it became necessary in 1967 to review both experience and progress under Executive Order 10988. President Johnson appointed a Review Committee for this purpose on September 8, 1967. The Committee reached agreement on a number of recommendations, however, total concurrence by all members could not be obtained on the final version of the report and it was never submitted to the President.

In 1969, shortly after taking office, President Nixon experienced pressure to revise Executive Order 10988 from both Federal agency and union officials. He appointed the Shultz Review Committee to study the situation and make appropriate recommendations. The Committee submitted its report on September 10, 1969. The report recommended promulgation of a new executive order containing changes to the existing program in six major areas. President Nixon approved the report and signed Executive Order 11491 on October 29, 1969, thereby giving major redirection to the Federal labor-management relations program.

Major innovations in Executive Order 11491 center on changes in types of unit recognition, centralization of the administration of the Federal labor-management relations program in the Federal Labor Relations Council, and ultimate resolution of negotiation impasses by a Federal Service Impasses Panel. Informal and formal recognition is abolished and exclusive recognition is accorded to a labor organization if it receives the vote of a majority of employees in a unit in a secret election. The Federal Labor Relations Council is the single authority for overseeing the program, interpreting the Order and settling policy issues while the Federal Service Impasses Panel is empowered at its discretion to settle an impasse or recommend resolution procedures to the parties involved.

It is significant to note that although there were substantial changes made in the program by Executive Order 11491, the basic underlying principles of Executive Order 10988 remain unchanged and continue to form the core of the Federal employee-management relations program.

Perhaps the real impact of Executive Order 11491 will be felt over the years in the Civil Service Commission, which until 1962 was largely responsible for protecting the employee in his labor-management relationship. With the advent and growth of unions in the Federal sector, the Civil Service Commission can expect to lose this and other major functions due to the impact of collective bargaining within the Federal sector.

NOTES

1. "Executive Order 11491, Code of Federal Regulations, Title 3," *The President, 1966-1970 Compilation,* Government Printing Office, Washington, D.C., 1971, pp. 861-875.

2. "Executive Order 10988, Code of Federal Regulations, Title 3," *The President, 1959-1963 Compilation,* Government Printing Office, Washington, D.C., 1964, pp. 521-528.

3. Harriet F. Berger, The Old Order Giveth Way to the New: A Comparison of Executive Order 10988 with Executive Order 11491, *Labor Law Journal,* XXI(2), February 1970, pp. 79-80.

4. *Report and Recommendations on Labor-Management Relations in the Federal Service and Executive Order 11491 of October 29, 1969*, Government Printing Office, Washington, D.C., 1969, pp. 17-22.

5. *A Policy for Employee-Management Cooperation in the Federal Service*, Government Printing Office, Washington, D.C., 1961, p. IX.

6. J. Joseph Loewenberg, Development of the Federal Labor-Management Relations Program: Executive Order 10988 and Executive Order 11491, *Labor Law Journal*, XXI(2), February 1970, pp. 75-78.

7. See Reference 4, p. 31.

8. *Ibid.* p. 32.

9. See Reference 1, p. 864-865.

10. See Reference 4, p. 33.

11. *Ibid.* p. 34.

12. See Reference 5, p. 14.

13. See Reference 4, p. 35.

14. See Reference 1, pp. 865-868.

15. Benjamin B. Naumoff, Ground Rules for Recognition Under Executive Order 11491, *Labor Law Journal*, XXII(2), February 1971, p. 100.

16. See Reference 4, p. 40.

17. See Reference 6, p. 80.

18. See Reference 4, p. 41.

19. See Reference 1, p. 871.

20. See Reference 3, p. 81.

21. See Reference 4, p. 42.

22. See Reference 1, p. 872.

CHAPTER 4.
THE SCENARIO IN EDUCATION, HEALTH, AND PUBLIC SAFETY

Teacher Militancy and Collective Negotiations

Lester S. Vander Werf, Sol M. Elkin, and John W. Maguire

MILLITANCY AND THE PROFESSION OF TEACHING

By Lester S. Vander Werf

As one who has gone on record advocating, over many years, increasing responsibility for, and corporate autonomy of, teachers, this writer views the present militancy of teacher groups with strangely mixed feelings and even alarm. The issue is not unions vs. professional organizations, since it is difficult at best to validate the differences between them. The worst of the semantic quibbling is suggested by the question: Can a union member call himself professional? The United Federation of College Teachers uses the phrase "professional unionism." Nor is the issue one of strikes or other work stoppages, although both the American Federation of Teaches locals and the National Education Association affiliates recently have been responsible for several of them. Finally, it is not a matter of dedication, for who would attempt to measure the statistically significant difference between the average dedication index of NEA members as opposed to AFT members.

The real issues involve what a profession is and does. While the term profession has been defined variously, nearly all definitions suggest specialized knowledge, a high degree of autonomy,

Reprinted by permission of INTELLECT and Lester S. Vander Werf, Ed.D., Distinguished Professor of Education, C.W. Post Center, Long Island University; Sol. M. Elkin, Chairman, Dept. of Education, Albion College, Albion, Michigan; and John W. Maguire, Dean, School of Education, Barry College, Miami, Florida, 33161.

admission by other professionals according to standards set by professionals, protection from those who fail to meet the standards, educating the public to its service importance as well as the standards, and others.

Traditionally, teachers' organizations have paid little attention to any of these except perhaps in a small way to specialized knowledge and only recently to autonomy. It is the nature of the growing autonomy as exemplified by negotiated agreements that we should examine and seek to draw some inferences. In order to do this it would not be improper to use as an example New York City, whose Board of Education and United Federation of Teachers negotiated, in the fall of 1968, with national impact, the most sophisticated and hard-nosed contract in the country.

As one reads the contract with its 600-odd items, one is impressed with the way the whole thing is put together, with only a smidgen of mutual trust shining through, and with as little as possible left to chance. Furthermore, there is the clearest bending of diction to purpose. One can "excess" a class by the number of students over the contracted limit. In this context, excess is a power word, a hard, brutal word, especially when a class is *excessed* administratively. Every category of teacher is listed and provided for by class size, teaching periods, relief from non-teaching chores, transfers, and similar matters. For example, a teacher can apply for transfer every five years, but those longest in service, of course, always have seniority. Nearly every category of school and special class is mentioned—each with its own vagaries, class limits, and restrictions on personnel.

A cluster teacher has a program of 20 45-minute teaching periods a week, with some non-preparation periods assigned by the principal. A teacher of the homebound works a six-and-a-half-hour day; a teacher of industrial arts or home economics in special service schools has 23 teaching, seven preparation, and five administrative periods; while one in a regular junior high school has 26 teaching, five preparation, and four administrative periods. One could go on about a dozen more examples of hardening of the categories.

How is this to be viewed? The first inference is that what is numerically limiting is likely to become maximum. A teacher's work is described as so many periods, period. Any committment beyond this will be viewed as harmful to all teachers, as suspected ingratiation, and, therefore, unpopular with union leaders as very "unprofessional." There is evidence that this happens rather frequently. If it seems commendable to set limits on class size—the first New York City contract set a precedent for this—does a profession set limits on everything else? Traditionally, professions have used service, not gain, as the ordering principle. Nor can service be measurable in hours. Could it not be argued that the more detailed the contract, the more the agreement is sprayed with minutiae, the farther removed from "professional" everybody gets? For, by virtue of the spelling out of detail, general principles are defined and, thus, restricted. This very restriction cramps professional style and flexibility.

Quite a different view was possible by observing the picket lines while the negotiations were being carried on during the strike. It is common knowledge that, when on strike, teachers tended to mimic the overt behaviors often cited for laborers on strike: the purple language hurled at non-striking colleagues, the slashing of automobile tires, and other quite unprofessional activities. Pressed for objective statements describing events, teachers will admit these things, but union officialdom rarely will. In free discussion, this nub appears like a club. Many teachers simply do not want to be associated with these behaviors or run the risk of being so associated.

What is it about strikes that seem to bring out the worst in some people? Perhaps the condition is just another reminder of how thin the line is that we all walk between our human and animal natures. None of these remarks should be interpreted as necessarily anti-strike, for there are times when teachers' perceptions reveal no alternative. In the past, teachers often were intimidated by boards of education and administrators. Yet, it seems unfortunate that our politics so prescribe our perceptions as to make misunderstanding—to say nothing of outright warfare—necessary.

There is still another item worth mentioning. Following the release of the Bundy report on school decentralization for New York City, the UFT, predictably and typically, supported the Board of Education in a negative response. With a common enemy, the parties of agreement often band together. Liberal perhaps in some ways, the union leadership became hidebound conservative on this issue for quite obvious reasons: if there were, in fact, to be 30 to 60 independent districts with authority to appoint, there would be powerful forces working against a monolithic union structure. However, the point is that a profession should attempt to thaw the frigidities of a system rather than to freeze in support of them.

It may be too early for teachers to question the results of this attitude. It is, of course, true, particularly in large cities, that teachers function in strong bureaucracies with their hierarchies of leadership, strict protocols of authority, and unbending, carefully defined structures. Under such an array of pigeonholes within tightly varnished boxes, teachers are discouraged from making waves, stepping up innovations, or developing imagination. Yet, now that teachers have forced themselves into power positions to effect the processes of decision-making, they find that, while in some ways their security is enhanced, freedom or independence is even less possible than formerly.

Because the AFT forced the NEA to a more aggressive stance, "professional" attitudes are placed in limbo for another eon. The "unity" of the profession has all but disappeared, what with the labor-management dichotomy blazing like a fiery cross on all hillsides. Educational administrators and teachers belong to different "professions." There are many signs that administrators will go it alone. Altogether, I am not at all sanguine that teaching will arrive in our time at anything like professional status. But, it is fair to ask what it would take to do so.

Ideally, it would take a deliberately planned relationship among the length of preparation, the ability to complete the preparation, and the salary the preparation would demand. This relationship does not exist presently, but would be a natural relationship in the sense that if the preparation were long enough and difficult enough, salaries would be higher. As it is, we have tended to develop salary schedules based on credit accumulation.

The first professional responsibility is preparation for the profession. Teachers now work at several different levels of preparation: teacher aides; substitutes, both temporary and permanent; and teachers with bachelor's degrees, master's degrees, sixth-year advanced certificates, and doctorates. While all of them do not apply in all school systems, there is no generally accepted notion of what a teacher's preparation ought to be either in length or content, although there is a trend among the 50 states to require five years (master's) of preparation for permanent certification. One of the first items then is for teachers to decide the guidelines for preparation. Once this professional responsibility is assumed, teachers could call an agency like the National Council for Accreditation in Teacher Education (NCATE) to help them firm up programs and eliminate the weak institutions.

If teachers can not agree on what kind of people they wish to have as colleagues, they are not likely to set up criteria for admission to teaching nor assume the responsibility for admission.

This, however, is the second major professional responsibility. Here we must distinguish between professional licensure and state certification. Certification is a civil service function and should concern itself with citizenship, health, age, applicability of tenure, etc. Certification should follow admission into the profession because if one can not be admitted, the civil service items are obviated. Admission to the profession suggests graduation from an approved school and the passing of examinations, either state or national. Admission by examination is the practice of many other professions now. Teaching is not a trade.

The third major professional responsibility is the elimination of incompetents. No college, however superior, will guarantee the character of its graduates forever. People do vary markedly in their responses to a code of ethics. Nor, for that matter, will the completion of a doctor's degree guarantee first-rate teaching. While teachers are loath to meet these issues, it seems odd that a group which spends its life making judgments about students seems most reluctant to judge its peers or to have its peers in the seat of judgment. If teachers want power, they could use it no more effectively than here. From the public's view, however, unless teachers go about this in a planned and determined fashion, there will be increasing resistance to across-the-board salary increments.

A profession should assume, of course, more than these three basic responsibilities. Yet, there is little indication, aside from an occasional small voice, that teachers will take these seriously. However, there are three "movements" that will be interesting to watch. The first is a possible merger of the NEA with the AFT. Overtures have been made and so far rejected; yet, the energies now expended in the competition could be used more fruitfully elsewhere. The second is the noise being made by NEA affiliates. The American Educational Research Association has left the NEA fold, while the American Association of School Administrators and the Association for Supervision and Curriculum Development, both large and powerful, have discussed separation and will do so again. The third is the behavior of state legislatures. States increasingly have permitted or demanded negotiation between teachers and school boards. With added contradictory pressures from many sides, American citizens will want to know if this trend is halted, reversed, or extended, and they may wish to add some pressures of their own.

ANOTHER LOOK AT COLLECTIVE NEGOTIATIONS FOR PROFESSIONALS

By Sol M. Elkin

Collective negotiations continue to spread throughout our educational system, and teacher militancy grows apace. It is no longer a matter of which major organization teachers favor. The differences between the National Education Association and the American Federation of Teachers are so blurred that merger between them is more a matter of "when" than "if."

And yet, one senses on the part of many teachers an unease, a hanging-back, a less than whole-hearted acceptance of the collective negotiations road we have chosen. Is it not unprofessional to join a labor-affiliated teachers' union? Is it not professional to strike? After all this time, there is still lingering fear that militancy will compromise our status as professionals.

Collective negotiation is a logical and reasonable outgrowth of the teachers' relationship to society. The thesis needs stating, not in order to swell organizational ranks, which are swelling in any event, but to aid teachers to take up defensible positions in this period of confrontation politics.

To understand the teachers' relationship to society, there is no need to raise once again the familiar question of whether teaching is a profession. We know that it is: teachers perform a socially useful service, we have access to a body of technical knowledge, we have a degree of personal autonomy in our work, we command a certain public respect. The term "teaching profession" is part of our language pattern. At the same time, we may be insufficiently aware that teaching, as a profession, relates differently to society than do the professions of medicine and law to which we so often compare ourselves.

The criteria of professional status—one can make a long list—include two which are critical and in which teachers differ from doctors or lawyers. These differences are inherent in our profession and are not subject to change. All sorts of consequences flow from these differences, which we do not consider sufficiently when we make superficial comparisons between ourselves and members of the "senior" professions.

It is depressing always to have placed before us as models the high-status medical and bar associations which we—consciously and unconsciously—try to emulate. Repeatedly, we define a profession in terms of what doctors and lawyers are and find, to nobody's surprise, that we fall short. Accordingly, we exhort one another to adopt more "professional" behavior, as though in this way we could achieve parity with medicine and law. Following this line of thought, collective negotiation is "unprofessional" and, therefore, out of bounds for teachers.

Our mistake has been to equate the concept of professionalism with the particular way in which medicine and law are practiced. It would be more realistic to recognize that the teaching profession has characteristics of its own which dictate for teachers a different relationship to society. In other words, we have been using the wrong yardstick.

One major criterion of a profession is the matter of access to an esoteric body of knowledge which is not readily available to the general public, and which can be acquired only by way of a long period of specialized training. There is such a body of practical and theoretical knowledge which we transmit to our teacher trainees through classroom instruction and student teaching. A structured program of teacher preparation certainly is a requirement for successful teacing.

Yet, the idea persists that anyone can teach, even without professional preparation. We must admit the suspicion has foundation. There is much that still is not known about the teaching and learning process. We also must grant that our present state of knowledge is not so voluminous or abstruse as to require a long and specialized training. Teaching is not the same locked mystery for the educated layman as are the specialized practices of medicine and law. Evidence of this may be found in the widespread employment of teachers with various kinds of special permits which have been granted upon completion of a portion of the regular preparation, or even none at all. To prohibit this practice would not alter the fact that it is possible to teach with little or no professional training. It is, on the other hand, not practical to practice medicine on this basis. No temporary permits are issued to first-year medical students.

Translating the matter into political terms, much of the power of professional groups derives from their monopoly over a vital body of knowledge. The tighter the monopoly, the greater is the power wielded by the group in molding legislation which concerns it. The influence of the American Medical Association on Congress and the state legislatures is an excellent case in point. Conversely, the body of knowledge about teaching and learning that is the exclusive possession of teachers is limited and, hence, is a limited source of power.

Let us assume an optimistic stance and anticipate a time

when advances in educational research and teacher education will produce the scientific knowledge we now lack, thus placing the teacher and the physician on an equal footing as possessors of esoteric knowledge, the acquiring of which requires long years of training. We then are brought face-to-face with another fact which is intrinsic to the educational enterprise, but not to the other professions.

The fundamental questions in education concern not how to, but what and why. Even if we could lay claim to scientific mastery of the teaching and learning process, the philosophical issues before us would continue to outweigh in importance the techniques used to implement them. Education is not so much a matter of expertise as it is of social decisions. To integrate or not to integrate; to reinforce religious training or ignore religion; to provide minority group students with models whom they can emulate or to assign faculty without regard to race—these are the issues that cause the really serious conflicts, not such questions of educational expertise as the best method of teaching reading or the virtues of the new mathematics vs. the old system.

In a democracy, the determination of such values is made by the community. The substantive issues of education are resolved outside the school. It can be no other way. The American public will not hand over to any professional group, no matter how high its standards, the power to determine what kind of education their children shall receive. It is society's prerogative to determine the goals of education, the portion of our resources we choose to allot to schools, or our conception of the educated man (one who knows Latin, or one who knows Swahili?), and this prerogative will not be, and should not be, surrendered to any single group within society.

By contrast, there are no serious philosophical differences regarding the aims of the medical profession. Few dispute the value of good health, and we all recognize it when we enjoy it. Since we agree on goals, exclusive possession of technique bcomes primary. Interestingly, new organ transplant procedures have raised a host of ethical and moral issues which the public appears determined to decide, via the courts and the legislatures. This is true also of issues of abortion, euthanasia, and birth control. The doctors retain their monopoly on techniques, but it is not the techniques which are at issue. All the skill and knowledge of the medical profession are not deemed sufficient to qualify doctors to make moral, ethical, and religious judgments on behalf of the rest of the citizenry.

Yet, such fundamental judgments are involved in the every-day education of children. The teacher can not expect to be allowed to make these judgments on behalf of society. The teacher's autonomy necessarily is circumscribed by decisions made outside the school, primarily by people who are not teachers.

Our second criterion of professional status is the degree of group and individual autonomy. As has been shown above, the relationship of the schools to American society limits teacher autonomy in substantive ways. Lay authority always has predominated and continues to do so today, whether that authority is represented by regularly elected school boards or by rump boards operating on the margin of legality. The current drive for community control of schools will increase lay involvement greatly.

We have always ceded to citizen groups the right to express their views on school policy. Our subjection to lay control nowhere is illustrated better than during our periodic appeals for money. In one school system, we see the spectacle of millage defeated six times running, and schools closing their doors for lack of funds. The people have spoken. The teacher ceases to teach.

We must remind ourselves that citizen involvement in the schools is a tenet of educational belief. We can not have it both ways. If we actively seek the widest possible lay involvement, we can not reject its impact upon teachers and teacher autonomy. And we have no viable option. Lay control of schools is a part of American custom and law, and is not going to change in the foreseeable future, except to intensify.

It is surprising that, in discussing teaching as a profession, the self-evident fact that the basic relationship of the teacher to the community is that of employee-employer is mentioned so rarely. Teachers are employed and paid by the community to do the job that the community wants done, at a salary the community is willing to pay. The individual teacher is compelled to accept conditions prescribed either by the local board unilaterally, or by mutual agreement with the teachers' organization.

By contrast, the physician and the lawyer are private entrepreneurs, working for a fee which is set through direct negotiation with patient or client. The teacher, unlike those in the senior professions, can not increase his fee as he becomes more competent or more modish. In fact, the whole thrust of the new teacher militancy is against merit pay and toward greater equality: every qualified teacher to be compensated equally, with only academic degrees and seniority yielding a higher return. In this situation, the road to advancement and higher pay lies out of the classroom. Promotion is gained by winning the approval of one's superiors in an organizational hierarchy—precisely the kind of recognition which professionals scorn. All this is scarcely conducive to individual professional autonomy of teachers.

By the very nature of schools, teachers function within a bureaucracy. Bureaucracy means rules and regulations, uniformity, hierarchical relationships. For example, schools must start and stop at a certain time. Courses must have a certain uniformity. Grades, textbooks, credits, and the whole structure of academic bookkeeping impose restrictions that narrow the professional latitude of the individual teacher. No matter how democratically these rules are formulated, once established, no serious deviation is possible. The inevitable result is restriction of the personal freedom of teachers, and this differs from the self-directed course of the physician or lawyer.

It may be argued that, in place of autonomy, the teacher has his academic freedom. The argument is largely spurious as it relates to elementary and secondary school teachers. It is true that, at the college level, the principles of academic freedom are well-established and reasonably well-defended. The college professor is a scholar whose freedom to search for the truth places upon him an obligation to utter it. In any event, college students are there voluntarily, and are deemed to be of sufficient age and maturity to be able to handle radical ideas. But at the lower levels, we encounter built-in limitations. Elementary and secondary teachers, as a group, have little claim to the role of researcher or scholar. Correspondingly, one might say that they are not obliged to enunciate new truths. Also, their students are there under compulsion, and they are very young too young, in the view of many, to be exposed to ideas divergent from those of their parents.

Such restrictions and limitations on personal autonomy seldom appear in writing, and only infrequently in the courts. But they do not have to—they are a part of the culture of the occupational group. Because society views the teacher as a transmitter of the culture, he does not take up the role of innovator readily. He must function within a system, in contrast to the free-enterprise naure of the medical and legal professions.

Lacking foundation in an esoteric body of knowledge, having a limited individual or group autonomy, being employees of large organizations, we must conclude that teaching, as a profession, finds itself in a different situation than either the medical or legal profession. Surely, then, it is self-defeating for us to urge one another toward more "professional" behavior, as though that would turn us into doctors and lawyers. We relate differently to society than they do. Thus, our behavior and our forms of organization must be different.

Fortunately, in a democratic society, teachers have available the same option as any other group of people who find themselves subject to forces which they can not influence personally—they can organize.

The next question which occurs is whether one has to be poor in order to be professional. For once, comparison with the American Medical Association may be truly apropos. Clearly, the AMA is ever-vigilant to protect physicians from any loss in income resulting from the extension of medical services. For example, when Congress decided to subsidize medical care for the elderly, doctors did not accept a reduction in pay or status. Under Medicare, fees remain high, and the physicians' status even may be said to have been reinforced due to the respect accorded them by Congress itself. In this area, the behavior of the AMA is no different from that of any other labor union.

It is natural for all occupational groups to seek to raise their status, enhance their influence, safeguard their security, and increase their income. We need not be concerned if our actions appear self-serving. We are no less professional nor less concerned for the general welfare for wanting to pursue our work under optimum conditions. The maintenance of high medical standards never has required financial sacrifice on the part of individual medical practitioners. But the employers of teachers, unlike the employers of doctors, are collective entities, and so it behooves teachers to collectivize their response. We need have no reservations nor offer apologies for such action.

Physicians, in giving their support to the AMA, go further. They claim that their professional organization has benefited the public by assuring high standards of medical service.

A parallel case can be made for the proposition that improvement in teachers' working conditions will lead to improvement in education, *i.e.*, higher pay will attract better teaches, smaller classes will permit more individualized attention to each child, and freedom from community harassment will free the teacher to teach. It is not possible, nor is it necessary, to determine the degree to which teachers' demands are motivated by the desire for personal ease or by the desire to improve the education of children—what matters is that the effect of such changes is to improve the educational program.

For teachers, as for physicians, there need be no conflict between professionalism and organized action to sustain a high income level. If, in fact, there is a similarity between teachers and doctors, it lies not in superficial status symbols, but in the willingness of each to utilize collective action where this seems to be necessary to safeguard incomes and job security.

There is no doubt that teachers, in fact, are realigning themselves in relation to society in terms of collective negotiations. The foregoing analysis suggests that, as professionals, we can accept this trend. It is the logical and necessary outgrowth of the type of profession that education is. Given the conditions of employment, union or union-like activity can be used to advance teacher interests and improve the ambience for education, without compromising our professional status. Perhaps, along the way, teachers can provide a standard of social service which doctors and lawyers will urge one another to emulate.

When teachers bring themselves to accept the need for organization, without ambivalence and without a sentimental hankering after things that might have been, we will find we have a stronger hand in shaping the educational establishment of the future.

PROFESSIONAL NEGOTIATIONS: STATE OR FEDERAL LEGISLATION?

By John W. Maguire

By 1965, California, Connecticut, Massachusetts, Michigan, Oregon, Washington, and Wisconsin had statutes governing the subject of teacher professional negotiations.[1] Since then, pressure has been brought on state legislatures to prepare similar legal codes, and several states have established such codes. Teacher organizations at the state level have been expending much time and effort on lobbying for legislation to cover negotiations. State affiliates of the National Education Association have listed a professional negotiations statute as a first-priority item in their legislative programs.[2] A professional negotiations statute will exist soon in all 50 states.

The laws now in force show great variation in negotiations coverage and procedures from state to state.[3] The situation may be considered somewhat analogous to the position of the American labor movement in the late 19th century and in the early part of this century, when each state legislated concerning labor regulation. This process had many hazards and created myriad problems.[4]

The National Labor Relations Act (1935), labor's "Bill of Rights," recognized the need for national legislation to protect the American worker from the whims and caprices of various state legislatures. The rationale for the act was the authority granted by the U. S. Constitution to "regulate commerce among the several states." Workers and labor officials took advantage of the provisions of the law to organize and to effect dramatic reforms in industries and trades.

Contrary to the prevailing belief at the time, the number and percentage of strikes, lockouts, and other work stoppages actually declined and, in general, industries whose workers were organized rapidly suffered least once orderly collective bargaining was implemented. From 1935 until today, highly organized industries have been plagued less and less by stoppages.[5]

Teacher organizations' attempts to get favorable legislation for professional negotiations at the state level well may be shortsighted. Leaders of the teaching profession must consider the long, difficult path which labor trod in the era of state legislative control.

Recent efforts produced state legislation resulting in recognition of the rights of teachers to negotiate collectively. Work stoppages, whether they are categorized as professional days, mass resignations, or strikes, have been prevented by establishment of routinized legal channels. However, the history of organized labor in the U. S. seems to indicate that national legislation would produce a more orderly process.

In addition to the lessons taught by labor's difficult struggle with state legislation, several other concerns also must be considered. Various power structure studies have indicated that conditions vary greatly from locale to locale. The influence of a power structure well may shape a particular state statute. The range of variety in findings in power structure studies from Hunter,[6] Kimbrough,[7] and Dahl[8] indicates an unevenness of legislation would be a natural outcome.

Uneven state legislation could create many problems for the mobile professionals of today. Teachers trained in various public and private institutions work in public schools of all of the states. The mobility of the student population across state lines in our public schools is a well-known fact. Further, state lines seldom are recognized as a formidable barrier when the national welfare is concerned. The commerce clause, seemingly, has no direct bearing on the teaching profession, but the interstate nature of the business of education in sale of textbooks, educational materials, and school equipment can not be denied. The interstate nature of the teaching profession well might be given serious consideration.

Many state statutes have taken major portions of their collective negotiations act verbatim from the Taft-Hartley Act (1947). States also have used precedents established by the National Labor Relations Board in deciding disputed cases in teacher negotiations before state appeals boards.[9] This also may be construed as lending support to the case for a Federal Statute.

The problem of application of the "equal protection" clause of the 14th Amendment to the U. S. Constitution also might be a factor to consider. State legislation frequently has been declared unconstitutional in civil rights cases when individuals or groups were denied equal protection of the law. Teacher organizations may choose to explore the possibility of entering into litigation when they consider a state law as failing to provide equal protection to a teacher or a group of teachers under a professional negotiations act.

Recent Federal legislation has removed education further from the realm of being a state function. The National Defense Education Act, the National Science Foundation, the Elementary and Secondary Education Act, and other national legislation have increased Federal involvement in, and control over, education at the state and local level. Restriction, regulation, and required compliance by state and local school officials to Federal statutes are common.[10] To argue that education today is exclusively a "state function" is to deny the facts. Since most teachers are affected either directly or indirectly under certain provisions of Federal statutes, the case for a national statute for professional negotiations has further validity.

American teaches need a "Bill of Rights," and are one of the last major groups in our society to recognize their need. Recent unrest underlines their awareness. A national professional negotiations statute would serve to give teachers equal protection of the law and establish a measure of orderly process in teacher-school board bargaining.

NOTES

1. Michael Moskow. "Recent Legislation Affecting Collective Negotiations for Teachers," *Phi Delta Kappan*, 47:3, November, 1965.

2. "FEA Legislative Program," *Florida Education*, 50:19, January, 1969.

3. Myron Lieberman and Michael Moskow, *Collective Negotiations for Teachers* (Chicago: Rand McNally, 1964).

4. John R. Commons, *et al., History of Labor in the United States,* Vols. II-III (New York: Macmillan, 1946).

5. Bureau of Labor Statistics, U. S. Department of Labor, "Work Stoppages in the U.S." (Washington, D.C., 1968).

6. Floyd Hunter, *Community Power Structure: A Study of Decision Makers* (Chapel Hill: University of North Carolina Press, 1954).

7. Ralph B. Kimbrough, *Political Power and Educational Decision Making* (Chicago: Rand McNally, 1964).

8. Robert A. Dahl, *Who Governs?* (New Haven: Yale University Press, 1961).

9. From a speech by Aubrey V. McCutcheon, Jr., Deputy Superintendent of Schools for Staff Relations and Chief of Labor Negotiations, Detroit, Mich., 1969: "Let's Quit Pussyfooting: A Shirt Sleeve Session on Negotiations Conducted by Experienced Negotiators, Fact Finders and Mediators."

10. Stephen J. Knezevich, *Administration of Public Education,* 2nd ed., (New York: Harper & Row, 1969).

The Implications of Police Unionism

Hervey A. Juris

Virtually unstudied and largely unobserved, the police employee organization has evolved over the last fifty years into a strong economic and political institution. The rapid growth of militant police unionism as a new political and economic force in the society has raised serious problems for the police agency administrator in the exercise of his professional responsibilities in the area of law enforcement and his executive responsibilities in the area of personnel management. It has also raised serious public

(C) The Law and Society Association. Reproduced from LAW & SOCIETY REVIEW, Vol. 6, pp. 231-245 (1971). Reprinted by permission of The Law and Society Association. LAW & SOCIETY REVIEW is the official publication of the Law and Society Association.

Hervey A. Juris is a member of the faculty at Northwestern University.

policy questions as to whether the protected right to organize and to bargain collectively which is being extended to all other public employees ought to be extended to the police without limitations. Underlying all these questions is the basic issue of whether official sanction should be extended to another entrant in the competition for control of local police operations.

This paper will argue that police unionism is an established institution in the society and that there is a need for both police executives and public officials to consider how they intend to approach this new power center. It will be suggested that there now exists a sufficiently large body of experience which should be examined before legislative bodies adopt guidelines for institutionalizing the relationship.

Police employee organizations can be traced back to the end of the last century (Hutchinson, 1969:10). Early attempts at unionization (in the sense of affiliation with organized labor and a desire for collective bargaining) ended, with scattered exceptions, with the 1919 Boston strike. However, from that time until the 1960s police employees remained highly organized. Local independent police-only organizations pursued their wage and benefit goals through legislative lobbying at the municipal and state levels. With the beginning of extensive public employee bargaining at the municipal level in 1961, police employee organizations began to assert themselves as economic organizations, pursuing collective bargaining where possible and occasionally engaging in job actions (such as slowdowns, working to rules, sick-calls) or strikes.

Civil rights demonstrations, student unrest, and anti-war protests have put tremendous pressures on police agencies and police officers. Amid a conflict between pressure group concerns and a general concern for law and order, public officials and police agency executives have attempted to define a response to crises consistent with the needs of society. Police employee organizations, however, have in some instances taken policy positions which have conflicted with those of the hierarchy or of elected officials. It is this competition for authority on the part of the union as a political and economic institution which has caused a great deal of concern among police executives and others. This concern with the potential role of the union has led some police agency executives to oppose police employee organizations, although recognizing that the reasons behind the militancy might reflect shortcomings in the agency itself. Usually this opposition is couched in terms of police employee organizations being in-

compatible with professionalism and the movement toward professionalism in the police service.

A Special Committee on Police Employee Organizations made
the following report to the 1969 convention of the International
Association of Chiefs of Police:

> The objectives of labor unions are by definition narrow in scope,
> immediate in nature, and almost entirely non-altruistic in outlook.
> There is a definite lack of evidence to indicate that any police union
> has ever gone on record in defense of raising the education require-
> ments for police officers or for any other phase of professionaliza-
> tion. The advancement of social or professional goals is definitely
> not an important part of union programs, and it is quite likely, that
> if police unionization were to become the rule rather than the excep-
> tion, the struggle for professional status would deteriorate into a
> struggle for immediate financial betterment (International Associa-
> tion of Chiefs of Police, 1969:19).

While their statement is probably quite accurate in its specu-
lation, it is probably quite irrelevant as a policy guide, for underlying the statement is an assumption that police officers are altruistic professionals in the same sense that self-employed physicians, lawyers, and accountants are assumed to be altruistic professionals. A more relevant model I would suggest is that set forth
by Archie Kleingarter in his *Professionalism and Salaried
Worker Organization* (Kleingartner, 1967). Kleingartner argues
that even though an employee may be told he is a professional, or
perceives himself as a professional, if in fact he is a salaried
employee of a large bureaucratic organization, he will react to this
need first and his professionalism secondarily. While Kleingartner was writing about nurses, teachers, and engineers, we see
this behavior in lawyers and doctors employed by city goverments[1]
and I would contend that this is the behavior we are seeing in
police employees as well.

Jack Barbash of the University of Wisconsin has articulated a
model explaining why employees form self-help organizations.[2]
Among the conditions he isolates are: the size of the organization
and its complexity; the efficiency-consciousness and the power-
consciousness of the supervisory staff; the felt need of employees
to redress daily on-the-job grievances; the felt need of employees
for an effective voice in decisions affecting them; and the need for
a reaction mechanism to cope with rapid change in the environment.

All of these factors are relevant to the police situation today.
As a large, semi-military, authoritarian organization, the police

department imposes its wishes on the individual officer through one-way communication and through discipline to a greater extent than through rewards. In addition, the ambiguities inherent in his daily decision-making responsibilities and those engendered by the organization itself as well as an increasingly hostile environment among the client population and elements of the liberal and academic communities have driven the men closer together. The fact that police employee organizations had been functioning for several years meant that they were prepared to move with the advent of public bargaining in the 1960s. The demonstration effect of other public employees' success, the declining utility of the security of a police career, and the relatively poor financial position of the police at the beginning of the last decade made collective bargaining an attractive alternative. Not only was there an opportunity for bargaining and a propensity for militant action, but the police also found themselves the beneficiaries of a great deal of unanticipated bargaining power because of the increasing concern for "law and order" and the implications of this issue for police political and economic power.

Had it not been for the influence of the 1919 Boston strike, we might not be so far behind in our research in this area. Unfortunately, the effect of that strike was to direct attention away from the police employee organizations as they existed toward speculative research as to the potential dangers of police unionism affiliated with the AFL-CIO.

The 1958 IACP monograph, *Police Unions*, saw the challenge as coming solely from affiliated organizations and failed to anticipate the challenge from the local police-only independents (International Association of Chiefs of Police, 1958). In 1960, Patrick Murphy defined unions as affiliated organizations, but Murphy did indicate that independent employee organizations might pursue personnel grievances (Murphy, 1960).

In 1968, using a functional definition of police unionism, Kay Hutchinson and I surveyed the 304 cities of over 50,000 population listed in the 1966 *Municipal Yearbook* (Juris and Hutchison, 1970). We defined a police union as an employee organization which deals with police agency management in a systematic way with respect to questions of wages, hours, and conditions of work. Of th 239 respondents, 214 reported a police employee organization. Ninety-nine of the 214 (or approximately one-third of the 304) reported they were engaged in a collective bargaining relationship with their police employee organization. Another 20% permitted the police employee organization to represent the membership on these issues in a relationship other than bargaining.

Furthermore we found that all of these organizations were police-only local units for purposes of representation. Where they were affiliated, it was usually with a state federation of police organizations, the Fraternal Order of Police, or the ICPA. Organized labor was a party in only 15 of the 214 cities.

Starting, then, from an assumption that some form of functional unionism in the police service is an accomplished fact, we must ask what is the potential impact of police unions on professionalism, the operation of the agency, and the formulation of law enforcement policy.

THE POTENTIAL IMPACT OF POLICE UNIONS ON THE PROFESSIONALIZATION OF THE POLICE SERVICE

Much has been made of the need to upgrade the personnel in the police service, as for example in the *Report of the President's Commission on Law Enforcement and Administration of Justice* (President's Commission, 1967: Chapter IV) or Charles Saunders' *Upgrading The American Police* (Saunders, 1970); and there has also been discussion of changing the nature of the job, as is proposed, for example, in Morton Bard's generalist-specialist research in New York City (Bard, 1969).[3] Critics of police unionization argue, however, that police unions would block the changes necessary to make police service what they prefer to call "more professional."[4] In particular they argue that patrolmen's unions would oppose higher education standards for hiring, new standards for promotion, changes in job descriptions, and provisions for lateral entry (International Association of Chiefs of Police, 1969).

If we accept Kleingartner's analysis with respect to salaried employees in a large bureaucracy and are prepared to enter a bargaining relationship with a police union (defined functionally hereafter rather than in the sense of AFL-CIO affiliation), then it is possible that within the context of the bargaining relationship there exists the potential for *quid pro quo* exchanges which would satisfy the officers' need for welfare and security while progressing toward some degree of professionalization as defined by the executives of the police agency. We see the potential for this kind of bargaining in the safety rules and entry requirements pursued by the Airline Pilots Association; the More Effective Schools program of the American Federation of Teachers; and the professional concerns being voiced by the Professional Air Traffic Controllers Organization. In Wisconsin, education incentive plans have been introduced in police agencies by means of the collective bargaining process, indicating at least potential in this direction. What is required, of course, is a strong executive branch willing to demand these *quid pro quo*. To date management has been somewhat derelict in these responsibilities.

Public managers argue that they are at a disadvantage because, unlike their private sector counterparts, they cannot take a long strike, thus increasing the union's relative bargaining power. To alleviate this situation we are currently experimenting with many impasse resolution procedures designed to provide equity without incurring the high public costs inherent in a strike.[5] Thus, some day the parties may have available to them fact finding, advisory arbitration with a prior agreement to accept the terms as binding, or compulsory arbitration.[6] With respect to the police particularly, Michigan, Rhode Island and Pennsylvania require compulsory arbitration as the last step.

THE POTENTIAL IMPACT OF POLICE UNIONS ON THE OPERATION OF THE POLICE AGENCY

The police agency administrator has long enjoyed *carte blanche* with respect to the internal operations of his agency, especially as they relate to personnel management. Furthermore, as the head of a quasi-military organization highly dependent on discipline and loyalty for its efficient operation, he looks askance at any challenge to his traditional authority. Balanced against this, however, is the realization on the part of many police officers that just cause and due process are the rule rather than the exception in personnel actions by managers, not only in the private sector, but also in other segments of the public sector as well.   196816

Given the ability to bargain collectively, it is to these needs that most police unions have addressed themselves. The most obvious challenge to traditional personnel management practices is the negotiation of grievance procedures whereby superior officer implementation of regulations can be effectively subjected to review by an employee who believes his rights have been violated.

Contracts have also abridged management flexibility in other ways. The 1969 New York City agreement provided portal-to-portal pay for officers assigned to another section of the city on temporary special duty, revised overtime provisions, and prohibited the rescheduling of off-days in order to avoid payment of overtime in a given week. While managerial flexibility was curtailed, these provisions also served to bring working conditions in the police service into equilibrium with working conditions in other occupations to which the patrolman might look as alternatives, an important labor market consideration.

Other bargaining demands by police unions which have been considered more threatening in their implications are often cited as *prima facie* reasons why police unions must be constrained. A careful review of these situations has led this author to conclude that the fault may lie less in the concept of collective bargaining than in the implementation of that concept by police agencies and the institutional and administrative environment which these agencies have created over time.

An example of how the parties may handle a policy disagreement within the context of a bargaining relationship is seen in the issue of one-man squad cars and the assignment of investigative duties to patrolmen in New York City. Both proposals were made by management in the interest of better manpower utilization. The union objected to each and wanted to discuss them within the context of the collective bargaining process. The city refused on the grounds that these were management prerogatives not subject to bargaining. The impasse was presented to an arbitrator who ruled that manning requirements and job duties were not bargainable issues.

An example of an issue handled outside the total context of bargaining can be seen in the question of tenure for detectives in New York City. Detectives serve at the pleasure of the chief of detectives, and may be returned to the patrolman rank at any time in their career. Management argues that this is necessary for incentive reasons and also because the nature of the duties of the detective bureau is such that they must be able to demote for misfeasance and malfeasance. The union argues that an individual suitable for promotion to detective should, after a probationary period, be able to obtain some measure of job security. The issue was not resolved in the bargaining process and was taken by the detectives' association to the city council in the form of a bill which would require just cause and due process before a detective could be demoted. The bill passed the council but was vetoed by the mayor. The policy issue raised is whether the union should have had access to the council, after being turned down by management with respect to a personnel issue of this type.

Herman Goldstein, in his "Administrative Problems in Controlling the Exercise of Police Authority" (1967), applies to the police agency the generally accepted management principle that an individual or organization with responsibility should be given the authority to carry out that responsibility and then be reviewed by higher authorities for the quality of execution. While he was discussing possible cases of police malfeasance, the principle is equally applicable here.

Largely because of earlier reform movements and concern from time to time with the issue of keeping the police out of politics, there exists a variety of models for the control of police agencies. As a result, police unions find they often have wide latitude with respect to avenues of appeal from the bargaining process. Among these are personnel commissions, city councils, mayor manager's offices, and, in some cases, the state legislature.

The problem then is to limit undesirable egress from the bargaining process so that management may deal with authority in personnel matters—a principle central to the success of a bargaining system. While recognizing that for political reasons little can be done with respect to instituting a rational administrative structure, still with respect to *personnel* duties it should be possible to allow the agency to establish its own bargaining posture and to hold the executive responsible for the ramifications of that posture. Where the council by law must retain these powers, it can still limit changes to the bargaining process, rather than lobbying, and be sure to include the chief or his representative as a consultant to, or member of, the bargaining committee.

Many of the threatening implications referred to above can be viewed in this perspective. For example, in the city of Boston the police union objected to name tags on uniforms, the assignment of traffic personnel to patrol duty, changes in the color of squad cars and uniform shirts, and the consolidation of precincts and streamlining of operations in general. In each case, the union went outside the bargaining process to accomplish its goals. The city council outlawed name tags. Appeal to the council delayed, but did not prevent, the redeployment of traffic personnel. The council approved a change in the color of squad cars, but backed the union on the question of shirt color. On the question of precinct consolidation, the union was able to block the city in the state legislature. Had there been some agreement among these agencies to limit the discussion of these issues to the bargaining process, management would have been in a better overall position to cope with the potential impact of police unions on the operation of this agency.

THE POTENTIAL IMPACT OF POLICE UNIONS ON LAW ENFORCEMENT POLICY FORMULATION

The impact of the discretionary power of individual police officers on the formulation of law enforcement policy at the street level is already well documented (Davis, 1969; Skolnik, 1966; Wilson, 1968). In this paper, however, we will be concerned with the more overt efforts on the part of police employee organizations to influence the law enforcement policy of the community through participation in elective and legislative politics, and through attempts at generating a set of signals distinct from those issued by city and agency officials to guide the exercise of discretion by individual members.

Public policy with respect to these issues is unclear. For years, the celebrated dictum of Mr. Justice Holmes had been predominant: "The petitioner may have a constitutional right to talk politics, but he has no constitutional right to be a policeman (*McAuliffe* v. *City of New Bedford*, 1892:220). This has been interpreted as limiting the rights of police officers to make critical public statements on policy issues, and as limiting their participation in elective politics—the latter because of possible misuse of their unique power and station in the society. However, as we shall see, this position has recently been substantially modified with respect to public policy statements.

The ambivalence of public policy with respect to political participation is best seen in the sometimes tacit, sometimes overt encouragement by police executives of participation by employee organizations in legislative political activity directed at larger appropriations for police agencies—especially as these appropriations relate to salary items, retirement systems, and welfare benefits. Given this official sanction and a functioning political organization, and given the leverage inherent in the public concern with law and order, it is not surprising that police employee organizations took advantage of their new constituencies to move into elective political action and public statements on issues of law enforcement policy, even though local regulations may have prohibited both.

This expanded activity with respect to public statements was reinforced by the changing Constitutional climate during the 1960s. In a line of cases from *New York Times Co.* v. *Sullivan* (1964) through *Pickering* v. *Board of Education* (1968) the Court moved from a virtual prohibition of public employee rights to the exercise of critical speech to a standard which has been interpreted as allowing critical statements so long as they do not include knowing falsity, disclosure of confidential information, or falsehoods which would impair the operation of the agency, destruction of an effective superior-subordinate relationship, or adversely affect work relationships in the agency.[7]

An example of the extent to which we have moved from Holmes's statement can be seen in a Maryland case, *Eugene C. Brukiewa* v. *Police Commissioner of Baltimore City* (1970). Brukiewa, the president of the Baltimore police union, had made comments critical of the department and the commissioner on a local television program. He was suspended by the department's disciplinary board which ruled that he had violated two departmental regulations relating to discussion of departmental business in public and criticism of superiors. A Baltimore city court upheld the suspension on the grounds that the regulations cited were clear and unambiguous. The Appeals Court overruled the city court on the grounds that the city did not show that the appellant's statements hurt or imperiled the discipline or operation of the police department, and were, therefore, within his right to make under the First Amendment and the decisions of the Supreme Court.

The Police Benevolent Association in New York City, from time to time in recent years, has, among other things, charged political interference with the operation of the department, warned of gaps in police protection, called for 100% enforcement of the law by officers regardless of signals from the commissioner and the mayor, and warned the public about changes in hiring standards for officers. At one point, police pickets paraded in front of city hall chanting, "We want Daley; Lindsay must go." Of course the most famous New York City case is the role of the PBA in the defeat of the civilian review board referendum. More recently they have been debating the implementation of the mayor's campaign to eliminate graft and corruption.

The police unions in Chicago, Newark, Syracuse, Cleveland, and elsewhere have spoken out on similar issues. The national Fraternal Order of Police from time to time issues statements on civil unrest and at one time called for the removal from the Kerner Commission of Herbert Jenkins, chief of police in Atlanta.

A case more directly related to collective bargaining occurred in the fall of 1970 in Waukegan, Illinois, where a group of officers, fired by the city for participating in a recognition strike, accused the mayor and chief of various indiscretions, from ticket-fixing to the coddling of vice activities. Perhaps even more significant than the process of accusation is the fact that several of the discharged officers ran for city council.

These examples might be termed the center of police political commentary. From the right come the voices of associations such as the Law Enforcement Group in New York City and from the left come the voices of groups such as the Afro patrolmen's associations. This spectrum of politial activity serves to point up a basic issue: Is society better served by more or less participation by police employee organizations in the public debate on law enforcement policy?

Police management views political activism as a challenge to its authority when issues of policy are raised but endorses it when legislative political activity results in large appropriations. Of the employee organizations of the left, center, and right, each feels it has a legitimate analysis and solution, an obligation to publicize it, and a protected right to do so. On the other hand, each is intolerant of political activity by the other two. Within the society the constituency of each group is tolerant of political activity by those with whom it agrees and intolerant of similar activity by its opponents. I would suggest that the policy most consistent with our pluralistic society and representative democracy would be to increase rather than decrease the number of voices contributing to the debate. While there are costs inherent in such a position, there are many who feel that the long-run bnefits have historically outweighed the short-run costs.

A natural extension of free speech and participation in legislative politics is participation in elective politics. Regardless of local prohibitions, many police employee organizations have backed candidates for public office. Notable successes (from the point of view of the employee organization) have included Yorty in Los Angeles, Stenvig in Minneapolis, and Gribbs in Detroit. Notable failures (again from the point of view of the employee organizations) have been the election of Lindsay in New York and Stokes in Cleveland.

No one questions the policeman's right to vote. Can he as an individual, however, make a contribution to an individual campaign? Can he distribute leaflets, canvass, or collect money for a candidate if he does so off duty and out of uniform? Can an officer ever be considered "out of uniform" if he is known by the merchants and citizens on his beat? If he is prohibited these activities as an individual, can he be prohibited these activities as a member of an organization? These are some issues which must be considered in adopting a policy with respect to elective politics.

Another aspect of participation in elective politics is participation in the election campaigns of those most intimately concerned with the administration of criminal justice in the community—the prosecutors and the judges.[8] In the theoretical construct of the criminal justice system, each level is expected to function independently: the police effect arrests, the prosecutor decides if a formal charge is warranted and prosecutes the case, the judge presides over the trial and passes sentnce. While in practice these are not independent events, still the question arises as to whether we want to make the interdependence overt through police union endorsments and campaigns for candidates. The same issue arises in campaigns for mayor and governor where the candidate states a position on the types of individuals he will appoint to civilian review boards, civil service commissions, parole boards, and other agencies which might have jurisdiction in the criminal justice area. These are raised as issues for discussion which must be considered within the context of free speech, political activity, and law enforcement policy formulation. There are no easy answers.

SUMMARY AND CONCLUSIONS

Police unionism in the functional sense is already upon us. To form an intelligent response to the challenge of police unionism, we must recognize it for what it is—first and foremost an organization of salaried employees in a large bureaucracy; concerned with the economic well-being, safety, and security of its members; and responding to management's necessary insistence on efficiency and authority. Secondarily, police unionism assumes the prerogatives of a professional organization in the sense that its members will speak through it to express opinions on the nature of law enforcement in the society. Furthermore, where an economic organization exists, there may also arise political organizations on the right and left which are concerned solely with policy.

Collective bargaining represents an opportunity to engage employees in participation in changes in the structure of the organization and within the organization. However, for bargaining to function in this sense, management must take a strong position and demand *quid pro quo* for the various benefits which ultimately will be negotiated. While management may argue that its authority is undercut by the union's appeal to the legislature and other branches of the executive, I would contend that the fault lies not with the bargaining construct or with the union which is exploiting an obvious weakness, but rather with the city which has failed to rationalize authority for bargaining within the government.

Police unions will likely become more active in legislative and elective politics. While some may object on the grounds that they consider the message the police preach to be inimical to their own perception of the well-being of society, we must remember that this is not a proper test of the right to free speech. Rather, we must strengthen the channels by which other minorities may communicate with their potential constitutencies.

Police unionism, because of the nature of the organization of the employer side of the market, will tend to be most potent at the local rather than the national level, thus lessening the potential differential impact of national as opposed to local organizations. Should federal funding change the structure of the delivery system of law enforcement services, I would alter this conclusion.

George Stigler, the noted economist, has said that it is a venerable tradition to judge public policy by its intentions rather than its achievements but that, venerable tradition or not, it is a tradition ill-suited to the formulation of intelligent public policy.

This admonition is particularly relevant to the determination of the proper response of public officials and police agency administrators to the challenge of police unions. Many of the 50 states have yet to take a clear-cut stand on the protected right of police employee organizations to be recognized and to bargain collectively with the city. A generation of police executives and supervisors must be educated in the practice of personnel management when dealing with an employee organization and organized employees.

There has been sufficient experience with police unionism and collective bargaining to allow the systematic collection of facts so that we may attempt answers to several of the unanswered questions:

a) what has been the actual impact of police unions on the three areas discussed above—empirical research is needed;

b) does the type of police-only employee organization affect bargaining or the potential for change;

c) can we distinguish among the various alternative structures of bargaining (from city autonomy to agency autonomy) as they might alter the impact of the union on management's ability to manage;

d) will splinter groups from the left or right have an impact—will this impact fall within or without the structure of bargaining;

e) should there be any limits on the scope of collective bargaining;

f) should supervisory employees be allowed to organize and bargain;

g) is compulsory arbitration of new contract conditions necessary in the protective services or will fact finding and advisory arbitration with optional prior agreement to accept the terms as binding suffice;

h) to what extent should police employee organizations be allowed to participate in elective and legislative politics?

NOTES

1. For example, doctors in New York City employed by the city and attorneys in Milwaukee, Wisconsin, employed by the city have organized for the purpose of collective bargaining.

2. This model has been articulated in seminars, lectures, and several mimeographed papers "for circulation only."

3. In fact, if we were to raise the education and skill requirements for the job of patrolman and not also expand the responsibility, authority, and discretion, the change might be self-defeating, given what we know about the dysfunctional aspects of upgrading personnel in a constant environment. See, for example, McGregor (1958) and March and Simon (1958). For a general discussion of police personnel problems and police unions, see Juris (1969: 311-320).

4. Professionalism is a difficult concept to grasp. We are conditioned to respond to the term as it is applied to medicine, law, and the ministry where it connotes intellectual training at a high level, specialized knowledge, practicality, self-organization, altruism, and an ethical code (see Kleingartner, 1967: 1-22). As applied to police, professionalism connotes occupationalism in the sense that a machinist refers to himself as a professional. This concept connotes minimum hiring and training standards and a commitment to excellent performance. One is entitled to be somewhat suspect of the commitment of police executives to professionalization in the former sense when one considers that at the executive level there are no nationwide minimum promotional standards, no specified training, and no lateral entry except at the level of chief or patrolman. Readers interested in this area would be well advised to read all of Kleingartner (1967), not only for content but also for the wealth of references. A more recent empirical study embodying these principles is found in Kleingartner (1969).

5. For a discussion of this point as it might apply to the private sector, see Stern (1964).

6. For an excellent disucssion of this issue, see Anderson (1970: 259-283).

7. From a legal point of view: *Georgetown Law Review* (1968); from an operational point of view: Mondello (1970).

8. I am indebted to Herman Goldstein for his pointing out the need to highlight this issue within the context of elective politics.

CASES

McAuliffe v. *City of New Bedford* 155 Mass. 216; 29 N.E. 517 (1892).
New York Times Co. v. *Sullivan* 376 U.S. 254 (1964).
Pickering v. *Board of Education* 88 S. Ct. 1731 (1968).

REFERENCES

ANDERSON, Arvid (1970) "Compulsory Arbitration under State Statutes," in The Proceedings of the Twenty-Second Annual Conference on Labor. New York: New York University Press.

BARD, Morton (1969) "Alternatives to Traditional Law Enforcement," Presented at the 77th Annual Convention of the American Psychological Association on September 2, 1969.

DAVIS, Kenneth Culp (1969) Discretionary Justice. Baton Rouge: LSU Press.

GEORGETOWN LAW REVIEW (1968) "The First Amendment and Public Employees: *Times* Marches On." 57 Georgetown Law Review 134.

GOLDSTEIN, Herman (1967) "Administrative Problems in Controlling the Exercise of Police Authority," 58 Journal of Criminal Law, Criminology and Police Science 160.

HUTCHISON, Kay B. (1969) "Municipal Police Employee Organizations: A Study in Functional Unionism." Master's thesis, University of Wisconsin.

INTERNATIONAL ASSOCIATION OF CHIEFS OF POLICE (1969) "Report of the Special Committee on Police Employee Organizations." Typescript.

JURIS, Hervey A. (1969) "Police Personnel Problems, Police Unions, and Participatory Management," in the Proceedings of the 22nd Annual Meetings of the Industrial Relations Research Association. Madison: IRRA.

———— and Kay b. HUTCHISON (1970) "The Legal Status of Municipal Police Employee Organizations." 23 Industrial and Labor Relations review 352.

KLEINGARTNER, Archie (1967) Professionalism and Salaried Worker Organization. Madison: Industrial Relations Research Institute University of Wisconsin.

———— (1969) "Professionalism and Engineering Unionism," 8 Industrial Relations 224.

McGREGOR, Douglas (1958) The Human Side of Enterprise. New York: John Wiley.

MARCH, James G. and Herbert A. SIMON (1958) Organizations. New York: John Wiley.

MONDELLO, Anthony (1970) "The Federal Employee's Right to Speak," 10 Civil Service Journal 16.

MURPHY, Patrick V. (1960) "Police Employee Organizations." Master's thesis, City College of New York.

President's Commission on Law Enforcement and Administration of Justice (1967) Report: The Challenge of Crime in a Free Society. Washington, D.C.: Government Printing Office.

SAUNDERS, Charles B. Jr. (1970) Upgrading the American Police. Washington, D.C.: Brookings.

SKOLNIK, Jerome H. (1966) Justice Without Trial. New York: John Wiley.

STERN, James (1964) "The Declining Utility of the Strike," 18 Industrial and Labor Relations Review 60.

WILSON, James Q. (1968) Varieties of Police Behavior. Cambridge: Harvard University Press.

Fire Fighter Strategy in Wage Negotiations

James A. Craft

Undoubtedly, the most significant development in municipal personnel and labor relations in the past decade has been the rapid growth of unionism among public employees and the concomitant emergence of bilateral negotiations over wages and other conditions of work. Given the extensiveness of negotiation activity in municipalities across the United States, it is somewhat surprising that there has been so little effort to examine systematically public employee union strategy and behavior in negotiations.[1] This is unfortunate because if we are to obtain a better

Reproduced from THE QUARTERLY REVIEW OF ECONOMICS AND BUSINESS, Vol. 11, (Autumn, 1971). Reprinted by permission of the Bureau of Economic and Business Research, University of Illinois, Urbana, Illinois, 61801.

understanding of the bargaining process in the public sector and promote the development of mature employment relations, we must have insight into all aspects of negotiating behavior.

It is the purpose of this article to provide a preliminary examination and analysis of the strategy and tactics employed by municipal fire fighters during wage negotiations. The specific objectives of the study are to review the types of strategies employed and to present a generalized analysis of when and why a strategy is implemented in negotiations. Fire fighters provide a particularly interesting group for examining, since (1) they have the longest consistent history of exclusively public employee unionism, with the International Association of Fire Fighters (IAFF) having been founded in 1918; (2) they have consistently emphasized the need for collective bargaining on wages; (3) they are a highly organized group;[2] and (4) they provide a critical service to the municipality.

The data and information on which this study is based were collected primarily from interviews with state and local officers of fire fighter organizations affiliated with the International Association of Fire Fighters and located in Indiana.[3] The interview data were supplemented by an extensive review of fire fighter journals, an examination of newspaper accounts of fire fighter negotiating activity, and observations of militant fire fighter activity in progress.

A PERSPECTIVE ON FIRE FIGHTER STRATEGY

For 40 years after the mid-1920s, organized fire fighters employed an accomodative and conciliatory strategy in dealing with municipal employers. It seemed to be characterized by the attitude that militancy was inappropriate and unnecessary to achieve their goals. The strategy emphasized political support of municipal leaders sympathetic to the fire fighter objectives and the development of community support for the needs of the public servant.The abortive Boston police strike of 1919 crystallized a strong public antipathy toward labor unions in the public sector in general, and militant job action by public protection employees in particular. The conciliatory approach was the only alternative if the fire fighter union movement was to remain viable (see [18]). In addition, this strategy was reinforced by the traditional "no strike" policy incorporated in the constitution of the IAFF and the strong responsibility for public safety implicit in the fire fighter's job.

Since the mid-1960s, however, significant alterations in the municipal labor relations environment have placed the fire fighters in a position in which they have found it possible to reconsider strategy alternatives in dealing with their employers. For example, there has been a rapid growth in the acceptance and implementation of colletive bargaining for municipal employees [7]. Also, a number of public employee interest groups (notably teachers and sanitation workers) have successfully employed militant tactics to achieve their goals and there has been little public repression of them or their unions. Finally, the fire fighters have found themselves in a declining relative economic position with the rise of widespread disparity between police and fire fighter salaries. Their customary srategy seems to have been ineffective in resolving this problem [4]. Given these events, the desire for a broader selection of strategy choices in dealings with their employers was reflected in the decision of the 1968 IAFF convention to eliminate the long-standing "no strike" clause from the union constitution.

The current fire fighter strategy in negotiations exhibits an interesting combination of the usual approach with a new emphasis on cautious militancy.

CURRENT STRATEGIES

At the present, two basic strategic approaches employed by fire fighters in wage negotiations can be identified. The most common approach, which is an outgrowth of the usual conciliatory approach, is a cooperative strategy. it emphasizes the use of educational and persuasive tactics in dealing with the employer. The second strategy is conflict oriented and stresses use of coercion and pressure. Although each strategy is fairly distinguishable in its basic orientation, each is directed toward the end of increasing the fire fighter wage level. Generally speaking, both strategies increase upward pressures on the wage level because of the expanded visibility of the fire fighters and their intensified interaction with the community and the elected city officials. Also, each strategy, though different in its approach, attempts to reduce the forces restraining upward wage adjustments (for example, public reluctance to increase taxes, council reluctance to reallocate money, and relative importance of pressures from other interest groups). Each strategy may be employed alone, but it seems to be increasingly common to combine them in the most advantageous mix in wage negotiations.

A COOPERATIVE STRATEGY

The cooperative strategy emphasizes the use of educational procedures in conjunction with rational persuasion to promote an
environment that will be receptive to fire fighter wage proposals.
The fire fighters provide extensive information and a logical
rationale for an increase in their wage level. The underlying assumption is that as the importance, value, and contribution of
the service is discerned by the public and by city officials, fire
fighter needs will receive a prompt and positive response.

When employing this strategy, fire fighter activity is directed
at two groups: (1) the community, and (2) the city officials (that
is, the fire chief, mayor, and city council). There is a twofold
objective in dealing with the community. First, the fire fighters
attempt to decrease the taxpayers' reluctance to grant increased
funds to the municipality for increased fire fighter wages. Second,
if the amount of money cannot be increased, they try to persuade
the community to exert pressure on the mayor or the council so
that they will realign priorities for budget allocations and increase
funds for fire fighters at the expense of other groups or programs.
At the minimum, it is expected that the community will be neutral and not hostile to union demands. When the fire fighters
direct their activities toward the city officials, the objective is to
have them revise priorities and reallocate funds in favor of the fire
fighters.

The cooperative strategy may include both long-term and
short-term behavior. Long-term behavior extends over the entire
year (with implications for even longer periods) and is not limited
to budget decisions periods.[4] The short-term behavior, in contrast, is focused in the budget decision period.

Long-Term Behavior

The long-term behavior is characterized by information-sharing
and educational activities at both the community and the council
levels. The union emphasizes buiding a reservoir of goodwill and
developing an "image" of the fire fighter as a community servant.[5]
He is presented as a highly skilled professional, dedicated to
safety and the public welfare, who often risks his life for the
protection of the community. Specific illustrations of activities
include publicizing fire-fighting activities in the newspaper, holding open houses for the public at fire stations, participating in
and leading community service projects (for example, muscular
dystrophy), holding elaborate community funeral services for

those killed on duty, and so forth.[6] In addition to this, local officers are encouraged to develop friendships with the mayor and council members so that those in decision-making positions can be kept abreast of fire fighter activity. Later, of course, this will provide the fire fighters with a direct channel to the decision-making authority to present their arguments. The image and goodwill are subsequently used in garnering community and city officials' support for wage proposals. At best, it is hoped that these parties will respond positively to wage proposals at budget decision time. At worst, it means that they will be neutral, and not hostile to fire fighter wage proposals.

Short-Term Behavior

The short-term behavior and tactics are characterized by direct persuasive activity and are concentrated in the budget decision period. The data generated by the fire fighter wage committee research in formulating the wage proposal for the year are used as the basis for rational persuasion to gain community and council support.[7] Of course, the receptiveness of the parties to the arguments will depend to some extent on the effectiveness of the long-term program in conditioning the public and council. Examples of short-term tactics used in dealing with the public include newspaper, radio, and television spot ads appealing to the community to support the fire fighter wagge increases proposed; door-to-door campaigns by fire fighters to present their arguments to the citizens and gather expressions of support on petitions; and the presentation of their arguments and detailed cost analysis of the wage proposal to citizen groups that review the budget and have influence with the council (for example, a taxpayers' association or a chamber of commerce).

In dealing with the fire chief and the elected mayor and council, two persuasive approaches are used: (1) the rationale of data in conjunction with fire fighter "needs," and (2) the encouragement of community expression of support. In the first case, the fire fighter union representatives meet with the chief and the mayor and later with the council to present their proposal and the justifying data. At a more informal level, it is not uncommon for fire fighter wage committee members to take city officials out to dinner to continue the discussion of the wage proposal. In the second case, the IAFF local encourages interested community groups (for example, firms that depend upon city fire protection and the central labor council) to express support publicly for the wage proposal during council delierations.

A COERCIVE STRATEGY

The coercive strategy places emphasis on the use of pressure tactics to obtain wage objectives from the employer. Whenever such tactics are threatened or actually employed, it is made clear by the union that they are directed at an uncompromising individual or group (for example, the mayor or council) and *not* at the community at large. Although such activity, especially job action, will affect the public, the fire fighters try not to alienate the community any more than is necessary.[8] The city officials provide readily available and visible targets as the head of the city bureaucracy and the formal employer of the firemen. These officials are, of course, responsive to political pressure from the community. The underlying assumption of this strategy is that the threatening or the actual taking of action which will affect the provision of fire protection to the public will cause the city officials to respond by revising priorities to meet the fire fighter demands. The stimulus for action is the expected or real pressure on the city officials from the community due to the actual or threatened change in provision of a critical service.

As contrasted with the cooperative strategy, the tactics are all short-range and are concentrated in the budget decision period. The pressure tactics are deliberate and may take on a sequential pattern whereby the intensity of the pressure on the council is increased step by step. For example, a likely series of activities might include (1) "packing" the council meeting with fire fighters to demonstrate solidarity on the wage proposal; (2) picketing the council meeting or the mayor's office; (3) starting strike rumors and taking a strike vote at a mass meeting of fire fighters; (4) a slowdown during which firemen refuse to carry out maintenance, inspections, and other non-critical duties; (5) a "sick-out" or "blue flu" with only partial operation of the fire service; and (6) a complete walkout or strike in support of wage demands. Activities (1) through (3) can be called "limited pressure" since they involve a threat to the city council but no job action.[9] Activities (4) through (6) can be designated "total pressure" tactics, since they involve direct job action and affect the provision of fire service.

THE STRATEGY MIX IN NEGOTIATIONS

Earlier, I noted that it seems to be increasingly common for fire fighters to employ both of these strategies in negotiations. Let us turn our attention to the question of when and how these two strategies are used.

My research findings indicate that virtually all fire fighter union locals employ the long-term tactics of the cooperative strategy consistently. Over the year, they use this to enhance their visibility and to create a favorable image and relationship with the employer and the public. In the budget decision period, most local unions continue with the short-term tactics of the cooperative strategy up to the period when the mayor submits his budget proposals and the council reviews a preliminary budget to consider it for adoption. At this point, one of three behavior patterns may emerge. Some fire fighter locals continue their short-term persuasive activities, others discontinue or reduce activity, and still others employ militant coercive tatics. The chart illustrates the strategy choices.

Strategy and the Wage Level
The field research indicates that the strategy selected at this point is to a great extent dependent on how nearly the wage goals and expectations of the fire fighters have been met in the wage prop-

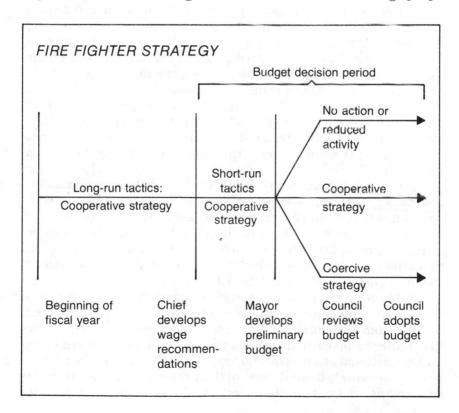

FIRE FIGHTER STRATEGY

osal the municipal representatives have made in negotiations or have placed in the preliminary budget. The fire fighters, like other organized employees, enter wage discussions with wage goals and expectations. They have formally defined a wage target that they hope, but generally do not expect, to achieve. In addition, and perhaps more significant in determination of strategy choice, there seems to be a minimal wage level that is acceptable to the majority of fire fighters in a local union.[10] Although the wage target in the cities studied was without exception above the current wage, the minimal acceptable wage was equal to or above the current wage—but not in excess of the wage target.

The minimal wage level that is acceptable for the ensuing fiscal year appears to be most significantly influenced by the fire fighters' desire for internal and external wage equity. Internal equity concerns the fire fighters' perception of their wage relative to the wage level of reference groups within the municipality—in particular, the local police. Given the tradition of wage parity between fire fighters and police that has existed in most large cities, the fire fighters feel strongly about the emergence of disparity (see [4 and 16]). This has been reinforced with the strong emphasis placed on parity by the IAFF.[11] The maintenance of parity and the elimination or reduction of disparity, if it exists, is the most critical element in determining the minimal acceptable wage. However, supplementing this demand for internal equity is the desire on the part of fire fighters to maintain or improve their wage position relative to fire fighters in the surrounding geographical area and in cities of similar size.[12] This factor becomes paramount if the fire fighters currently enjoy a parity wage with the police.

The emphasis on parity and external equity may be moderated to some extent, however, by two factors: (1) extensive moonlighting activity and (2) the apparent security consciousness of fire fighters. Moonlighting, or multiple job holding, seems to be common among fire fighters. In a number of cities investigated in this study, the interviewees estimated that 90 percent or more of the fire fighters held second jobs. Given their work schedule, most fire fighters expect to hold a second job and many younger men even see the fire department job as a "second job." The combined income from both jobs, in most cases, far exceeds that which the fire fighter could earn on any full-time job given his limited skills and educational attainment. So long as the fire fighters' wages do not lag excessively behind those of their reference groups, they are less willing to exert militant action and seem more willing to accept smaller wage increases if they have good second jobs which allow them generally to maintain their standard of living.

The perceived importance of the economic security benefits affects the minimal acceptable wage, since many fire fighters feel that these benefits are one of the major economic attractions of the job.[13] Generally, state or municipal law provides excellent retirement plans, disability insurance, and family security programs that are superior to the plans the men could find in private industry. Interviews with local fire fighter leaders indicate that if the number of "security conscious" men in the local union (for example, those who feel that the security benefits are the most important attraction of the job) is large, the level of the minimal acceptable wage is restrained.[14] The fire fighters seem to be willing to settle for a smaller wage increase rather than risk jeopardizing these benefits through actions that might result in their discharge. Logically, this might be even more significant when these men have good incomes from second jobs.

Strategy Decision Rules

The data obtained from interviews and observation of fire fighter negotiations indicate that, in general, the choice of strategy during the final part of the budget decision period appears to be best understood in terms of some simplified decision rules.

The first decision rule appears to be that if the wage proposed by the municipality is equal to or exceeds the minimal acceptable wage, but is less than the wage target, the union continues with the cooperative strategy. This strategy has proved successful in obtaining at least a generally acceptable wage and it is maintained to try to persuade the council to meet the wage objective. The coercive strategy is not employed, since a majority of fire fighters will not support it. Second, if the wage proposed by the municipality is approximately equal to or exceeds the wage target, then the goal has been achieved and little further action by the fire fighters, except support activity, is necessary. Finally, however, if the wage proposed by the municipality is less than the minimal acceptable wage, the fire fighters see little hope for upward revision, and there is little possibility of arbitration, then they adopt the coercive strategy to obtain a wage level equal to or exceeding the minimal acceptable wage.

When the coercive strategy is adopted, the fire fighters generally employ "limited pressure" tactics initially to try to force an increase in the municipal wage proposal. If this is not effective, then they will take one of two courses of action: (1) accept a compromise solution where the actual or expected value of the compromise is about equal to or better than the minimum acceptable wage, or (2) employ "total pressure" tactics. In the first case, this may mean that the fire fighters accept the proposed wage plus other concessions which will benefit them financially (for example, increased uniform allowances, reduced work hours, better insurance, increased longevity pay). If this type of compromise is impossible or unavailable, the fire fighters will accept ad hoc arbitration of the wage dispute—if they expect that the outcome of the arbitrtation will bring the new wage to their minimum acceptable level or will give them other benefits to compensate for a lower salary.[15]

The second course of action, employing "total pressure" tactics, is chosen when no compromise is available and/or when actual or expected value of a compromise is less than the minimal acceptable wage. The fire fighters hope to put immediate and powerful pressures on the municipal government to force an upward revision in the proposed wage.[16]

If this is not successful in promoting a satisfactory increase in the proposed wage, the fire fighters may be expected to accept a compromise solution if available, when the actual or expected value to them approximates the minimal acceptable wage level. If such a solution is not forthcoming at this stage, or if they feel that it would not meet their needs, then one of the two following actions occurs: (1) the fire fighters return to work by force of a court injunction with the problem yet to be resolved,[17] or (2) large numbers of fire fighters are dismissed or they resign from the department.[18]

STRATEGIC CHOICE: A CASE STUDY

At this juncture, an example may be useful to illusrate fire fighter strategy selection. For this purpose, the 1969 wage negotiations between the city of Gary, Indiana, and IAFF Local 359 will be examined briefly. In these negotiations, the entire range of fire fighter strategy was employed.

Although Indiana has no enabling legislation for public employee collective bargaining, its public employees are in fact highly unionized and there is some form of union activity to influence wages in all of the larger cities. The fire fighters are perhaps the most highly organized group of municipal employees with 51 local unions throughout the state that include over 90 percent of the full-time municipal fire fighters in Indiana as members. The Gary local union, IAFF Local 359, was founded in

1933 and is one of the oldest, strongest, and most militant locals in the state. It, like most other IAFF affiliates, has usually relied on an accomodative strategy and limited pressure tactics to achieve its wage goals. Consistent with that of the IAFF, its constitution contained a "no strike" clause until late 1968. The local seems to have been reasonably effective in past salary discussions with the city council, since Gary fire fighters have had high salaries relative to other cities in the state.

Background Events

In 1968, the Gary fire department and the local fire fighters' union seemed to be characterized by internal conflict and confusion. This appeared to be due to the advent of a new municipal administration, a new fire chief, new policies regulating operations of the department, and the uncertain stand of the IAFF with regard to militant tactics including job action. Partly as a result of these uncertainties and divisions, the fire fighters obtained only a small wage increase of $420 from the financially troubled Gary city council.[19] Although the small increase (about 2.5 percent) was a face-saving victory, it created problems that were to affect negotiations in 1969. In particular, the small increase placed the Gary fire fighters in a position of both internal and external wage inequity. Their salaries fell below local police salaries and Gary fire fighters lost their position as a salary leader in northwestern Indiana.

After the August 1968 IAFF convention, the Gary local deleted the "no strike" clause from its local constitution with the full approval of the IAFF. The local union's wage committee began to develop wage proposals with the following objectives in mind: (1) to eliminate or reduce internal and external wage inequities, and (2) to try to achieve the IAFF wage goal of $10,000 a year.[20] The local developed a wage target proposal of a $3,000 increase. In an interview with the local president, however, it was indicated that the fire fighters would really have been willing to settle without job action for a $1,500 increase. This was the minimal acceptable wage increase.

1969 Wage Negotiations

Throughout the year the fire fighters employed elements of the cooperative strategy to increase their chances for a large wage increase. In the budget decision period, the chief recommended a $2,000 wage increase, but the mayor recommended only a $1,000 increase to the council. Both recommendations fell short of the target increase proposed by the union, and the mayor's recommendation fell short of the minimal acceptable increase. In July, when the council was formally to consider fire fighter wages, it became apparent that neither the target nor the minimum acceptable objectives would be achieved. The union began to employ limited coercive tactics. It carried out the following activities: (1) the council meeting was "packed" with large numbers of fire fighters to demonstrate support for a large wage increase; (2) mass membership meetings were held to discuss the problem; and (3) a strike vote was conducted when the council offer of a $240 increase for privates and $480 increase a year for others on the force was tendered.

The council immediately asked the fire fighters for further negotiations and obtained a restraining order prohibiting the strike. During the ensuing negotiations, the union receded from its original demand and adopted the chief's $2,000 wage increase recommendation as their stated goal. In order to place more pressure on the council, the wives and children of the firemen picketed the main Gary fire station and effectively blocked the use of the fire equipment. The police cleared the pickets and arrested two of the women. Shortly thereafter, the council passed a budget providing for a $600 wage increase for fire fighters and refused to consider any further increase. A permanent injunction was issued against any fire fighter strike.

The fire fighters, recognizing that their wage demands were not going to be met, exerted total pressure tactics. They ignored the injunction and went on strike. The union demanded additional increases in wages for the next year and renewed negotiations with the council. The council, however, remained adamant. Indeed, it stated that Indiana law prohibited any alteration in the city budget that had been adopted after a specified date—which by now had passed.

The strike lasted five days during which at least one spectacular fire and several smaller ones occurred involving an estimated loss of over a million dollars in property. During the strike the fire fighters tried, with no success, to obtain arbitration of the 1970 wage increase. Finally, under the overwhelming pressure of a court injunction, lengthy hearings to determine if all the fire fighters should be subject to contempt proceedings, the issuance of arrest warrants for the local union leadership, threats of dismissal, the citation of numerous fire fighters for disciplinary action, and no movement by the council on the wage issue, they returned to work.[21]

CONCLUDING COMMENTS

In this article we have seen that fire fighter strategy in wage negotiations with municipal employers has been changing in recent years. The old accomodative and conciliatory strategy has evolved into a sophisticated procedure emphasizing public relations and rational persuasion that I have called the cooperative strategy. In addition, the fire fighters have recently added a militant choice to their strategy alternatives which includes numerous coercive activities—the ultimate being the strike. In addition to identifying current strategies and tactics in wage negotiations, I have examined them in terms of when they are employed relative to the budget decision period and why they are employed with regard to fire fighter wage objectives.

Upon reviewing the current strategies and tactics, it becomes clear that they are strongly influenced by the characteristics of the public sector and the specific nature of the fire fighter's job and its relationship to the community. First, the strategies reflect the *political* (rather than the economic) environment of public sector wage decision-making. Illustrations of this include the fact that fire fighters conduct activity over the entire year that is designed to affect their wages during the budget decision period. Much of this activity is reminiscent of the usual lobbying and interest group ingratiation that is characterisic of the political decision-making process. In addition, when total pressure tactics are used, the fire fighters generally take care not to alienate the public, if at all possible, since it is the source of political strength and they must return to the public each succeeding year. Second, the *ambiguous nature* of the public employer is reflected in the fact that the strategy choices are directed toward several distinguishable groups of individuals. In effect, the fire fighters negotiate or try to influence a number of parties during the successive stages of wage negotiations (for example, the community, the fire chief, the mayor, and the city council).Successful dealings with any and/or all of these groups may have important positive impacts on the resulting wage package. Finally, the *critical nature* of the fire fighter job and the long history of public sentiment against militancy by public protective employees (many times embodied in restrictive legislation) noticeably affects strategy selection and the use of militant tactics. This is reflected in the extensive use of cooperative strategies with the heavy emphasis on educational and lobbying tactics. Also, this is manifested in the strong reluctance by fire fighters to take complete strike action and their general willingness to accept voluntary arbitration if it is available. Such action, of course, is only rarely, if ever, seen in the private sector in wage negotiations. It is also less common in negotiations between municipalities and employees in less critical public occupations.

In conclusion, it seems reasonable to expect that in the foreseeable future the coercive strategy—including the strike—will become more commonly employed in wage disputes even though it is not favored by the fire fighters or the community. The basic reasons underlying the expected growth of coercive activity include (1) the rapid growth of disparity between fire fighter and police wages in municipalities in recent years, (2) the success of fire fighters and other public employees who have used coercive tactics in wage negotiations, and (3) the very rapid growth in collective bargaining in municipalities and the inevitable problem of inexperienced negotiators on both sides in the context of an uncertain developing relationship.

NOTES

1. One of the few studies that does have some discussion of public employee tactics in negotiations is [17].

2. Fire fighters appear to be the most highly organized municipal employee group. See [19].

3. Twenty-five structured interviews were conducted in 12 of the largest cities in the state of Indiana. I wish to thank the officers of the Indiana State Association of Fire Fighters for providing documents and useful insights into the problem and procedures of fire fighter negotiations.

4. The concept of the "budget decision period" will be used throughout the article. It is the period of the year when formal activity is carried out in formulating the operating budget for the ensuing fiscal year. It is divided into three time segments for our purposes. Its early stages begin when the mayor asks the fire chief to present budget needs for the next year. The second stage occurs when the mayor draws up the preliminary budget. The final stage begins when the city council reviews the preliminary budget and ends when it completes the budget for the next year.

5. The quality of the image of the fire fighter is seen as having a significant relationship to improvement in salaries and working conditions. At the 1968 IAFF convention, Resolution 101 was adopted to establish an IAFF Public Relations Department to enhance the fire fighter image. For the perceived importance of image-building and public relations, see [3 and 1].

6. One unusual program was developed in Dayton, Ohio. There the fire fighters, working with the welfare and service organizations, were

trained to be counselors for the communities they serve. It was noted that such community counseling activity might pay off by helping to win a pay disparity fight. See [10].

7. For an excellent detailed example of this type of behavior, see [6].

8. For the fire fighter's perception of the importance of maintaining favorable public sentiment during a strike, see [8].

9. For some informative illustrations of the use and effectiveness of limited pressure tactics, see [9].

10. Fire fighters are a close-knit and cohesive group. The cohesiveness is caused by their peculiar occupational subculture (irregular work hours, high interaction and mutual interdependence of living together and on the job, and a dangerous occupation with need for extensive coordination). This closeness and high interaction promotes extensive and intimate discussion among and within work groups. From it emerges an informally developed and generally accepted wage or package of economic benefits most fire fighters feel they must get as a minimal acceptable wage.

11. The IAFF convention in 1968 adopted a strong resolution calling for wage parity between fire fighters and police. Also see [2].

12. The emphasis placed on this is illustrated in [2].

13. Indeed, some seem to feel that this is the most important economic benefit in the fire fighter's job.

14. The "security conscious" men would include the fire fighters with long service who feel that they have a heavy investment in the benefits they are to receive later, and those without other adequate insurance and security plans for their families.

15. For an example of the fire fighters submitting a wage dispute to arbitration and not getting what they expected (with the result being a strike over the arbitrator's decision), see [5].

16. Examples of this can be seen in the 1969 strikes of Local 311 in Madison, Wisconsin, and Local 1186 in Vallejo, California. See [11 and 13].

17. For a recent illustration of this, see the result of the strike by Sacramento, California, Local 522 [15].

18. This occurred in the fire fighter strikes in Atlanta, Georgia, in 1966, and in Kalamazoo, Michigan, in 1969.

19. This put the basic salary for a Gary fire fighter at $7,440 a year.

20. In early 1970, at least 72 cities or districts were reported to have annual salaries of $10,000 or more for their fire fighters. See [14].

21. Although the coercive strategy had been ineffective in getting an immediate wage increase, the fire fighters did obtain some face-saving gains. A bipartisan blue ribbon committee was established to make recommendations on fire fighter wage increases in the immediate future. Also, this committee made recommendations which eventually resulted in a city ordinance recognizing the right of the fire fighters' union to bargain collectively and enter into written agreements with the city— something that no other city in Indiana has.

REFERENCES

1. Albert E. Albertoni, "Public Relations—365 Days a Year," *International Fire Fighter*, Vol. 53 (February 1970), p. 18.
2. William D. Buck, "Fire Fighter and Police Salaries," *Public Management*, Vol. 47 (August 1965), pp. 187-91.
3. _____, "A Successful Public Relations Program," *International Fire Fighter*, Vol. 50 (May 1967), p.3.
4. James A. Craft, "Fire Fighter Militancy and Wage Disparity," *Labor Law Journal*, Vol. 21 (December 1970), pp. 794-803.
5. Harold W. Davey, "The Use of Neutrals in the Public Sector," *Labor Law Journal*, Vol. 20 (August 1969), pp. 537-38.
6. Don J. Dougherty, "Local 385, Omaha, Wins 15 Percent Hike," *International Fire Fighter*, Vol. 50 (February 1967), pp. 6-7.
7. Joseph P. Goldberg, "Changing Policies in Public Employee Labor Relations," *Monthly Labor Review*, Vol. 93 (July 1970), pp. 5-14.
8. International Association of Fire Fighters, *A Public Relations Handbook for Union Fire Fighters* (Washington, 1970), pp. 24-25.
9. *International Fire Fighter*, Vol. 51 (January 1968), pp. 8 and 9.
10. _____, Vol. 52 (January 1969), pp. 4-17.
11. _____, Vol. 52 (May 1969), p. 10.
12. _____, Vol. 52 (August 1969), p. 7.
13. _____, Vol. 52 (September 1969), p. 7.
14. _____, Vol. 53 (May 1970), p. 18.
15. _____, Vol. 53 (December 1970), pp. 5 and 21.
16. William Lang, "Fire and Police Salaries—Another Viewpoint," *Public Personnel Review*, Vol. 26 (July 1965), pp. 164-68.
17. Michael H. Moskow, J. Joseph Loewenberg, and Edward C. Koziara, *Collective Bargaining in Public Employment* (New York: Random House, 1970), especially pp. 261-76.
18. Sterling D. Spero, *Government as Employer* (New York: Remsen Press, 1948), pp. 228-44.
19. Jack Stieber, "Employee Representation in Municipal Government," in *Municipal Year Book, 1969* (Washington: International City Mangement Association, 1969), pp. 36-37.

CASE #1
Municipal Labor Relations
in a Legislative Void:
The Texas Case

I. B. Helburn

The presence of severe restrictions against collective bargaining by public employees in Texas has led to the development of substitutes and supplements to bargaining. Two patterns of arriving at wages and working conditions are described: the persuasive-political process and the negotiation process. Also reviewed are the implications of these methods, the use of informal grievance procedures in preference to the written steps, and the fact that legal strike penalties are not often or severely imposed. The advent of legalized bargaining is seen as a certainty with its ramifications dependent on present attitudes and the nature of such legislation, whether mandatory or permissive.

INTRODUCTION

Present restrictions against collective bargaining by public employees in Texas are severe, with public employee organizations in an underdeveloped state. Nevertheless, there are unmistakable signs of existing and potential collective activity as employee organizations learn to maneuver within existing legislation and to concentrate their efforts on the passage of more permissive law. This article deals with the present state of municipal employer-employee relations in Texas, the particular accomodations that have been made to existing legislation, and future problems and implications.

Dr. Helburn is an Assistant Professor of Management in the Graduate School of Business, the University of Texas.

Materials for the article were gathered from newspaper reports, earlier reports of Texas public employee unionism, extensive personal interviews and telephone conversations with union and municipal management officials throughout Texas, and a questionnaire survey of mayors or city managers, as appropriate, of cities thought to have public employee organizations. Of the 68 cities surveyed, including all over 20,000 plus smaller municipalities where applicable, 57 responded, a rate of 83.8 per cent.[1]

Legal restrictions on public employee activities in Texas are unique, incorporating "the most inclusive and severe strike ban of any state," [2] plus additional bans on the recognition of public employee organizations for the purpose of collective bargaining[3] and the signing of such agreements by public officials.[4] However, the law does give the right to join or refrain from joining a public employee organization without penalty.[5] Such organizations may represent employees in the presentation of grievances over wages, hours, and other conditions of work.[6]

More recent legislation permits municipalities of 10,000 or more to voluntarily authorize checkoff, provided the employee gives written consent. Cities are empowered to collect fees to defray administrative costs.[7]

Two additional pieces of legislation have impact on police and fire fighters. The State Firemen's and Policemen's Civil Service Act authorizes municipalities of 10,000 or more to adopt civil service on a local option basis.[8] The act includes alternatives to the more normal union-management grievance procedure in the form of appeals to a Civil Service Commission.[9] Automatic suspension, fines from 10 to 100 dollars, and/or jail sentences of up to 30 days are penalties for striking, which is a misdemeanor.[10] Local civil service laws are common throughout Texas, particularly in the larger cities.

Article XI, Section 5 of the Constitution, gives home rule cities the authorization to frame and amend their charters. Municipalities over 5,000 thus have the power to provide for a number of means of citizen participation in the affairs of government, including the referendum, which allows private citizens to require the city government to put propositions to the electorate for a vote.[11] Fire fighters and policemen in a number of cities have used this procedure to gain wage increases or hour reductions denied by city officials. Thus, as discussed later in the paper, the procedure takes on importance as a tactic in municipal employer-employee relations.

THE EXTENT OF
MUNICIPAL EMPLOYEE ORGANIZATION

Three organizations predominate in Texas: the American Federation of State, County, and Municipal Employees, AFL-CIO (AFSCME); the International Association of Fire Fighters, AFL-CIO (IAFF); and the Texas Municipal Police Association (TMPA). The AFSCME has approximately 8,000 members throughout the state, with organizations in 13 Texas cities.[12] Local 1550 includes employees of the municipalities of Houston and Pasadena, Harris County and the Harris County Hospital district, and the Deer Park Independent School District (non-instructional personnel). With a membership of approximatly 4,500, the local is one of the largest in the international union. A second AFSCME "super local" of about 650 members includes employees of Port Arthur, Nederland, Port Neches, Beaumont, and Orange County. Thus, the bulk of the AFSCME membership is concentrated in the Houston-Galveston-Beaumont triangle, an area that is heavily industrialized with oil refineries and shipping and which has had many private sector unions for some time.

The Laborers' International Union, AFL-CIO (LIU), with locals in San Antonio and Lubbock, has the only other significant organization among municipal employees in the state at this time, excluding police and fire fighters. The LIU also includes the Lubbock city police department and the Lubbock county sheriff's department in a local union. Four of eight municipally owned transportation systems are unionized by the Amalgamated Transit Union, AFL-CIO: Dallas, San Antonio, Wichita Falls, and Amarillo.

Fire fighters, where organized, are members of the IAFF, with 49 locals throughout the state, including all major cities.[13] Policemen appear to belong to the Texas Municipal Police Association or a local organization, thereby staying aloof from affiliation with national organizations. Present exceptions include the Lubbock police organizations and El Paso Local 119, International Association of Police Officers, one of three El Paso police organizations. While TMPA officials have noted over 130 local chapters, the present study identified only 20. However, it is possible that chapters exist in the smaller communities not included in the study.

As expected, public employee organizations of all types were found more often in cities over 50,000 than in the smaller cities. Additionally, police and fire fighters were more likely to have some form of organization than were other types of municipal employees, and to be better organized. Data for 20 police and 27 fire fighter organizations showed 85 and 75 per cent respectively with memberships of at least 75 per cent of the total eligible, while only one of 11 municipal unions showed that degree of organization. Municipal unions tended to be more highly organized in cities under 50,000, with these cities being in the Houston-Beaumont-Galveston area. It is likely that heavy private sector industrial unionism in the area, plus the lesser diversity of municipal employees in the smaller cities in the area, have both contributed to the success of the AFSCME.

REGOGNITION AND CHECKOFF

The ambivalence of Texas public employee law is reflected in figures showing recognition and the granting of checkoff. While a close relationship might be expected between formal recognition for grievance purposes and the granting of checkoff—certainly a significant form of recognition in itself—this is not the case. Table 1 shows three basic trends. First, checkoff is more prevalent than recognition among all types of organizations. Second, many recognized organizations have not been granted checkoff rights. Third, municipal employee organizations have had greater success in gaining recognition and checkoff, again due likely to the existence of a number of locals in heavily unionized areas of the state.

TABLE 1
Formal Recognition and Checkoff Rights

Employee group	Police		Fire		Municipal	
	No.	%	No.	%	No.	%
Formal recognition	5	21.7	6	25.0	6	40.0
Checkoff rights	8	34.8	11	45.8	12	80
Number of formally recognized groups with checkoff	2		4		6	

GRIEVANCE PROCEDURES

When discussing grievance procedures, distinctions must be made between public safety employees (police and fire fighters) and other municipal employees and between paper and practice procedures. Particularly where municipal employees are concerned, the presence of specific written procedures is not necessarily an indication of actual practice. Such procedures may be included in city ordinances, in administrative regulations adopted or ratified by council, or in simple statements of work policy and/or conditions issued by the municipality. Where levels in the procedure are specified, they generally involve the supervisor concerned, department head, city manager, mayor, or civil service director, and finally city council or commission. In actuality, the immediate supervisor and council or final appeals authority may seldom be involved.

A change in procedures in El Paso shows many of the reasons for the more informal procedures that have evolved there and elsewhere. El Paso AFSCME Local 59 formerly had a grievance system that included stewards at operating levels. If a union steward could not settle a problem with the supervisor concerned, the union considered the case at an open meeting and decided upon further appeals to the Civil Service Commission.[14] This was prior to the employment of a full-time business agent in December, 1964. Since that time, the business agent has become involved to a great degree, and the importance of the stewards has diminished. The business agent, sometimes with other local officials, will look into a problem at the operating level, and if it cannot be solved satisfactorily, bring it to the attention of the Director of Personnel and Civil Service. Some problems or grievances are discussed directly with the Director. The union business agent recalled only six or eight grievances that had been taken to a Commission hearing since he had become business agent.

Three primary reasons explain the use of this more informal system. First, the business agent is paid to service union members and has both time and experience to do so. Second, union leaders feel that the business agent, employed by the union and not the city as is the case with a steward, can speak with more independence and authority. Finally, the union spokesman and the Director of Civil Service and Personnel have developed a good working relationship and are thus generally able to find acceptable solutions to potential or current problems.[15]

Where a more formal procedure is in effect, it generally involves the union business agent and departmental head first, then the city manager. Thus, in fact, both formal and informal processes seem to involve the same sets of municipal officials. Where line supervisors at the first step and appeals panels at the final step are specified, they are often omitted (supervisors) or unnecessary (panels). What appears to be most critical is the relationship established between union and management officials, with a good relationship leading to increased use of informal procedures. Thus, there are parallels in this respect between public and private sectors. The major difference may be decreased emphasis on problem solving at the very lowest level for organized municipal employees in Texas.

The use of grievance procedures by public safety employees does not appear to be as prevalent as by other unionized municipal employees, with major reasons for the difference lying in the use of civil service regulations and the nature of the work. Because of civil service regulations there exist two systems for processing grievances. Those that do not fall under civil service may be handled in the same way as municipal employees' grievances, with the final level being the mayor, city manager, or city council in most cases. However, it appears that by and large grievances can be settled within the department.

The most likely explanation for the relative absence of grievances—at least for the fire fighters—lies in the nature of the work. An individual station house in the larger cities is commanded by a lieutenant or captain. The officer and his crew eat, sleep, work, and train together with little real distinction between ranks. Because of this close relationship, problems are generally solved within the station before they become major. If this is not the case, then the district chief, deputy chief, and fire chief may be involved prior to people outside the department. Thus, there are numerous opportunities for settlement and, unless the matter is extremely serious, such as discharge or suspension, a solution is often found.

CHANGES IN WAGES AND WORKING CONDITIONS

As with many of the grievance procedures, form must be separated from substance when discussing the procedures for considering employee requests and the final embodiment of these requests. While a signed contract is illegal, there are substitutes.

The Texas City *Employees' Work Policy* begins with the following statement: "Statement of Policy, City of Texas City, as to Conditions of Employment, Including Wages, Hours, and Working Conditions of Texas City Employees." The City of Orange *Employee Handbook* is similar to the Texas City publication in many respects, containing information about grievance procedures, employee responsibilities, and with the exception of current pay scales, conditions of work and fringe benefits. Yet, the Texas City handbook is in large measure the product of negotiations between union and management officials; the City of Orange does not have an organized group of municipal employees and, while there are IAFF and TMPA groups, activity which could be classified as negotiations does not take place.[16] Thus, the final form in which wages and other conditions of employment are presented is not always indicative of the way in which these conditions were determined. However, it is possible to delineate two patterns of arriving at wages and working conditions.

WAGES AND WORKING CONDITIONS: THE PERSUASIVE-POLITICAL PROCESS

In its purest form, the persuasive-political process involves four factors:
1. the understanding that there will be no overt negotiations between union and management,
2. the presentation, in written and/or oral form of requests to the municipal governing body,
3. meetings between the union business agent and possibly other union officials with elected and appointed individuals in city government, and
4. the use of a variety of approaches designed to increase the possibility of acceptance of employee requests for improved wages and conditions of work.

Again the El Paso procedure provides a good example. The July 16, 1970, request from AFSCME Local 59 was in the form of a letter with attachment addressed to the Mayor and City Council. The letter requested consideration of improved wages, increases in paid vacations, increases in allowed paid sick leave, the institution of a shift differential, improvements in the hospitalization insurance, and study of the classification schedule to reduce inequities. These requests were coordinated with the IAFF local and Local 119, International Association of Police Officers, so that requests from all groups were identical. (In this respect, the El Paso case is atypical, as it has not been usual in Texas for municipal and public safety employee groups to coordinate requests.)

The requests were followed by conferences between union officials and the Mayor, individual councilmen, the Director of Civil Service and Personnel, and others who might have influence or play a direct role in the formulation and passage of the final municipal budget. Particularly in meetings with elected officials, the ultimate appeal to the electoral process—whether made explicit or left implicit—exists as a silent partner of employee representatives. While individual employee organizations do not make endorsements of mayoral or council candidates, they are involved in endorsements made by the central labor body. Where labor has strength in a given community and can command votes, the endorsement and its implications must be considered by those wishing to run initially for or be reelected to public office.

These talks may be supplemented by a number of more visible tactics designed to bring pressure upon the governing body. The most obvious, the strike or work stoppage, will be discussed later in this paper. However, this tactic, when used in conjunction with the request procedure, generally occurs after a budget recommendation rather than during the deliberations leading to the recommendation.

The more distinct possibility is threat of a strike or variant thereof. In 1969, the promulgation of a revised salary schedule for El Paso police and fire fighters was in part the result of a strike threat by these employees. While the revised schedule would have been effected anyway, it appears as though this came about earlier than the city officials desired because of pressures brought by the public safety groups.[17]

In 1967, the Fort Worth City Council included raises in the budget where none had been previously included by the City Manager, following a walkout threat by municipal employees, members of AFSCME Local 1552.[18] In 1969, sanitation employees threatened to strike rather than continue to carry trash cans from houses to the curb for the same rate of pay as for simply emptying those cans already on the curb. Resolution of the problem came from a committee of city, sanitation department, and employee representatives, thus avoiding the strike.[19] The 1969 Fort Worth situation was related to a specific set of undesirable working conditions rather than a request for a general wage increase. Nevertheless, it is an indication of the possibility of pressure from employees. Here the more normal (for Fort Worth) arms length approach was abandoned in the face of both a specific problem and a specific strike threat.

Other forms of pressure may also be applied, particularly by public safety employees who, so far as can be determined, have not yet struck in Texas. However, their use of the referendum has had an impact. In Beaumont, elections held in 1962,[20] 1965,[21] and 1967[22] resulted in pay increases for police and fire fighters. In 1964, fire fighters had their hours reduced without an election but after the necessary petitions had been filed.[23] In 1969 and 1970, these employees received raises without resorting to the referendum, but the local IAFF President felt that earlier successes had some influence in later decisions made by municipal officials.[24]

A search of *The Texas Fire Fighter*, publication of the Texas State Association of Fire Fighters, showed 23 instances between 1959 and 1971 where the referendum was threatened or used by fire fighters to gain wage increases or hours reductions. This list is incomplete, and probably weighted in favor of successful outcomes, but there were 17 reported successful elections.

Thus, even without actual bargaining, there are alternatives that have been used by public employees throughout the state. Talks with union and management officials plus questionnaire returns suggest that particularly when wages were concerned, public employee organizations have often been successful in influencing budget recommendations.

WAGES AND WORKING CONDITIONS: THE NEGOTIATION PROCESS

Despite the prohibition of a public employee organization as a collective bargaining agent, there are instances in Texas where the union-management relationship can only be described as one of collective bargaining. In Texas City, the *Employees' Work Policy* has replaced an earlier, illegal agreement,[25] but negotiations still continue, with the Mayor and selected commissioners bargaining for the city after the commission as a whole has set guidelines for its bargaining representatives.[26] In Pasadena, the results of negotiations are embodied in a *Memorandum of Understanding* which reads like a union-management contract, except for the omission of a clause recognizing the union as a collective bargaining agent. Bargaining occurs in other jurisdictions, most notably San Antonio, with the municipally owned transit system and ATU involved.

Based on questionnaire returns and interviews, there is little doubt that, in general, the persuasive-political process dominates in Texas both because of the legal environment and the more conservative nature of the public employees, particularly police and fire fighters. What is hard to determine, however, without being present in a myriad of sessions in a variety of locations throughout the state, is where the process falls into the gray area between persuasion and negotiation. When individual council members are visited by union officials, how often are promises of support exchanged—support for a wage increase in return for support of a councilman's pet project or campaign for reelection? This, if and when it occurs, is negotiation in itself. Or, for example, when union-management study committees are named to bring joint recommendations to the city council, as has been done in Houston, how should this be classified? One cannot always speak with certainty about the relationship between two parties, and in some cases the parties themselves will disagree in the application of a descriptive label.

WORK STOPPAGES

Table 2 summarizes the strike experience of Texas municipalities in the 1966-1970 period. A number of trends are evident. First and most obvious is the propensity to strike among sanitation workers, both organized and unorganized. Data indicate that the presence of a union is not a necessary condition for a strike where sanitation workers are concerned. Only in the Galveston strike was the AFSCME, the strongest municipal union in the state, involved.

In most instances, wages were noted as a primary issue, but there have also been other serious problems. Two other important trends may be noted, particularly in view of Texas law. The strikes have resulted in increased communications between the parties, with a negotiated settlement involved in many instances. Moreover, in many instances, employees involved in work stoppages were given little or no punishment, although the law is specific in the application of penalties to striking public employees. Of course, the definition of a particular work stoppage as a strike must first be made by municipal officials, and stoppages have often been defined as "sick-ins," protest days, and prolonged absences in order to avoid the imposition of the specified penalties.

The problem some officials see is one of uninterrupted services to the taxpayers rather than simply compliance with the law. In this light, increased communications and the lack of punishment may be seen as an attempt to improve or normalize a disruptive situation rather than worsen it. Obviously the approaches taken by city officials may vary depending on their philosophical/political attitude toward unionism, the history of the relationship, union strength, availability of a substitute work force, and the criticality of services performed by the striking workers.

CURRENT PROBLEMS

Like unions elsewhere, public employee organizations in Texas have been concerned with wages, hours of work, fringe benefits, and other working conditions. Unlike many areas, Texas law made it necessary for employee organizations to develop substitutes and supplements to the bargaining process. Political pressures, public relations techniques, use of the referendum, quasi-bargaining techniques, and collective bargaining covered with a veneer of legality have all played a role, as has the strike, actual or threatened.

On the other side of the coin, the ambivalence of municipal officials regarding organizational and representational activities of their employees emerges as a distinct and possibly critical trend. Public officials have on occasion expressed the opinion that in the next few years public employees will gain the legal right to bargain collectively. Even now, some employee organizations have been recognized officially or unofficially through the granting of checkoff or the use of substitute bargaining procedures. Yet there appears to be a great reluctance to grant legal recognition for grievance purposes. If this reluctance were to be dissipated by the passage of more permissive legislation, the chaos that is sometimes predicted as a result might perhaps be minimized. But, to the extent that the ambivalence is representative of a more deep-seated attitude, the problems of transition from unilateral to bilateral decision-making would be greater.

Another problem concerns the variety of approaches to the setting of wages and working conditions. Employees have at times by-passed the civil service or personnel offices in favor of pleas to the City Council if this approach seemed more expedient. Here the problem becomes one of substitution of a political for a nonpolitical process. While final recourse to the governing political body, at least for approval of a settlement, is not likely avoida-

TABLE 2 Municipal Strikes in Texas: 1966-70

Date	Municipality	Length of strike (calendar/ work days)	Approximate Number of Employees Involved	Department Involved	Union	Major Issue(s)	Settlement	Disposition of Strikers
September 1966	Austin[1]	4/2	65	Sanitation		Wages—immediate increase	No immediate increase—wage increase already budgeted for October 1966.	Workers offered employment for immediate return, others to be resigned with loss of accrued sick leave & vacation benefits.
October 1966	Dallas[2]	1/1	675	Dallas Transit System	ATU	Refusal of the System to bargain with the union.	Employees returned under a court injunction. DTS will not bargain.	Return to work, no punishment.
July 1967	San Antonio[1]	10/6	275	Sanitation and Street	LIU	Wages, check-off, overtime	Negotiated settlement	Loss of accumulated sick leave and one week's pay.
February 1968	Pampa[1]	6/5	25	Sanitation		Wages	Wages and fringes increased	Return to work, no punishment
June 1968	Odessa[1]	2 hours	40	Sanitation		Wages and hours	Mutually agreed upon settlement	Return to work, no punishment
August 1968	Lufkin[3]	5/5	28	Sanitation, Street, Water and Sewer		Wages	Employees given one week to report to work, wages improved.	Wages lost during time out. One or two not rehired by city.

TABLE 2 Municipal Strikes in Texas: 1965-70 (continued)

Date	Municipality	Length of strike (calendar/ work days)	Approximate Number of Employees Involved	Department Involved	Union	Major Issue(s)	Settlement	Disposition of Strikers
August 1968	Lubbock[4]	8/6	200	Sanitation and Public Works	LIU	Time and one-half for overtime, shorter routes.	Overtime pay as of 10-1-68, as close to an 8 hr. day as possible until then	Strikers rehired and allowed to make up lost day prior to October 1, 1968.
September 1968	Galveston[4] [5]	4/4	150	Sanitation	AFSCME, General Drivers & Helpers AFL-CIO	Wages	Agreement on wage improvements	Strikers allowed to return to work & make up lost pay if trash promptly cleaned up
June 1969	Corpus Christi[4]	4/3	140	Sanitation	CUMA	Hours of work, overtime pay, removal of department head, civil service status	Negotiated settlement of removal of supervisor, civil service status, improved minimum wage, continued talks on work week.	No punishment, no pay for days not worked but employee can credit it against leave time.
July 1969	Corpus Christi[4]	8/7	140	Sanitation	CUMA	Civil service status, increased pay plus earlier issues	Civil Service Commission approved civil service for sanitation employees	Strikers fired, all but one allowed to return as new employees with loss of earlier accrued benefits.

TABLE 2   Municipal Strikes in Texas: 1966-70 (continued)

Date	Municipality	Length of strike (calendar/work days)	Approximate Number of Employees Involved	Department Involved	Union	Major Issue(s)	Settlement	Disposition of Strikers
August 1969	Marshall[1] [3]	2½/2½	30	Sanitation		Wages, revised pay periods	Most employees returned to work. No promises made by city except future consideration or requests.	Organizers terminated—strikers lost wages while out.
September 1969	San Antonio[4] [5]	14/14	450	San Antonio Transit System	ATU	Wages and working conditions	Negotiated improvements in wages and fringes	Strikers returned with only loss of wages while on strike.
November 1969	Houston[4]	1/1	6	Porters at dog pound		Wages, working conditions	Increase in wages, immproved conditions.	Return to work, no punishment
August 1970	Longview[3]	5/5	38	Sanitation		Wages, grievance system, working conditions	No changes in pre-strike conditions	All except 5 or 6 ringleaders rehired with only loss of week's pay

[1] Data taken from questionaire returned by municipal official.
[2] Data based on telephone conversation with Wilson C. Driggs, General Manager, Dallas Transit System.
[3] Data based on telephone conversations with respective city managers.
[4] Data based on newspaper accounts from local papers.
[5] Data based on interviews with management officials concerned.

ble, there may be advantages to settling wage and working conditions questions by means that at least initially minimize politics as far as possible. There would appear to be some value in making wage decisions based on comparison with other job classifications and/or similar-sized municipalities where the facts, if not the final decisions, would not be distorted or misrepresented for purposes of public appeal.

The strike provisions of the law raise additional questions. In Texas, as elsewhere, the prohibition coupled with possibilities of harsh penalties has not eliminated stoppages. In fact, the present study shows that not only is the imposition of penalties avoided in the case of some work stoppages, but an additional activity of questioned legality—collective negotiations—is adopted, at least on an *ad hoc* basis as an expedient way to settle the dispute, or possibly to eliminate the threat of a pending dispute. In the public sector the strike serves a political function rather than the economic function it serves in the private sector, forcing the elected municipal or county official to respond to pressure from inconvenienced taxpayers.[27] Thus, it is not surprising that a method holding promise of a quick solution is adopted at the time of a strike rather than the imposition of penalties, which could well prolong the stoppage. Certainly alternatives to the strike in the form of dispute settlement procedures should be considered as part of a revision in present law, particularly if bargaining were to be legalized.

The political ramifications of the public employee strike tie together with the problem of involvement of Texas public employees in the political process. Neither the presence of state and local versions of the Federal Hatch Act nor the fact that endorsements are made by central labor bodies rather than by individual local unions eliminates political activities by these locals. The central labor body endorsement may represent only the tip of the iceberg of political activity. For example, while the Fort Worth IAFF local does not endorse local candidates itself, it does participate in endorsement decisions of the central labor body. In addition, members of the local will interview council candidates to determine their positions on issues of importance to the fire fighters. Within the local, by use of newsletters or other means, members will be encouraged to vote for specific candidates; and the women's auxiliary, usually the wives, will campaign openly for candidates approved by the IAFF local. The practice in Fort Worth does not appear to be atypical of the big city unions.

The Beaumont IAFF Local 399 recently took a public position

in a recall election involving city council members. Because this
type of election is technically classified as an issue election as
opposed to an individual battle for an elected seat, the union's
stance was found to be in accordance with the civil srvice regulations.[28] However, there may be few practical differences between
the types of elections, so that the implications of this kind of open
political activity are similar to those of participation in electoral
politics.

The increase in public employee activity has additional, possibly more direct ramifications for taxpayers. Whether by bargaining or other means, these employees are receiving sizable increases in wages in many parts of the state. Part of this is due to
the aggressiveness and improved techniques used by these
groups in their own behalf, while part of the reason may be found
in the accumulation of economic pressures during the years when
public employees did not drink heavily from the trough of public
revenue. The funds for such increases must ultimately come from
the taxpayer, who may find himself torn between the desire for
high quality services, such as adequate police protection, and the
desire to keep his tax obligation to a minimum. When the elected
official is included in the mix, on occasion as the man in the
middle, the problems of adequate wages and working conditions
for public employees become too complicated for easy solution,
thus leading full circle to part of the reason for heightened
employer-employee conflict.

FUTURE PROSPECTS

Several things might happen to change the nature of employer-
employee relations as they now exist in Texas. The most drastic
change would involve new legislation legalizing public sector collective bargaining and the resulting agreements. Such a change
in Texas might involve permissive legislation—legalizing, but not
mandating collective bargaining between political jurisdictions
and their employee organizations—rather than mandatory
negotiations at the request of either union or management as is
the case in some states. However, even legislation of a permissive
type would almost certainly result in an acceleration of the present trend of closer union-management relations and would put a
premium on patience, understanding, and realism on the part of
both union and management officials.

Even without changes in the law, modification of present
union or association practices might make these organizations a

more powerful force. One possibility is inherent in the activities of AFSCME Local 1550, the 4,500 member Houston-based local which includes employees of five political jurisdictions. The local demands a large voice in the Harris County AFL-CIO (its chief business agent has been president of the central labor body), including its endorsements for political candidates. In addition, the local has the financial resources to afford full-time business agents for its membership regardless of which political subdivision serves as the employer. A similar "super-local" has evolved in the Beaumont-Port Arthur area with the amalgamation of five of the seven area AFSCME locals. Similar reorganization might be a possibility in the Galveston-Texas City area with three locals, and eventually elsewhere in the state as the public employee union movement expands. With greater financial resources such unions might increase their participation in politics (thus possibly compounding a present problem), their full-time representation, and their strength in either the grievance representation or negotiation processes.

A similar tactic on a lesser scale is available to public safety employees. While police and fire fighters have at times cooperated in the presentation of demands or requests for improvements or a referendum campaign for higher wages, this cooperation does not appear to be widespread or continuous. If these groups are ever able to put aside historical differences over parity in wages and hours and to cooperate in their dealings with municipal management and their appeals to the general public, they might find more success in obtaining higher wages and fringe benefits, particularly in a period when the public is very conscious of the issue of "law and order."

An extension of this would be the cooperation of all three groups of public employees at the municipal level—municipal employees, police, and fire fighters. Although this has happened in El Paso where the IAFF and the AFSCME have coordinated with the local police union (but not with the other two police organizations), such cooperation does not appear likely because of the more conservative, professional nature of the nonunion police organizations in the state. The unionization of police, a possibility but not a likelihood, might change this, but there are no indications that this is about to happen. Another variant on the above theme would be to have police associations stand by themselves while receiving aid in bargaining from a local union. This is the pattern in Texas City where the AFSCME representative aids both the police association and the IAFF, and where many members of both of these departments belong to both their own organizations and the AFSCME. Again, however, this arrangement is atypical.

PUBLIC POLICY IMPLICATIONS

There can be little doubt that the increased interest shown by public employees in their conditions of work will not abate in the future, and that public employee organization, regardless of the law, will attempt to translate interest into influence in a variety of ways. If this occurs, the potential for both constructive and destructive union-management relations is heightened. In observing the experience of other states, the shift in Texas from rural to urban representation, and the union attempts to gain more permissive legislation, the conclusion is reached that passage of such legislation is a certainty, with only the date of passage a question.

The choice for Texas legislators may well be one of constructive law passed after considerable thought and study of accumulated experience or legislation hurriedly enacted as a response to a specific incident or set of incidents. The former would appear to offer more long run potential for all concerned, including the general public.

NOTES

1. Below are the number of cities and respondents for each size category used. The number before the slash represents total cities in the category; the number of respondents follows the slash: up to 20,000 12/8; 20,001-50,000 31/26; 50,001-100,000 14/12; over 100,000 11/10.

2. Chester A. Newland, "Public Employee Strikes: Administrative Change and Political Protest," *Public Affairs Comments,* XIV, May 1968, p. 2.

3. *Vernon's Annotated Revised Civil Statues of the State of Texas,* Article 5154c, Sec. 2.

4. *Ibid.,* 5154c, Sec. 1.

5. *Ibid.,* 5154c, Sec. 4.

6. *Ibid.,* 5154c, Sec. 6.

7. *Ibid.,* 6252-3a. Only Fort Worth and Beaumont collect fees to defray administrative costs.

8. *Ibid.,* 1269m.

9. *Ibid.,* 1269m, Sec. 16-20.

10. *Ibid.,* 1269m, Sec. 27.

11. See Institute of Public Affairs, *Texas Council-Manager Charters,*

The Institute of Public Affairs, The University of Texas, Austin, 1961, pp. 55-57.

12. Interview with Don McCullar, Area Director, AFSCME, Brownwood, Texas, December 15, 1970.

13. International Association of Fire Fighters, *Directory of Recording Secretaries* IAFF, Washington, D.C., May 1970. Information about an additional local in Harlingen is taken from *The Texas Fire Fighter*, XII, June-July 1970, p. 5.

14. Chester Newland, *Public Employee Unionization in Texas*, Institute of Public Affairs, The University of Texas, Austin, 1962, p. 5.

15. J. D. Givens, Business Agent, Local 59, AFSCME, and James H. Ewell, Director of Civil Service and Personnel, City of El Paso, both interviewed in El Paso, Texas, on July 23 and 24, 1970, respectively. Both emphasized their working relationship and ability to solve problems.

16. Information concerning the City of Orange was taken from questionnaire responses and the *Employee Handbook*.

17. James H. Ewell, *op. cit.*

18. Interview with W. A. Driver, Business Agent, Local 1552, Fort Worth, Texas, July 17, 1970.

19. *Idem*. Additional information was received from Charles W. Binford, Assistant to the City Manager, City of Fort Worth, in a letter dated June 24, 1970.

20. *The Texas Fire Fighter*, V, April 1962, p. 1.

21. *Ibid.*, IX, January 1966, p. 1.

22. *Ibid.*, XI, January 1968, p. 1.

23. *Ibid.*, VII, May 1964, p. 1 and July 1964, p. 1.

24. Interview with Louis Herbert, President, Local 399, IAFF, Beaumont, Texas, July 28, 1970.

25. Newland, *Public Employee Unionization in Texas*, p. 22.

26. Interview with Kenneth Nunn, Secretary-Treasurer, City of Texas City, Texas, July 29, 1970.

27. For an excellent discussion of the differences between public and private sectors see George H. Hildebrand, "The Public Sector," *Frontiers of Collective Bargaining*, (John T. Dunlop and Neil W. Chamberlain, eds.), Harper & Row, New York, 1967, pp. 125-164.

28. Louis Herbert, *loc cit.*

This article has been adapted from a monograph *Public Employer-Employee Relations in Texas: Contemporary and Emerging Developments*, published by The Institute of Public Affairs, The University of Texas.

CASE #2
Nurses and Pennsylvania's New
Public Employee Bargaining Law
John Schmidman

For many years, officials and legislators, as well as experts in labor law have attempted to come to grips with the problem of public employee strikes. Should they be allowed—what alternatives to a strike exist or to the legalization of that privilege? In this article, the author presents the results of a detailed study which was finalized before the passage of P. L. 195, which granted Pennsylvania public employees the right to collective bargaining and a "limited" right to strike.

On October 21, 1970, the Commonwealth of Pennsylvania bcame a show case state in regard to public employee bargaining. For it was on that date that the Public Employe Relations Act (Act 195), governing collective bargaining in the public sector, took effect. This law has been praised by such diverse groups as the Pennsylvania State Education Association, the Pennsylvania AFL-CIO, the Pennsylvania School Boards' Association, and the Pennsylvania Nurses' Association as being the most "realistic" and "workable" of any comparable public employee bargaining law in the nation.[1] While Act 195 does contain certain flaws, it nonetheless has established bargaining rights among public employees, and it gives an extremely broad definition to public employer and employee. Under the Act, a public employee is any individual working for the Commonwealth of Pennsylvania and its political

Reproduced from the November, 1971 issue of the LABOR LAW JOURNAL, published and copyrighted (1971) by Commerce Clearing House, Inc., 4025 W. Peterson Avenue, Chicago, Illinois 60646. Reprinted by permission of the author and Commerce Clearing House, Inc.

John Schidman is an Assistant Professor of Labor Studies at The Pennsylvania State University in University Park, Pennsylvania. The author wishes to thank the National Science Foundation and the Pennsylvania Nurses' Association for their assistance in this study. However the views expressed herein are solely his.

subdivisions, state-related institutions, non-profit organizations and institutions, and any charitable, religious, scientific, literary, recreational, health, education or welfare institutions receiving grants or appropriations from local, state or federal governments. It does not cover police or firemen as they are covered by Act 111 of June 27, 1968, which provides for compulsory arbitration in the event of a collective bargaining impasse.

Probably the two most influential groups lobbying for the passage of a public employee bargaining law were the Pennsylvania AFL-CIO and the Pennsylvania state Education Association (PSEA). The Pennsylvania AFL-CIO had its strength mainly in the House of Representatives, while the PSEA found its greatest influence to lie in the State Senate. The bill that emerged is largely the result of a compromise between these two organizations. However, these were not the only groups actively lobbying for and having an influence on the final shape of the Act. The Pennsylvania School Board's Association was undoubtedly the major force behind the fact that the agency shop is illegal under Act 195. Also active in obtaining the inclusion of non-profit institutions under the definition of public employer was the Pennsylvania Nurses' Association (PNA). Although the road for the PNA has ben a long and hard one since the Act took effect, it has not met with the success of other groups in winning exclusive bargaining rights for those individuals it claims within its jurisdiction, that is, nurses in the hospitals of Pennsylvania.

While public school teachers, state employees, municipal employees and others have been extremely active—and successful—in drives to win negotiation rights, the Pennsylvania Nurses' Association has been slower and is just now beginning to catch up.[2] The slight propensity of nurses to bargain collectively for the salaries they receive, on the hours which they work and over the conditions they work under can be directly correlated to two essential factors: (1) the structuring of Act 195 itself, and (2) the inherent nature of the nursing profession and the PNA.

A BRIEF DESCRIPTION OF ACT 195

The Public Employee Relations Act is administered by the three member Pennsylvania Labor Relations Board (PLRB) which also has jurisdiction over the Pennsylvania Labor Relations Act. Membership on the Board is a part-time position, and each member is selected by the Governor for a six-year term with the consent of the State Senate.[3] When Act 195 took effect, the Board found itself virtually deluged with election and recognition petitions.[4] At one point, its backlog was in excess of six hundred cases. It does not have the personnel even yet to handle the case load it faces and must rely on *per diem* Trial Examiners rather than full-time personnel.

In addition to the broad definition given to public employers and public employees under the Act, the law also provides for bargaining rights of a sort for individuals at the lowest level of supervision. Due to the unique nature of public employment, the General Assembly[5] felt that these employees were unlike first level supervisors in private employment. Under Act 195, these persons have all the rights of the people they supervise, save for the most important one. That is, a public employer is not under any duty to bargain with a unit of first level supervisors, but, using the language of Act 195, he is only under an obligation to "meet and discuss"[6] with such individuals or their representative. The Act also states that professional employees may not be included in the same unit as non-professionals unless they so vote.

Act 195 contains a "limited" right to strike. It is limited in the sense that there are certain specified procedures that must be gone through before a group of public employees may in fact strike. If an impasse has been reached after twenty-one days of negotiations, the parties must notify the Pennsylvania Bureau of Mediation. There is the added proviso that this date must be no later than one hundred-fifty days before the budget submission date of the public employer. If no agreement is reached during the next twenty days, the Bureau of Mediation so notifies the Pennsylvania Labor Relations Board which may at its discretion appoint a fact-finding panel of either one or three members. If one or both of the parties refuse to accept the recommendations of the fact-finding panel, these recommendations are then made public. If the Board does not deem fact-finding to be appropriate, the public employees may then stike.

However, there is the added limitation that a public employer may go into the state court having jursidiction and seek an injunction ordering the striking employees back to work, claiming that the strike is creating "a clear and present danger or threat to the health, safety or welfare of the public."[7] The inclusion of the word "welfare" raises real doubts as to whether there is in fact an actual right to strike. In some cases, judges have denied such employer requests and in other cases have granted them. In one central Pennsylvania school district which cuts across two counties, an unusual situation existed where the judge in one county refused the school board's request for an injunction, and the judge in the other county granted the enjoining order.

ACT 195 AND THE NURSES

In spite of the long way the PNA has come in recent years, its membership still sees it all too often as a "professional" organization. The metamorphosis of the Pennsylvania State Education Association is much in contrast with the case of the PNA. The PSEA long ago lost its company union syndrome. In most school districts in Pennsylvania, there is little difference in approach and tactics between local unions of the American Federation of Teachers (AFT) and local branches of the PSEA. The PSEA has finally realized that labor relations and collective bargaining in the public sector is a confrontation between employer and employee organization. The PSEA initially hoped to have a separate agency administer Act 195 fearing that the state Labor Relations Board would be too prounion, that is pro-AFT. It now realizes that an employee organization is an employee organization, and its staff seems to be less annoyed when they are referred to in the press as a teahers' union.

One advantage that teachers, whether they be Union or Association members, have had that the PNA did not was an extensive organization in addition to a staff and membership who had some notion of what bargaining was about. Even while actively lobbying for the passage of Act 195, the PNA was still referring to collective bargaining as its "economic security program," and claimed as members a small percentage of the 80,000 nurses in the Commonwealth.

The manner in which Act 195 defines first level supervisors has handicapped the PNA in its organizational efforts to date. In the petitions for recognition which they have filed thus far with the PLRB, the PNA has sought representation for only registered nurses and head nurses. In some cases, they have managed to have head nurses included in the unit determined, and in others hospital administrators have been able to have them defined as supervisors.

The PNA has also been troubled by the intervention of other employee organizations in their organizing efforts. In order for the PLRB to order a representation election in a proposed unit, the employee organization must have a showing of interest of at least thirty per cent. In order for a second employee organization to intervene, it must demonstrate a showing of interest of at least fifteen per cent. In the event of a joint petition for certification on the part of a public employer and emloyee organization, only a one per cent showing of interest is needed for a second organization to intervene. There have been hospitals in which the Laborers International Union, Service Employees International Union and Drug and Hospital Local 1199 have sought to organize the non-professional hospital employees much to the consternation and confusion of the PNA.

The only other organization of professional health care employees which is realistically facing the inevitability of collective bargaining in the hospitals of the Commonwealth is the Pennsylvania Association of Nurse Anesthetists (PANA). This is an organization of about 1,450 members which can claim an almost one hundred per cent affiliation of nurse anesthetists in the Commonwealth. It must be admitted however that this high percentage of affiliation is largely due to the fact that the PANA plays a vital role in the certification process by which an individual becomes a Certified Registered Nurse Anesthetist. Thus far however, the PANA has sought to opt out of bargaining in hospitals in which the PNA has filed petitions for recognition, the one major exception to this being the anesthetists employed at the state hospitals.

THE NURSING PROFESSION

To understand the immense problems facing the PNA in its attempt to organize the nursing profession in Pennsylvania, one has to recognize that there is something much deeper than the mere structure of ACT 195 which makes the task an extremely difficult one. This lies in the inherent nature of the nursing profession. William M. Baird has claimed that there are three major barriers preventing the establishment of collective bargaining on the part of professional nurses.[8] He first cites the legal framework, mentioning the lack of coverage under the National Labor Relations Act as well as a lack of coverage under most state laws governing labor relations in the public sector. Secondly, he maintains that the negative attitudes of hospital administrators toward collective bargaining are comparable to those "which in the past have been held by management in other industries in the early stages of collective bargaining."[9]

Professor Baird further claims that the third barrier is the structure of the labor market for registered nurses. He describes hospitals as monopsonists, and states that nurses themselves have demonstrated little mobility. Although there is little statistical evidence to prove or disprove this contention in Pennsylvania, there is a general feeling amongst the PNA, hospital administrators, and registered nurses themselves that there are three jobs for every two working nurses in the state.

Pennsylvania hospital administrators are no less anti-collective bargaining for nurses or other hospital employees than are their counterparts in other states. But boards of school directors in the Commonwealth as well as the majority of school superintendents are also of the old school, and yet bargaining in school districts went on even before the passage of Act 195. Pennsylvania hospitals to a great extent do dictate the wages which are paid private duty and office nurses, and with the exception of industrial nurses, they face little competition in hiring professional nursing staffs.

With the passage of Act 195, the question is now whether or not the PNA will successfully make use of this piece of enabling legislation. It is difficult to pick up a newspaper in Pennsylvania today that does not contain some article on the movement towards collective bargaining among public employees, unfortunately all too often in terms of some threatened or actual strike. It would seem that nurses also ought to be aware of what is going on among other public employees in the Commonwealth, but as the head of one school of nursing mentioned to the author, "Nurses realize that they have responsibilities which far exceed their rights." It would seem that this Florence Nightingale image permeates every school of nursing in the state whether connected with a university of a hospital, and that there is something inherent in the training that nurses receive that causes them to double think collective bargaining out of existence.

With these problems in mind, a grant was obtained from the National Science Foundation to attempt to discover the attitudes of nurses toward collective bargaining. While the results of this study are by no means meant to be all-inclusive or definitive, they do indicate areas which must be dealt with on the part of those who would seek to organize professional nursing staffs for the purpose of collective bargaining. The fact should be noted that this study, as does any survey research project, contains flaws and also the fact that the data were accumulated one year before passage of Act 195.

The data collected from the survey were grouped into four general areas. One was biographical, seeking to discern the effects of age, marital status, and years spent working in the nursing profession on the attitudes of nurses toward organizing for collective bargaining, and to then relate these biographical areas to the specific attitude clusters studied in the survey. Another cluster of questions concerned itself with the employment situation and factors related to the work performed. The third group sought to obtain information in regard to authority and professionalism in medical institutions. The fourth cluster consisted of the attitudes toward the effectiveness of bargaining as a device to improve the economic and professional status of nurses.

A list of all the active nurses in the Commonwealth was obtained from the Pennsylvania Board of Nurse Examiners.[10] District Six of the PNA was chosen for the survey. District Six consists of nine counties in southwestern Pennsylvania, and it provided a cross section of both urban and rural areas. It includes greater Pittsburgh as well as areas in Fayett and Green Counties which are more representative of typical Appalachia. A random sampling of ten per cent of the 12,000 active nurses in District Six was chosen to receive the mail questionnaire, and 491 nurses responded to it.[11]

SURVEY FINDINGS

Because of the large number of items dealt with in the questionnaire, an effort was made to reduce them to a smaller and hopefully more workable number. However, after three rotations it was found that factor analysis, our choice of analytical tool, explained only sixteen per cent of the variance, and we thus were forced to return to the original correlation matrix. The fact that factor analysis turned out to be useless as a tool for analysis was a warning to us of the confusion on the part of nurses in the state in regards to collective bargaining.

Biographical Data
In regard to the biographical data accumulated, a major goal was to discover the effects of age, marital status and years in the nursing profession on the proclivity for membership in the PNA. A second purpose was to relate these biographical measures and membership in the PNA to the specific attitude clusters studied in the body of the survey.

The nurses ranged in age from 24 to 66. Of those surveyed nineteen per cent were single, seventy-one per cent were married and ten per cent were either divorced or separated.[12] The survey demonstrated that older nurses, those who had been in the profession for a longer period of time, and those in higher positions in the institution in which they worked were significantly less likely to be members of the PNA. Marital status was not correlated to membership in the PNA to any significant degree. Of the sample taken, 174 were members of the Association and 317 were non-members. The average age of the PNA member was 28 years, while the average age of the non-member was 36 years. As a tentative conclusion, one might say that the longer a person is in the nursing profession, the greater their dissatisfaction with the Association.

Interestingly enough, none of the biographical findings correlated significantly with any of the attitude clusters found in the body of the survey. The significance of this finding cannot be under emphasized. Neither age, position, nor membership in the PNA distinguished nurses on their attitudes as measured in the survey. This finding has two ramifications: (1) the attitude findings seemingly apply to the nursing profession as a whole regardless of age, position and membership factors; and (2) if members of the PNA are indistinguishable from non-members on their attitudes toward collective bargaining, the employment situation, and authority and professionalism, what indeed does membership in the PNA mean for the individual nurse?

Employment—Work Factors
A cluster of questions throughout the survey concerned themselves with the employment situation and factors relating to the work performed. In general, the nurses surveyed were significantly agreed that they would stay in their present institution, that they would continue to work as a nurse, that their work position allowed them to do the work they felt best prepared for, and that there was employment security in being a nurse. However the nurses surveyed were surprisingly neutral on the adequacy of their pay, the adequacy of their chances for promotion, and whether they would recommend nursing as a career to a friend.

A general picture of the work situation suggests that nurses in Pennsylvania are very satisfied with their position in society, with the respect they receive, with the content of their jobs, and with the institutions they are employed by, but decidedly are not enthusiastic about their pay nor their chances for promotion. These findings, as stated before, apply to the entire sample, not just to younger nurses or members of the PNA.

"Company Line" Attitude
One problem often encountered in organizing groups of professional employees is the "company line" attitude present in the

minds of such individuals. In nursing, two key words have often been used as reasons for a lack of organization for the purpose of bargaining: (1) necessary medical authority and (2) professionalism. A second group of questions attempted to survey the attitudes of nurses on these subjects. Generally, the findings indicate that nurses are significantly negative on the propositions that organization for collective bargaining and activism are against good medical practice or are unprofessional.

The nurses disagreed significantly with the statements that hospital administrators are paying as much as is possible, that a raise in pay can be directly related to increased patient costs, that a concern with pay is equivalent to a lack of professionalism, and that hospital administrators are willing to bargain collectively with their nursing staffs. They further significantly disagreed with the proposition that the necessary medical authority will be destroyed if nurses are organized, and that militant nurses are being inconsistent with their nursing duties.

Within this cluster, the questions are all significantly inter-correlated. While the majority of nurses are consistently in favor of collective bargaining, there is a group of nurses who are consistently anti-collective bargaining. The key concept in this area is whether or not the nurse believes that the hospital administration is paying nursing staffs as much as possible. Nurses who agreed with this statement showed a conservative or traditional attitude on the other measures in this attitude cluster. Nurses who disagreed with the statement on pay showed a consistently activistic concern with the other measures in this cluster.

A general evaluation of this cluster reveals that nurses significantly rejected the idea that activism or economic organization is an anathema to their profession. They also seemingly stand ready to challenge administrators and physicians in areas in which they feel themselves competent. However, attitudes are not always translated into behavior, and it must again be pointed out that members of the PNA showed no difference in attitudes on these issues than did those nurses who are not members of the Association.

Effectiveness of Bargaining

If collective bargaining has not been practiced by nurses in Pennsylvania, it is not because the average nurse feels antagonistic towards it as a technique. Rather the nurses surveyed viewed collective bargaining as a useful tool in improving their salaries, working conditions, as an aid in improving the quality of medical care, and as having served other professions well.

Some lack of knowledge was found when specific questions about collective bargaining practices were asked. For example, when asked about higher nursing salaries in other states, most nurses weren't able to state whether or not collective bargaining had played any significant role. They agreed that the state legislature should pass a bargaining law, and that the PNA should be concerned with collective bargaining.

While nurses expressed generally positive attitudes on all aspects of collective bargaining, it was this area which also brought about the greatest split in opinions. A small group of nurses were definitely adamant in their opposition to any kind of collective negotiations. This small group was not specifically concentrated in older nurses or those in higher positions but was filtered through all levels.

Only two exceptions were found to the trend of "positive" acceptance of collective bargaining, and both of these items were "tainted" with the word "union." In fact the word "union" appeared only twice on the entire questionnaire, both times in reference to collective bargaining. In a complete negation of the consistent agreement on the benefits from and usefulness of collective bargaining, the nurses violently disagreed with two specific statements. The first concerned the possibility of bargaining effectively without becoming a union in fact, and the second concerned the PNA's seeking assistance from the Pennsylvania AFL-CIO in getting a bargaining bill passed in the General Assembly.

A summation of this particular attitude area would therefore suggest the following: (1) nurses are ready for collective bargaining in Pennsylvania with a minority violently opposed, and (2) the mere mention of organized labor seems to drive down any consensus on collective bargaining and brings about a negative reaction.

ARE THE DATA DATED?

The results of the survey are possibly open to challenge on several grounds. First of all, survey research itself certainly is not a perfect research technique. It might well be that in spite of the random sampling in District Six of the PNA that the nine county area itself is atypical. Finally, as was mentioned earlier, the data were collected one year prior to the passage of Act 195.

No pretence has been made that the survey was designed to

provide anything in the way of absolute answers, and it only has served to illustrate the attitudes of nurses toward collective bargaining. At the present time, about one-half of all the petitions for recognition which the PNA has filed with the PLRB have come from District Six. Thus, if it is not typical of the attitudes of nurses in Pennsylvania, the bias is a pro-bargaining one. The lack of PNA petitions for recognition as compared with other organizations of public employees as well as its drop in membership of 2,000 nurses since the survey was conducted would indicate that the directions in which nurses view collective bargaining has not changed radically.

CONCLUSION

One lesson to be learned from the experience, to date, of the PNA under Act 195 is that a law establishing collective bargaining rights for public employees is merely enabling legislation. During the lobbying which immediately preceded the passage of Act 195, one received the impression from a number of public employees and their officers in the Commonwealth that once the Act became law all would be well. They failed to take into account the notion that Pennsylvania's law was intended to institutionalize conflict, not do away with it. They failed to realize that the interpretation of such a law would change over the years, and most importantly they failed to recognize the fact that bargaining would occur only if they were strong enough internally to force it upon public employers.

Thus, while Act 195 was viewed as some sort of panacea by the PNA, they failed to realize the ramifications which bargaining would have on their Association and its members. The Act is now in existence, and it has thus far created more problems for the PNA than they previusly had thought possible. While certain sections of the Act have made it more difficult to organize a hospital than say a school district, the basic reason for the slow start of the PNA lies in its failure to shake off tradition and find a new sense of direction. Or to paraphrase Thomas Wolfe, they can't go home again.

NOTES

1. The one exception that is heard around the state is when reference is made to Hawaii's Act 171 covering labor relations in that state's public sector.

2. In the past two years, membership in the PNA has dropped from 11,500 to about 9,500. The major reason to which the PNA accredits this drop is a recent increase in dues.

3. At the present time, the Board is made up of two attorneys and an International Representative of the Laborers International Union of North America. The terms of one of the two attorneys expired in June, 1971, and the other, who is the Chairman of the Board, has served in that position without appointment since June, 1969. While this is legal under Pennsylvania law, it does add to the instability which one currently finds in the administration of Act 195.

4. It is possible to obtain recognition as the exclusive bargaining representative under Act 195 without an election. This occurs when the employer and employee organization file a joint request for certification and no other organization intervenes.

5. In Pennsylvania, the term General Assembly means both the State Senate and House of Representatives.

6. P. L. 195, Section 704.

7. P. L. 195, Section 1003.

8. "Barriers to Collective Bargaining in Registered Nursing." LABOR LAW JOURNAL, Vol. 20, No. 1, January, 1969, pp. 42-46.

9. Cited at footnote 8, pp. 43-44.

10. The Board of Nurse Examiners uses the word "active" to mean nurses currently working in the nursing profession.

11. Of extreme interest were some of the letters and notes which accompanied some of the 491 responses. A typical note was, "it's difficult for me to answer fairly the questions on collective bargaining, and I know of no institute in the state where it's used." Some of the notes were somewhat hostile, questioning the purpose of the survey, who had authorized it, what were it ulterior motives, and whether it was a ploy paid for by some "labor union under a fancy name."

12. The people coding the questionnaires, wanted to know whether members of religious orders should be classified as single or married. Given the progressive positions which certain factions of the Catholic Church have recently taken, a decision was made to classify them as single, for purposes of this survey only of course.

AN EXPERIENTIAL EXERCISE:
The Nurses' Strike

The newspaper headline—STRIKE PINPOINTS RIFT OVER ROLE OF NURSES IN HEALTH CARE—revealed a major conflict at the Metropolitan Hospital. This encounter would affect patients, employees, managers, and many others before it would release its tension and be resolved by the procedures of labor relations.
Question: What are the basic issues underlying this breakdown of normal organizational relations?
Question: What methods will be used to bring this volatile encounter under control and final resolution?

DESCRIPTION OF THE CONFLICT

Officials of the Nurses' Union served notice that they would walk out at 7:00 a.m. Saturday if they did not have a contract by that time. The strike took place as scheduled.

BACKGROUND DATA

- Last month, the Metropolitan Hospital withdrew recognition of the union as the official bargaining representative.
- 300 nurses out of 500 joined the strike.
- The Hospital has 911 beds with a 73 percent occupancy rate.
- 41,000 patients a year are treated in the emergency rooms.
- The nurses are paid a starting salary of $12,528 and to $14,679 in five years.

Contract negotiations broke down six months ago and nothing has happened in the interim to resolve this dispute. Among the key demands by the nurses in negotiatons are:

- maternity leave
- use of seniority in the assignment of work hours
- time off for continuing education—five days per year
- performance evaluations subject to review and change through the grievance procedure
- extended vacation and sick leave

- an 8 percent increase in salary and uncapped COLA
- a union shop clause

The negotiators for the hospital have responded in part to some of these demands, for example:

- Management maintains the right to assign nurses to schedules.
- Educational leave granted at supervisor's discretion: one day the first year and two days the second year.
- The hospital will permit nurses only to add written comments on performance evaluation.
- Management will grant one additional day of vacation time— this would give a nurse four weeks of vacation and nine days of sick leave after 10 years.
- Management has offered a raise of approximately 5 percent in each of three contract years.

The strike is now in its twelfth day and the hospital is operating at 30 percent capacity. Although the parties are spending long hours at the bargaining table, there is no resolution in view.

A major underlying issue has begun to surface: the nurses' role. They want to change their role from ". . . simply handmaidens of physicians" to ". . . equal members of a health care team, providing a type of care that is different from, but nonetheless as important as, that provided by more highly trained physicians who make three to ten times the money nurses earn." So, although the specific demands are important to the nurses, this underlying view of their role and themselves needs to be dealth with.

ANALYSIS CHECKLIST

1. The basic issues are _____
2. The alternative solutions are _____
3. The impact of each solution is _____

EXPERIENTIAL EXERCISE

1. Invite several nurses and a hospital administrator to class to review this encounter and to debate the merits of the alternative solutions you have arrived at.
2. Design a questionnaire to be completed by nurses at a local hospital. This should include questions which elicit their view

of their present working conditions in contrast to desired working conditions. Analyze the variance.

3. Identify key roles in this situation and permit the students to volunteer to role-play the role they feel most comfortable with. For example:

> Chief negotiator for hospital
> Chief negotiator for nurses
> Advisory team of nurses
> Advisory team of management staff
> Advisory team representing patients.

Present arguments for each position and suggest procedures for the resolution of impasses.

PART II

COLLECTIVE BARGAINING— STRUCTURE AND PROCESS

PART II
COLLECTIVE BARGAINING—
STRUCTURE AND PROCESS

As in the private sector, once a public sector union has secured representation rights, its core function becomes that of negotiating improvements in wages, hours, and working conditions for its members. However, before a union can begin the process of negotiation, a decision must be made as to which employees it will represent. "Unit determination" is the term used to describe the procedure in which certain criteria are applied in deciding the composition of a bargaining unit. The litmus test is known as an "identifiable community of interest" among the employees. Here a number of variables will be considered, among them similarity of skills, duties, wages and working conditions, the pertinent collective bargaining history, if any, among the employees involved; the extent and type of union organization; the employees' own desires, and the appropriateness of the units proposed in relation to the organizational structure of the agency or department. In this manner the structure is established for the process of negotiations.

The first two readings in Chapter 5 deal with different aspects of bargaining structure, from the management and union vantage point respectively. Roger Mansfield discusses multiemployer bargaining, a strategy to neutralize divide-and-conquer tactics used by unions, wherein a public agency is isolated by a strong union, which gains a lucrative contract through pressure tactics and then "whipsaws" other public employers, claiming that they must match the gains secured from the first employer.

Stephen Hayford next takes up the problem of deciding whether an employee with a supervisory job title really has supervisory responsibilities or is only nomimally acting in that capacity. The distinction is crucial in determining the bargaining rights status of foremen or supervisors. Normally, an irreconcilable conflict of interest develops when bona fide supervisors are also union members. Imagine, if you will, the situation in which an office supervisor is elected president of a union and then has to lead a strike vote against agency management!

The next two selections offer insights into the severe fiscal constraints facing the actors at the state and local government levels. Arvid Anderson attempts to assess the degree of responsibility with which public employees, public employee unions, and collective bargaining settlements should be saddled for New York City's financial plight. Donald Wollett presents the management stance in New York State government negotiations which faced similarly bleak monetary prospects.

Public sector unions, many of which have mixed memberships and also represent private sector employees, often have an experience advantage in dealing with public employers, who often are neophytes at the game of bargaining. The unions have had extensive negotiating experience in private employment and attempt to exploit this management weakness. In the next reading, Blair Curry, John Sweeney, and Charles Blaschke spell out the computerized mathematical simulation technique they have devised to aid educational administrators in mapping out a cost-effective bargaining strategy.

A term cropping up often in public sector literature is "productivity bargaining," the bargaining position gaining increasing popularity with public managers in which unions commit themselves to increase output and efficiency as an alternative to substantial layoffs and as a condition precedent to wage increases. The idea that public employees' services are not as measurable as the rivets from a factory machine is fast losing its currency. Paul Staudohar relates an experiment in Orange County, California where the police association and the city negotiated a productivity agreement resulting in a substantial decrease in crime statistics.

The final reading in Chapter 7, that by Paul Gerhart, describes the influence of environmental factors upon collective bargaining results by analyzing a sample of 262 local government-labor agreements. Not surprisingly, he concludes that negotiating results in the form of improved wage, hours, and fringe benefits as well as noneconomic issues such as job security and work rules are systematically related to numerous external characteristics.

The third case in the book deals with a federal employee union's successful efforts to obtain national exclusive recognition. Marvin Levine, who was personally involved in this case, explains how the National Association of Air Traffic Specialists was able to convince the Federal Aviation Administration that a comprehensive national bargaining unit encompassing 3,000 employees was preferable to 346 separate, fragmented entities.

Next, James Freund cites Philadelphia's uphill battle to reconcile increasing citizen demands for more and better services
with rapidly escalating budgetary costs in that urban metropolis.

Finally, the experiential exercise, again taken from an actual
situation, depicts the pressures at work in a police slowdown in a
suburban jurisdiction near a large, metropolitan area, and asks
how you would handle the situation.

CHAPTER 5.
BARGAINING UNIT DETERMINATION

The Advent of
Public Sector
Multiemployer Bargaining
Roger W. Mansfield

INTRODUCTION

Many authors have compared the practice of collective bargaining to human systems of behavior such as marriage, business, and politics; the similitude being that each of these follow certain commonly accepted guidelines, although the specific form is determined by many factors that vary from place to place and from time to time. The purpose of this paper is to explore an emerging bargaining form, that of multiemployer bargaining in the public sector. More specifically, the paper attempts to present some of the possible reasons for the use and acceptance of multiemployer bargaining as a public sector labor-management tool.

Multiemployer bargaining is not a new concept; it has been used in major segments of private industry for some time. As a result, this paper first attempts to present the various bargaining typologies which commonly fall under the multiemployer heading. Emphasis then shifts to a historical discussion of the evolution of private sector multiemployer bargaining. Drawing on the experiences of the private sector 30 to 35 years ago, similarities are then made with the emerging trends toward the use of mul-

Roger W. Mansfield is an analyst in the City Manager's Office for the city of Redondo Beach, California.

tiemployer bargaining in the public sector today. Concluding remarks center around the need for approaches which will help jurisdictions respond more fairly to the demands of public employee unions without compromising the interests of taxpayers and public service recipients.

BACKGROUND

What is multiemployer bargaining? Frank Pierson in his article, "Multi-Employer Bargaining," identifies several of the union-employer relationships which are commonly classified under the multiemployer bargaining headng.

The first of these bargaining relationships is industry-wide bargaining. In its pure form, industry-wide bargaining exists when one or more unions, acting together, bargain with an employer association over wages and working conditions for an entire industry. The contract or agreements apply to all firms or employers in the industry. Industry-wide bargaining in this form is rare in the United States. However, in the railroad and bituminous coal industries something close to it exists.[1]

More common than systems of industry-wide bargaining are regional and local systems. In these, employers in a city or wider geographical area join together to bargain for the industry in that area or region with the union or unions representing their employces. Pierson states that what distinguishes between these bargaining types is who is represented by the spokesman for the two parties and what proportion of the industry in the area is covered. Negotiations are on a local area basis when the bargaining representatives speak for a majority of an industry's employers and employees in a given community or locality. Bargaining becomes regional when the coverage goes beyond a local area, but falls short of being industry wide in extent. Several examples of the local arrangements are evident in the brewing, printing and publishing, and retail trade industries. Examples of regional arrangements are industries like the pulp and paper, hosiery, and fishing industries.[3]

The chief purpose of these various multiemployer relationships is to fix uniform scales of wages and uniform working conditions within an entire industry, area, or community. Uniformity may not be achieved; and where it is achieved, it may not last or may be interrupted. But uniformity is still the goal.[3]

The historical development and use of these multiemployer bargaining approaches is traced by Wilson Randle and Max

Wortman in their book *Collective Bargaining.* The authors state that most multiemployer associations in this country were founded around 1900. The primary goal of these organizations was to oppose the trend toward unionism evolving at that time. However, by the 1930's, the basic philosophy of these associations changed with the passage of the Wagner Act, which caused them to operate within the new public policy framework favoring collective bargaining.[4]

During the period from 1935 to 1947, trade unionism expanded at unparalled rates. Throughout this decade unionism radically changed its position in the United States. From a small minority, representing little more than ten per cent of the nonagricultural wage-earning and salaried population, it rose in these years to a minority empowered to speak for forty per cent.[5]

Concurrent with the rapid rise in union membership was a significant shift in the relative and absolute power of the unions. In an article by Leo Wolman entitled, "Industry-Wide Bargaining," he notes that the transformation in the position of organized labor had swift practical consequences. Union policies and practices which previously affected only the fringes of American industry now went to its very heart. Single unions or combination of them had the power to shut off the flow of goods and services or to determine the conditions under which it was allowed. It was also the first time that organized labor was strong enough to shut down an entire industry or a substantial part of an industry in order to effectuate policy.[6]

Wolman contends that with the rise and spread of organized labor and the concurrent disapearance of the limited strike, the public increasingly faced the threat of industrial paralysis and crises that endangered their health and safety. Also, that it was only natural that such a great shift in the relative and absolute power should place the public's view of the union movement in a new perspective. Therefore, it was to be expected that a public which viewed the behavior of a relatively weak minority with equanimity and indifference began to take seriously the same practice in the hands of a larger and much more powerful union.[7] This increasing apprehension about the growing monopolistic tendencies on the part of organized labor manifested itself in the passage of the Taft-Hartley Act of 1947. The Taft-Hartley Act placed restrictions on organized labor and sought to balance the bargaining rights of management and labor.[8]

Since the passage of the Taft-Hartley Act, the trend from single employer to multiemployer bargaining has continued.

Randle and Wortman in their efforts to describe the reasons for this trend have offered the following possibilities. The strength of unionization is cited as the prime factor. From this source have come the continuing bargaining ambitions on the part of unions and the defensive alignment of employers into associations and multiemployer groups. This trend toward larger and more centralized units, in turn contributed to a defensive alignment of the unions into larger bargaining structures. The growth and recognition of collective bargaining, itself, contributed to a standardization of conditions and gave encouragement to collective bargaining. The industry-wide production drives of World War II are also mentioned as contributing toward multiemployer bargaining thinking and action. In addition, the War Labor Board with its Wage Stabilization Program imposed wage ceilings that caused a cluster of rates to accumulate around the ceilings and thus gave added uniformity to wage structures. Finally the development of wage pattern negotiation significantly contributed to multiemployer and association bargaining.[9]

Today's private sector employers associations have developed across industry lines into what are called federated metropolitan employer bargaining associations. These associations attempt to aid their member firms and associations through collective bargaining and the improvement of their employment relations policies. Several examples of this type of association are the Associated Industries of Cleveland, the Employers' Association of Greater Chicago, the Mountain States Employers' Council, and the San Francisco Employers' Council.[10]

Having briefly described the various types of private sector multiemployer bargaining relationships and their historical evolution, discussion will now shift to the emerging use of this approach by public sector employers.

What is the nature of multiemployer bargaining relationships now appearing in the public sector? From the limited literature presently available on public sector multiemployer bargaining, it would appear that most of these evolving relationships fall under Piersons's classification of localized multiemployer bargaining. Under this typology employers band together on a localized or larger area to bargain with the union or unions representing their employees.

Since the literature on the American experience with this approach is so scarce, the exact extent of usage is unknown. However, the National League of Cities and United States Conference of Mayors have documented the first use of this approach in

the Twin Cities area of Minneapolis and St. Paul.[11] The only other
governmental agencies known to be using this technique are the
cities of Pleasanton, Livermore, and the Valley Community Services District in California.[12]

The limited documented experiences with multiemployer
bargaining seem to indicate that there are three primary reasons
for its use. These reasons are as follows: The geography causes
the parties to draw on the same labor pool; there exists a common
union or unions that represent a majority of the employees; and
the increasing awareness of municipal and other governmental
officials that they are at a distinct disadvantage at the bargaining
table when dealing with the full-time professional union
negotiators. In addition to these expressed reasons for the advent
of multiemployer bargaining, it is felt that in some important
repects one can compare multiemployer bargaining in the public
sector today, with multiemployer bargaining relationships in the
private sector 30 to 35 years ago. Evolving trends of that time are
now appearing, as government gains more experience in collective
bargaining with public employees.

In examining what has happened in the public sector, one
finds some interesting similarities. The first of these similitudes
has been the rapid growth in size and power of the public unions.
Like the growth period from 1935-1947 in the private sector, the
period from 1962 to the present has been a major growth period
for public sector unions. From 1962 to the present, public sector
unionism has grown from 1.2 million, or seven per cent of the
total United States union membership, to nearly 2.5 million, or
11.8 per cent of the union membership, and is still growing.[13]

The prime factors for this growth, according to Harry Cohany
and Lucretia Dewey, authors of the article "Union Membership
Among Government Employees," are: the passage of Kennedy's
Federal Executive Order 10988 in 1962 which sanctioned union
organization at the federal level and had wide repercussions for
state and local levels as well; the long standing wage differentials
between private and public employers; the results achieved by
many militant unions; and the need for a mechanism whereby
employees, especially professionals, could participate in decision
making from which they had previously been excluded. They also
note that technology, population, urbanization, and changing
concepts of governments role have also had their effects, leading
toward greater public sector unionization.[14]

With this growth in size of public sector unions, there has
been a concurrent increase in the power of the unions. The power

of the public sector unions is evolving much as it did in private industry. At the outset, it was noted that unionization was accepted with equanimity and indifference, but as the power of the unions became increasingly disproportionate, there came cries that this power be mitigated. This cry was answered with the passage of the Taft-Hartley Act of 1947. In the public sector, the same power syndrome seems to be evolving. During the early 1960's militancy among public employees was met with acquiescence by our society generally. The example of the student war protestors, the civil rights movement and so on, left its mark on the fireman, hospital worker, teachers, and others. Conduct of questionable legality had achieved results where more conventional means had failed.[15] However, this conduct and power is increasingly coming under closer scrutiny as more individuals' health and safety are threatened. Or, as George Skelton and William Endicott have pointed out in their recent *Los Angeles Times* article entitled "The Public's Servants—How Big? And How Powerful?" some are now fearing that if this power trend continues the public servant corps may someday overwhelm the electorate it serves. They note that bureaucracy has never shown a willingness to diminish itself, even when the need for which it was created has long since vanished, and they fear that its steady growth in size and power could render the private citizenry powerless to effectively deal with it. Before this happens, it is felt that changes in the structure of bargaining will be necessary. The purpose of such restructuring would be to ensure that a particular interest group, public employee unions, do not gain a substantial competitive advantage over other interest groups in pressing its claims on government.[16]

The second likeness between the public and private sectors has been the trend toward centralized bargaining units. Randle and Wortman note that in the private sector there was a trend towards larger business units with greater centralization of control, which contributed to a defensive alignment of unions into larger bargaining structures.[17] Through centralization, unions are attempting to standardize wages, hours, and working conditions in the labor market, in order to eliminate competition between individual workers or groups of workers. Randle and Wortman also state that centralization occurred because of an expanding technology and improved transportation services which enlarged the area of competition; and local labor markets are becoming increasingly interdependent through wage standardization programs. As a result of this movement toward larger bargaining units, there is a tendency toward increasing multiemployer as well as multiunion collaboration in collective bargaining.[18]

During the late 1960's, the public sector widely used a form of regional centralization such as councils of governments and associations of governments as an approach to planning and problem solving. This was primarily due to the growing number of problems which transcended local jurisdictional boundaries and the areawide planning incentives attached to federal and state grants in aid.[19]

Joseph Zimmerman in his article entitled "Meeting Service Needs Through Intergovernmental Agreements" states that city and county officials have increasingly attempted to meet these joint problems and common needs through the use of formal and informal agreements. The dominant motive for entering into these agreements is to take advantage of economies of scale. Other reasons cited are the lack of facilities, the lack of qualified personnel, meeting an urgent problem, ciizen demand for service agreements, civil service avoidance, and keeping the service out of politics. Zimmerman feels that the use of agreements is a limited form of functional consolidation based on a partnership approach, whereby administration is centralized and policy making is decentralized.[20] Although the original purposes of many of these regional associations and agreements may not have been to deal with labor relations and collective bargaining, they do represent the ability and willingness to establish cooperative approaches to matters of area-wide concern. These associations have demonstrated that they can deal with activities involving more than one policy or program area; membership consisting predominantly of elected officials or appointed representatives of constituent local governments; and funded by local cooperation. As collective bargaining and labor relations become more of a problem for governmental jurisdictions, it is felt that this demonstrated ability to work together will lend itself to the creation of multiemployer relationships. A recent example of where this has taken place has been the creation of the Southwest Labor Relations Council in Southern California. The Council was set up by the South Bay City Managers Association to handle the growing problems associated with current day labor relations in the Southern California area.

The third similarity between the private and public sectors has been the increasing amount of labor relations legislation which is adding uniformity and giving encouragement to collective bargaining. The Wagner Act, which was passed in 1935, gave collective bargaining rights to most employees working in the private sector. However, it was not until 1962 that the federal government granted some form of collective bargaining to its employees. Similarly, only the state of Wiscnsin had provided bargaining for employees of its local units of government by 1962. Since 1962, the scene has changed dramatically; twenty-two states have passed laws granting collective bargaining to state and local employees. Nixon's Executive Order 11491 replaced Kennedy's Executive Order 10988 and updated and expanded the framework for federal employee bargaining.[21] Also, recent legislation such as the Fair Labor Standards Act and the Equal Employment Opportunities Act seem to be directed toward the union goal of uniformity. These statutes seek to protect and encourage organization among the unorganized and no doubt provide a moral and legal imperative in that direction. However, comprehensive statutes are generally not enacted until union organization is substantial. Thus, one might say that organization seems as much of a cause of legislation as an effect.

The fourth similarity between the two sectors has been with wage and price controls. During the 1940's the War Labor Board imposed wage ceilings that caused a cluster of rates to accumulate around the ceilings and gave added uniformity to wage structures.[22] One must wonder how much of an effect Nixon's 1971-1973 Economic Stabilization Program has had on added wage uniformity in the public sector. It is doubted that the impact of Nixon's program on wages would be as far reaching as the War Labor Board's since the program was not in effect as long. However, it is felt that there was a tendency for wages to move toward the imposed wage ceilings.

The fifth likeness between the private and public sectors has been the development of wage pattern negotiations by unions. By wage pattern negotiations it is meant that the employee labor organizations are developing common demands and positions which are presented to a number of jurisdictions. The organization then plays the actions of one of the jurisdictions against the other. In California, the Los Angeles County Division of the League of California Cities has identified this as one of the developing problems in the labor management relations in this area. One means they suggest for combating this situation is the exchange of correct information, including the cities' positions and proposals; and the use of total compensation figures for an accurate accounting of personnel costs to facilitate effective meeting and conferring.[23] The actions suggested and being taken by area wide associations like the Los Angeles County Division of the League of California Cities seem to resemble the actions by private sector multiemployer bargaining associations during the 1930's and 40's.

What have been the advantages and disadvantages of multiemployer bargaining based upon public sector usage? In discussing the alleged advantages and disadvantages of public sector multiemployer bargaining it should be noted at the outset that collective bargaining relationships do not operate exactly the same in any two situations since they are usually the result of different situations and pressures. Consequently, the following advantages nd disadvantages are based on generalizations from the limited documented public sector experiences found in the lierature.

Proponents of multiemployer bargaining usually aver the following characteristics of the multiemployer relationship:

1. Most multiemployer associations have typically aided in the development of job specs, pay plans, and daily personnel policies.
2. Negotiations and preparations are simplified for the member jurisdictions of the multiemployer association.
3. Since the association does most of the "hard nose bargaining," the CAO and personnel staff are able to work with employee representatives on personnel program activities not directly related to collective bargaining in a more harmonious atmosphere than might be the case.
4. Multiemployer bargaining has brought expertise to the bargaining table.
5. There appears to be an equalization of bargaining between the member jurisdictions and unions which contributes to a better competitive position for each group.
6. Multiemployer bargaining tends to reduce the provincialism on both sides of management and labor by forcing employers and employees to evaluate the area situation as a whole during negotiations and imposes the necessity of compromise as a price of whatever uniformity is achieved.
7. Wages and earning levels do not appear to have risen more rapidly under multiemployer bargaining.
8. Wide salary differentials for similar positions seem to have been eliminated.
9. Unions seem to achieve greater stability in their political structure and greater uniformity of contract interpretation.[24]

Opponents of multiemployer bargaining are also able to present strong arguments against it. These arguments usually center around the following:

1. The jurisdiction may lose direct control over a significant budgetary item-personnel service.
2. There may be inequitable apportionment of costs to maintain the association.
3. More time may be involved in the negotiation of the contract.
4. The entity established to conduct multiemployer bargaining programs may usurp the jurisdictions authority in handling of the personnel function.
5. During the establishment of the multiemployer association, or shortly thereafter, the wages, hours, and terms of employment usually rise to the highest cost firm in the association.
6. There may be possible restrictions on terminating the agreement once it is entered into.
7. It may imply the facilitation of the establishment of make work rules and full crew laws which may impair efficiency.
8. Strikes have not been eliminated and the consequences are more severe when they do occur.
9. Between negotiations the union may obtain concessions through the administrative machinery of the contract by whip-sawing grievances from one firm to another until the most favorable outcome is obtained.[25]

In analyzing the arguments for and against multiemployer bargaining, it is easy to see how heated battles could develop over attempts to outlaw, weaken, or strengthen it through legislated public policy. However, the documented public sector experiences with multiemployer bargaining seem to play down the negative aspects of the approach, relative to its redeeming characteristics.

CONCLUSION

There is no one "best" system of collective bargaining. What may work well in one place may be entirely inappropriate in another. Consequently, the purpose of this paper was not to present multiemployer bargaining in a context that it might be the public jurisdiction's panacea to its labor management problems. Rather, the purpose of the paper was to explore the use of multiemployer bargaining as a labor management tool which might be used under certain circumstances to counter-balance the growing power of the public sector unions.

In examining multiemployer bargaining systems, it is apparent that there is a need for local and regional efforts to relate to state-wide developments. Labor unions that are dealing with municipalities on a state-wide basis utilize settlements from municipalities in other regions, as evidenced in the recent Southern California Rapid Transit strike where wage comparisons were being made with other major metropolitan cities as New York and San Francisco. Consequently, the entity created to handle the bargaining program should have current and up-to-date information on other municipal developments as suggested by the Los Angeles County Division of the League of California Cities. In addition, it is felt that contract administration and general personnel administration should be vital parts of any total labor management programs established. In this way, it is hoped that governmental jurisdiction may be able to respond more fairly to the demands of public employee unions, without compromising the interests of the taxpayers and recipients of public services.

NOTES

1. Frank Pierson, "Multiemployer Bargaining," in *Unions, Management, and the Public,* pp. 346-347.
2. *Ibid.*
3. *Ibid.*
4. Wilson Randle and Max Wortman, *Collective Bargaining,* p. 109.
5. Leo Wolman, "Industry-Wide Bargaining," in *Industry-Wide Collective Bargaining,* p. 15.
6. *Ibid.*
7. *Ibid.*
8. Jessie Fredin, *The Taft-Hartley Act and Multiemployer Bargaining,* pp. 1-3.
9. *Op.cit.,* Randle and Wortman, p. 104.
10. *Ibid.* p. 109.
11. _____, *Cities Join Together for Bargaining: The Experience in Minnesota and British Columbia,* U.S. Conference of Mayors, National League of Cities and National Association of Counties, September 1971, pp. 1-16.
12. Joint Powers for Labor Relations Consolidated Bargaining, Cities of Livermore, Pleasanton, and the Valley Community Services District, May 1, 1973.
13. _____, *Statistical Abstract of the United States: 1974,* p. 365.
14. Harry Cohany and Lucretia Dewey, "Union Membership Among Governmental Employees," in *Collective Bargaining in Government,* pp. 5-11.
15. *Ibid.*
16. George Skelton and William Endicott, "The Public Servants—How

Big? And How Powerful?" *Los Angeles Times*, (September 10, 1974), p. 1.

17. *Op.cit.*, Randle and Wortman, p. 15.

18. *Ibid.* pp. 15-16.

19. _____, *The Municipal Year Book 1973*, International City Management Association, p. 63.

20. Joseph Zimmerman, "Meeting Service Needs Through Intergovernmental Agreements," in *The Municipal Year Book 1973*, pp. 79-88.

21. Joseph Loewenberg and Michael Moskow, *Collective Bargaining in Government*, p. 1.

22. *Op.cit.*, Randle and Wortman, p. 102.

23. _____, *Report of the Task Force on Action Plan Implementation*, Los Angeles County Division of the California League of Cities, August 6, 1974 p. 4.

24. Based on readings in the bibliography.

25. Based on the total readings in the bibliography.

REFERENCES

Anonymous, *Statistical Abstract of the United States: 1974*, U.S. Bureau of the Census, 95th edition, Washington, D.C., 1974.

_____, *The Municipal Year Book 1973*, International City Management Association, Washington D.C., 1973.

_____, *Report of the Task Force on Action Plan Implementation*, Los Angeles County Division of the California League of Cities, August 6, 1974.

_____, *Cities Join Together for Bargaining: The Experience in Minnesota and British Columbia*, U.S. Conference of Mayors, National League of Cities and National Association of Counties, September 1971.

_____, Joint Powers Agreement for Labor Relations Consolidated Bargaining, Cities of Livermore, Pleasanton, and Valley Community Services District, May 1, 1973.

Bakke, W. W., Clark Kerr, and Charles Arnold, *Unions, Management, and the Public*, Harcourt, Brace and Co., New York, 1960.

Cohany, Harry and Lucretia Dewey, "Union Membership Among Government Employees," *Collective Bargaining in Government*, pp. 5-11.

Fredin, Jessie, *The Taft-Hartley Act and Multiemployer Bargaining*, University of Pennsylvania Press, Philadelphia, 1948.

Kaye, S.P., and A. Marsh, *International Manual on Collective Bargaining for Public Employees*, Praeger Publishers, New York, 1973.

Loewenberg, J.J., and M. H. Moskow, *Collective Bargaining in Government*, Prentice-Hall, Inc., Englewood Cliffs, 1972.

Pollak, Otto, *Social Implications of Industry-Wide Bargaining*, University of Pennsylvania Press, Philadelphia, 1948.

Randle, Wilson and Max Wortman, *Collective Bargaining,* Houghton Mifflin Co., Boston, 1966.

Skelton, George and William Endicott, "The Public Servants—How Big? and How Powerful?" *Los Angeles Times,* XCIII, September 10, 1974, pp. 1, 14-15.

Warne, C., *Industry-Wide Collective Bargaining,* D.C. Heath and Co., Boston, 1950.

Wellington, H. H. and R. K. Winter, Jr. *The Unions and the Cities,* The Brookings Institution, Washington D.C., 1971.

Warner, K.O., *Collective Bargaining in the Public Service: Theory and Practice,* Public Personnel Association, Chicago, 1967.

Wolman, Leo, "Industry-Wide Bargaining," *Industry-Wide Collective Bargaining,* D.C. Heath and Company, Boston, 1950, pp. 13-22.

Zimmerman, Joseph F., "Meeting Service Needs Through Inter-governmental Agreements," *The Municipal Year Book 1973,* International City Management Association, Washington D.C., 1973, pp. 79-88.

An Empirical Investigation of the Public Sector Supervisory Bargaining Rights Issue

Stephen L. Hayford

There is at the present time wide diversity in the collective bargaining rights protection afforded supervisors in the public sector. Legislators, commentators, and practitioners in the field of public employee labor relations all are currently engaged in a vigorous debate over the issue of the proper bargaining rights status of supervisory employees. The strong possibility that some form of federal public employee collective bargaining legislation (covering all levels of government employees) will be approved by Congress in the foreseeable future adds urgency to this debate.

Reproduced from the October, 1975 issue of the LABOR LAW JOURNAL, published and copyrighted (1975) by Commerce Clearing House, Inc., 4025 W. Peterson Avenue, Chicago, Illinois 60646. Reprinted by permission of Stephen L. Hayford, Assistant Professor of Public Sector Labor Relations, School of Public and Environmental Affairs, Indiana University, and Commerce Clearing House, Inc.

This continuing public policy discussion is the focus of this research.

In another study the author delineated four primary approaches to the treatment of supervisory bargaining rights presently being implemented at the state and federal levels. Those approaches can be categorized as follows:

Exclusion—All Supervisors, jurisdictions where all supervisors are excluded from any form of statutory[1] bargaining rights protection;

Exclusion—Bonafide Supervisors, jurisdictions where only bonafide supervisors are excluded from bargaining—in these governmental units many employees who have been classified by the public employers as "supervisors" have not been so categorized by the respective administrative agencies for the purpose of the statutes;

Full Bargaining Rights—Autonomous Units, jurisdictions where supervisors have statutory rights comparable to rank and file employees but are separated into autonomous bargaining units;

Meet and Confer—Autonomous Units, jurisdictions where there is statutory protection for supervisors in units separate from rank and file employees but without an employer obligation to bargain with them.[2]

The divergent approaches reflected above are based to a great extent upon differing views as to the functions, organizational status, identity group, and collective bargaining-related desires of supervisors in public employment. Much commentary has appeared in recent years concerning the proper bargaining rights status of those individuals.[3] Despite this exchange, the issue upon which it has focused has not been resolved. Among the reasons for this state of non-resolution is the fact that the existing literature lacks a data base upon which to make broad public policy conclusions.

A legal framework that seeks to serve as the basis for a viable system of public sector labor relations must assign roles and rights to front line supervisors that accurately reflect those individuals' actual functions, status, identity group, and desires. This study is an empirical investigation into those key factors. It will produce data-based conclusions and policy recommendations as to an optimal statutory approach to the supervisory issue. Hopefully, this study is reresentative of the type of research that must be conducted if a workable solution is to be found to the public sector supervisory bargaining rights controversy.

DESCRIPTION OF THE STUDY

The sample group was draw from selected municipalities and public school districts in the state of Iowa. Questionnaires were administered to upper level agency managers,[4] front line supervisors,[5] and rank and file employees[6] in those employing units. Public employees in six functional areas were included in the sample group: police and firefighters, public educators, clerical employees, skilled employees, and unskilled employees. Of 288 questionnaires administered, 266 usable questionnaires were obtained.

The attitudes of all respondents were examined as they pertained to the role description (i.e. the functions, organizational status, and identity group) of front line supervisors, and the proper bargaining rights status of front line supervisors. As with the remainder of the study, the focus of this segment was upon the attitudes of the front line supervisors in the sample group.

The study also examined the collective bargaining-related attitudes and desires of front line supervisors. In this context two questions were examined: (1) if allowed to bargain collectively, would front line supervisors choose to do so; and (2) if allowed to bargain collectively, would front line supervisors prefer to be placed in autonomous bargaining units or to be placed in the same units with rank and file employees?

THE BONAFIDE SUPERVISOR—
LESS THAN BONAFIDE SUPERVISOR DISTINCTION

Prior to the analysis of the data, the respondents in the front line supervisor classification were categorized as either bonafide supervisors (individuals with supervisory titles who possess consequential managerial authority and responsibilities) or less than bonafide supervisors (individuals with supervisory titles who do not possess consequential managerial authority or responsibility). This bifurcation of the front line supervisory group is central to the entire study.

Each supervisory respondent answered the following five questions. These questions center upon the front line supervisor's role in labor relations and personnel management.[7] Respondents who answered the five questions in the manner indicated below were classified as bonafide supervisors. Any other pattern of response resulted in placement of the individual in the less than bonafide supervisor category.

1. How many employees work directly under your supervision? *one or more*

2. Do you have authority to resolve your subordinates' employment related complaints and grievances? *yes*

3. Does higher level management frequently overturn your decisions on personnel matters? *no*

4. Are you regularly consulted with by higher level management for your ideas and input as to departmental personnel policy before a decision is made? *yes*

5. Are you usually directly informed by higher level management of policy changes that directly affect you in the performance of your job? *yes*

RESULTS OF THE STUDY

Role Description Attitudes

The attitudes of respondents as to the role description of front line supervisors were elicited by eleven Likert Scale statement-response items. These statements were structured around the concept of the supervisors' labor relations and personnel management responsibilities and authority; their organizational status and community of interest; their place in the management communication system; and the deference paid them by rank and file employees. To provide a basis for the scoring of the responses to these statements and the testing of several of the major hypothesis incorporated in the study, the researcher constructed two polar model definitions of the front line supevisor's role of description.

The management identity model clearly identifies with the management group, has an important role in labor relations matters and status concomitant with such a role.

The rank and file identity is not clearly a member of the management group. The community of interest is more closely aligned with rank and file employees than with management. There is no important role in labor relations matters and concomitantly lower status.

A respondent who indicated strong agreement on all eleven statements with the management identity model accrued a role description attitude score of fifty-five (55). Conversely, a respondent who indicated strong agreement on all eleven statements with the rank and file identity model generated a role description attitude score of eleven (11).[8] The role description attitude scores of respondents were contrasted along the dimensions of organiza-

TABLE 1
Mean Role Description Attitude Scores
By Organizational Level

Organizational Level	Mean Role Description Attitude Score	F Value
Upper level agency managers	43.76	49.11*
Bonafide supervisors	42.70	
Less than bonafide supervisors	35.26	
Rank and file employees	39.69	

*significant at the 0.001 level

tional level; functional area of employment; size of the city in which the respondent was employed; and the presence or absence of a collective bargaining agreement in the respondent's employing unit.

Organizational Level

There were statistically significant differences in the role description attitudes expressed by upper level agency managers, bonafide supervisors, less than bonafide supervisors, and rank and file employees. One way analysis of variance[9] and t-tests for differences between means[10] were the two primary statistical techniques utilized in this and the remaining phases of the study. As reported in Table 1, upper level agency managers and bonafide supervisors expressed the highest (in the direction of the management identity model) mean role description attitude scores. Less than bonafide supervisors reported the lowest (in the direction of the rank and file identity model) mean role description attitude score of all respondents.

Multiple comparison t-tests were performed to determine between which organizational levels the significant attitudinal differences obtained. The results of that analysis are reported in Table 2. Significant inter-level differences were found to exist between every group except the bonafide supervisors and the upper level agency managers. The respondents in these two organizational levels, who viewed front line supervisors as being much more strongly identified with management than did the less than bonafide supervisors and rank and file employees, did not differ significantly in terms of their attitudes as to the functions, organizational status, and identity group of front line supervisors.

TABLE 2
t-Tests For Inter-Organizational Level Comparisons
of Role Description Attitude Scores

	Bonafide Supervisors	Less than Bonafide Supervisors	Rank and File Employees
Upper level agency managers	1.48	10.80*	6.96*
Bonafide supervisors		10.09*	6.00
Less than bonafide supervisors			3.21*

*significant at the .05 level (t $_{.05, 6, \circ \circ}$ = 2.64)[11]

Functional Area

No statistically significant differences were detected in the mean role description attitude scores expressed by respondents in the police, firefighter, public educator, clerical employee, skilled employee, and unskilled employee functional areas. Additional analysis showed that the front line supervisors in the six functional areas did not differ significantly in terms of their role description attitudes.

Other Dimensions

As with functional area of employment, city size and the presence or absence of a collective bargaining agreement did not prove to be important determinants of an individual's attitude as to the role description of front line supervisors.

ATTITUDES AS TO THE PROPER BARGAINING RIGHTS STATUS OF SUPERVISORS

All respondents were presented with the statement, "Front line supervisors should be allowed to bargain collectively." Five response options were available and were scored as follows: (1) Strongly agree, (2) Agree, (3) Undecided, (4) Disagree, or (5) Strongly disagree.

Thus, an individual who strongly opposed a grant of bargaining rights protection to supervisors generated a supervisory bargaining rights status attitude score of 5. An individual who strongly favored a grant of bargaining rights protection to supervisors generated a supervisory bargaining rights status attitude score of 1.

The subject attitudes of respondents were contrasted along

TABLE 3
Mean Supervisory Bargaining Rights Status Attitude Scores By Organizational Level

Organizational Level	Mean Bargaining Rights Status Attitude Score	F Value
Upper level agency managers	3.16	14.81*
Bonafide supervisors	2.38	
Less than bonafide supervisors	2.06	
Rank and file employees	2.18	

*significant at the .001 level

TABLE 4
t-Tests For Inter-Organizational Level Comparisons of Supervisory Bargaining Rights Status Attitude Scores

	Bonafide Supervisors	Less Than Bonafide Supervisors	Rank and file Employees
Upper level agency managers	3.50*	6.17*	5.06*
Bonafide supervisors		2.10	1.22
Less than bonafide supervisors			.086

*significant at the .05 level (t $_{.05, 6, \circ \circ}$ = 2.64)

the dimension of organizational level. There were significant differences in the subject attitudes expressed by upper level agency managers, bonafide supervisors, less than bonafide supervisors, and rank and file employees. As reported in Table 3, upper level agency managers were most strongly opposed to a policy position that would allow front line supervisors to bargain collectively. Less than bonafide supervisors most strongly favored a grant of bargaining rights protection to front line supervisors.

As reported in Table 4, multiple comparison t-tests showed that significant attitudinal differences obtained only between upper level agency managers and the three remaining organizational levels. Thus the attitudes of bonafide supervisors, less than bonafide supervisors, and rank and file employees were more favorable than those of upper level agency managers toward a policy position that would allow front line supervisors to bargain collectively. Notwithstanding the above observations it is important to note that none of the four organizational level groups expressed attitudes strongly opposing a statutory grant of bargaining rights protection to supervisors.

SUPERVISORS' COLLECTIVE BARGAINING DESIRES

The 132 front line supervisors in the sample group were asked to answer the question, "If supervisors were allowed by law to bargain collectively would you choose to have an organization represent you in collective bargaining with your employer? (check one)" Two response options were available and were scored one point for yes, zero points for two.

To determine whether a statistically significant majority of either bonafide supervisors or less than bonafide supervisors would choose to bargain collectively if allowed by law to do so, confidence interval tests for proportions were performed.[12] As reported in Table 5, a highly significant majority (86.1 percent) of the less than bonafide supervisors indicated that they would choose to exercise a statutorily-granted right to bargain collectively. In contrast, only 46.7 percent of the bonafide supervisors (which was not a significant majority) responded in the affirmative to the above question.

TABLE 5
Collective Bargaining Desires of
Front Line Supervisors

Category	Number of Responses	Number of Yes Responses	Percentage of Yes Responses	Lower Limit of Confidence Interval	Upper Limit of Confidence Interval
Bonafide supervisors	60	28	46.7	34.1	59.3
Less than bonafide supervisors	72	62	86.1*	78.1	94.1

*significant at the .05 level

TABLE 6
t-Test for Collective Bargaining Desire Scores of
Bonafide and Less than Bonafide Supervisors

Category	Mean Collective Bargaining Desire Score	t-Statistic
Bonafide supervisors	.492	4.67*
Less that bonafide supervisors	.847	

*significant at the .5 level (t $_{.05 \circ \circ}$ = 1.96)

As indicated in Table 6, the mean collective bargaining desire score for the bonafide supervisor group was .492 and for the less than bonafide supervisor group .847. A t-test for differences between means showed that there was a significant difference in the collective bargaining desires expressed by the two supervisory groups. An additional t-test showed that there was a significant difference in the collective bargaining desire scores of the front line supervisors in the six functional areas of employment. These mean collective bargaining desire scores were as follows:

firefighters	— 0.91
unskilled employees	— 0.86
skilled employees	— 0.69
clerical employees	— 0.60
police	— 0.55
public educators	— 0.50

The fact that front line supervisors in the firefighter and unskilled employee categories expressed the strongest desires to bargain collectively may be accounted for in part by the high percentage of those respondents who fell into the less than bonafide supervisor category (firefighters—82 percent and unskilled employees—72 percent).

SUPERVISORS' UNIT PLACEMENT PREFERENCES

The final phase of the study centered on the type of bargaining units in which bonafide supervisors and less than bonafide supervisors would choose to be placed if they elected to exercise a statutorily-granted right to bargain collectively. Supervisor respondents were presented with the following question and response options (the response options were scored as indicated):

"If you were allowed by law to bargain collectively and you elected to do so, what type of bargaining unit would you choose to be placed in? (check one)" *(5)* an autonomous, supervisors-only bargaining unit; *(1)* a mixed bargaining unit, with rank and file (non-management) employees; *(3)* undecided.

As with the supervisors' collective bargaining desires, confidence interval tests for proportions were performed to determine whether a statistically significant majority of either bonafide supervisors or less than bonafide supervisors indicated a preference for placement in autonomous or mixed bargaining units. As reported in Table 7, thirty-five of the sixty bonafide supervisors in the sample group indicated a preference for placement in autonomous bargaining units (with nineteen respondents favoring a mixed unit placement and six responses of "undecided"). This constituted a non-significant majority of 58.3 percent. Thirty-nine of the seventy-two less than bonafide supervisors in the sample group indicated a preference for placement in mixed units (with twenty-four respondents favoring an autonomous unit placement and nine responses of "undecided"). This constituted a non-significant majority of 54.2 percent.

TABLE 7
Unit Placement Preferences of Front Line Supervisors

	Bonafide supervisors	Less than Bonafide Supervisors
Number of Responses	60	72
Number of Mixed Unit Preference Expressions	19	39
Number of Autonomous Unit Preference Expressions	35	24
Percentage of Mixed Unit Preferences		54.2
Percentage of Autonomous Unit Preferences	58.3	
Lower Limit of Confidence Interval	45.8	42.8
Upper Limit of Confidence Interval	70.8	65.6

TABLE 8
t-Test for Unit Placement Preferences of Bonafide Supervisors
and Less Than Bonafide Supervisors

Category	Mean Unit Placement Preference Score	t-Statistic
Bonafide supervisors	3.53	3.60*
Less than bonafide supervisors	2.58	

*significant at the .5 level (t $_{.05, \circ \circ}$ = 1.96)

Thus, while there appeared to be a tendency for bonafide supervisors to prefer autonomous unit placement and a similar tendency for less than bonafide supervisors to prefer placement in mixed bargaining units, these predilections were not of a statistically significant nature.

As indicated in Table 8, the mean unit placement preference score for the bonafide supervisor group was 3.53 and for the less than bonafide supervisor group 2.58. A t-test for differences between means showed that there was a significant difference in the unit placement preferences expressed by the two supervisory groups. A similar test indicated that there were no significant differences in the unit placement preferences of the front line supervisors in the six functional areas of employment.

CONCLUSIONS

The conclusions made herein are specifically relevant to the Iowa municipal sector (including public education) and more generally to public sector jurisdictions where collective bargaining statutes have only recently been enacted. Furthermore, because of their data-based nature, these conclusions are germane to the ongoing debate in all jurisdictions of the public sector as to the role description, the proper bargaining rights status, and the collective bargaining-related desires of front line supervisors.

Bonafide supervisors generally viewed themselves (and all front line supervisors) as being more closely identified with the management group than with rank and file employees. The study showed that if allowed by law to bargain collectively a majority of bonafide supervisors would not choose to do so. The unit placement preference of this group is less clear. However, there did appear to be a tendency among the bonafide supervisor groups to prefer placement in autonomous bargaining units.

The attitudes of bonafide supervisors as to the proper bargaining rights status of front line supervisors did differ from the strong management identity model somewhat. The attitudes in support of such a statutory grant of bargaining rights expressed by the bonafide supervisor group appear to differ significantly from those held by the upper level agency manager group. This phenomenon does appear to be part of an overall pattern, however, in which, as noted above, respondents in all four organizational levels expressed attitudes either in agreement with or, at the extreme, only "undecided" on a policy position that would guarantee front line supervisors the right to bargain collectively.

Less than bonafide supervisors generally viewed themselves (and all front line supervisors) as being more closely identified with rank and file employees than with the management group. If allowed by law to bargain collectively a majority of less than bonafide supervisors indicated that they would choose to do so. As with bonafide supervisors, the unit placement preferences of less than bonafide supervisors is somewhat unclear. However, there did appear to be a tendency among the less than bonafide supervisor group to prefer placement in mixed bargaining units. Finally, less than bonafide supervisors as a group held attitudes most strongly in favor of a statutory grant of bargaining rights to all front line supervisors.

IMPLICATIONS

The previous commentary in this subject area has failed to produce a clear picture of the role description of the front line supervisor in public employment. Neither did those commentators concern themselves extensively with the collective bargaining desires and unit placement preferences of such individuals. This ambiguity and inconclusiveness may have resulted in large part from the failure of those individuals to bifurcate the front line supervisor group in the manner done herein. The distinction between bonafide supervisors and less than bonafide supervisors is central to the conclusions drawn above and the policy recommendations made below.

The diversity in the role description attitudes and collective bargaining-related desires expressed by bonafide supervisors and less than bonafide supervisors in this study bears one highly

significant implication. In the public sector there can be no presumption that employees with supervisory titles are indeed
bonafide supervisors who should be accorded statutory treatment
different from rank and file employees. That there is often a
presumption of bonafide status in many jurisdictions, without
any extraordinary attention being paid to the questionable status
of many supervisory employees, is evident from the statutory
language and interpretative decisions in effect in several of the
states with comprehensive public employee legislation.

The statutes in New York, Massachusetts, and Michigan,
among others, do not even contain a definition of the term
"supervisor."[13] Those laws grant full bargaining rights protection
to all supervisory employees in autonomous units and there is no
evidence that the administrative agencies in the three states have
drawn the bonafide/less than bonafide distinction in unit determination decisions.

The presence of a presumption of the bonafide status of many
supervisors is evidenced by the definition of "supervisor" contained in the Iowa *Public Employment Relations Act.* That definition specifies that "all school superintendents, assistant superintendents, principals, and assistant principals. . ." are to be considered supervisors for the purpose of exclusion from the statute's
coverage.[14] Thus, the determination of supervisory status in public education bargaining units is made in the statute rather than
being made on a case-by-case basis by the Iowa Public Employment Relations board.

One of the major proposed public employee collective bargaining statutes presently before Congress, H.R. 9730, would very
likely result in the creation of a presumption of bonafide status
for most all supervisory employees. H. R. 9730 would grant bargaining rights protection to state and local empoloyees by simply
striking from the Labor-Management Relations Act the exclusion
of the states and their political subdivisions from the definition of
"employer." Thus, the determination of supervisory status would
be made under the Taft-Hartley definition of supervisor by an
administrative agency (the NLRB) which is bound by almost three
decades of precedent to a policy of excluding most all supervisors
from bargaining rights protection.[15]

The results reported above suggest that front line supervisors
in public employment cannot be viewed as a single homogeneous
group. Bonafide supervisors and less than bonafide supervisors
are unique from one another in terms of their identity groups,
communities of interest, collective bargaining desires, and unit

placement preferences. General theorizing as to the attributes and proper bargaining rights status of all public sector front line supervisors, without the bonafide/less than bonafide distinction being drawn, is an exercise of little value.

In formulating statutory and interpretative approaches to the supervisory bargaining rights issue, state legislatures, administrative agencies, and Congress must be very sensitive to the distinct characteristics of the two types of supervisory employee. Failure of those policy makers to very carefully and fully consider the bonafide/less than bonafide delineation will likely result in the promulgation of a statutory framework within which the supervisory bargaining rights issue will remain a source of controversy and disruption.

POLICY RECOMMENDATIONS

Based on the above conclusions, the writer maintains that an effective statutory structure should provide that true, bonafide supervisors (as defined and discussed in this study) be excluded from bargaining rights protection. This recommendation is made notwithstanding the persuasive arguments put forth that all but the top echelon of public employees should be allowed to bargain collectively and the lack of negative reports from the five states pursuing such a policy.[126]

The role of the bonafide supervisor in contract administration is a major basis for this policy stand. The heart of a viable labor relations structure lies in effective contract administration. Although the general emphasis in public sector labor relations has yet to switch from contract negotiation to contract administration, it is a widely accepted fact that, in mature bargaining relationships, the key person in day-to-day contract administration is the bonafide supervisor. The formidable long run problems inherent in weakening this first line of management-labor communication and cooperation by allowing such individuals to bargain collectively are apparent.

It cannot be disputed that efficient public administration requires that legitimate management personnel retain a strong commitment to the management point of view and to the achievement of the governmental unit's goals and objectives. Even in contexts other than contract administration (e.g., production maintenance, evaluation of subordinates, enforcement of standards), the division of the management structure wrought by allowing bonafide supervisors to bargain collectively would likely result in decreased managerial effectiveness on the part of the supervisory group.

The majority of bonafide supervisors surveyed in this study did not express a desire to bargain collectively. Their strong identification with the management group makes it improbable that a grant of bargaining rights protection would be of value to those individuals. There is little rational basis for allowing bonafide supervisors to bargain collectively if they do not desire to do so.

The exclusion of bonafide supervisors from bargaining rights protection as proposed herein would not withhold such protection from individuals with supervisory titles who are determined to be less than bonafide supervisors. Supervisors who fall into this category are not really managers, and the traditional arguments supporting supervisory exclusion from statutory coverage do not hold for such individuals. Because of their obvious common community of interest, a policy of placing less than bonafide supervisors in appropriate mixed bargaining units with rank and file employees would seem most appropriate. The attitudes and desires of the less than bonafide supervisors surveyed in this study and discussed above support this statutory approach.

A proscription of bargaining rights protection for bonafide supervisors would require a modification of the view presently held by many higher level public sector managers of the front line supervisor's organizational role. This reorientation would consist primarily of an acknowledgement by public management that many individuals with supervisory titles are "supervisors" in name only.[17] These less than bonafide supervisors can no longer be considered a part of the legitimate management group.

Designation of an individual as a supervisor must be accompanied by a real grant of managerial authority and responsibility. Supervisory titles can no longer be granted capriciously, as they often have been in the past. This concession may be difficult to make initially. However, the findings of this study suggest that the long run result of this realignment of the management and non-management groups should be the elimination of most of the problems attendant to an exclusion of front line supervisors from bargaining rights protection.

The exclusion of only bonafide supervisors can best be implemented by the stringent application of a rigorous definition of the term "supervisor." Several of the comprehensive state statutes incorporate this type of approach. The Connecticut *Municipal Employee Relations Act* contains the following language relating to supervisors:

In determining whether a supervisory position should be excluded from coverage under this act, the board shall consider, among other criteria, whether the principal functions of the position are characterized by not fewer than two of the following: (A) performing such management control duties as scheduling, assigning, overseeing and reviewing the work of subordinate employees; (B) performing such duties as are distinct and dissimilar from those performed by the employees supervised; (C) exercising judgment in adjusting grievances, applying other established personnel policies and procedures and in enforcing the provisions of a collective bargaining agreement; and (D) establishing or participating in the establishment of performance standards for subordinate employees and taking corrective measures to implement those standards.[18]

In a similar manner, which serves to restrict the number of individuals who are excluded from its coverage, the Wisconsin *State Employment Relations Act* prefaces its standard LMRA-type definition of supervisor with this qualifying phrase ". . . any individual whose principal work is different from that of his subordinates. . ."[19]

Attempts to exclude by statute all individuals in particular supervisory classifications[20] are a mistake. The body most qualified to make the bonafide supervisor/less than bonafide supervisor distinction is an appropriate administrative agency staffed by competent and experienced individuals. The test for satisfaction of the statutory definition of supervisor must be formulated so as to clearly distinguish between "working foremen" or "leadmen" and bonafide supervisors whose managerial responsibilities and authority clearly separate them from their subordinates. Because of the presence of many individuals in public employment with supervisory titles who do not have consequential management responsibility or authority, a workable statutory and interpretative apoproach must require substantial proof of "bonafide" supervisory status before an individual can be excluded from bargaining rights protection.

SUMMARY

The writer has advanced the view that only supervisors who possess consequential managerial responsibilities and authority should be excluded from statutory bargaining rights protection. If a policy such as the one advocated herein is adopted in comprehensive public employee collective bargaining statutes (state or federal), then it is probable that the factors which have prompted many public sector supervisors to seek statutory bargaining rights protection will diminish in importance.

Furthermore, much of the debate over supervisory bargaining rights could be dispensed with if only true, bonafide supervisors were excluded from statutory coverage. Hopefully, the conclusions and recommendations produced by this study will contribute to the development of a viable policy approach to the perplexing issue of supervisory bargaining rights in the public sector.

NOTES

1. When this term is used the author has in mind jurisdictions which are regulated by Executive Order 11491 and municipal ordinances as well as comprehensive state public employee bargaining statutes.

2. Stephen L. Hayford and Anthony V. Sinicropi, "The Bargaining Rights Status of Supervisors in the Public Sector," accepted for publication in *Industrial Relations* (May 1976).

This article presents an exhaustive review and analysis of the statutory treatments afforded public sector supervisors in the several states with comprehensive public employee collective bargaining statutes and the federal government.

3. See for example: Joseph P. Goldberg, "Labor Management Relations Law in Public Service," *Monthly Labor Review* 91 (June 1968) p. 51; Harry H. Rains, "Collective Bargaining in the Public Sector and the Need for Exclusion of Supervisory Personnel," LABOR LAW JOURNAL 23 (May 1972) p. 284; Edward Reith and Harold S. Rosen, "Problems in Representation of Supervisors," *California Public Employees Relations* 9 (March 1971) p. 3; Harry H. Wellington and Ralph K. Winter, *The Unions and the Cities* (Washington: The Brookings Institution, 1971) p. 113.

4. For purposes of this study, upper level agency manager is defined as the head of an agency or department or his immediate subordinate. In public education these terms refer to the school system superintendent or his immediate subordinate.

5. For purposes of this study, front line supervisor is defined as an employee at the first or second lowest level of the management hierarchy. In public education this term refers to principals or assistant principals.

6. For purposes of this study, rank and file employee is defined as a non-management employee who is subordinate to a front line supervisor.

7. The labor relations and personnel management aspects of the supervisor's role were focused upon because these are the two concepts most often referred to in the various statutory definitions of the term "supervisor."

8. A standard five point response scale (strongly agree, agree, undecided, disagree, strongly disagree) was utilized.

9. Leonard S. Feldt and Tse-Chi Hsu, "The Effect of Limitations on the Number of Criterion Score Values on the Significance Level of the F-Test," *American Educational Research Journal* 6 (November 1969), pp. 515-527.

10. John E. Freund, *Mathematical Statistics* (Englewood Cliffs: Prentice-Hall, Inc., 1971), pp. 318-320.

11. When multiple two-way t-tests are performed there is a greater probability that significant differences will be found in one or more of the comparisons. To compensate for this fact the test t-statistic (2.64) in Table 2 and Table 4 was taken from Dunn's Table for Multiple Comparison t-tests.

12. Freund, *Mathematical Statistics*, pp. 275-276.

13. Hayford and Sinicropi, "The Bargaining Rights Status of Supervisors in the Public Sector."

14. *Iowa Public Employment Relations Act*, S.F. 531, Secs. 1-29, eff. 7/1/74, Section 4(2).

15. Stephen L. Hayford, "An Investigation Into the Role Description and Collective bargaining-Related Desires of Front Line Supervisors In Public Employment in the State of Iowa" (Ph.D. diss., University of Iowa, 1975).

16. Hayford and Sinicropi, "The Bargaining Rights Status of Supervisors in the Public Sector." Those five states are Hawaii, Minnesota, New York, Massachusetts, and Michigan.

17. Stephen L. Hayford and Anthony V. Sinicropi, "Collective Bargaining and the Public Sector Supervisor," accepted for publication in the *Public Employment Relations Library* (PERL) series.

18. Connecticut General Statutes, Title 7; 1965, P.A. 159, as amended, Section 7-471(2).

19. Wisconsin Statutes, Chapter III, Sub. Chapter V; L. 1971, Chapter 270, effective April 30, 1972, Section 111.81(19).

20. E.g. principals, assistant principals, police sergeants, fire captains.

CHAPTER 6.
ADJUSTING TO
LIMITED RESOURCES

Local Government—Bargaining and the Fiscal Crisis: Money, Unions, Politics, and the Public Interest
Arvid Anderson

"The money is in Washington, the power is in Lansing, and human problems are at the local level of government."[1] So stated Detroit Mayor Gribbs in 1970. The truth of his remarks has been underscored daily during the 1970s as major cities and smaller local governments have struggled with fiscal and labor problems.

My message is written from the deck of the Titanic while it is listing and still afloat. Now I know what happened to the Titanic, but I believe that rescue efforts have improved in the last 60 years, and New York and other cities are hoping to avoid the fatal iceberg of bankruptcy in the second half of the 1970s. While New York has stayed alive in 1975, it will not be out of the fix in 1976, and it is unlikely to be out of it for several more years without continued and substantial help from governments with the money and the power—Albany and Washington.

In this paper I will examine some of the developments in New York City's fiscal crisis and their effect on collective bargaining. The impact of the crisis on the city was brought to national attention last October by the President's speech to the National

Arvid Anderson is on the staff of the Office of Collective Bargaining for the city of New York.

Press Club, which the *New York Daily News* headlined as: "FORD TO CITY: DROP DEAD." Happily, the President changed his mind after originally opposing aid to New York City, and the Congress authorized loans that have enabled the city to work toward a rational solution of its problems.

Clearly, the fiscal crisis in New York has chilled the public's attitude there and in other large cities toward public employee unions and collective bargaining, and it has prompted a reexamination of the collective bargaining process as opposed to the traditional political role of the legislature and executive in determining conditions of employment for public employees.

One sign of the fiscal impact has been the reassessment of the strike as a weapon to deal with bargaining impasses. At the conclusion of last September's teachers' walkout in New York City, Al Shanker stated, "A strike is a weapon you use against the boss who has money. This boss has no money."[2] The realization that an effective New York City transit strike would have a destructive effect on the city's economy and also deal a crippling political blow to New York's effort for fiscal stability has had a major inhibiting effect on strike talk during the transit negotiations. But a strike possibility still exists since the problem is not yet resolved.

While New York City did experience a three-day wildcat sanitation strike to protest substantial layoffs, there has been no repetition of such incidents in spite of the fact that 15 percent of the city's workforce, comprising more than 45,000 employees, have been laid off, retired, or separated from the workforce during the past year,[3] However, a major New York City municipal hospital strike has been authorized for May 24, 1976, to protest hospital closings and cut-backs in service.

EMERGENCY FINANCIAL CONTROLS

The fiscal crisis in New York brought about the Financial Emergency Act, which in turn created the Emegency Financial Control Board, a unique combination of elected officials and appointed private citizens: the mayor, governor, state comptroller, city comptroller, and three private businessmen appointed by the governor.[4] The most important assumption in the city's new fiscal plan mandated by the new law is that there would be no wage increases above the 1975-76 levels for municipal employees for the duration of the plan. The effect is, at least implicitly, to freeze wages and prohibit wage bargaining for the next three years.

These actions have put a damper on the city's collective bargaining process and have raised the question of how viable the bargaining process will be for the next three years for the city and also for the State of New York.

Although this legislation provides that "nothing contained in this act shall be construed to impair the right of employees to organize or to bargain collectively," the reality is that there now exists substantial limitations on the city's financial and legal ability to negotiate. During the teachers' negotiations and strike last September, both the New York City Board of Education and Mr. Shanker pleaded for the "real" employer to please stand up. Since the strike settlement, the Emergency Financial Control Board definitely has stood up and has initially rejected the terms of the teachers' contract, requiring the parties to renegotiate its terms. One of the critical factors in determining whether that contract ultimately will be approved concerns the issue of whether increments in a teaching schedule are to be included in the cost of settlement. Apparently, they have not been counted, but clearly, no budget can ignore the impact of annual increments.

On May 18, the Emergency Financial Control Board also returned the transit settlement to the Transit Authority and the Transport Workers Union for renegotiation on the ground that the Transit Authority had not demonstrated that the settlement (which has been described as modest, providing only for a cost-of-living adjustment on the basis of one cent for each 0.3 change in the Consumer Price Index) was in compliance with the wage-freeze provisions of the Financial Emergency Act.[5] The Emergency Financial Control Board directed the parties to renegotiate the agreement and to clearly condition any cost-of-living increases on productivity savings so as to self-finance and also to possibly defer payment of any such increases.

One of the salutary benefits of the fiscal crisis is the increasing attention to productivity and productivity bargaining in public employment. Thus, the Emergency Financial Control Board has had a direct impact on two of the largest bargaining units in New York City, the teachers and the transit workers. Although neither are strictly speaking city employees—the Transit Authority being a state agency and the school boards being a separate employer (under the Taylor Law)—they are fiscally dependent upon the city. The wage patterns ultimately established by the Emergency Financial Control Board in the teacher and transit negotiations will influence all future city negotiations with its 200,000 other employees.

WAGE-DEFERRAL AGREEMENTS

Most municipal unions in New York City, as a result of emergency legislation, voluntarily entered into agreements deferring contractual wage increases that were to have been paid during fiscal 1975-76. The expectation is that such wages will be paid in 1978. In consideration of such wage-deferral agreements, the city pledged not to exercise its right to lay off or terminate, for economic reasons, full-time per annum permanent employees covered by the agreements for the period from September 1, 1975, to August 31, 1976, except in the event of "extreme necessity." Nevertheless, the continued fiscal crisis raises the possibility that further layoffs may be required.

However, the mayor's projected budget for 1976-77 contemplates that the (deferred) increases will be paid commencing in September 1976. The city maintains it has no funds to pay increased wages beyond that point, although this week it announced increases for a number of key budget personel, not subject to collective bargaining, who have not had increases for a number of years.

Whether the city will be able to maintain a hard wage freeze for the duration of the fiscal emergency is open to question, especially in light of the substantial wage increases we have witnessed in the private sector. Federal pay policies and those of many local governments are based on comparability with private-sector rates, and by the fourth year, New York City could be confronted with pressures for significant catch-up increases that would, in turn, affect its financial position in 1978 and thereafter. In the interim, the wage freeze, by removing incentives for improved employee performance, may adversely affect productivity as well as the city's ability to remain competitive in the labor market.

OTHER EFFORTS

In addition to the legislative wage-freeze and wage-deferral policies, the city has adopted a policy of attrition, meaning that if an employee leaves because of retirement, resignation, or is otherwise separated, he is not replaced except in the most urgent cases.

Another example of the change brought about by the fiscal crisis has been the bargaining away of existing benefits. New York City unions agreed not to oppose the expiration of state legislation requiring the city to pay one-half of the employee's share of pension contributions. The effect of this has been that most city employees found their take-home pay reduced from 2 to 2.5 percent as of April 1, 1976.[6] It is possible that there may be a reduction of an additional 2 to 2.5 percent on July 1, 1976, if the state legislature does not act.

To deal with the overwhelming fiscal crisis, unions "have given at the office." Employee and city pension fund trustees, pursuant to new state and federal legislation protecting such actions, voted to commit some $3.7 billion worth of pension trust investments toward the purchase of city and state securities.[7] More than one billion of that sum represents direct employee contributions to pension funds.

Union decisions to make such investments were based on the simple premise of self-preservation. They realized that the failure to invest would undermine the pensions and job security of all persons now employed at the price of giving uncertain protection to the pension benefits of those persons now retired. It is worth noting that when the public employer needs the assistance of municipal labor union leaders to secure approval of the investment of pension funds in municipal and state securities, no arguments about management rights are being raised about such bargaining. As is often the case, political and fiscal realities override legal rights.

Individual unions have modified their agreements and yielded particular benefits secured during more affluent days. For example, the summer-hours clause whereby employees were dismissed an hour earlier during two summer months has been given up in bargaining. Firemen, who received an extra day off for the donation of blood, gave up that benefit. A reduction in the number of men on a truck has occurred in the fire department.

There also has been a severe limitation on overtime work and pay for all city employees, as well as a virtual freeze on promotions and a delayed payment of employee obligations already accrued. All this has meant not only a reduction in employee benefits, but, of course, also reduced services to the public. Sanitation pickups are less frequent. Schools, hospitals, libraries, fire stations, and police precincts have been closed.

Another example of how the bargaining game has been changed is the effort of the city to recapture 18 additional days from the work schedule of police in New York City. More than two years ago, at the city's insistence, the patrolmen's tours of duty were increased from eight to eight-and-a-half hours per day, which resulted in an average decrease of 18 workdays per year for each patrolman. Because of recent reductions in the police force caused by layoffs and attrition, the city wants to revert to the prior work schedule, which would enable it to put more policemen on the streets. That matter is now before an Office of Collective Bargaining impasse panel.[8]

LEGAL CHALLENGES

It must also be noted, in the litany of what has been taken away, that the city has given the required two-year notice of its intention to withdraw from the Social Security system, a measure vigorously opposed by city unions and even by another mayoral pension commission.[9] This proposal for unilateral withdrawal from the Social Security system has been attacked as violating the city's duty to bargain changes in wages, hours, and conditions of employment. No legal action concerning this issue has been commenced, but the constitutionality of the debt moratorium has been upheld by the appellate division and will undoubtedly be appealed to the state's highest court and possibly to the United States Supreme Court.[10]

The constitutionality of the wage-freeze legislation also has been sustained to date, but further appeals are pending. The views of the appellate courts in New York have caused great concern over the viability of collective bargaining agreements. The Appellate Division, First Department, in a ruling affecting the City of New York and the Uniformed Sanitationmen's Association, rejected the union's claim that a clause in the labor agreement, providing a pay rate based on annual days of work, was a work-guarantee clause.[11]

After making that dispositive factual ruling, the court then engaged in very extensive dicta to the effect that a municipal employer could not by a labor contract limit its right to abolish positions or to lay off employees. The court cited with approval the following language of another appellate ruling:

"Even were we to accept the concept that a public employer may voluntarily choose to bargain collectively as to a nonmandatory subject of negotiation, the public interest or welfare in this case demands that the public employer's job abolition power remain unfettered. Regardless of fault the fact remains that the fiscal crisis facing the City of Long Beach threatens its very ability to govern and provide essential services for its citizens. The city must not be stripped of its means of survival."

These determinations were also influenced by the fact that the state legislature had declared that the city was in a state of financial emergency.

The Patrolmen's Benevolent Association, in an attack on the constitutionality of the wage-freeze legislation in another proceeding, has argued that while the state clearly has the right to declare a fiscal emergency and thus to impair the obligation of contracts despite the provision of Article 1, Section 10, of the United States Constitution, the state and the city have not equitably applied the contract-impairment concept to all of their creditors.[12] The PBA argued that a wage deferral in the case of the PBA amounts to a permanent loss of a 6 percent wage increase, which means that the police would be receiving 94 percent of their contractual obligations while other creditors, such as the utility companies and bondholders, would be receiving 100 percent payment on their contracts.

The point argued by the PBA is that labor contracts must be given the same credence as all other contracts of a municipal employer and may not be derogated on the ground of fiscal emergency while other creditors are paid in full, even if some payments are delayed or interest reduced. The final word of the courts has not been spoken on the issue of whether a collective bargaining agreement has less claim to constitutional protection than that afforded other contracts, whether for debt service, contractors, or suppliers. A major decision concerning this issue is expected next month from New York State's highest court.

WHO IS RESPONSIBLE?

Are public employees, public employee unions, and collective bargaining settlements responsible for the fiscal crisis and the threat of default in New York and other cities? Certainly wage costs and bargaining settlements are a substantial part of any municipal budget—at least 50 percent and in some instances 70 to 80 percent, depending upon the nature of the service. Obviously, substantial increases in wage costs add to municipal budgets. The Conference Board, a respected management research agency, in its January issue of the *Conference Record*, rejects as "wishful thinking" the notion that New York City can solve its problems by eliminating "waste and extravagance in the employment area."[13]

The statistics analyzed by the Conference Board are taken from the Bureau of the Census and the Bureau of Labor Statistics and reveal that New York City per capita expenditures for local government services, while high, are lower than those of Boston, San Francisco, and Miami, and approximately equal to those of Philadelphia, Atlanta, and Washington. Other statistics developed from the Department of Commerce, the Census, and BLS indicate that New York City municipal salaries rank fourth among the first 13 cities of the nation, and when adjusted for the high cost of living in New York City, rank tenth. Among nonteaching employees, New York City salaries rank eighth, and when adjusted for the cost of living rank 16th.[14]

Similarly, wage increases for municipal workers over a period of time indicate that New York City settlements have not been significantly in excess of those granted in either the public or private sector. For example, in the fiscal years 1971 to 1976, the average salaries of nonuniformed New York City employees increased by 44.7 percent and of uniformed employees by 48.5 percent.[15] During a similar five-year period, the average annual increases in major collective bargaining agreements in the private sector throughout the country totaled 43.5 percent. Similar settlements were made for New York State employees. The statistics show that New York City settlements have been based upon comparability with persons doing like work in public and private employment.

Thus, these and other figures indicate that the rise in public-sector wages has not been very different from that in the private sector and cast doubt on the allegations that collective bargaining in the public sector accounts in large measure for the financial difficulties of cities. What has happened is that *particular wage* increases or unusually high pay scales, as those for certain San Francisco craft workers, have received so much attention that other reasons for public payroll increases have been largely overlooked.

If the high cost of labor or labor settlements is not adjudged to be solely responsible for the fiscal crisis, what are the other causes? The January *Conference Record* refers to a "culture of poverty," concluding that New York, which has approximately 3 percent of the nation's population, contains roughly 10 percent of the nation's welfare load.[16] These numbers mean a direct city budgetary burden of about $1 billion, including welfare and medicaid. When the total annual costs related to providing services of all kinds for the poor are computed, they come close to $2 billion, according to the Conference Board. This clearly places an unfair burden on New York City as compared to the rest of the nation.

Recent statistics demonstrate that 63 percent of the city's welfare mothers were not born in New York: 34 percent were born in Puerto Rico and 29 percent in other states.[17] New York State legislative efforts to enact residency requirements, as a means of barring federally mandated welfare claims, have been held by federal courts to be unconstitutional. To further illustrate the New York welfare dilemma, I ask you to visualize a federal law that would mandate the suburban ring of Maryland and Virginia, which surrounds Washington, D. C., to assume a substantial share of the welfare costs of the nation's capital

Clearly, New York City and New York State taxpayers are bearing a very large percentage of everyone's burdens. With such crushing welfare costs, no matter how efficient New York City government might become, additional aid from the state and federal governments is needed to help balance the city's budget. As for charges of welfare rip-offs and bungled administration, both New York City and New York State administrations have made clear that they would be overjoyed with a federal takeover of the entire program.

WHAT IMPACT?

What are the conclusions to be drawn from the impact of the fiscal crisis on bargaining in New York? One is that the adversity of the fiscal crisis established the conditions for the application of collective bargaining principles by which city and state government officials, in cooperation with union, banking, and commercial interests, joined together to stave off default, to win financial assistance and time for a new fiscal plan, and to secure aid from the state legislature and loans from the federal government. The New York City labor unions are represented on the Emergency Financial Control Board by a labor observer.

William Ellinghaus, a Control Board member and former Big MAC chairman, is quoted as saying, "I have found the municipal labor unions to be the most practical people in this crisis. They understood the problem more quickly than the city administration." Felix Rohatyn, Big MAC chairman, declared, concerning the role played by labor in holding off default, "It could not have happened without Vic Gotbaum."[18]

The above references are made not to give singular praise to the leaders of organized labor, but to emphasize the spirit of cooperation between all of the interest groups—banks, labor unions, and political leaders—who realize that they each have much more to lose if they do not cooperate. This is not to suggest that there will not be a renewal of the political battles between the city and state officials and the legislature, or confrontations between any of the participants. What has happened to date is a demonstration of statesmanship or, if you prefer, enlightened self-interest to prevent default. In sum, what has happened to date is a recognition of the effectiveness of the collective bargaining process as a tool to deal with major fiscal crises.

We also see that the fiscal crisis and the legislature have imposed substantial limitations on bargaining with respect to wages and pensions for some time to come. Collective bargaining has also been struggling to cope with some of the fiscal problems, but, unfortunately, most of the major economic problems are beyond solution at the collective bargaining table and beyond the resources of New York City and other large cities. They require, as has been demonstrated, fiscal and political decisions at the state and national level. Clearly, until the federal government takes effective action to deal with the problems of inflation, recession, unemployment, and unequal distribution of services, burdens, and responsibilities that it mandates to be provided at the local level, there will be continuing struggles over money, layoffs, and service cutbacks.

The failure of the federal government to deal with urban problems will not mean that the issues will go away; rather, it will mean that many city and state employees, instead of working and earning a living from tax dollars, will collect unemployment compensation, welfare, food stamps, and medicaid from those tax dollars. Unfortunately, they will not be providing any useful public services to an ever-dwindling number of taxpayers.

The public reaction toward unwise, untimely, and illegal public employee strikes and related union political actions have differed from jurisdiction to jurisdiction. Mayor Wes Uhlman of Seattle successfully rebuffed firefighter efforts to recall him from office because of his opposition to their bargaining proposals.[19] San Francisco voters changed the local law and the criteria for determining police and fire salaries, and also the method for fixing the wages of prevailing-rate employees, following police and fire strikes last year in that city. The result was wage cuts for the highest paid craft employees, followed by a strike. Their calls for a general strike fell on the deaf ears of their fellow, lower paid municipal trade unionists and private-sector union members.[20]

These events may be evidence of only a temporary public reaction to public employee unions and collective bargaining, but

I am not sure. The jury is still out as to whether there will be a widespread turn-away from the process for establishing employment conditions for public employees. It is my hope that in the long run the majority of the public will realize that it is not in the public interest to again politicize the bargaining processes and that it is wiser to adopt comprehensive and effective collective bargaining laws for resolving the employment problems for state and local employees.

Even with comprehensive bargaining laws, the failure to use them properly may invite unwise legislative action. For example, Mayor Abraham Beame is now faced with the process of totally reordering his fiscal plan and laying off as many as 8,000 additional employees as a result of a state legislative override—the first in 104 years—of a governor's veto of a bill requiring the city to spend at least 20 percent of its budget for education.[21] The success of the teachers union in lobbying for such a measure, despite the New York fiscal crisis, has induced police and fire unions to seek similar state legislation barring further layoffs from their ranks.

The city has taken the position that the state law is unconstitutional as a violation of home rule, and a court test has begun. The teachers say that they are employed by a separate governmental entity and thus not subject to the home-rule provisions of the state constitution. We cannot predict the outcome of this conflict, but can only hope for a reasonable compromise.

Whatever the ultimate decision as to the best means for determining employment conditions for public employees, the message of the 1970s for local governments and particularly for urban America is clear: "The money is in Washington, the power is in the State Capitol, but the human problems" must still be dealt with by local governments.

NOTES

1. GERR, No. 361, B-12, Aug. 10, 1970.
2. *The New York Times,* Sept. 17, 1975, p. 28.
3. *The New York Times,* May 17, 1976.
4. New York State Law, Ch. 868 of the Laws of the 1975 Session.
5. *The New York Times,* May 1, 1976.
6. *The Public Employee Press,* Vol. XVII, No. 21, Dec. 5, 1975, p. 2.
7. *The Public Employee Press,* Vol. XVIII, No. 9, May 7, 1976, p. 4.
8. Office of Collective Bargaining, Patrolmen's Benevolent Association and the City of New York, Case # I-124-75.

9. *The Chief*, March 26, 1976, p. 1, col. 4.

10. *New York Law Journal*, May 6, 1976, Vol. 175, No. 88, p. 1, *Flushing National Bank v. Municipal Assistance Corporation for The City of New York*.

11. *New York Law Journal*, March 10, 1976, Vol. 175, No. 47, p. 1, *DeLury v. City of New York*, 370 NYS 2d 600 (NY 1975) 77 LC Sec. 53,760.

12. Appellate Division, First Department, *Patrolmen's Benevolent Association against The City of New York*, Index No. 10012175.

13. *The Conference Board Record*, Vol. XIII, No. 1, Jan. 1976, "New York Is Really Something," p. 3.

14. U. S. Department of Commerce, Bureau of the Census, *City Employment in 1973* (Washington: May 1974); see also *City Employment in 1974*, GE 74, No. 2 (Washington: June 1974), and *Local Government Employment in Selected Metropolitan Areas and Large Counties*, GE 74, No. 3 (Washington: Aug. 1975).

15. Office of Labor Relations, New York City.

16. *The Conference Board Record*, cited at note 13.

17. *The New York Times*, Nov. 16, 1975.

18. *The New York Times*.

19. GERR, No. 613, July 7, 1975, p. B-4.

20. *Wall Street Journal*, April 15, 1976, p. 34.

21. *The New York Times*, April 15, 1976.

State Government—Strategies for Negotiations in an Austere Environment: A Management Perspective
Donald H. Wollett

When I was practicing law in New York City, largely on the management side, my colleagues and I used to jest about typical marching orders from chief executive officers which usually sounded something like: "Don't give them anything, but for God's

Reproduced from the August, 1976 issue of the LABOR LAW JOURNAL, published and copyrighted (1976) by Commerce Clearing House, Inc., 4025 W. Peterson Avenue, Chicago, Illinois, 60646. Reprinted by permission of the author, the Industrial Relations Research Association and Commerce Clearing House, Inc.

Donald H. Wollett is the Director of Employee Relations for the state of New York.

sake, as well as the corporation's, don't have a strike." The Governor of the State of New York does not talk this way, but in the 14 months that I have spoken for him in negotiations with unions representing 180,000 state employees, the bottom line of his instructions could be translated into about the same words.

This is not lightly given counsel. The Carey administration is committed to the proposition that collective bargaining is the best way to resolve conflicts of interest between employees and employers and solve problems of the workplace, in both the private and public sectors. Nor is this an easy injunction to follow at a time when real earnings have been severely eroded by a rising cost of living and employee expectations are high.

Assume the following facts: Inflation has sent the costs of government up; recession has impaired the growth of revenues; the tax base has shrunk; hidden legacies of past mismanagement have been uncovered. In fiscal 1975-76 there was a serious budgetary gap between income and expenditures. The projected budget for 1976-77 is balanced, but precariously. Salary and fringe-benefit demands cannot be met without drastically curtailing services to the public or seeking major increases in a severely burdensome tax structure. Given these fiscal realities, state management's objective at the bargaining table is to yield nothing or next to nothing without provoking job action.

This has been the setting for negotiations in New York State. In the hope that our experiences may have general and instructive value, I propose to tell you how we operated.

Our strategies have been predicated upon two articles of faith. First, collective bargaining is a flexible instrumentality that can be made to work in an austere environment. Second, trade unions and the employees whom they represent will take "no" for an answer provided they are persuaded that (a) the economic crisis is "real," (b) they have a stake in the solution of the economic problems of the governmental enterprise, and (c) they are not being singled out, not being discriminated against—that sacrifice is being shared by all, not fastened upon a few.

MANAGEMENT MUST ACT LIKE MANAGEMENT

In the private sector, the chief executive officer is accountable to the owners of the enterprise, not to its employees. In the public sector this is not wholly true. Employees in the enterprise are also among its owners—the voting, taxpaying constituency. The chief executive officer of a government is both a manager and a politician. Public-sector union pressures are directed toward evoking his responses as a politician. But, if collective bargaining is to work, the chief executive officer must act first as a manager, although he understands that hard choices, if they are politically unpalatable, may ultimately drive him from office.

Absent collective bargaining, the terms and conditions of state employment are fixed in the main by legislation—special self-interest bills that public-employee organizations can manipulate through the political process. Collective bargaining is intended largely to displace this way of doing business. But it works only if all parties—the governor, the legislature, and the unions—recognize that public-sector collective bargaining becomes a sham if it is politicized. Unions should accept the legitimacy of management's acting like management.

But it is unrealistic to expect them to forgo the use of conventional political pressures to achieve their economic ends unless management has the courage to demonstrate their futility. This means that public management must not permit the unions to collect political debts at the bargaining table. It also means that management must resist efforts by the unions to end-run the bargaining process by taking to the legislature proposals that they have lost at the table.

I do not wish to push the logic of this position too far. Some problems endemic to the workplace have such overriding and general social significance that they may be better dealt with legislatively, *e.g.*, industrial injury and disease, health and safety, sexual and ethnic discrimination.

MANAGEMENT SELF-DISCIPLINE

The operational and structural arrangements should be similar to those that obtain in the private sector. The dimensions of the chief negotiator's authority should be derived directly from the governor. The sole responsibility to deal with the unions and the authority within those dimensions to make agreements should be fixed in the negotiator. End runs should be prohibited. The governor must set the tone. His door should be shut to the unions; only the chief negotiator's door should be open. This role should apply to all top gubernatorial aides and agency heads.

Management must also maintain internal discipline. Let me give a personal example. On February 2, 1976, Albany was hit by a blizzard. Many employees were unable to get to work. The Director of State Operations decided that state offices in the Albany area should be shut down. The question then arose as to whether or not the day of absence should be counted against employee leave accruals, specifically five-day personal leave. Historically, so-called snow days have been counted, time off has been recorded as personal-leave time, and employees who manage to get to work are not entitled to compensatory time off. This time one of the governor's key advisers, in the belief that reversal of past practice would redound to the governor's political advantage, persuaded him to take that position.

Since we had a proposal on the bargaining table to reduce the five days' personal leave time to three days, and since the effect of the governor's decision was to add a day, our position at the bargaining table on this matter was fatally undermined. Happily, this was the only breakdown in discipline that occurred, and the damage was not irreparable. Indeed, its occurrence may have served to tighten ranks as we moved toward the critical days of negotiations.

A TOTAL STRATEGY

Management must keep in mind at all times the impact of agreements with one union on the political imperatives of other unions. The twin phenomena of "me-too-ism" and "one-upsmanship" belong in the forefront of the bargaining strategy. State police troopers will not accept less money than prison guards; prison guards will want some advantage over maintenance workers; registered nurses will want more than licensed vocational nurses; and university professors will want the world.

In New York State we are substantially advantaged in dealing with these problems by our nonproliferated unit structures. We have five broad horizontal units that cut across agency and departmental lines:

Administrative Services Units, 40,000 employees; represented by the Civil Service Employees Association (CSEA); communication equipment operators, examiners, office support staff, such as secretarial and clerical personnel.

Institutional Services Unit, 47,000 employees; representd by CSEA; employees providing therapeutic and custodial care to persons in state institutions, *e.g.,* therapy aides.

Operational Services Unit, 25,000 employees; representd by CSEA; craft workers, maintenance and repair personnel and machine operators.

Professional, Scientific, and Technical Services Unit,

39,000 employees; representd by CSEA; employees who are primarily licensed professionals. *e.g.*, engineers, cartographers, kosher-food inspectors, bursars, psychiatrists.

Security Services Unit, 9,000 employees; represented by Council 82, American Federation of State, County and Municipal Employees; prison guards and security personnel other than state troopers, such as narcotic correction officers, lifeguards, and park and parkway patrolmen.

We have three vertical units:

State University Professional Services Negotiating Unit, 18,000 employees; represented by the United University Professions, Inc., affiliated with the American Federation of Teachers, AFL-CIO; all faculty and nonteaching professional staff of the State University system, including faculty, librarians, bursars, guidance counselors, environmental health and safety officers, museum curators, and pharmacists.

State Police Troopers, 3,300 employees; represented by the State Police Benevolent Association; all noncommissioned officers, investigators, and troopers of the Division of State Police.

State Police Officers, 100 employees; represented by CSEA; all captains, lieutenants, and majors in the Division of State Police.

By contrast, Los Angeles County, for example, has approximately 50 units covering over 60,000 employees. Obviously, the problem of devising a strategy to blunt me-too-ism and one-upsmanship is much more difficult in a Los Angeles County type situation than it is in the one in which we operate in the State of New York.

Management must reduce employee expectations to realistic levels, thus making it possible for union representatives to take acceptable positions and survive politically. This is a subliminal strategy that requires a public relations campaign designed to implant in the public subconscious the fiscal setting of the negotiations. Despite its obvious importance, most public managements lack the capacity to execute a full-blown public relations strategy. We in New York are not an exception. We do our best with limited resources. Again let me personalize.

Our theme was austerity—belt-tightening and survival. We were benefited by the continuous financial crisis in New York City with its fall-out impact on the state's fiscal situation, as well as such threatening events as a 3 percent reduction in force at the start of the fourth quarter of the fiscal year. Obviously, these events were not a part of any plan, but were fortuitous circumstances that worked to create a climate hospitable to low-cost settlement. However, we arranged for frequent repetition of the theme by as many sources as we could reach.

Other things happened that we did not expect. For example, Senator Warren Anderson, majority leader of the Republican-controlled State Senate, responding to Governor Carey's call for legislation imposing a wage freeze, said that the employees had the right to have the governor's representatives say "no" at the bargaining table, rather than to have the legislature say "no" by enacting a freeze. This was interpreted as a signal that an appeal by the unions from our position at the bargaining table to a legislative hearing, which is the final step under our statute for resolution of a bargaining impasse, would be unproductive.

We did two other things: First, we developed a set of affirmative management demands, utilizing the labor-relations directors of state agencies to set forth the felt needs of their operational people. We carefully sifted these, resolved inconsistencies, removed ambiguities, and excised all demands except those which could be justified by compelling operational problems or by a desire to return specified state benefits to comparable levels in the private sector. We initiated negotiations instead of waiting for the unions to come to us, and we publicized them in the media at the outset, making such statements as:

"The State has presented a set of proposals to eliminate employee benefits which exceed those found in the private sector. A report from the Division of the Budget demonstrates that some employee benefits are excessive. For instance, in the first year of State service a new employee is entitled to 42 days of leave with pay, including five days of personal leave. In 1974-75 paid leave, not including time off for union business, cost the State $384 million. There can be some dollar savings in this area and some increases in productivity by recapturing 14 million manhours of work without increasing the number of State employees who presently work 37 1/2 hours a week to 40 hours a week. Our proposals will save the State $28 1/2 million in out-of-pocket costs."

Finally, we gave public exposure to unrealistic positions taken by the unions where we felt that it was warranted. Thus, when the Civil Service Employees Association proposed salary increases ranging from 25 to 36 percent at an aggregate cost to the state of $460 million per annum, we did not hesitate to issue a critical press release, pointing out that these demands could not be met without raising taxes by that amount or laying off over

40,000 employees (or some combination of the two). Without exception, mass media editorial comment urged CSEA to abandon these unrealistic positions and adjust to the realities of the bargaining environment.

RISKS

Management must be prepare to take risks. First, there is the risk of unpopularity. The execution of these strategies will not be greeted with universal acclaim. For example, I received a letter from one employee in which he said, among other things:

"Your attitude in the present negotiations of no salary increase and your insistence of [sic] taking away fringe benefits already enjoyed from previous contracts sounds like the ravings of a very sick person. . . . Your tactic of negotiating through the press and looking for public sentiment is one of the dirtiest deals ever imposed upon the state employees. . . . I sincerely hope that the Governor and the public see you for what you really are and that you eventually will be dismissed in complete disgrace."

The Governor's fan mail was equally unenthusiastic. One employee wrote:

"Why your vicious attack on state civil service employees, even before the election ballots were cold? What happened to all those surplus funds those bums in Albany were sitting on, according to your campaign oratory? Regretfully I believed you, and for the first time in 38 years wish I could recall my vote."

Another employee wrote: "I would like you to know that I voted for you, but I would vote for my pet dog for governor before I would vote for you again."

A second risk is legal. The execution of strategies which are conceived to be sound from a labor relations point of view should not be inhibited by legal doctrines of doubtful validity. For instance, the New York Public Employment Relations Board has held that the failure of a public employer to continue, during negotiations for a new agreement, terms and conditions of employment established by an expired contract or by past practices constitutes a refusal to negotiate in good faith.[1]

The employer, according to this decision, must maintain the *status quo* unless and until either (a) the union agrees to discontinuance or (b) statutory impasse procedures, including a legislative hearing, have been exhausted. This doctrine prevents a public employer, even where it has given the union notice and has bargained to an impasse, from unilaterally modifying matters within the mandatory scope of bargaining.

The *Triborough Doctrine*, as it is known, has not been tested in the courts. In our view it will not survive judicial scrutiny because the statute is not intended to deprive an employer of the benefits of the bargain made with respect to the contract expiration date. Accordingly, we decided to ignore *Triborough*. We advised the unions that the benefits generated by the collective bargaining agreements would, if we were at impasse at the time of their expiration, be terminated. This gave us leverage that a more cautious strategy would have lacked.

Finally, if public management is to pursue aggressive strategies, it must take a hard look at the possibility of strike action and be prepared to take a strike if bargaining objectives cannot otherwise be attained.

The New York statute, the so-called Taylor Law, contains the most severe strike penalties in the country. Strikers are automatically placed on probation for one year; they are subject to discipline, including discharge; they are docked two days' pay for each day they are on strike. The strike is subject to injunctive relief, which the New York courts grant with regularity, and a noncomplying union may be severely punished by fines and jail sentences for the leaders. Furthermore, the union may lose its right to have dues deducted from the employees' salary checks.

These sanctions are of course no guarantee against strike action. What they do is increase the cost to the employees and to the unions of strike acion. This means, theoretically, that since the price is up, the number of strikes will be down. But strikes will and do occur where the employees feel strongly enough about the issues to pay the higher price. Accordingly, if public management pursues an aggressive strategy, it must prepare for strike action.

Strikes by public employees are weapons of political embarrassment. They do not typically inflict significant economic harm, except on the strikers. The question in each case is whether or not interruption of the service provided will generate political pressures on the chief executive officer that will move him toward settlement.

Thus, for example, a strike by the faculty of a state university is of little consequence. Failure to maintain the service may make ripples, but no waves. It is not necessary or even desirable to get hard-nosed at the bargaining table to the point of stressing that strike action may do the employer more good than harm since it will save money.

Exactly the opposite is true of a state correctional system. A strike in penal institutions is a grave matter. Operations must be maintained, and a union representing prison guards must be made to understand that you have the will and the ability to do precisely that.

REALISTIC EXPECTATIONS

Management must prepare to meet employee expectations that are realistic. Management should identify those areas of significant employee concern about which something can be done, thus creating feasible trade-offs without violating fiscal constraints or crippling operations. Three illustrations drawn from our recent New York experience make the point.

(1) A long-standing grievance of the members of the Operational Services Unit stems from the practice of discriminating against labor-class employees who are laid off. Employees in other classes have the right, after one year of credited service, to be laid off pursuant to seniority rules and to be placed on a preferred rehiring list. Labor-class employees do not acquire these rights until they have five years of credited service. The reason for the discrimination is political—a management desire to be free to lay off and rehire on the basis of patronage considerations.

(2) Some members of the Administrative Services Unit felt sorely abused when the New York State Lottery was abruptly closed last December because of defects in the conception and management of the "game plan," and all the employees were laid off with three weeks' notice.

(3) The correctional officers in the Security Services Unit have jammed our grievance docket with cases claiming that work directly affecting the health, safety, or security of inmates has improperly been assigned from time to time to civilian personnel, thus depriving prison guards of overtime opportunities and, according to their allegations, creating hazardous conditions.

A management that is pushing for a no-cost settlement must be prepared to make concessions with respect to matters of this sort.

TIMETABLES

Where multiple sets of negotiations are in progress, management must work to a timetable. What should be the order of settlement?

In orthodox whipsaw strategy, you would go after the weakest adversary first. But this will not work here because patterns established with weak unions are not likely to have any impact on strong unions. What is needed is agreement with a union that has clout.

In our case we turned to the PBA, representing the State Police troopers. There were four reasons for this. First, PBA had just stood off an election challenge to its status as the bargaining representative by a three-to-one margin. As a consequence, it was secure. Second, PBA has strong, effective, and realistic leadership. Third, the State Police have a proud history of rising to emergencies. Fourth, they have a strong professional (no-strike) tradition and are held together by the amalgam of a nomadic and hazardous job.

The choice proved to be a wise one. The agreement with PBA established a pattern of extending the operative provisions of the present agreement, with no increase in the salary schedule or in fringe benefits. The only economic benefit was to service the present salary schedule by paying increments to eligible employees (which amounts to an increase in the aggregate payroll of about 1.25 percent).

The Memorandum of Agreement with PBA was signed February 9, 1976. The pattern was extended to the four units of 147,000 employees represented by the Civil Service Employees Association on March 12, and was accepted by Council 82 of AFSCME, representing the 9,000 members of the Security Services Unit, on April 29. Thus, the pattern is now established in six of the eight units (160,000 employees) with whom we have collective bargaining relationships.

The price for these settlements was to meet some of the employee concerns which neither pierced our fiscal ceiling nor crippled operations. Thus, we agreed to nondiscriminatory treatment of labor-class employees; to give notice of closedowns of agencies, facilities, and major departments; to create a committee to deal with labor-displacement problems patterned after the Armour Automation Committee established in the meat packing industry in 1959; to give permanent employees preference over provisional and temporary employees in layoff situations; and, except in emergencies, to assign correctional officers' work in the prison system to members of the Security Services Unit.

DO THESE STRATEGIES WORK?

This question cannot be answered categorically.

It is clear, as far as our experience in New York State is

concerned, that we complied with our marching orders and achieved our objectives: no increases in salary schedules or fringe benefits; some concessions in areas of special concern to employees, concerns which could be met with little or no cost; no job actions, with our collective bargaining systems alive and well.

It is not clear that these strategies were a *sine qua non* of ending up on target. Perhaps we were just lucky. I'm sure that many observers will say so. On that point I am reminded of the 1962 World Series between the New York Yankees and the San Francisco Giants. With the series tied at three games apiece, the seventh and final game in Candlestick Park moved to the bottom of the ninth, with the Yankees leading one to nothing, the tying and winning runs on base, two out, and left-handed Willy McCovey at bat. McCovey hit a vicious line drive, which Bobby Richardson, the Yankee second baseman, who was positioned 30 feet to the the right of second base, caught off his shoe tops. Thus, the Yankees won their 20th World Series since 1921. If Richardson had not been playing out of his normal position, the game and the series would have gone the other way. So the familiar cry went up, "The damned Yankees are lucky." But the late Branch Rickey was fond of saying, "Luck is the residue of design." I find it ego-gratifying to believe that Mr. Rickey was right.

Nor can one accurately assess the long-range consequences of pursuing these strategies. In this business there is always next year, and the question remains: "Did we pay too high a price in terms of employee morale and attitudes?" It is axiomatic that sometimes a deal is too tight and results in consequences that cost more than the agreement is worth. My judgment is that the price was about right. My evidence is the ratification-vote results, which were as follows:

Sixty-three percent of the State Police troopers approved the agreement.

In the four basic CSEA units, one agreement was ratified three-to-one, another two-to-one, a third five-to-two, and the final one seven-to-five.

The Security Services Unit agreement has not yet been ratified, but the 24 members of the negotiating committee approved it unanimously, suggesting that it has broad-based political support.

These data are by no means conclusive, but I find them reassuring, as I do the fact that our relationships with the union leaders seem to me to have been improved by our experiences in the crucible of hard bargaining.

There is also the question of the political cost to the first Democratic administration in New York State in 16 years. I do not feel competent to answer this question, although it does seem clear to me that our negotiations next year must turn to more constructive and dynamic directions than we have managed in the past two years of fiscal crisis.

There is one conclusion with which I do feel comfortable. Collective bargaining is not an alchemic vehicle. It will not transmute tin into gold, rain into sunshine, or chicken excrement into chicken a la king. The function of collective bargaining, as I understand it, is to protect and advance the interests of employed occupational groups. Within those limitations, it can be made to work in any kind of environment to prevent injustice, to keep compensation levels at or close to comparability standards, to maintain due process in the shop, and to keep management on its toes.

NOTES

1. *Matter of Triborough Bridge and Tunnel Authority,* 5 PERB 3064 (1972).

CHAPTER 7.
TACTICS
AND RESULTS

The COST-ED Model:
A New Economic Tool That Can Be Used
To Aid Negotiations

Blair H. Curry,

John M. Sweeney,

and Charles L. Blaschke

The COST-ED Model is a computerized mathematical simulation of how educational decisions and patterns of school operations affect costs. The various reports prepared from information programmed into the Model can aid the administrator in making sophisticated economic analyses of his programs and can show relationships among facilities, schedules, staff allocation, materials, and costs. Such analyses can also provide the negotiator with an objective, quantified picture of the economic implications of alternate contract proposals and rational arguments for the adoption of one or another alternative.

INTRODUCTION

Squeezing better educational results from shrinking tax funds demands strong, sound school management.

The school administrator has final responsibility for the effectiveness with which tax dollars for education are spent. This responsibility, however, often exceeds his actual power to control

Blair H. Curry is Director of Marketing and John M. Sweeney is Director of Production for the Economic Analysis Division of Education Turnkey Systems, Inc. Charles L. Blaschke is President of Education Turnkey Systems, Inc.

school operations. He must accommodate the pressures of union leaders, educational experts, neighborhood representatives, state legislators, and others in exercising what is left of his discretion on behalf of the children and the community at large.

Pragmatism demands the recognition that most school decisions are arrived at subjectively through a process of considering a variety of ideas, suggestions, and demands. The overriding of broad, managerial considerations by pressures from the strongest vested interest groups of the moment has played no small part in our schools' current fiscal crises.

The wise administrator strives to keep his prerogatives in line with his responsibilities. He knows he must do this by strengthening and maintaining his store of management information so that the economic impact of all decisions can be considered.

He can do this by controlling the language used in the decision-making process, by full command of all the key facts, and by building good community and governmental relations. Proper use of COST-ED modeling and analysis in proposal definition and evaluation, in provision of a functional and operational accounting for current school operations, and in establishment of "learning per dollar" goals and commitments can help him attain all these sources of strength.

As fiscal pressures lead to tax revolts despite worsening school conditions, it is evident that the power to influence decisions will be increasingly enjoyed by those who offer efficient economic solutions to school problems. If a rash of wanton cost cutting and staff trimming is to be avoided, it is imperative that the currently prevalent system of demands, counter-demands, and crisis-precipitating actions give way to constructive, cost-conscious cooperation. Use of COST-ED tools can play a contributory role in helping crystallize this transformation.

Such tools can also clarify collective negotiations by giving the negotiators visible alternative costs for proposals and the trade-off effects of those proposals. This allows administrators to make reasoned judgments and gives them an objective basis on which to sell that judgment to negotiating adversaries and taxpayers.

THE COST-ED MODEL: WHAT IT IS

The COST-ED Model is a computerized mathematical simulation of how educational decisions and patterns of school operations affect costs. It traces the contribution to total school costs of decisions on class size and instructional materials expenditures, of teachers' salaries, and of school building design parameters. In all, over 3600 distinct cost-influencing factors may be considered in a COST-ED model.

A model may be designed to represent a complete district's costs, or just those of an individual school. A COST-ED model may be used to allocate costs to individual programs of instruction within a school, or even to distinct elements of the instructional process within a course. The level of detail at which it may be used is flexible, depending upon the analytical objectives selected.

Once built, a COST-ED model may be run on a computer to determine the "what if" cost impact of changes in any of hundreds of cost-influencing factors. Computer reports are prepared showing a ranking of all manageable factors according to their relative power in affecting total costs. Other computerized analyses provide anwers to such questions as: How much will a change here affect a cost subtotal there? or, How much of a change here is equivalent to (or needed to offset exactly) a change there?

Considerations of educational effectiveness may be brought into COST-ED analyses through use of historical measurements or informed judgments of the results expected from new programs. A reading-level gain, for instance, may be related in COST-ED analysis to the total costs of the reading program; the result is an accountable measure of the cost per unit of achievement. COST-ED analyses can establish the learning gain before it is justified on a results-per-dollar basis.

COST-ED FOR PROGRAM EVALUATION

Through the application of the model, the education planner who is experimenting with various instructional programs has a tool to analyze the economics of each pilot program in terms of its cost and the achievement resulting from that program. He can then determine how the pattern of cost incurrence differs from program to program. For example, an administrator may be considering mathematics and readng programs which include the following design features: a ratio of professional teachers to students of 1 to 600, 32 paraprofessionals relying heavily on the use of audio-visual and other automated capital-intensive means of instruction. This program will be characterized by relatively high cost increases in certain areas (e.g., audio-visual equipment) and

drastic reductions in others (e.g., total cost for teachers) compared with other less radical programs, such as the current
school district program. Using available data on the economics
and effectiveness of various instructional programs, the administrator can project the economic cost as well as possible benefits to
be achieved if other schools were to adopt and implement specific
programs. In this sense, the administrator can use the model for
budgetary planning as well as for program planning and evaluation.

COST-ED FOR PROGRAM SIMULATION

In other instances where the administrator cannot afford to conduct an expensive pilot or demonstration program to determine
the cost effectiveness of an instructional program, he might want
to use the COST-ED Model as a simulation device to project the
nature of the economics and total cost of the proposed program,
using data gathered elsewhere on effectiveness. In simulating the
proposed program, he could relax certain existing constraints
within the school system to determine what he would be saving if
he did not have to abide by these constraints, which may unduly
increase cost without increasing effectiveness. For example, if an
instructional program demonstrated and tested elsewhere indicates that through the use of paraprofessionals and automated
means of instruction operating twelve hours a day, certain results
are achieved but existing school regulations or traditions preclude the hiring of paraprofessionals or the operation of school
facilities for twelve hours a day, then he will have a factual basis
for determining the cost of not using the most efficient configura-
tion of the learning system.

Using a COST-ED model of the ongoing instructional program as a basis, the administrator could simulate the effects of
many recent education proposals (e.g., team teaching, differentiated staffing, learning centers, twelve-month school year) on his
own cost structure.

COST-ED AND THE PROGRAM BUDGET

Like the accounts of a well-designed Planning-Programming-
Budgeting System, COST-ED analyses are management-oriented,
not auditor-oriented. In fact, COST-ED analysis is a simple but
sophisticated form of the "Planning-Programming" use as-

sociated with the type of cost information gathered in a PPBS accounting structure.

COST-ED reports group expenditures by function or purpose of expenditure before splitting them into categories of staff or facilities. In this critical feature they differ markedly from a school budget, which fails to show how much money is used to support reading instruction or is spent on teachers doing non-teaching work. At the same time, COST-ED analyses show the surreptitious impact on fund allocations among educational purposes that arise from salary or price changes in various cost categories.

Because of this difference, COST-ED dollar figures may be used to answer questions and support judgments that would otherwise require an unaffordable effort with standard budgets. The questions they answer and the judgments they inform are those that are oriented toward program evaluation and planning for change.

COST-ED AND NEGOTIATIONS

The school administrator knows that spiraling teachers' salaries may have repressive effects on other portions of his instructional budget, but can he quantify these effects and demonstrate them at the bargaining table?

If all parties involved in the collective bargaining process were to approach the bargaining table with the same frame of reference—a common language—then a more rational discussion of demands and counterdemands would be possible. COST-ED Analysis provides just such a common language in which the economic effects of all decisions can be reviewed, in which all parties can present their case *quantitatively*. Although negotiators have made efforts to do this, too often the process was one of educated guesswork, perhaps because the laborious, time-consuming calculation involved deterred such efforts.

In this respect, COST-ED Analysis prepares two computer reports that are useful in the formulation of rational negotiation arguments: 1) an Economic Factor Ranking and 2) a Custom Trade-Off Analysis.

The first of these, the Economic Factor Ranking (Table 1), provides visualization of the equal-cost trade-offs implied by a particular bargaining demand. This report presents a rank ordering of all key cost determinants within a school system with respect to their impact on total cost. It also presents ways by which each of these cost determinants (factors) could be changed

TABLE 1
National Average COST-ED Economic Factor Ranking–Education Turnkey Systems

Level: Elementary
Program: Academic

Rank of 25	Data Group	Cost Factor	Refer.	1% savings		Initial value		1% addl cost		Cost Impact Relation		Relative Power
				\multicolumn{6}{c}{Cost factor value for change in cost per student year}						
1	Instruction	Staff ratio	Teacher	27.9358	:1	27.3000	:1	26.6925	:1	Neg	Acc	100
2	Classroom tchr	Annual salary		8830.1758	$	9025.0000	$	9219.8203	$	Pos	Lin	95
3	Classroom	Peak use %		93.1856	%	100.0000	%	106.8144	%	Pos	Lin	30
4	Classroom	Raw unit rqmts		30.4779	Unit	33.070	Unit	35.5361	Unit	Pos	Lin	27
5	Classroom	Unit acq cost		18.9630	$	20.6100	$	22.2570	$	Pos	Lin	26
6	Student flow	Dropout rate		0.0631	%	1.0300	%	1.9799	%	Pos	Acc	22
7	Principal & staff	Annual salary		28700.0000	$	31673.6992	$	34647.3945	$	Pos	Lin	22
8	Classroom	Useful life		56.0187	Yrs	50.0000	Yrs	45.1495	Yrs	Neg	Acc	21
9	Classroom	Overhead %		54.6237	%	62.5450	%	70.4662	%	Pos	Lin	16
10	Classroom	Bond maturity		17.1317	Yrs	20.000	Yrs	22.8683	Yrs	Pos	Lin	14
11	Classroom	Interest rate		5.4307	%	6.3400	%	7.2492	%	Pos	Lin	14
12	Instruction	Plan. Factor	Teacher	0.1703		0.2005		0.2307		Pos	Lin	14
13	Classroom	Op cost/unit-day		0.0027	$	0.0033	$	0.0039	$	Pos	Lin	12
14	Classroom tchr	Fringe rate		6.3534	%	8.7000	%	11.0466	%	Pos	Lin	8
15	Classroom	Maint cost/$-yr		0.0122	$	0.0171	$	0.0220	$	Pos	Lin	7
16	Dist. admin. staff	Annual salary		42930.1797	$	61884.8398	$	80839.5000	$	Pos	Lin	7
17	Multipurpose rm	Raw unit rqmts		3.3389	Unit	5.8680	Unit	8.3971	Unit	Pos	Lin	5
18	Instruction	Other hour cost	Totals	0.0104	$	0.0199	$	0.0294	$	Pos	Lin	4
19	Principal's area	Raw unit rqmts		2.4830	Unit	5.0120	Unit	7.5410	Unit	Pos	Lin	4
20	Classroom furn.	Raw unit rqmts		22.6972	Unit	59.0800	Unit	95.4628	Unit	Pos	Lin	3
21	Instruction	Bk-av hour cost	Totals	0.0023	$	0.0118	$	0.0213	$	Pos	Lin	3
22	Instrctnl. Eqpt.	Raw unit rqmts		2.5948	Unit	18.9900	Unit	35.3851	Unit	Pos	Lin	2
23	Kitchen	Raw unit rqmts		Low		2.2670	Unit	4.7960	Unit	Pos	Lin	2
24	Kitchen	Useful life		High		50.0000	Yrs	15.4312	Yrs	Neg	Acc	1
25	Dist. Admin. area	Raw unit rqmts		Low		2.1500	Unit	6.7519	Unit	Pos	Lin	1

to cause a "1% saving" (lower cost) and a "1% additional cost." For example, in the school system described by Table 1, the student:teacher ratio (class size) in instruction is the most important (#1 ranked) determinant of total cost. If that class size were increased from its current "initial" system-wide average value of 27.3 students per class to 27.9358 students per class, total per-pupil costs would go down by 1%.

In a negotiating session, for example, an administrator with a fixed budgetary constraint could point out that an increase in the average annual teacher's salary (the second-ranked factor) from $9,025 to $9,219.82 would have to be offset by one of the following actions:

- an increase in class size (factor #1) from 27.3 to 27.9 students per class;
- a reduction in teacher planning time (factor #12) from .2005 hours per hour of instruction to .1703 hours per hour of instruction;
- a reduction in the money spent per day to keep the teacher's classroom lighted, heated, and cleaned (factor #13) from .33 cents per square foot to .27 cents per square foot. Operationally, this may take the form of less frequent sweeping;
- a reduction in the annual expenditures for books and audiovisual software (factor #21) from 1.18 cents per student-hour in instruction to .23 cents per student-hour in instruction;
- a reduction in the per-pupil investment in audiovisual equipment (factor #22) from $18.99 per student to $2.95 per student;

or some combination of these or other factors.

To amplify upon each of these equal-cost trade-offs, the COST-ED Model prepares Custom Trade-Off Analyses, such as the one shown in Table 2. Each Custom Trade-Off Analysis presents ten equal-cost alternatives based upon changes in selected factors. Equal cost alternative 6, for example, indicates that, in a school system with a fixed budgetary limit of $783.85 per pupil, a 2% increase in the average annual teacher's salary could force nearly a 75% reduction in expenditures per student-hour for books and audiovisual software. Furthermore, if, through hiring practices, the *average* annual teacher's salary could be reduced by 5% (equal cost alternative 4), it would be possible to increase spending on books and audiovisual software by over 186%, nearly a threefold increase.

TABLE 2
National Average COST-ED Custom
Trade-Off Analysis–Education Turnkey Systems

Level: Elementary
Program: Academic
Trade-off of: Classroom teacher annual salary
Against: Totals; bk-av hour cost instruction
Subject to: Totals; total cost/stu-yr = $783.85l8
Remaining Unchanged

	Classroom teacher annual salary		Totals bk-av hours cost instruction	Corresponding percentages of change from initial values
Initial Values:	$ 9025.0000	and	$0.0118	
Equal cost alternative 1:	4512.5000	and	0.2314	-50.0 and 1860.6
Equal cost alternative 2:	6768.7500	and	0.1216	-25.0 and 930.3
Equal cost alternative 3:	8122.5000	and	0.0557	-10.0 and 372.1
Equal cost alternative 4:	8573.7500	and	0.0338	-5.0 and 186.1
Equal cost alternative 5:	8844.5000	and	0.0206	-2.0 and 74.4
Equal cost alternative 6:	9205.4961	and	0.0030	2.0 and -74.4
Equal cost alternative 7:	9476.2461	and	Negative	5.0 and Low
Equal cost alternative 8:	9927.4961	and	Negative	10.0 and Low
Equal cost alternative 9:	11281.2500	and	Negative	25.0 and Low
Equal cost alternative 10:	13537.5000	and	Negative	50.0 and Low

In addition to serving as a persuasive tool at the bargaining table, COST-ED reports can be used to illustrate the thinking that influenced acceptance of particular alternatives, and thus serve as a means of convincing school board members of the soundness of the completed argument. Later, the reports can be used to show the taxpayers numerically the decisions and compromises that, of necessity, went into the school district budget. Decisions can be justified on the basis of the greatest good for the greatest number of students or similar grounds, rather than on the basis of someone's intuition.

Other COST-ED reports designed to verify data and describe the economic characteristics of an instructional program are also available and may be tangentially useful during negotiations. They each have a particular use and include: Cost Analysis Summary, a one-page digest of the key characteristics of a program; Client Data Listing, a review of all the factors and values that were used to construct a client's model; Program Cost Analysis, breakdown of total costs by function, resource type, and specific characteristics of each resource; Sensitivity Analysis, which illustrates how responsive the total cost per student-year is to changes in each subfactor or program facet; Custom Sensitivity Analysis, which shows how changes in one area affect requirements in any other economic factor or cost subtotal; and Program Comparison Summaries, which give summarized descriptions of several alternative programs for ready comparison.

Thus, COST-ED Analyses represents a blended method of systems analysis and cost accounting that can be useful to school districts and other public employment units. This economic tool can aid negotiations, help sell the contract to both sides, and later help sell the budget to the voters. It also provides an economic basis for the concept of accountability, which is currently in vogue. It must be remembered, however, that although COST-ED and similar systems are useful tools, they are no substitute for sound educational values, and they must be used in conjunction with an honest concern for the dignity and worth of all human beings involved in the learning situation.

An Experiment in Increasing Productivity of Police Service Employees

Paul D. Staudohar

The role of government has expanded to the level of employing nearly a fifth of the civilian labor force. Yet demands on government continue to increase, and key indicators such as crime, air pollution, and traffic congestion suggest that some services are not keeping pace with problems. Public employee wages are increasing rapidly and are likely to continue to do so in the future despite the much acclaimed taxpayer rebellion. In view of this gloomy prognosis, public policy is shifting toward emphasis on decreases, or at least reductions in the rate of increase, in costs of providing public service, while at the same time seeking to avoid a concomitant lowering in quality of service. This policy redirection is based on the premise that, with other things equal, a jurisdiction that raises rates of output per employee requires fewer employees to perform a given level of service, or can perform a higher service level with the same number of employees.

Increases in the crime rate, even in the face of a steady rise in numbers of police personnel, are of particular concern to the citizenry, and programs to increase police output are being given special attention. Costs of police service are high and climbing. Annual cost of placing an additional officer in a police car with a partner 24 hours a day has been estimated to exceed \$175,000.[1] Of encouragement, however, is that potential for improvement in performance of police service is significant, as illustrated by a study showing that total police expenditures varied by over a factor of four for cities of similar crime rate and size.[2] Approaches to productivity improvement that are being tried in police service include: (1) changes in technology, e.g., making more extensive

Reprinted from PUBLIC ADMINISTRATION REVIEW, (C) 1975 by The American Society for Public Administration, 1225 Connecticut Avenue, N.W., Washington, D.C. All rights reserved. Reprinted by permission of the author and publisher.

Paul D. Standohar is a Professor of Business Administration at California State University, Hayward.

use of computers to provide data on criminal records, missing persons, automobile thefts, and the like; (2) changes in organization, e.g., combining of police services in nearby communities to generate economies of scale, and rescheduling of work within an agency; and (3) increasing employee motivation, e.g, creating psychological incentives, through financial reward or job enrichment, which can increase individual or group output. With personnel accounting for about four-fifths of police costs in most jurisdictions, accent on optimizing human resource use is vital to attempts at increasing overall productivity of police departments.

This article examines an experiment in the third category above, involving an attempt to increase employee motivation through a group incentive plan. The plan is contained in a 1973 agreement between the City of Orange, California, and the City of Orange Police Association which provides for salary increases if there is a reduction in four crimes—rape, robberty, burglary, and auto theft—over periods of time set forth in the agreement. It is the first such agreement involving police in the nation, and its announcement received national publicity.[3] Discussed below are features of the incentive plan and an analysis of experience under it. Prior to this, however, it is appropriate to examine some of the unique problems presented by productivity measurement in the public sector in general and police service in particular. This is done to indicate certain measurement criteria in light of which the Orange incentive plan can be assessed.

THE MEASUREMENT PROBLEM

The National Commission on Productivity has identified two reasons for productivity of police being particularly hard to measure: (1) the basic data on crime statistics and police output are weak; and (2) the effect of police activity on deterrence of crime is difficult to determine.[4] To these it might be added that difficulty of measurement of police output is complicated by the need, in some instances, to relate it to overall output of a larger system of providing service.[5] This problem is illustrated by the measurement of police output whose overall effectiveness is a function of other components of the system of justice, such as the ultimate prosecution of apprehended criminals by the courts. Despite an increase in the number of arrests, the courts may be unable to process the extra load of cases, thereby negating the potential contribution to efficiency of the system of justice made by the police. Thus, to the extent that inputs and outputs of agencies within a system are related, it is useful to coordinate productivity efforts among them and to measure the output of each agency in terms of the overall effects on service.

Underlying the complexity of output measurement is the qualitative side of public service. It can be misleading to attribute improvements in operation of, for instance, public schools and sanitation service simply to larger numbers of pupils per class and tons of garbage collected. Despite a productivity improvement in quantitative terms, quality of education may be impaired if decreased personal attention by the instructor impedes student progress. Tons of garbage collected might increase at the same time more waste is strewn about and more noise made by the collection process. Complexity of estimation of output grows with the number of qualitative factors involved. Optimally, each qualitative factor should be isolated, have a weight assigned to it, and be indexed so that the factors will be additive to reflect a total result. Qualitative factors that might be considered in interpreting police productivity, as expressed in terms of say arrests or number of crimes reported, are reduction in response time, outcome of apprehended offenders' court cases, indication of citizen reactions to the propriety of various services provided, and overall feelings of citizen security.

Finally, local conditions should be considered in interpreting productivity data. Measurements can vary among jurisdictions on the basis of socioeconomic characteristics such as population density, median income, public attitudes toward certain crimes, and rate of unemployment. A degree of noncomparability may therefore exists in productivity data from jurisdictions that vary socioeconomically unless the data are adjusted to take account of this difference.

ORIGINS OF THE ORANGE PLAN

The City of Orange is a rapidly growing middleclass community located in the center of Orange County, a mile from Disneyland and 40 miles from Los Angeles. Population is estimated at 84,600 as of January 1, 1974, up from 77,000 in 1970. Of the city's labor force, three-fourths work in Orange County and one-fourth in Los Angeles County. Median family income of Orange residents as of January 1, 1974, was $16,682. Principal racial composition, according to the 1970 census, is about 87 per cent white and 11 per cent Spanish-American.

Following passage of the Meyers-Milias-Brown Act of 1968,

which provided for meeting and conferral by local government agencies with recognized employee organizations on matters of wages, hours, and other terms and conditions of employment, the City of Orange negotiated successive one-year agreements with the City of Orange Police Association in the spring of 1970, 1971, and 1972. During 1973 negotiations, in response to a proposed wage increase by the association, the city suggested the possibility of a police performance incentive plan.[6] The idea for the incentive plan was conceived by the city manager who had been trying to find a way to justify higher salaries for police without alienating taxpayers. He felt the police force was relatively well educated and capable. The average number of semester units of college and university work per policeman was about 75 units, and the crime rate in Orange was lower than in nearby cities.

The city manager discussed the types of crimes to be used in the plan with the police chief. In trying to determine which crimes might be used, the chief examined the seven "Part I" crimes designated by the Federal Bureau of Investigation, which include homicide, forcible rape, aggravated assault, robbery, burglary, larceny, and auto theft. The crimes of rape, robbery, burglary, and auto theft were chosen because they were felt to be "repressible" in that the police have more control over them. Homicide was thought to be essentially "nonrepressible" because it is a crime of passion usually occurring among family members. Larceny frequently involves theft within a business firm, while assault is a crime of passion often occurring spontaneously in or just outside bars; each of these crimes is less susceptible to police control.

THE AGREEMENT

The incentive plan became part of a two-year agreement between the city and police association reached on May 30, 1973. In the opinion of the city manager, "The high level of education and intelligence of the police personnel created the kind of environment that made negotiation of the incentive plan possible." Apart from the productivity incentive, salary increases were provided of 7.5 per cent in July 1973 and six per cent in July 1974. The pertinent sections of the agreement read:

> . . . (I)f the crime rate for rape, robbery, all burglaries (including burglary from auto), and auto theft are reduced by 3% for the period from July 1, 1973 to February 1, 1974, as compared to the same crimes for the period July 1, 1972, through June 30, 1973, an additional salary increase of 1% shall be granted effective March 1,

1974. Or, if the same crimes are reduced by 6% as compared to the base period, an additional salary increase of 2% shall be granted effective March 1, 1974. If the population increases in increments which exceed 1500 persons, these same comparisons shall be made and the percent reduction of crimes shall be computed on the number of these crimes per 1000 population. State Department of Finance population estimates shall be used for the computation of these population figures.

And, if the crime rate has been reduced 8% for a period of 20 consecutive months beginning July 1, 1973 as compared to the base period of July 1, 1972 through June 30, 1973, salaries shall be increased 1% on March 1, 1975. If the crime rate has been reduced 10%, salaries shall be increased 2%. If the crime rate has been reduced 12%, salaries shall be increased 3% on March 1, 1975. If the population increases in increments which exceed 1500 persons these same comparisons shall be made and the percent reduction of crimes shall be computed on the basis of the number of crimes per 1000 population.

Monitoring — Radio call slips, regardless of the source, which indicate that a police report is necessary, shall be given to the Watch Commander on duty, who shall place a copy of the call slip in a folder kept in the Watch Commander's office.

At the end of each watch, these call slips shall be compared to the reports submitted by the officers by the on-duty Watch Commander, who shall reconcile any differences.

Once every two weeks, a member of the City Manager's staff shall review the disposition of the call slips with the Administrative Captain as to accuracy and disposition. Each month, the number of cases which prove to be unfounded through investigation shall be subtracted from the total. This will be done according to the Manual on Uniform Crime Reporting, and shall coincide with the same statistical data submitted to the California Bureau of Criminal Statistics.

The Monthly Crime and Clearance Report indicates each month the number of offenses reported unfounded, and the number of actual offenses. Each month, these reports and the statistical data relating to the four repressible crimes shall be reviewed by the Chief of Police for accuracy.

Initially affected by the agreement were 113 sworn and 23 nonsworn police personnel through the rank of lieutenant.[7] (Although the bargaining unit covered by the agreement does not include sergeants or lieutenants, these groups were included in the incentive plan by the city).

EXPERIENCE UNDER THE AGREEMENT

On March 1, 1974, police in Orange earned a two per cent salary increase, which was the maximum possible in the first phase of the plan. Receiving the increase were 139 sworn and unsworn personnel. Computation of the increase was based on a comparison of the number of reported crimes per thousand population from the period July 1, 1972, to February 1, 1973, with data on reported crimes from July 1, 1973, to February 1, 1974. (The original agreement provides that the comparison period be July 1, 1972, to June 30, 1973, but the parties changed the comparison period to from July 1, 1972, to February 1, 1973.) In the first period there were 13.0364 reported crimes per thousand people, while in the second period the rate dropped to 10.739 per thousand. Based on these figures the decrease in reported crime was 17.62 per cent, well over the 6 per cent decrease required for the maximum salary hike. Interestingly, the reported incidence of robbery and auto theft actually went up, while rape and burglaries were down. Particularly influential was the decrease in burglaries, which account for about 80 per cent of the activity in the four categories, and which more than offset increases in reports of other crimes measured.

The average salary increase for employees covered by the agreement was approximately $21 per month. An informal understanding between the city and police association provides for a 15 per cent differential between certain job classifications. For example, a sergeant is paid 15 per cent more than a master patrolman, and a lieutenant is paid 15 per cent more than a sergeant. Since master patrolmen receive the two per cent salary increase due to their inclusion in the bargaining unit, sergeants' and lieutenants' wages were adjusted upward to maintain the differential. Salaries of captain and above, which are classifications involved in monitoring the incentive plan, were not affected.

Following the initial pay increase under the plan, the incidence of reported crimes continued down, but not by as much as during the first phase. On March 1, 1975, the plan ended with covered employees earning a three per cent pay increase, the maximum possible, for reducing the crime rate by 12.56 per cent over the plan's 20-month duration. This was barely over the 12 per cent decrease necessary to receive the maximum. As in the first phase, robbery and auto theft rose while rape and burglary dropped.

APPRAISAL OF RESULTS

To what can the apparent success in reducing numbers of reported target crimes in Orange be attributed? The plan's monetary incentive has had some affect in motivating police to be more effective. There appears to be a "Hawthorne effect" in existence, and employee morale is high. Credit also seems due to the department's Crime Prevention Bureau set up in 1973 in conjunction with the incentive plan. If a crime pattern begins to form, the bureau will inform those potentially involved of how to deal with the hazard. For example, if there is a burglary pattern at construction sites, the bureau will send a letter to building contractors making suggestions for minimizing losses. Victims of home burglaries are informed of how to prevent them in the future. Also, literature is sent to people in the community asking them to close their garage doors and keep cars locked. Officer teams of three are sent out to give talks to local groups on residential burglary, consumer fraud, self-defense for women, and gun safety. The idea is to get people thinking about preventing crime and to estabish a closer and more personalized relationship between police and the community through better communication. Not only does rapport between the police and citizenry appear to have improved, but police are talking to each other more. Because nearly everyone in the depàrtment benefits from a decrease in reported crime, they tend to cooperate more to get results. Between shifts, personnel who specialize in investigation of various types of crimes can be found in group discussions.

In addition to the bureau, a Special Enforcement Team was also established in conjunction with the incentive agreement. It consists of a sergeant and four patrol officers, and is designed to promote coordination in crime reduction efforts. The teams have been particularly successful in undercover work.

A critical examination of the incentive plan and experience under it shows that there has been an increase in the number of sworn police personel during the agreement. From the start of the plan to November 1974, sworn personnel went from 113 to 118, and remained at the higher level when the plan ended. The reduction in reported crimes may therefore be in part due to the increase in staff.

Another consideration is that reported crimes do not constitute the total number of crimes committed, since crimes go unreported because of a citizen's lack of confidence in the ability of the police department to solve the crime, alienation from police, or fear of being drawn into the net of an investigation. One way to find out about unreported crimes is to make a household survey to ask persons whether crimes committted against them were not reported. It could be that a higher or lower percentage of total crimes are being reported in Orange since introduction of the incentive plan. No information on unreported crimes was available, however. Nor were data tabulated on qualitative aspects of the incentive plan, such as citizen complaints or feelings of citizen security. The plan does not link reported crimes and their resolution by police to the broader system of criminal justice. However, greater complexity occurs when additional variables have to be factored in, and there is the advantage to simplicity, especially in a pioneering program, of engendering understanding by employees, administrators, and the public.

The watch commander plays a key role in monitoring the plan. Radio call slips indicating that a police report is necessary are given to him. At the end of the shift the watch commander on duty is to compare the slips with reports submitted by the officers. It is then the responsibility of the on-duty watch commander to reconcile any differences between slips and reports. A conflict of interest arises, because the watch commanders are covered by the incentive plan in that all personnel up through lieutenant get the same percentage pay adjustment whether in or out of the bargaining unit. While the watch commander's conflict of interest is probably more potential than real, it raises some doubt over the authenticity of the monitoring process.

It should be noted that the incidence of Part I crimes in Orange, other than the four target crimes, showed a substantial increase in numbers of reported occurrences during the first phase of the incentive plan. While homicide dropped, aggravated assault and larceny were up. Larceny is by far the largest single type of crime committed in Orange. Particularly due to the rise in larceny, the result of the comparison in the totals of reported Part I crimes of all types for the time period is that reported crimes have actually risen somewhat. However, because larceny is essentially a nonrepressible crime, and the rate of increase in reported larceny in nearby jurisdictions exeeded that in Orange during the period in question, the overall Part I figures can be discounted in terms of evaluating the results of the incentive plan.

CONCLUDING REMARKS

Experience with the police performance incentive plan in Orange indicates success in reducing the reported total of four target crimes. The results, however, are moderated by noting that although the total reported crime rate went down, individual rates for robbery and auto theft increased. Noteworthy too is that the crime figures are only for those crimes reported to the police, not for crimes which actually occurred. The potential weakness in the monitoring process points up the need for an external auditing of crime data to insure that conflicts of interest do not lead to spurious results.

Despite shortcomings, the Orange plan is an innovative experiment which will hopefully stimulate similar schemes in other cities. Future efforts should seek to refine and improve the model. There is no single best way to attempt to increase police productivity through a group incentive plan. Police departments differ from one another, as service emphasis, local environment, and the role a department seeks to play make what might work in one city an unwise choice in another. Dealing with an employee organization adds a further dimension, which may make it desirable to implement the creation of the plan through productivity bargaining, as in Orange. Perhaps a common denominator to such plans is that to implement them effectively will largely depend on successful community relations. There will likely have to be more emphasis on crime prevention. The results in Orange indicate that people, through the way they cooperate with the police, play a large role in determining the level of effectiveness of public safety in the community.

NOTES

1. *Opportunities for Improving Productivity in Police Services*, Report of the Advisory Group on Productivity in Law Enforcement (Washington, D.C.: National Commission on Productivity, 1973), p. 1.

2. *The Challenge of Productivity Diversity: Improving Local Government Productivity Measurement and Evaluation*, Part 1—Overall Summary and Conclusions, June 1972. Prepared for the National Commission on Productivity by the Urban Institute and the International City Management Association (Washington, D.C.: General Services Administration, 1973), p. 23.

3. *Wall Street Journal*, October 2, 1973, p. 1; *Business Week*, No 2312, January 4, 1974, p. 37; *Newsweek*, Vol. 83, No. 13, April 1, 1974, p. 69; and *Time*, Vol. 104, No. 12, September 16, 1974, p. 86.

4. *Second Annual Report of the National Commission on Productivity, March 1973* (Washington, D.C.: U.S. Government Printing Office, 1973), p. 48.

5. See Robert C. Lind and John P. Lipsky, "The Measurement of Police Output: Conceptual Issues and Alternative Approaches," *Law and Contemporary Problems*, Vol. 36, No. 4 (Autumn 1971), p. 569.

6. Negotiation of this type is known as "productivity bargaining," a ". . . process which seeks to treat production as a central collective

bargaining consideration and explicitly recognizes the trade off between measures to improve labor productivity and the sharing of resulting benefits."*First Annual Report of the National Commission on Productivity, March 1972* (Washington, D.C.: U.S. Government Printing Office, 1972), p. 9.

7. Nonsworn personnel include job categories of record clerk, secretary, police clerk, dispatcher, and clerk stenographer.

Determinants of Bargaining Outcomes in Local Government Labor Negotiations
Paul F. Gerhart

This paper analyzes a sample of 262 local government labor agreements to assess the impact of unions in the public sector. The agreements are used to construct an index of bargaining outcomes, and this index is related to a number of environmental characteristics through the concept of bargaining power. Estimates obtained in multiple regression equations indicate that union influence on bargaining outcomes depends on such factors as the size of the metropolitan area, the level of public sector strike activity, the international affiliation of the union, and the governmental function involved. In addition, the author finds that the inclusion of mandatory penalties in laws prohibiting

Reprinted with permission from the INDUSTRIAL AND LABOR RELATIONS REVIEW, Vol. 29, No. 3, pp. 331-351, April, 1976. (C) 1976 by Cornell University. All right reserved.

Paul F. Gerhart is Assistant Professor of Labor and Industrial Relations at the University of Illinois. This article is based on research initiated while he was a graduate research assistant working on The Brookings Institution Studies of Unionism in Government. He wishes to express his appreciation to the Ford Foundation, The Brookings Institution, and the Institute of Labor and Industrial Relations at the University of Illinois for their support of this research. In addition, the author wishes to thank John Burton, James Chelius, Milton Derber, and Walter Franke for their comments on earlier drafts of this paper.

strikes by public sector employees reduces union impact on bargaining outcomes, but that a no-strike policy without penalties has an impact that is not significantly different from that of common law prohibitions. Finally, public sympathy toward bargaining by municipal and county employees appears to be a better predictor of outcomes than the presence of a statute requiring bargaining by the employer.

It is easy to overemphasize the role of personal and accidental factors in collective bargaining. It is difficult to discern the persistent and underlying forces at work in the bargaining process. Yet the provisions of agreements—the policies agreed upon by unions and managements—fundamentally reflect the more enduring features of the environment of the collective bargaining relationship. This fundamental fact must be perceived or collective bargaining will appear capricious.[1]

Each collective bargaining relationship is unique, and therefore the labor agreement growing out of it is also likely to be unique. As Dunlop and others before him have realized, however, the uniqueness of the agreement is not a random event. This study attempts to develop a model that relates a number of the "features of the environment" to variations in bargaining outcomes in the local government sector and to determine empirically which of the features may have important impacts on bargaining outcomes.[2]

To assess the role and probable impact of unions in the public sector, other researchers have conducted numerous surveys, gathering information on union membership, representation rights, public sector collective bargaining laws, and similar features of the environment. In this study, an alternative and completely independent measure of union influence is developed—the outcome of bargaining as reflected in the collective agreement. It is clear, however, that the validity of both types of measures—the features of the environment and bargaining outcomes—is open to question. Thus, a study of the relationship outlined by Dunlop— between the environment surrounding collective bargaining and the provisions of the negotiated agreement—would be of some value. If there is a systematic relationship between the environmental features and bargaining outcomes, that relationship would be evidence for the validity of both of the measures. Further, such a study would indicate whether it would be possible to control bargaining outcomes through manipulation of certain features of the environment.

A MODEL

Bargaining power can be expressed as a set of ratios (taken from Chamberlain and Kuhn):[3]

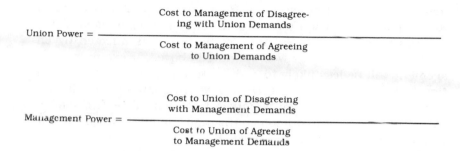

$$\text{Union Power} = \frac{\text{Cost to Management of Disagreeing with Union Demands}}{\text{Cost to Management of Agreeing to Union Demands}}$$

$$\text{Management Power} = \frac{\text{Cost to Union of Disagreeing with Management Demands}}{\text{Cost to Union of Agreeing to Management Demands}}$$

The concept of "cost" includes not only pecuniary but psychological and political costs as well, whether real or perceived, actual or anticipated. Differences in the environment may affect one or more of these costs. A state collective bargaining statute, for instance, probably reduces the political cost to management of agreeing to a demand for recognition by a majority union. Furthermore, the statute may require recognition after an election. Therefore, management's cost of continued disagreement is likely to be much higher in the presence of a statute since it risks "unfair practice" charges. Together, these changes raise the union power ratio. On the other hand, the effect of a statute is likely to be the opposite on the union's costs of agreeing and disagreeing. Therefore, the management power ratio is lowered and the net effect on the relative bargaining power of the parties shifts in favor of the union. Although this example is highly simplified, it illustrates how hypotheses can be generated using the Chamberlain cost ratios.[4]

Environmental factors can affect the costs of agreeing or disagreeing, and, hence, the relative power of the parties, either directly or indirectly. *Indirect* effects are those associated with specific issues, those in which unions attempt to negotiate a particular provision at a particular time because they see a connection between the provision and the immediate (or future) welfare of their members.[5] For instance, job security issues become of

interest when employment within the enterprise becomes un-
steady; work rules are needed when technology is changing. The
greater the level of interest in such issues, the more willing the
membership is to engage in activities to achieve specific union
demands. These activities, if effective, stand to increase the cost
to management of continuing to disagree and, perhaps, reduce
management's cost of agreeing. Hence, union power is in part a
function of the level of interest the union has in a particular issue.

Management's interest in specific issues is affected by environmental features, as well. As noted above, for example, management will be less likely to resist a union demand for recognition in a state where a collective bargaining law specifically provides for it. The path by which environmental features affect
bargaining power and outcomes through the interests of the parties is labeled "indirect" in Figure 1.

Direct effects of the environment on relative bargaining power
are unrelated to the interests of either party in specific issues.
The incidence of strikes in nearby jurisdictions, for example,
affects the credibility of a union threat to strike for job security,
work rules, or any other demand. Thus, the anticipated cost of
continued disagreement perceived by management is, *ceteris
paribus*, likely to be greater where strike incidence is higher.

FIGURE 1
*The Impact of Environmental
Features on Bargaining Outcomes*

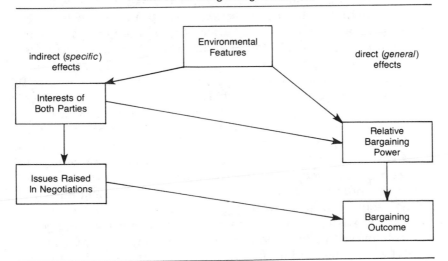

Summarizing, the features of the environment considered in this study are expected to influence bargaining outcomes either indirectly, through their effects on the interests of the parties in specific provisions, or directly through their impact on the relative power of the parties.[6]

Obviously, direct bargaining power can be used with respect to any issue in bargaining. Indirect power, however, may appear to be limited in its applicability to confrontations on the specific issue from which it is derived. The availability of indirect power would, however, reduce the quantity of direct power necessary to achieve union goals concerning that issue. Thus, the quantity of direct power available for use on *other* issues would be enhanced, and the overall bargaining outcome would be more favorable to the union. Assume, for instance, that the union possesses some stock of power assets derived in a direct fashion.[7] In the absence of a collective bargaining statute, some of these assets would have to be used to obtain recognition. With a bargaining statute, the relative bargaining power of the parties would be altered by a change in the level of interest management would have in the recognition issue. Direct power assets of the union, which would have been used to secure recognition, could now be used to alter other provisions of the bargaining outcome. Thus, environmental differences that alter the relative bargaining power of the parties, directly or indirectly, will alter the overall bargaining outcome, not simply limited aspects of it.

One final caveat is important. The model employed here is static, a limitation imposed by the cross-sectional data available for the study. Many interesting propositions involving feedback from the contract to relative bargainin power, of course, cannot therefore be tested. In addition, care must be used in interpreting the results since the direction of causality is not always as clear as the model suggests. Even with this shortcoming, however, research utilizing the static model will help to establish which environmental features are worthy of incorporation in a more complex model. At this exploratory stage it would be inappropriate to discard potential variables arbitrarily, but it will become evident below that future research along these lines will profit by a reduction in the number of variables investigated.

THE BARGAINING OUTCOME

A major task in this study has been the development of an operational definition of bargaining outcomes that can be linked to a

theoretical model. Chamberlain indicates that "union penetration of managerial areas [can be measured] . . . by seeking to
establish the number of areas where unions now share . . .
decision-making power and by attempting to estimate the importance of their share. . . ."[8] The definition of bargaining outcomes adopted for this study involves a listing of issues present in
the agreement as well as a measure of how each issue is resolved
in the agreement.[9] Margaret Chandler used a similar approach to
define management rights and Kochan and Wheeler also incorporated both aspects into their measurement of bargaining outcomes.[10] This definition is necessary for two interrelated reasons.
First, union influence (which is what the bargaining outcome
purports to measure) can be increased either through greater
union influence on the same number of issues or through an
expansion of the number of issues over which the union exercises
influence. Second, tradeoffs between the two dimensions occur in
the bargaining process. Management's willingness to increase
wages in order to buy out restrictive work practices is one example of such a tradeoff.

Another problem in operationalizing the bargaining outcomes concept is obtaining a valid measure of it. The written
agreement is the only practical measure available to researchers
on a scale necessary for statistical analysis, but practitioners are
aware that the formal bargaining outcome in the written agreement can be substantially different from the real outcome—the
range of issues over which the union has significant influence.[11]
An extensive discussion of this problem is beyond the scope of
this paper. It is safe to assume, however, for this particular sample of agreements that the formal bargaining outcomes *are* a valid
measure of the real outcomes.[12] In similar analyses using different
sets of data, this problem should be carefully considered.

Quantifying the bargaining agreement by reducing it to a
single index number appears to require assumptions about the
relative values—or weights—that negotiators attach to particular
issues and their resolution.[13] For a particular negotiator, such a
set of values does exist and presumably could be discovered. To
extend the same value structure across a group of negotiators in
different environments, however, would require rather heroic,
and probably incorrect, assumptions.

The solution to the weighting problem used here, which is
based on a statistical theorem set forth by S. S. Wilks,[14] is identical to the solution applied by Stalnaker to the problem of appropriate weights for questions on students' examinations.

In the usual testing situation we have a series of correlated item or part scores, X_1, X_2, X_3, . . . X_n, which are combined in some linear fashion to get a total score. We might say S _ k_1X_1 ° k_2X_3 ° k_3X_3 . . . ° k_nX_n, where the weighting factors are expressed by k. It can be shown mathematically that as n becomes larger the k's may take on almost any values, within reasonable limits, and the correlation between two sets of scores obtained by the use of different values for the k's becomes perfect. The relative order of the individuals tested bcomes invariant for different weights as n becomes large. The more interrelated the items are, that is the more narrow and homogeneous the field being tested, the smaller n can be and still maintain a given high correlation. Generally speaking, when items on a restricted subject-matter test number around one hundred, the use of weighting factors, regardless of how they are arrived at, is rarely of any practical significance.[15]

In this study, 158 items from the agreements were analyzed—a number sufficiently large to make Wilks's theorem operative.[16] An outline of the contract items analyzed appears in the Appendix. Points were assigned to a particular contract clause from a union negotiator's perspective in such a way that the greater the penetration of the management prerogative, the greater the number of points assigned. The sum of the points for a particular agreement is the contract index (CI).[17] The formula for scoring the agreements allowed for a maximum CI (the ideal contract from the union point of view) of 100 points. The CI scores used in this analysis have a mean of 33, a range of 6 to 55, and a median of 35. The distribution meets a chi-square test for normality at the .05 level.

SAMPLE, ANALYSIS, AND RESULTS

A random sample of 262 agreements covering nearly all functions and occupations found in local government was analyzed. (Teacher and transit agreements were excluded.)[18] The agreements were initially negotiated by affiliates of the American Federation of State, County, and Municipal Employees (AFSCME); Service Employees (SEIU); Laborers (LIU); and Teamsters (IBT) between 1962 and 1968 and all remained in effect during 1968 when this sample was selected. The research departments of these unions, at that time, maintained files of current agreements and after an exhaustive search conducted in connection with the Brookings Studies of Unionism in Government, it was concluded that affiliates of these four unions had negotiated all

TABLE 1
Features of the Environment
and the Bargaining Unit

Independent Variables	Frequency [a]

1. Employer type

COUNTY	= 1	where unit consists of county employees	43
SCHLDIST	= 1	where unit consists of nonprofessional school employees	68
SPLDIST	= 1	where unit consists of special district employees	19

Base: units consisting of city employees [b]   132

2. Bargaining unit size

MEDSIZE	= 1	where the unit has 25 to 100 employees	118
LARGSIZE	= 1	where the unit has over 100 employees	63

Base: unit under 25 employees   67

3. Employer size

LOGPOP   natural log of the population of the jurisdiction   cont

4. Metropolitan area size

SMSASMLL	= 1	where SMSA is under 500,000	50
SMSALARG	= 1	where SMSA is 500,000 or more	110

Base: jurisdictions not within an SMSA   102

5. Age of bargaining relationship (years elapsed since first contract)

YOUNGREL	= 1	where relationship is under 3 years old	55
OLDREL	= 1	where relationship is over 10 years old	50

Base: First agreement was negotiated 3-10 years before current agreement   143

6. Governmental function

		where *majority* of unit employees work in	where *minority* of unit employees work in	
HWYMAJ	= 1	highways and streets		36
HWYMIN	= 1		highways and streets	54
HSPMAJ	= 1	1 hospitals		5
HSPMIN	= 1		hospitals	1
HLMAJ	= 1	health		2
HLMIN	= 1		health	10
POLMAJ	= 1	police		7
POLMIN	= 1		police	17
SEWMAJ	= 1	sewage		3
SEWMIN	= 1		sewage	57
SANMAJ	= 1	sanitation		10
SANMIN	= 1		sanitation	41
HSEMAJ	= 1	housing		5
HSEMIN	= 1		housing	6
WRTMAJ	= 1	water		8
WRTMIN	= 1		water	36
UTLMAJ	= 1	utilities		3
UTLMIN	= 1		utilities	23
WLFMIN	= 1		welfare	8
FIRMIN	= 1		fire	17
PKSMIN	= 1		parks	62
AIRMIN	= 1		airports	9
ADMMIN	= 1		administration	13
NATMIN	= 1		natural resources	14
CORMIN	= 1		corrections	6
LIBMIN	= 1		libraries	9

Base: education, nonprofessional employees

7. Statutory bargaining obligation

BARGLAW	= 1	"mandatory" law at time of negotiations	129
CONFLAW	= 1	"meet and confer" law at time of negotiations	22
BARGENV	= 1	"mandatory" law effective by 1971	170
CONFENV	= 1	"meet and confer" law effective by 1971	26

Base: no law regarding bargaining had been passed   66

TABLE 1
Features of the Environment and the Bargaining Unit

	Independent Variables	Frequency [a]
8. Anti-strike legislation		
NOSTRLAW = 1	statute prohibits strikes; penalties *not* prescribed	99
STRIKPEN = 1	statute prohibits strikes; penalties *are* prescribed	54
Base: strike policy based on common law		109
9. Bargaining structure		
OCCUPTNL = 1	where the unit comprises a narrow occupational group	57
DEPT = 1	where the unit comprises most jobs within a department	79
Base: comprehensive units comprising most job classes of the employer		126
10. Form of government [c]		
MANAGER = 1	where council-manager form of government is used	35
11. Civil service		
CIVILSER = 1	where a civil service commission exists	37
12. Management negotiator		
COUNCNEG = 1	where elected council or board members participate	137
13. Union political activity		
POLSUCC = 1	where union supported with endorsements, funds, or manpower a majority of incumbent elected council or board members	74
POLFAIL = 1	where union supported opponents of majority of incumbents	39
Base: where union supported no one for majority of council or board seats		48
14. International union affiliation		
SEIU = 1	where local is Service Employees affiliate	39
LIU = 1	where local is Laborers' affiliate	35
IBT = 1	where local is Teamsters affiliate	55
Base: where local is AFSCME affiliate		133
15. Per capita revenue [c]		
REVENUE = 1	per capita revenue of the employer	cont
16. Unionization ratio		
UZLOW = 1	where proportion of the unit unionized is under 65 percent	16
UZMED = 1	where propostion of the unit unionized is 65-90 percent	68
17. State strike activity index		
STRIKACT	total nonfederal public employee strikes 1965-68 standardized for total nonfederal employees	cont
18. Pattern variable		
STATENDX	mean contract index for all *other* agreements within the same state that were analyzed for this study	cont

a Frequency indicates the number of times the variable was equal to 1. May not sum to 262 because of missing data. "Cont" indicates variable was continuous.
b Choice of base category was arbitrary. The base is indicated only where it is not obvious.
c Data available for cities only.
Sources (listed by variable number):
1. Labor agreement.
2. Union and management questionnaires.
3. Derived from U.S. Bureau of the Census, *Census of Population: 1960, Subject Reports, Characteristics of the Population* (Washington, D.C.: G.P.O., 1960).
4. Ibid.
5. Union and management questionnaires.
6. Labor agreement and management questionnaire.
7. Derived from Bureau of National Affairs, *Labor Relations Reporter, State Labor Laws*.
8. Ibid.
9. Management questionnaire and labor agreement.
10. *1967 Municipal Yearbook* (Washington, D.C.: International City Management Association, 1967). pp. 164-89.
11. *1966 Municipal Yearbook* (Washington, D.C.: International City Management Association, 1966). pp. 98-155, and management questionnaire.
12. Management questionnaire.
13. Union questionnaire.
14. Labor agreement.
15. Derived from U.S. Bureau of the Census, *1967 Census of Governments* (Washington, D.C.: G.P.O., 1967).
16. Union and management questionnaires.
17. Based on Bureau of Labor Statistics strike files analyzed by Charles Krider in connection with the Brookings Institution's Studies of Unionism in Government.

but a handful of the agreements then in existence in the local government sector excluding teacher and transit agreements.[19]

Table 1 lists eighteen features of the environment or the bargaining unit that were expected to have some impact on the relative bargaining power of the parties. In carrying out this study, hypotheses with respect to each of these variables were developed using the model above. These specific hypotheses have been omitted from this paper for brevity.[20] Table 1 also contains definitions of the variables as well as the frequencies with which specific categories of the variables were encountered. Fourteen of the features were measured using sets of dummy variables after the fashion described by Suits because most of them were of a nominal or ordinal nature.[21] For those that were intrinsically continuous, such as SMSA size, the use of dummy variable sets was appropriate because a linear relationship between the variable (or any simple transformation of it) was not anticipated. The problem that resulted from using sets of variables to represent environmental features was a large number of discrete variables (fifty-seven). Even though there were few high correlations among these variables, the sheer number of variables suggested that multicollinearity might be a problem. Thus, a straightforward regression of all eighteen variables on CI simultaneously seemed unlikely to be fruitful and, instead, three separate steps were used in the analysis.

The variables were classified as exogeneous (#1-6), controllable (#7-14), and endogenous (#15-18).

Exogenous Variables. The first six variables were labeled exogenous because there was no a priori reason to believe they were influenced by any of the other twelve variables. The results from the regression containing only these six variables (Equation 1) appear in Table 2.

It was anticipated that the CI would be correlated positively with *metropolitan area size* (#4) because of a greater tolerance for unions in these areas. In this case, the cost to management of continued disagreement would be greater. Table 2 shows that, as anticipated, the CI was 5.36 points higher on the average in small SMSAs than in jurisdictions outside SMSAs. Contrary to the hypothesis, however, the mean CI for this sample was even lower in large SMSAs than in non-SMSA jurisdictions. Perhaps increases in metropolitan area size beyond some critical point lead the employer to become substantially more sophisticated or cause

TABLE 2
Regression of Exogenous Variables
on Bargaining Outcome (Equation 1)

Variable [a]	Coefficient	Standard Error	Beta Coefficient	t-Value	Overall F Ratio	F for Significance at .05 Level
1. Employer type					0.09	2.65
COUNTY	-0.94	2.19	-0.03	-0.43		
SCHLDIST	-0.67	2.24	-0.02	-0.30		
SPLDIST	0.41	3.01	0.01	0.14		
2. Bargaining unit size					0.71	3.04
MEDSIZE	1.33	1.64	0.06	0.82		
LARGSIZE	2.69	2.20	0.11	1.23		
3. Employer size					3.58	3.89
LOGPOP	-1.06	0.56	-0.15	-1.89		
4. Metropolitan area size					9.28*	3.04
SMSASMLL	5.36	1.89	0.20	2.84*		
SMSALARG	-2.27	1.55	-0.11	-1.46		
5. Age of bargaining relationship					0.35	3.04
YOUNGREL	-0.81	1.56	-0.03	-0.53		
OLDREL	-1.24	1.64	-0.04	-0.76		
6. Governmental function					1.76*	1.56
HWYMAJ	2.02	2.69	0.06	0.75		
HSPMAJ	3.84	4.78	0.05	0.80		
HLMAJ	-18.97	7.33	0.16	2.54*		
POLMAJ	-5.59	4.06	-0.08	-1.38		
SEWMAJ	17.46	6.01	0.18	2.91*		
SANMAJ	-1.34	3.73	-0.02	-0.36		
HSEMAJ	-9.56	5.43	-0.12	-1.76		
WTRMAJ	0.43	4.09	0.00	0.10		
UTLMAJ	2.96	5.75	0.03	0.52		
HWYMIN	2.19	2.58	0.08	0.85		
HSPMIN	-8.88	9.79	-0.05	-0.91		
POLMIN	-0.79	2.92	-0.01	-0.27		
SEWMIN	2.74	2.97	0.10	0.93		
SANMIN	-2.83	2.94	-0.09	-0.96		
HLMIN	2.46	3.80	0.04	0.65		
HSEMIN	12.48	5.12	0.18	2.44*		
UTLMIN	-0.11	3.11	-0.00	-0.03		
WTRMIN	0.66	3.39	0.02	0.20		
WLFMIN	7.56	4.49	0.12	1.68		
FIRMIN	-4.63	3.32	-0.11	-1.40		
PKSMIN	-0.07	2.03	-0.00	-0.14		
AIRMIN	0.77	4.18	0.01	0.19		
ADMMIN	-6.22	3.37	-0.13	-1.85		
NATMIN	1.38	3.14	0.03	0.45		
CORMIN	-5.69	5.13	-0.08	-1.11		
LIBMIN	2.37	3.60	0.04	0.66		

a Definitions of variables appear in Table 1.

* Significant at the .05 level.

the bargaining relationship to become more political. Employer sophistication implies greater relative power; a more political relationship implies that a wider range of issues will be handled informally, outside the contract negotiation process.

The hypothesis with respect to *employer size* (#3) was similar: a positive correlation with CI was anticipated not only because of a greater tolerance for unions in big cities but also because thee is greater "organizational distance" between negotiators and administrators in larger employers. Hence, it was expected that both parties would have a greater interest in formalizing the agreement. The opposite result was obtained: the larger the employer, the lower the CI. Although the coefficient was not significant at the .05 level, its size relative to its standard error strongly suggests that the relationship found here was not due to sampling error.[22]

The other variable in the exogenous group that contributes to explaining the variance of CI is *governmental function* (#6). Any particular function of government (such as streets, sanitation, hospitals) has common characteristics across different public employers that are important in determining the needs, interests, and goals of individual workers. The nature of the work, work location and conditions, occupations of the workers, skill levels, education and professional interests, closeness of supervision, and "essentiality of service" to the public are examples of such characteristics that may lead to systematic differences in bargaining outcomes.

Table 2 shows that the governmental-function set was significantly and consistently useful in helping to explain variations in the CI. A consideration of the individual coefficients, however, is beyond the scope of this paper.[23] *Ex post* it is noteworthy that the coefficient of SEWMAJ (units where sewage workers comprise a majority of the bargaining unit) is so substantial. In light of the 1965 Milwaukee Sewerage District strike as well as the more recent San Francisco city employee strike (1974), sewer workers may have been overlooked as one of the most powerful public employee groups. The effects of their strikes can be immediate and substantial. The increasing concern over pollution adds to the political dimension of a threatened sewage strike.

Bargaining units size (#2) probably affects the availability and usefulness of alternative informal channels to resolve potential collective bargaining issues. Furthermore, the larger the bargaining unit, the greater the costs it might be able to impose on management in the event of continued disagreement. Of course, the cost to management of agreeing would also be greater, particularly with regard to economic issues. The hypothesis was that, on balance, larger units would negotiate higher CI scores. The coefficients had the anticipated sign and pattern but were not significant.

Four *employer types* (#1) are included in this study—cities, counties, school districts, and special districts. (Only blue-collar employees are included for school districts.) These employer types differ from one another (1) in the extent to which authority to make personnel decisions is diffused; (2) in the way in which managers obtain their positions—election or appointment; and (3) in the political importance attached to elective positions in the governmental units.

Unions should be most powerful vis-a-vis city officials because (1) city government tends to be centralized; (2) the executive, or at least the legislative, officials are elected; and (3) elective positions in city government are likely to be steps in a political career. Counties, special districts, and school boards are relatively more powerful vis-a-vis unions than are cities, because one or more of these attributes does not apply.

Employer type is highly correlated with the governmental function variables so that it is not statistically important in any equations where the function variables are included. Whether the employer is a city, county, or district may therefore be more important than the statistical results imply. Do sewer workers, for example, achieve better agreements because they are sewer workers or because they are often employed by special districts? A clearer understanding of the institutional relationships would be necessary to answer this question.

Finally, *the age of the bargaining relationship* (#5) was expected to be correlated positively with the CI; but no relationship was found. This result is consistent with the findings of Kochan and Wheeler.[24]

Controllable Variables. Equation 2 was developed by retaining the significant exogenous variable sets[25] and adding the controllable variables—those determined directly by public policy makers, unions, or employers. These results are listed in Table 3.

As discussed in preceding examples, a *statutory bargaining obligation* (#7) on public employers was expected to enhance union power and the contract index. The hypothesis was correct; the average effect of such a law in this sample was to raise the CI by nearly six points. This finding is consistent with the Kochan and Wheeler results.[26] As anticipated, a law requiring only that the employer "meet and confer" had a much smaller effect, which was not statistically significant. (The inference that the statute has the effect implied here will be questioned below, however, in connection with Equations 4 and 5.)

Anti-strike legislation (#8) was expected to lower the cost to management of continued disagreement because, presumably, such legislation inhibits public employee strikes, at least at the margin. At the time the data for this study were collected, public employee strikes were legally prohibited in all the jurisdictions investigated. In some state, the prohibition was based on common law interpretation; in others, it was based on specific statutory provisions. For analytical purposes, I have distinguished

TABLE 3
Regression of Controllable and Significant Exogenous Variables on Bargaining Outcome (Equation 2)

Variable [a]	Coefficient	Standard Error	Beta Coefficient	t-Value	Overall F Ratio	F for Significance at .05 Level
4. SMSA size	b				5.19*	3.04
6. Governmental function	b				2.36*	1.56
7. Statutory bargaining obligation					4.11*	3.04
CONFLAW	1.08	2.31	0.03	0.47		
BARGLAW	5.86	2.06	0.29	2.83*		
8. Anti-strike legislation					2.88	3.04
NOSTRLAW	1.27	2.10	0.06	0.60		
STRIKPEN	-3.75	1.69	-0.15	-2.22*		
9. Bargaining structure					2.30	3.04
OCCUPTNL	-3.17	1.55	-0.13	-2.03*		
DEPT	-1.88	1.40	-0.08	-1.36		
10. Form of government					0.54	3.89
MANAGER	-1.46	1.89	-0.04	-0.77		
11. Civil service					2.30	3.89
CIVILSER	-4.08	2.69	-0.08	-1.52		
12. Management negotiator					0.83	3.89
COUNCNEG	-1.22	1.34	-0.05	-0.95		
13. Union political activity					2.39	3.04
POLSUCC	-0.04	1.64	-0.00	-0.00		
POLFAIL	-3.77	1.98	-0.12	-1.91		
14. International affiliation					4.93*	2.65
SEIU	-0.83	1.85	-0.03	-0.45		
LIU	-7.16	1.88	-0.24	-3.82*		
IBT	-0.83	1.44	-0.03	-0.53		

a Definitions of variables appear in Table 1.
b Individual variable coefficients omitted for brevity. All individual variables are included in the equation, however.
* Significant at the .05 level.

three types of anti-strike policy: common law, statutory prohibition without specified penalties for violations, and statutory provisions that include automatic penalties for violation (such as the Ohio Ferguson Act).

The results in Table 3 show that the statutes with automatic penalties against strikers or their unions (STRIKPEN) have a depressing effect on union power. There is no significant difference, however, between states with no-strike laws without specific statutory penalties (NOSTRLAW) and states that rely on common law to outlaw strikes. Where legislation is being considered, then, it should make little difference to union or management proponents whether the statute specifically prohibits strikes or not. What is critical is whether penalties for engaging in strikes are explicit. The additional bargaining power that a bargaining statute gives to unions is substantially reduced by a no-strike statute with penalties. (Compare the coefficient on STRIKPEN and BARGLAW in Table 3.) Thus, unions in states with no statutes regarding bargaining or strikes are nearly as well off as unions in states with bargaining laws and statutory strike penalties. Both groups are better off than unions in states with meet-and-confer laws coupled with strike penalties.

A priori, hypotheses regarding the relationship between *international union affiliation* (#14) and the CI are not obvious. Several distinct differences among the international unions in the sample, however, may be reflected in bargaining outcomes. The American Federation of State, County, and Municipal Employees (AFSCME) is almost wholly a public employees' union with only a small number of members employed by private employers. The other three unions—Service Employees, Laborers, and Teamsters—primarily represent employees in the private sector. Private sector craft unions, particularly the building trades with which both the Teamsters' and Laborers' locals are usually closely allied, have historically enjoyed close political connections with local public officials. If the political connections were established outside the framework of collective bargaining, however, one would perhaps expect to find a smaller *formal* bargaining outcome. Coefficients on the three private sector unions would therefore be expected to be negative.

The results show there are no significant differences between the CI of agreements negotiated by AFSCME, the SEIU, or the Teamsters, but that the mean CI of the Laborers' locals is substantially and significantly below these three. Further research into the institutional orientations of the four unions, the Laborers in particular, would be necessary to determine why this pattern exists.

Bargaining structure (#9) may vary from a single occupational class of employees in a single department to a comprehensive unit of all employees of the local governmental body. In practice, the comprehensive unit is rare in the public sector, since white-collar employees and uniformed forces—police and fire—are nearly always excluded. The three principal types of structure observed in this study were the intradepartmental *occupational* unit, *departmental* units comprised of all blue-collar employees within a single department, and *comprehensive* units covering nearly all classes of blue-collar employees in all departments.

It was observed in connection with the Brookings Studies of Unionism in Government that a united comprehensive unit of public employees, such as the AFSCME Council 33 in Philadelphia has considerably more political impact than fragmented occupational or departmental units such as those in St. Louis and Cleveland. Principally on the basis of these observations, it was hypothesized that comprehensive units would achieve higher CI scores than occupational units, with departmental units falling between them.[27] The results in Table 3 show that the coefficients on bargaining unit structure (OCCUPTNL and DEPT) have the predicted relative size and sign but are not significant as a group. (OCCUPTNL is significant in Equation 2 but loses significance in other formulations of the model.) It was discovered in equations not presented here, which omit the governmental function variable, that the unit structure variable is important. Thus it seems clear that the lack of significance in this equation is due, for the most part, to the correlation of unit structure with the governmental function variables. If the assumption that unit structure is principally determined by the function of government is correct, then unit structure, by itself, does not contribute to an explanation of differences in the CI.

The most obvious proposition regarding the impact of *union political activity* (#13) is that a union that is successful in electing its friends will reap the benefits in a more favorable bargaining outcome. An alternative proposition is that the politically successful union will negotiate very limited formal agreements because of the availability of informal channels of influence with public officials. Although Local 46 of the Service Employees International Union has probably organized more Chicago city employees than any other single union, for example, it has never negotiated a written agreement with the city.

The data, however, suggest that political activity by a local union does not enhance its bargaining power, and, furthermore, that such activity can be harmful if the supported candidates lose.[28] In Equation 2, POLFAIL (political support for candidates who lost) has the predicted sign but is not statistically significant at the .05 level. (In other equations not reported here, the coefficient is stable and sometimes significant.) A union policy of backing only "sure winners" or of remaining neutral in elections appears to be wise.

This finding is not completely compatible with the Kochan and Wheeler conclusion that candidate endorsement may be associated with a more favorable bargaining outcome. Since neither their data nor the statistical results presented here strongly support our varying conclusions (the Kochan-Wheeler coefficient was not significant in the final analysis, either), the different results may be due simply to sampling error. On the other hand, there may be a real difference in the effect of political activity conducted by firefighters (the group to which the Kochan-Wheeler study was limited) and local government employees, generally.

The principal impact *civil service* (#11) can have on the scope of bargaining is through its power to limit the discretion of the management negotiator by exercising its own prerogatives. If a civil service system exists and if a legislative body has given it the prerogatives to set wages, hire, allocate jobs, adjudicate discipline cases, and determine fringe benefits, there is little left for the union and management negotiators to discuss. However, not all civil service commissions have such broad powers, and not all commissions who have such powers exercise them independently.

The results indicate the existence of a civil service commission tends to be associated with a smaller CI. Although the coefficient is not significant in Equation 2, there, and in other equations not reported here, it is consistently large in the predicted direction.[29]

Form of government (#10) was expected to show that council-manager governments yield a more favorable bargaining outcome, for both structural and procedural reasons because they foster the formal centralization of power within a city and this, in turn, promotes more formal procedures in all types of city business, including labor relations. "Buck passing," common in decentralized governments, is more difficult and less likely. Furthermore, in a machine style environment (usually associated with nonmanager forms of government) the union attempt to change a system of operation from one of informal understandings to one including formal written agreements might require more power than most unions in such environments wield.

The results do not support this hypothesis. That is, there is a slight tendency for the CI to be *lower* in council-manager forms of goverment than in other forms. (Only cities and counties were used in the analysis of this variable.) A possible explanation was provided by Kochan and Wheeler whose results were compatible with these: greater dispersion of power among local officials in a given unit of government provides more opportunities for the union to play one interest off against another. In neither the Kochan-Wheeler study nor this one, however, was the coefficient significant, and so the importance of the variable is probably not great.

The *management negotiator* (#12) can be part of the executive or legislative branches of a government unit. It was anticipated that if the legislature or policy-making body were directly involved, a more favorable bargaining outcome would result, partly because the part-time, amateur character of the individuals serving on legislative-policy boards leaves them less skilled as labor negotiators than full-time professional executives and partly because the discretion to agree with union proposals is greater.

The results indicate, however, that the involvement of the policy body (COUNCNEG) does not have an effect on the scope of bargaining. The coefficient is actually negative for this sample (although not significant) indicating that on the average such participation actually lowered the CI. This finding is contrary to the Kochan-Wheeler finding that council participation enhances bargaining outcomes significantly. Perhaps, again, there is a difference, related to local government politics, between the effect of council involvement on firefighters and on other city employees.

Endogenous Variables. The last four variables added (Equation 3) may be, in part, determined by some of the preceding variables; furthermore, the direction of cause between these variables and CI is less clear than for the preceding variables. Hence, conclusions regarding the extent to which these variables *determine* bargaining outcomes can be defended with less vigor. The relationship between each of these variables and CI is, however, definitely of interest and will be considered, but the precise formulation of the relationships among the variables will be left to future research.

The *unionization ratio* (#16) was used as a proxy for the

support given to the union by the employees in the bargaining unit. A positive correlation with the CI was anticipated, but, as Table 4 shows, the relationship is virtually nonexistent. Others have had mixed results with the variable; so its performance here was not surprising.[30]

The bargaining *pattern* (#18), *strike activity* (#17), and the *per capita revenue* (#15) are three closely related variables that, together, are of considerable importance in Equation 3. The multi-collinearity among these variables makes it impossible to determine, using statistical tools alone, which of the three is the most important, however. As anticipated, each of the three is positively correlated with CI. Alone, each is significant and statistically important, but when combinations of the variables appear together, their coefficients are unstable. In the equation reported here, the pattern variable appears most important. Strike activity has the expected sign but is insignificant in the presence of the variables representing statutory bargaining obligation. (Simple *r* for STRIKACT and BARGLAW is .29; for STRIKACT and CON-

TABLE 4

Regression of Endogenous and Significant Exogenous
and Controllable Variables on
Bargaining Outcome (Equation 3)

Variable [a]	Coefficient	Standard Error	Beta Coefficient	t-Value	Overall F Ratio	F for Significance at .05 Level
4. SMSA size	b				4.86*	3.04
6. Governmental function	b				2.75*	1.56
7. Statutory bargaining obligation	b				2.68	3.04
8. Anti-strike legislation					2.00	3.89
STRIKPEN	-2.42	1.71	-0.10	-1.42		
14. International union affiliation	b				5.21*	2.65
15. Percapita revenue					0.22	3.89
REVENUE	0.048	0.101	0.03	0.48		
16. Unionization ratio					0.05	3.04
UZLOW	-0.46	2.28	-0.01	-0.20		
UZMED	0.25	1.30	0.01	0.19		
17. State strike activity					1.40	3.89
STRIKACT	2.57	2.17	0.08	1.18		
218. Pattern					6.28*	3.89
STATENDX	0.362	0.145	0.20	2.50*		

a Definitions of variables appear in Table 1.

b Individual variable coefficients omitted for brevity.

* Significant at the .05 level.

FLAW r is -.35.) In equations not presented here, REVENUE is important in the absence of the statutory bargaining obligation and pattern variable (r for REVENUE and BARGLAW is .35). Whether the apparent importance of REVENUE is spurious or not depends on how one conceptualizes the model. It is possible that statutory bargaining obligations and bargaining patterns are a function of how much revenue is available, that is that bargaining and a larger CI occur when the public can afford them. Alternatively, it may be that REVENUE is raised to meet already negotiated commitments. If the latter is true, REVENUE should be viewed as an effect rather than a cause of a larger CI.[31]

PUBLIC POLICY ENVIRONMENT

The close relationship among these variables and the statutory bargaining obligation suggests that there may be some underlying factor, such as public tolerance or sympathy for public sector collective bargaining, which all these variables reflect. Kochan and Wheeler attempted to measure this concept (which they considered part of the "political environment") by incorporating in their analysis the percent voting Democratic in the jurisdiction, but they found the variable to have little value. Here, an alternative variable was inserted in an effort to measure voter sympathy. It purports to measure what the voters or legislature think the law *should* be rather than what the law is. The label "public policy environment" is used to distinguish the concept from public policy as evidenced in existing statutes. The presumption is that a statute reflects what the public wants with respect to public policy, but generally lags behind the public will by some interval. Thus, it was anticipated that a measure of voter sympathy at the time of negotiations could be obtained by observing the law within that jurisdiction some period *after* the actual negotiations had been completed. A new set of policy environment variables (CONFENV, BARGENV) was created on the grounds that they would more accurately reflect the influence of voter sympathy on the bargaining process than the legislation in existence during negotiations (CONFLAW, BARGLAW). The new set measures the state statutes in existence in 1971.[32]

Table 5 presents the results of Equations 4 and 5 using the alternative measures—statutory bargaining obligation and public policy environment. The performance of the latter is clearly superior. Not only are the variables themselves more significant; every other variable except one is more significant in Equation 5,

TABLE 5
Regressions Including the Impact of Public Policy Environment and Statutory Bargaining Obligation on Bargaining Outcomes

Variable [a]	Statute (Equation 4)		Environment (Equation 5)	
	Coefficient (Standard Error)	Overall F Ratio	Coefficient (Standard Error)	Overall F Ratio
4. SMSA size	b	5.05*	b	5.67*
6. Governmental function	b	2.80*	b	3.18*
8. Anti-strike legislation				
STRIKPEN	-2.43 (1.66)	2.13	-5.04 (1.70)	8.76*
14. International union				
affiliation	b	3.38*	b	3.44*
17. State strike activity				
STRIKACT	2.34 (2.10)	1.24	4.70 (2.17)*	4.69*
18. Pattern				
STATENDX	0.369 (0.143)*	6.65*	0.227 (0.145)	2.46
7. Statutory bargaining				
obligation		3.24*		
CONFLAW	0.65 (2.36)			
BARGLAW	3.82 (1.50)*			
7A. Public policy				
environment				7.76*
CONFENV			6.30 (2.61)*	
BARGENV			6.08 (1.55)*	
R 2	.462		.482	
Equation F Ratio	5.38*		5.83*	

a Definitions of variables appear in Table 1.
b Individual variable coefficients omitted for brevity.
* Significant at the .05 level.

and the overall fit for the equation is better. Thus, there is support for the proposition that the public policy environment is more important in determining bargaining outcomes than actual bargaining statutes. One implication of this finding is that legislatures that react to voter sympathy with respect to public sector bargaining laws have less influence on the relative bargaining power of the parties than is apparent on the surface. This is not to say that statutes are irrelevant; on the contrary, because agreements in states with bargaining statutes tend to be more homogeneous than those in states without laws.[33] Furthermore, the argument that laws provide structure and procedural devices producing more equitable outcomes cannot be ignored. Statues are likely to have an important impact in specific cases. Their general effect, however, is less important than that of the underlying public tolerance or sympathies that generate the laws.

GENERAL CONCLUSIONS

The evidence presented in this study supports Dunlop's position that collective bargaining is not "capricious," that the provisions of collective bargaining agreements "fundamentally reflect the more enduring features of the environment of the collective bargaining relationship." While it may seem trite to the practitioner, we now have evidence of a somewhat systematic nature that shows that the outcome of the collective bargaining process is related to a number of characteristics surrounding the process. On the other hand, only half the variance in the dependent variable has been explained by the variables available in this study. The most obvious implication of a large error term in the model is that important explanatory variables are absent from the equation. For example, there is no information on the labor market conditions prevailing at the time of negotiations. Transient political considerations may be even more important than economic conditions. In addition, the historical development of the relationship between the parties and their bargaining strategies and abilities may also explain some of the difference in relative bargaining power. These variables were beyond the scope of this study.

While it seems obvious that the above considerations are important, a larger portion of the error term is probably attributable to the imprecise measure of many of the concepts already included in the study. This criticism is applicable to the technique of contract analysis, itself, as a means of measuring union influence. That is, unions use what power they have to represent constituent interests in many ways; the negotiation of formal labor agreements is only one of these ways. The shortcoming of the contract-analysis technique is that it measures only one of these uses of union power. To the extent that union emphasis on formal bargaining varies systematically in some unknown way with one or more of the independent variables, the results are misleading. The general agreement of the results of this study, however, with much of the common knowledge of industrial relations practitioners is reassuring in this regard. Notwithstanding its shortcomings, the idea of measuring the scope of bargaining quantitatively appears to have some merit.

APPENDIX

Recognition Clause

Unit Definition

Union Security Provisions
  Compulsory membership
  Nondiscrimination clause
  Paid time for union business
  Superseniority
  Use of public facilities
  Checkoff
  Contracting out

Wage Provisions
  Hourly (weekly) rates [b]
  Daily or weekly guarantees
  Call-in pay
  Report pay
  Shift or other premiums
  Holidays
  Overtime
  Severance pay
  Longevity

Hours Provisions
  Maximum or schedule
  Split shift
  Off-days schedule
  Overtime scheduling

Fringe Provisions
  Paid holidays
  Paid vacation
  Paid sick leave
    Uses
    Cumulation
    Pay for nonuse
  Military service
  Jury Duty
  Other leave
  Training allowances (reimbursement)
  Pension provisions
    Contributory or not
    Retirement eligibility

Social security
Hospital-medical-surgical
  Paid or contributory
  Famiy or employee only
Major medical
  Paid or contributory
  Family or employee only
Life insurance
  Paid or contributory

Job Security
  Seniority
  Bumping rights
  Promotion rights
  Transfer rights
  Scope of seniority unit

Job Evaluation—Union Role

Facilities, Clothing, Equipment

Work Rules
  Manning requirements
  Maximum work load (case load)

Civil Service Contract Relationship

Management Prerogatives Clause

Joint Committees (Bipartite)

No Strike Clause

No Lock-out Clause

Impasse Procedure for renegotiation

Grievance Procedures
  Time limits
  Arbitration

Duration (Termination) of Agreement

---

a This is not a complete list of all items analyzed; some detail has been omitted for brevity. The analysis form, coding procedure, frequencies of particular types of clauses, and precise formulation of the various contract indexes are available from the author.

b Wage *levels* were not used; this variable simply indicates whether or not rates or rate changes were included in the agreement. Comparison of wage rates across employers and occupations was beyond the scope of this study. Since the wage rate is one issue among many which could have been included in the contract index, its omission does not substantially reduce the validity of the index.

NOTES

1. John T. Dunlop, *Collective Bargaining, Principles and Cases* (Chicago: Richard D. Irwin, 1949), p. 74.

2. At the suggestion of the editors, I have substituted the term "bargaining outcomes" for the "scope of bargaining." The concept is identical to the one I discussed in a previous article, "The Scope of Bargaining in Local Government Labor Negotiations," *Labor Law Journal*, Vol. 20, No. 8 (August 1969), pp. 545-52, and in "The Scope of Bargaining in Local Government Labor Agreements" (Ph.D. dissertation, University of Chicago, 1973). However, since the term "scope of bargaining" is used by some in a manner other than the way I have previously defined it and since the term "bargaining outcomes" was used in a recent article in this journal to refer to what appears to be the same concept, I have adopted the new terminology. See Thomas A. Kochan and Hoyt N. Wheeler, "Municipal Collective Bargaining: A Model and Analysis of Bargaining Outcomes," *Industrial and Labor Relations Review*, Vol. 29, No. 1 (October 1975), pp. 46-66.

3. Neil Chamberlain and James Kuhn, *Collective Bargaining*, 2nd ed. (New York: McGraw-Hill, 1965), pp. 170-71.

4. There is some similarity between this model and analysis and that employed by Kochan and Wheeler, "Municipal Collective Bargaining." The concept of relative bargaining power derived through the Chamberlain ratios, though not directly observable, is relied upon in both our studies as the link between the "environment" and "bargaining outcomes." The empirical measures of environment and bargaining outcomes differ considerably, however.

5. Neil W. Chamberlain, *Collective Bargaining* (New York: McGraw-Hill, 1951), pp. 317-18.

6. The interest in specific issues is not observed empirically in this study. It is merely a conceptual link between the environment and the bargaining outcome. Also, in the empirical work, it will be apparent that few features are "pure," contributing only directly *or* indirectly to bargaining power. All features tested in this study probably have some influence on bargaining outcomes through both paths.

7. See James Belasco, "Collective Bargaining in City X," in Keith Ocheltree, ed., *Government Labor Relations in Transition* (Chicago: Public Personnel Association, Report No. 662, 1966), pp. 41-43.

8. Neil Chamberlain, *The Union Challenge to Management Control* (New York: Harper, 1948), p. 74. See also Neil Chamberlain and Donald Cullen, *The Labor Sector* (New York: McGraw-Hill, 1971): "The question of which subjects the employer should bargain over is not radically different from the question of how to resolve disagreements over the subjects he already agrees are bargainable (p. 219)."

9. My previous article ("The Scope of Bargaining in Local Government Labor Negotiations") referred to these two dimensions respectively as the

"breadth" and "depth" of union penetration into managerial prerogatives.

10. Margaret K. Chandler, *Management Rights and Union Interests* (New York: McGraw-Hill, 1964), especially pp. 108-12; Kochan and Wheeler, "Municipal Collective Bargaining," especially pp. 49-51 and Appendix.

11. Some academics have recognized the problem as well. See, for example, Milton Derber, W. E. Chalmers, and Ross Stagner, "The Labor Contract: Provision and Practice," *Personnel*, Vol. 34, No. 4 (January-February 1958), pp. 19-30.

12. This problem has been discussed at length in Gerhart, "The Scope of Bargaining in Local Government Labor Negotiations," and "The Scope of Bargaining in Local Government Labor Agreements." Let it suffice here to note that if the measure used were invalid, the "noise" introduced would cause insignificant results, so that no relationship would be found between the measured bargaining outcome and the predictors used in the model.

13. The suggestion for this step, upon which all of the subsequent analysis rests, was made by Arnold Weber. It may be feasible to develop a multivariate analysis using several dependent variables. Less information loss would occur in such a model but it would present numerous specification problems.

14. S. S. Wilks, "Weighting Systems for Linear Functions of Correlated Variables When There Is No Dependent Variable," *Psychometrica*, Vol. 3, No. 1 (March 1938), pp. 23-40.

15. John M. Stalnaker, "Weighting Questions on the Essay-Type Examination," *The Journal of Educational Psychology*, Vol. 29, No. 7 (October 1938), p. 486.

16. To test Wilks's theorem empirically, nine different weighting schemes were developed, using a range of different perspectives that union negotiators might take. (Many more would have been possible, of course, but nine seemed sufficient to test the theorem.) Nine different contract scores were thereby generated for each of the 262 contracts in the study. The lowest r in a correlation matrix of the nine scores was .84. Furthermore, few significant differences in the coefficients on independent variables were noted when these alternative formulations of the dependent variable were used in the model. See Gerhart, "The Scope of Bargaining in Local Government Labor Agreements," pp. 340-45 for a more detailed discussion.

17. The formula for the calculation of CI is available on request.

18. The focus of the Brookings Studies of Unionism in Government, of which this research was a part, was on local government labor relations but excluded teachers and transit, because transit has had a unique history of being privately owned and operated, and, at the time, considerable research with respect to teachers had already been completed.

19. I am indebted to these unions for their cooperation in the study. At the time the data were collected, these four unions had negotiated ap-

proximately 835 agreements at the local level. While affiliates of the Firefighters, Firemen and Oilers, various building trades, and other independent unions had negotiated a handful of agreements by 1968, the population from which this sample was drawn represented in excess of 90 percent of all local agreements (exclusive of teachers and transit) then in existence.

The largest number of the agreements were negotiated in 1967. Multiple-year agreements were rare at this time in the public sector, but through automatic renewal clauses and so-called "evergreen" clauses (whereby the agreement was to remain in effect until either party gave notice of an intent to terminate) a large portion of the agreements in the sample were still effective in 1968, even though they were over a year old.

20. As noted in Table 1, data on the selected features were derived from the U.S. Bureau of the Census, *1967 Census of Governments* and *1962 Census of Governments* (Washington, D.C.: G.P.O. 1968-70 and 1962-64); *1966-, 1967-,* and *1968 Municipal Year Book* (Washington, D.C.: International City Management Association, 1966, 1967, and 1968). In addition, through the cooperation of the four unions listed previously, questionnaires were mailed to union and management negotiators. The response rates to the questionnaires were, respectively, 62 and 82 percent. Where missing data apeared, the mean value for the variable was inserted for the regression analysis.

21. Daniel B. Suits, "Use of Dummy Variables in Regression Equations," *American Statistical Association Journal*, Vol. 52, No. 280 (December 1957), pp. 548-51. A set of dummy variables is used to represent a single concept. Each dummy is set equal to 1 only if the observation falls into the category represented by it. If the observation falls into the category not represented by a dummy, all dummy variables equal 0 for that observation. The category not represented by a dummy is the "base" category against which the others are measured so that in this study the coefficient on a particular dummy variable represents the mean difference in the contract index between the category represented by the dummy and the base category. The choice of base category is arbitrary.

22. The log form of the population variable was appropriate here because relative, not absolute, differences in employer size were expected to be correlated with bargaining outcomes. An alternative, categorized version of this variable was used in some equations not reported here in order to test for a nonlinear relationship between employer size and bargaining outcomes. Its performance was somewhat less useful than the log form of the variable reported. Finally, several variations of an employer size variable based on the total number of employees on the employer payroll were substituted in equations not reported here. In no instance did the coefficients of these versions of the variable suggest there was a relationship between employer size and bargaining outcomes.

23. Multicollinearity among the functions, particularly public works (highways, sewage, sanitation, utilities, water, and parks), presented problems. Individual coefficients were unstable, and Table 2 is somewhat

misleadng for the reason. Note also that the significance of the set (F ratio) is enhanced as other variables are added to the equation. Furthermore, in equations not reported, the significance of other variables was found to *fall* in the absence of the governmental function set indicating some comfounding among this and other variables.

24. Kochan and Wheeler, "Municipal Collective bargaining," Table 5, p. 60.

25. Dummy variable sets representing a single conceptual variable, such as governmental function, were treated as a group, except in the case of the statutory policy regarding strikes. Whether the variable set was retained or not depended on the overall F ratio for the variable set. The .95 confidence level for two-tailed distributions was used throughout the analysis.

26. Kochan and Wheeler, "Municipal Collective Bargaining," Table 1, p. 54.

27. This hypothesis must be tempered by reference to the skill level of the employees involved. Clearly, from private sector experience, we know that a small group of strategic employees can impose considerable cost on management—perhaps as great as a large group. This proposition assumes that all other relevant variables (such as skill level) are held constant.

28. These statistical results differ slightly from those reported in Paul F. Gerhart, *Political Activity by Public Employees at the Local Level: Threat or Promise* (Chicago: International Personel Management Association, 1974), pp. 47-48, since they are based on somewhat different data and formulations of the variable. The conclusions, however, are essentially the same.

29. A more refined analysis, taking into account in the scope of the duties of civil service commissions, revealed that commissions that have the authority to set wage rates have a substantial and significant impact on the scope of bargaining while the commissions that are limited to administering examinations and adverse actions appeals have virtually no effect. See Gerhart, "The Scope of Bargaining in Local Government Labor Agreements," pp. 221-23.

30. See David B. Lipsky and John E. Drotning, "The Influence of Collective Bargaining on Teachers' Salaries in New York State,"*Industrial and Labor Relations Review*, Vol. 27, No. 1 (October 1973), p. 34.

31. In addition to the variables reported here, the existence of rival unions, a history of layoffs within the jurisdiction, and variables reflecting the extent of bargaining in other jurisdictions within the same county were investigated. None appeared to have any importance.

32. Note that measuring voter sympathy in this manner permits the variables (BARGENV and CONFENV) to reflect *both* the impact of the environment *and* the impact of the law in those states where a law had been passed before negotiations. Only 45 observations were collected from states that changed the statutory bargaining obligation for employers between the time of negotiations and 1971. Hence, by defini-

tion, BARGENV is highly correlated with BARGLAW, and CONFENV with CONFLAW. This is not relevant to the question of which concept—voter sympathy or law—is the more important in determining bargaining outcomes, however. The real test is whether the 45 observations from states that modified their policies are more like those from states with laws at the time of negotiations or are more like those from states that had not yet adopted any bargaining statute by 1971. That is, is it more proper to classify observations on the basis of voter sympathy in the state as revealed in the subsequent passage of laws *or* on the basis of statutes in existence at the time negotiations took place? In statistical jargon, the more proper classification will be determined by the goodness of fit of the alternative equations.

33. See Gerhart, "The Scope of Bargaining in Local Government Labor Negotiations."

CASE #3
The Mechanics of Securing National Exclusive Recognition in the Federal Service; The NAATS Experience
Marvin J. Levine

In cases in the private sector involving a determination of the appropriate bargaining unit, the National Labor Relations Board has received requests by unions for nationwide bargaining units. Its policy has been to deny such requests as being inappropriate. For example, in *Transcontinental Bus System, Inc., and Amalgamated Transit Union and Brotherhood of Railroad Trainmen,* 178 NLRB No. 110, 72 LRRM 1214 (1969), the petitioners requested a national unit of bus operators. The bus company disagreed with this position, contending that the separate units then in existence constituted the appropriate unit for bargaining purposes. The board, in ruling against the union demand, stated:

> There is an obvious similarity of working conditions among the bus operators in the various subsidiaries and divisions, but there are also substantial differences in terms and conditions of employment among them. Because of local conditions, what is important to operators in one section of the country may not be equally important

---

Reprinted by permission of PUBLIC PERSONNEL MANAGEMENT from PUBLIC PERSONNEL MANAGEMENT, January-February, 1974, pp. 44-52.

to operators in another area. Wage rates, and their means of computation vary considerably in different units.

In the federal government, the assistant secretary of labor for
labor management relations is authorized by Executive Order
11491 to issue rulings in unit determination controversies which
arise in the federal government. He has indicated his belief that
decisions issued in the private sector are not controlling under
E.O. 11491. Yet, he did not completely eschew the relevance of
private industry standards when he said, "I will, however, take
into acount the experience gained in the private sector under the
Labor Management Relations Act, as amended, policies and practices in other jurisdictions, and those rules developed in the
federal sector under the prior Executive Order."

Section 10(b) of E.O. 11491 indicates that a bargaining unit
will not be considered appropriate unless it "will ensure a clear
and identifiable community of interest among the employees concerned and will promote effective dealings and efficiency of agency
operations."

This article will describe the events which led to a precedent-
setting decision in December, 1971, by the assistant secretary. He
approved a national unit of air traffic control specialists covering
approximately 3,000 employees who were employed by the Federal
Aviation Administration at 346 continental and international
flight service stations. Thus, exclusive recognition at the national
level was effectuated for the first time, with the National Association of Air Traffic Specialist (NAATS) gaining the right to repre-
cent the flight service station personnel.

The body of this article consists of the post-hearing brief
written by the author and submitted in support of the NAATS
representation petition. It should be noted that a number of the
arguments were successfully utilized by the Professional Air Traffic Controllers Association in their subsequent petition for a national unit of air traffic controllers.

This approach which features legal maneuvering and shows
the actual post-hearing brief employed is unconventional vis-a-vis
the present public sector labor relations literature, so it should be
of interest to practitioners in this rapidly evolving area.

SYNOPSIS OF EVENTS

Raymond J. Malloy, Associate Staff Counsel for the American
Federation of Government Employees, in his post-hearing brief
summarized the chronology of events as follows:

On December 4, 1970, the National Association of Air Traffic Specialists, hereinafter referred to as "NAATS," filed a petition (LMSA Form 60, AS 1; Tr. 8-9) with the Washington, D.C. Area Administrator requesting an election among, and certification as the exclusive representative for, the "non-supervisory Air Traffic Control Specialists GS-2152 Series . . . employed at Flight Service Stations" employed by the Federal Aviation Administration, hereinafter referred to as 'FAA," and specifically Air Traffic Control Specialists GS-2152 Series employed by the FAA at Centers and Terminals. This petition was docketed as Case No. 22-2145. The American Federation of Government Employees, hereinafter referred to as "AFGE," and the National Association of Government Employees, hereinafter referred to as 'NAGE," timely intervened in this case. Both of the Intervenors timely filed strong challenges to the status of NAATS as a labor organization and to the adequacy and validity of its showing of interest. The Intervenors both made repeated requests for a hearing to fully expose the grounds for such challenges. By administrative fiat the requested hearing was denied and the challenges were rejected. On April 7, 1971, the Regional Administrator consolidated Case No. 20-2414, a petition filed by NAGE on January 22, 1971, for a unit of Air Traffic Control Specialists employed at the Wilkes-Barre Flight Service Station, with Case No. 22-2145, and issued a Notice of Representation Hearing for April 27, 1971.

A pre-hearing conference with representatives of all parties and the Hearing Officer was held in the Area Administrators Office on April 20, 1971. The hearing in this matter was held before Hearing Officer Earl T. Hart, on April 27 and 28 and May 6, 1971, in Washington, D.C. A full record was developed and all parties fully participated and presented evidence. The Regional Administrator extended the time for the filing of briefs to the close of business on June 17, 1971.

Both AFGE and NAGE either had negotiated agreements or had gained exclusive recognition at 48 of the 346 FSS facilities included in the NAATS petition and they claimed that contract or election bars existed at these installations.

TEXT OF THE NAATS POST-HEARING BRIEF.

1.

A CLEAR AND IDENTIFIABLE COMMUNITY OF INTEREST EXISTS AMONG ALL NON-SUPERVISORY AIR TRAFFIC CONTROL SPECIALISTS EMPLOYED AT FLIGHT SERVICE STATIONS AND AT INTERNATIONAL FLIGHT SERVICE STATIONS. THE SAME COMMUNITY OF INTEREST IS LACKING AMONG

PERSONNEL EMPLOYED AT CENTERS AND TERMINALS AND THEY THEREFORE SHOULD BE EXCLUDED FROM THE NATIONAL BARGAINING UNIT SOUGHT BY THE PETITIONER.

One of the criteria established by Section 10 (b) of Executive Order 11491 for the determination of an appropriate bargaining unit for purposes of exclusive recognition indicates that "a unit may be established on a plant or installation, craft, functional, or *other basis* (emphasis supplied) which will ensure a clear and identifiable community of interest among the employees concerned. . ." Any unit should include individuals who share certain things, such as skills, working conditions, common supervision, or functions, to such a degree that it makes sense for them to deal collectively with management through a single voice. Conversely, no unit can be appropriate if its members are so divided by different interests arising from their work, skills, or functions that it is unreasonable to assume that they can speak with a single voice. The interests of the employees should be of prime importance in unit determinations. Employees in the same or closely related jobs and employees having similar wages, hours, and working conditions have the same collective bargaining interests. The purposes of the present Executive Order can be realized most fully if the employees grouped in the unit have a mutual interest in the objects of collective bargaining to be sought by the labor organization which will represent them in negotiations.

Mr. William H. Boatright, Chief of the Flight Service Station, Operations and Procedures Branch, Air Traffic Service, Federal Aviation Administration, Washington, D.C., by his testimony underscored the importance of the interchangeability of employees at geographically dispersed FSS facilities as a factor illustrating their skill homogeneity. Boatright, who transferred between six Flight Service Stations in 23 years of FAA experience, indicated no difficulty in these transfers, even if they occurred between an international and continental facility. (Tr. 87.) His testimony conclusively established the skill homogeneity and easy transferability from one Flight Service Station to another of FSS specialists without extensive retraining. In fact, during his own experience, he was transferred on one occasion on an emergency basis from the Childress, Texas FSS to one at Hobart, Oklahoma, and ". . . entered on duty the first hour I was there." (Tr. 87.) The longest period of reorientation required was that subsequent to his transfer in the spring of 1951 from an International FSS to the Childress, Texas FSS, when it took him less than twenty days to get an "area rating" and weather observer certificate. (Tr. 86, 87.) Petitioner submits that this expeditious interchangeability of employees regardless of location is due primarily to skill congruencies and is a vital factor in supporting the concept of a single, national bargaining unit.

Boatright pointed out two important differences in the job duties and operating requirements between FSS specialists and controllers at terminals and centers on cross-examination by AFGE counsel:

Q. "Could you tell me, Mr. Boatright, what difference, if any, there is between position descriptions for air controllers working at terminals and air route traffic control centers compared to these position descriptions in A-6?" (Tr. 71.)

A. "The main difference, and there may be a few, but the primary one is the flight service station personnel do not control nor separate aircraft. Air route traffic control centers and towers do control aircraft and separate aircraft. Flight Service Specialists perform preflight briefing duties, where the other two do not, and there is many others. . ." (Tr. 71.)

He also mentioned that the Air Traffic Service issues different procedures manuals for each of the three options, station, terminal, and center and that ". . . a station specialist does not refer to the controller manuals to do his job." (Tr. 72.)

Moreover, he emphasized the marked difference in training requirements between the three options by recounting that in an instance he was familiar with, a FSS specialist had not qualified for full-time duty *two years* (emphasis supplied) after transferring to a tower to become an air traffic controller. (Tr. 93.)

In addition, FSS specialists undergo a different training regimen than air traffic controllers, besides having different responsibilities. Quoting from the testimony of Joseph Feldman, a FSS specialist with 26 years of experience at three different FSS's:

". . . there are other increments in the flight service stations which do not apply to air traffic controllers. They don't have teletype work, they don't have weather observing, they don't have pilot briefing and this in itself is quite extensive in its preparation. The air route traffic controller does know procedures, and navigation and airways, whereas the flight service station, in addition to those three elements, has to know the rest." (Tr. 208, 209.)

The air traffic controller at centers and terminals also has a greater area of responsibility than the FSS specialist which is demonstrated by higher GS ratings carrying higher salaries. (Tr. 209.) The separate and distinct duties of FSS specialists and controllers at terminals and centers is further corroborated by a Civil Service Commission publication (FAA Exhibit 5) and a Department of Transportation brochure (FAA Exhibit 4).

Feldman also stated:
1. Air traffic controllers at centers and towers could separate air traffic without assistance from FSS's, thereby illustrating the lack of integration between the three facilities; (Tr. 210,211).
2. Controllers peformed more important duties than FSS specialists; (Tr. 222, 223).
3. The three options carry three different job descriptions; (Tr. 228.)
4. FSS specialists neither ever controlled nor separated air traffic; (Tr. 228.)

5. Flight Service Station specialists were located in *entirely sepa-rate and distinct* (emphasis supplied) facilities from centers and terminals; (Tr. 229.)
6. FSS specialists used a manual related solely to their unique duties; (Tr. 229.)
7. Centers and terminals utilized separate manuals from those in service at FSS's; (Tr. 230.)
8. The skills required of FSS specialists were "separate and apart" from those employed in centers and terminals; (Tr. 230.) and
9. Combined station towers are considered terminal facilities, not Flight Service Stations. (Tr. 236.)

He also mentioned that it took him thirteen months just to learn three "sectors" of the then ten required "sectors" to move from a FSS specialist position to that of a control center air controller in 1957, at a time when the present radar requirement was not a prerequis-ite, (Tr. 197,199.) and that it might take two years to successfully master all of the transfer requirements. (Tr. 190.) Even a NAGE witness admitted that it would take just "less than a year" for a specialist to become a controller. (Tr. 541)

Frank Kleuber, a FSS specialist since 1957, corroborated much of Boatright's and Feldman's earier testimony. During a fourteen year period, he served at both continental and international FSS's; an IFSS at San Francisco, California, and three stints at Carlsbad, New Mexico; Blythe, California, and Phoenix, Arizona. (Tr. 259, 260.) He contended that:

1. Job responsibilities and job descriptions at all 346 FSS's, inter-national and continental, were primarily the same; (Tr.; 275,276.)
2. FSS specialists used an "entirely different" manual than is used for terminals and centers; (Tr. 279.)
3. An intensive training period of from 18 to 24 months would be necessary for a FSS specialist to qualify as a full performance center controller. (Tr. 279,280.)

The lack of a community of interest between FSS duties and those of the terminal or tower and control center options was made crystal clear when he further stated:

". . . The tower chief, for instance in San Francisco, told me more than one time it would be much easier for him to hire a man off the street and break him into the tower option than it would be to take a man out of the flight service and put him . . ." (Tr. 269,270.)

Testimony was also elicited that more stringent physical examina-tion requirements are imposed on termnal and center controllers than FSS specialists because of the more demanding and stressful nature of controller duties and that, on several occasions, control-lers, due to physical problems, transferred to the less demanding duties at FSS's. (Tr. 250-258.)

One other distinction between FSS specialists and controllers at terminals and centers is, albeit a semantic one, nevertheless significant in demonstrating that FSS specialists maintain a separate identity within the FAA. Edward Curran, Director of Labor Relations for the FAA, answered in response to the Hearing Officer's inquiry as to whether the term "specialist" could be applied to center and tower controllers, that, "The common jargon within the FAA and among the work force is that controllers are understood to mean those people employed in terminals and centers. Specialists are those employed in the Flight Service Stations." (Tr. 297.) The separate treatment afforded FSS personnel as distinct from controllers was also graphically outlined by the Corson Committee Report whose recommendations to FAA concerning welfare, job training, early retirement and duties specifically excluded FSS personnel. (Tr. 485.)

Petitioner submits that three witnesses, Boatright, Feldman, and Klueber; the latter two presently active FSS specialists, with a combined total of 63 years of service at continental and international FSS's have provided a preponderance of evidence to prove the homogeneity and separate identity of FSS specialist positions regardless of location in sharp contrast to the basic skill and duty disparities between specialists and controllers at terminals and centers. Moreover, petitioner emphatically stresses that the testimony of these three witnesses, particularly that of Boatright, who wrote the Flight Service Procedure Handbook when working in the Air Traffic Service Manual Development Division, contains a much higher credibility quotient than the one intervenor witness who left active FSS service in 1958 (Tr. 515.) after a total of three years' experience as a FSS specialist. (Tr. 540.) This same witness confirmed the earlier testimony of Boatright, Feldman, and Klueber that FSS specialists are not authorized to separate and control air traffic. (Tr. 543.) Then again, his competence to describe recent developments at Flight Service Stations is subject to serious reservations since after testifying at length concerning the vital function of "flight following" at FSS's, he admitted that he was unaware that "flight following" was abolished as a FSS function over two years ago. (Tr. 562.)

2.

A NATIONAL UNIT OF NON-SUPERVISORY FLIGHT SERVICE STATION SPECIALISTS IS THE "MOST" APPROPRIATE UNIT TO "PROMOTE EFFECTIVE DEALINGS AND EFFICIENCY OF AGENCY OPERATIONS" UNDER EXECUTIVE ORDER 11491.

Meaningful collective negotiations require that the employee representative be brought face-to-face with management representatives who are able to deal authoritatively with the problems to be discussed. Therefore, appropriate units should lie within some as-

certainable organizational boundary, within which the management represetative can make authoritative decisions on a significant range of probable topics for negotiation. If the choice is between
a local unit and a national unit, the local unit shuld not be ruled
appropriate simply to satisfy a rule that local responsibility is best if,
in fact, the local manager has little or no authority to make binding
commitments in negotiations. The FAA Director of Labor Relations,
Edward Curran, indicated that this was a serious problem under
local exclusive recognitions because local contract negotiations ran
into difficulty due to an alleged lack of authority on the part of the
facility chief to deal meaningfully with employee representatives.
(Tr. 431, 432.) This impediment could be removed by national unit
bargaining with top echelon FAA representatives authorized to enter
into binding negotiations with officials of the certified labor organization.

The FAA organizational hierarchy features a chain of command
whereby the FSS system is subject to centralized administrative
control characterized by national policy determination. Witness
Boatright verified that FAA headquarters in Washington, D.C.
originate policy in his answers to the following two questions:

Q. "Is it true that regional directors implement the *national* (emphasis supplied) policy as set forth by the administrator and
with his office?"

A. "Yes." (Tr. 161)

Q. "Is it not a fact therefore whereas before there were seven regions
and now there are going to be eleven, you will simply have eleven
regional directors implementing the *national* (emphasis
supplied) policy in eleven regions?"

A. "Yes." (Tr. 161)

The chain of command within the FSS system follows this seq-
ence. The FSS chief supervises facility operations with all personnel
reporting to him. Then the chief reports to the air traffic division
chief in the regional office who in turn reports to the Regional
Director who then reports to the FAA Administrator. (Tr. 79, 80.)

The following response by the FAA Director of Labor Relations on
cross-examination by Intervenor NAGE provides ample evidence of
FAA's national policy-making role in the labor relations area:

Q. "I believe you testified last week that you review contracts which
have been executed by operational people in the field on a facility
basis. Would you explain what your function is in connection
with reviewing of these contracts?" (Tr. 399.)

A. "My office has the responsibility for reviewing contracts
negotiated at the local level and approving them or seeing that
they are approved on behalf of the Administrator." (Tr. 400.)

The FAA Office of Labor Relations is also called upon frequently by field management people to provide assistance in local negotiations and assigns people to participate in contract negotiations on behalf of the FAA by furnishing technical labor relations assistance. (Tr. 401.) The Director of Labor Relations of the FAA is also responsible for developing a *national* (emphasis supplied) contract negotiations policy and has the authority to overrule a regional chief or a facility on a matter of policy and contract negotiations. (Tr. 402.) The centralized nature of policy formulation was once more evident as a result of the following interchange:

Q. "But the working conditions would vary greatly from facility to facility?" (Tr. 405.)

A. "I am not sure that I could say that working conditions in that broad a sense vary greatly from facility to facility. . . . The only *national* (emphasis supplied) policy on the matter in the air traffic service is that people must have an obligation and an opportunity to work on all shifts so that they remain proficient. . ." (Tr. 405.)

Q. "Does the method of training differ from facility to facility?" (Tr. 406.)

A. "To my knowledge, not basically. In other words, we have *standard* (emphasis supplied) procedures that we try to achieve. . ." (Tr. 406,407.)

Q. "What about administrative leave? Would that vary from facility to facility?" (Tr. 406.)

A. "We have a *general* (emphasis supplied) policy on the so-called administrative leave. There are certain things under which it can be granted. I don't think I could fairly say that it would vary unless the circumstances vary." (Tr. 406, 407.)

Labor Relations Director Curran, who responded to the above questions, himself acted as management spokesman during contract negotiations at the Tulsa, Oklahoma tower in either late 1966 or eary 1967. (Tr. 395)
This centralized administrative superstructure would lend itself readily to the negotiation of a national contract in the event a single, national unit was determined as appropriate. Small, fragmented units were recognized under the old executive order when the scope of bargaining was considerably narrower than it is today. One expert in public sector labor relations predicts that *national unit bargaining* (emphasis supplied) will be the trend of the future in these remarks:

"It is all too easy to say that the existing units are appropriate considering the limited scope of bargaining, since there is not now bargaining over wage rates or pensions on an agency-wide basis and there is, therefore, little harm in establishing units on a departmental or agency basis. But what will happen when the scope of bargaining is expanded, as it will be some day, along the lines established under the postal corporation act. Will it be possible at that time to establish broad occupational units, or at least, agency-wide units so that you would have the equivalent of national bargaining on such items as salaries, pensions, welfare plans, vacations, holidays, and sick leave policies?" (Arvid Anderson, Chairman of the New York City Office of Collective Bargaining, in address keynoting the Federal Bar Association Council on Labor Law and Labor Relations Conference on Collective Bargaining in the Federal Sector, Washington, D.C., April 29, 30, 1971.)

The deficiencies inherent in a multiplicity of local units in the Navy Department were described by the head of Labor and Employee Relations Division of Navy's Office of Civilian Manpower Management as a "necklace" which "hangs like an albatross around the neck of Navy." He said that one of Navy's biggest labor relations problems is the fact that it has 536 exclusive units. This fragmentation was due to the "community of interest" policy of unit determination first contained in E.O. 10988. Attilio Di Pasquale urged the Assistant Secretary of Labor to adopt the standard of New York State's Taylor Law when approving future bargaining units. Under the Taylor Law a unit must meet the following qualifications before it will be approved by the New York State Public Employee Relations Board: (1) The employees involved must have a community of interest; (2) The public employer at the level of the unit must have the authority to agree or to make effective recommendations with respect to the terms and conditions to be negotiated . . . Di Pasquale stated:

"It is reported that the PERB has construed this statutory criterion to require the designation of as few units as possible, consistent with the overriding requirements that employees be permitted to form or join employee organizations of their own choosing."

Stated differently, the PERB policy is that fragmentation of public employer's employees into small units is to be avoided. To avoid fragmentation, the Board has adopted the "most appropriate unit" policy.

This differs from the approach adopted under E.O. 10988 in that any unit, so long as it was appropriate under the community-of-interest guideline, was to be approved even though more appropriate units could be conceived. Di Pasquale believes this policy led to the "albatross" of fragmented units which now threatens to blunt managerial effectiveness in the Navy Department. (Comments by Attilio Di Pasquale, head of Labor and Employee Relations Division of Department of Navy's Office of Civilian Manpower Management at Federal Bar Associa-

tion Council on Labor Law and Labor Relations Conference on
Collective Bargaining in the Federal Sector, Washington, D.C.,
April 29, 30, 1971.) FAA Labor Relations Director Curran noted
potentially the same problem of excessive fragmentation of bargaining units when he opined that a national exclusive unit of
FSS and IFSS specialists would promote effective dealings in
agency operations in that one contract would in fact be
negotiated as against the possibility as it now stands of 346
separate contracts. (Tr. 482, 483, 484.) He said that he honestly
feared that the FAA would be faced with 346 different units and
contracts under the presnt local exclusive recognition structure.
(Tr. 499.)

The slightly different approach adopted by E.O. 11491 might
well lead the Assistant Secretary into measuring proposed units
by the standards of the Taylor Law. This new approach, as embodied in Sec. 10(b) adds "effective dealings" and "efficiency of
agency operations" to the community of interest standard carried over from the old order and is more equitable in that
employer considerations as well as employee rights are taken
into account in the determination of appropriate units.

Excessive fragmentation now present in the Navy Department
and potentially so in the 346 Flight Service Stations might well
produce other consequences inimical to federal sector labor relations stability. There is the distinct probability that public
employers would be whipsawed as labor organization bargaining
strategy would concentrate on gaining a highly favorable contract at one facility and then bludgeoning management at the
many other facilities, where contract expiration dates are dissimilar under local exclusives, into conformity with the most
expensive contract provisions. The potential for heightened
labor-management conflict would increase due to the precedent
set by such highly favorable contract settlements since many
local union leaders could be whipsawed into very militant bargaining postures in order to satisfy membership pressure for
comparable contract gains. Moreover, the multiplicity of local
units may produce a succession of union leaders each more
militant than the others but consistently unable to satisfy a
diverse constitutency as the whipsaw phenomenon accelerated
in the manner of a thundering landslide.

3.

INTERVENOR LABOR ORGANIZATIONS HAVE NOT FUL-
FILLED THE BASIC DUTY OF FAIR REPRESENTATION
FOR THE EMPLOYEES WHERE THEY HAVE LOCAL
EXCLUSIVE RECOGNITIONS.

Section 10(e) of E.O. 11491 reads as follows:

"When a labor organization has been accorded exclusive recognition, it is the exclusive representative of employees in the unit and is entitled to act for and to negotiate agreements covering all employees in the unit."

The petitioner brings to the attention of the Assistant Secretary, the fact that the intervenors have 48 existing local exclusive recognitions but have been able to negotiate only six contracts between them under both executive orders. (FAA Exhibit 8) They therefore have not afforded employees at the facility level the benefits normally obtained by effective labor organizations and therefore, this type of bargaining unit is not conducive to the fulfillment of the primary duty of fair representation implicitly assumed by all labor organizations. The question may well be asked of the forty-two facilities where there are local exclusives but where no contracts have been negotiated, "What function are these labor organizations serving?" Presumably they are receiving dues payments from their members ostensibly to be used to protect the economic interests of FSS employees. Yet, no concrete benefits have been achieved!

4.

PETITIONER DOES NOT RECOGNIZE ELECTION, CERTIFICATION, OR CONTRACT BARS AT FSS FACILITIES WHERE LOCAL EXCLUSIVES WERE GRANTED PRIOR TO THE EFFECTIVE DATE OF EXECUTIVE ORDER 11491.

Under the old executive order the agency would determine the appropriate unit, as the following language of Section 11 indicates:

"Each agency shall be responsible for determining in accordance with this order whether a unit is appropriate for purposes of exclusive recognition."

This no longer is the procedure under E.O. 11491. Sec. 10(b) (4) reads:

"Questions as to the appropriate unit and related issues may be referred to the Assistant Secretary for decisions."

Therefore, based on the language of the E.O. 11491, technically the only existing contract, certification, or election bars would exist at those local exclusives accorded recognition after January 1, 1970, the effective date of the new order, where the Assistant Secretary ruled on the appropriateness of the unit, not the agency. Therefore, in the event the petitioner obtains national exclusive recognition through a representation election, the local exclusives at forty-two facilities should be eliminated by permitting the employees to vote for or against the petitioner. The *Report and Recommendations on Labor-Management Relations in the Federal Service* issued in October, 1969, as a prelude to the formulation of the new executive order urged exactly this:

"When national exclusive recognition has been granted in an appropriate national unit, no recognition should be granted to any other labor organization for employees within the national exclusive unit. . ." (p. 21.)

In conclusion, Petitioner submits that FSS specialists are a homogeneous occupational classification which maintains a separate and distinct identity within the national air traffic system from controllers at terminals (towers) and centers due to differential skills, training requirements, and areas of responsibility; that a national unit of FSS specialists excluding terminal (tower) and center controllers is the most appropriate unit to facilitate the representation and collective interests of said FSS specialists within the purview of Section 10(b) of Executive Order 11491 which describes an appropriate unit as one "which will ensure a clear and identifiable community of interest among the employees concerned and will promote effective dealings and efficiency of agency operations;" that the centralized administrative structure of FAA emphasizes national policy determination and control over FSS operations which organizational hierarchy would facilitate the negotiation and implementation of a single, national contract for all non-supervisory FSS specialists; that the inability of intervenor labor organizations to negotiate contracts at seven of every eight FSS facilities suggests a basic failure to fulfill the duty of fair representation incumbent upon all labor organizations; and that the only valid election, certification or contract bars presently extant are those local exclusive recognitions where the Assistant Secretary has made a determination as to the appropriateness of the unit under Executive Order 11491, and even these local residual units would best be absorbed in a national unit to promote labor relations stability.

DECEMBER 27, 1971—THE FINAL DECISION

The assistant secretary concluded that the NAATS petition was not timely filed as to those flight service stations covered by current agreements and it was, therefore, barred from including such stations. The assistant secretary also found that NAATS was barred from including those flight service stations where the exclusive bargaining representative had been recognized or certified within the twelve-month period immediately preceding the time NAATS filed its petition. The assistant secretary concluded that, except in unusual circumstances such units should not be disturbed because to do so would lead to instability and uncertainty in labor relations. As to exclusively recognized units encompassed by the NAATS petition where the evidence established the existence of a collective bargaining history, but no bar at the time the NAATS petition was filed, the assistant secretary determined that such employees would be entitled to a self-determination election in their respective units. However, where no collective bargaining history was established, he found that such units would be examined, and if found inappropriate, would be included properly under the NAATS petition. Regarding the election bar issue, the assistant secretary found that employees who had participated in a self-determination election during the twelve-month period immediately preceding the time NAATS filed its petition were not barred from being included in the unit sought by NAATS, since the NAATS petition was neither for the same unit nor a subdivision of the unit which was involved in the election.

In all the circumstances the assistant secretary found that the unit petitioned for by NAATS, which included all the FSS employed at flight service stations except those employed at stations where procedural bars existed, was appropriate. Such employees constituted a homogeneous group with a community of interest which differed from that of the activity's other employees. In reaching this conclusion, the assistant secretary noted that the training, skills, and functions of these employees were clearly distinguishable from all other occupational groups employed by the activity, including air traffic control specialists (ATCS) employed at control towers, control centers and combined station towers. The assistant secretary also rejected the contention that the unit sought by NAATS was inappropriate because it excluded teletype operators and clericals who, in some instances, worked at the same installation and under the same supervision as the FSS. In this regard, the assistant secretary noted that interests of the FSS were sufficiently distinguishable from those of the clerical and teletype opeators to entitle the FSS to separate representation.

The assistant secretary found that a nationwide unit of the FSS at flight service stations was appropriate in that all specialists had the same basic skills and working conditions; there was transferring of FSS between flight service stations; and all significant policies affecting the FSS were promulgated at the national level. In these circumstances, the assistant secretary concluded that there was a sufficient community of interest between all of the FSS and that they, therefore, constituted an appropriate unit for the purpose of exclusive recognition. Accordingly, he directed an election in a nationwide unit.

The assistant secretary found that the unit sought by NAGE, limited to the FSS employed at the activity's flight service station at Wilkes-Barre, Pennsylvania, was not appropriate, noting that all major policies and actions regarding personnel and labor relations matter were determined at either the regional or national level. The assistant secretary further noted that the FSS at Wilkes-Barre had the same basic skills and similar terms and conditions of employment as the FSS employed at other stations, and that there was no evidence that the Wilkes-Barre employees had any interest that distinguished them from the FSS at other service stations. In dismissing NAGE's petition, the assistant secretary stated that Wilkes-Barre employees would have an opportunity to vote in a more comprehensive unit as to whether or not they desired union representation.

CASE #4
Wage Pressures on City Hall:
Philadelphia's Experience
in Perspective
James L. Freund

Fiscal woes have plagued America's cities for generations, but only in recent years have the crises become so painfully acute. At the same time that citizens are demanding more and better services, school systems are forced to shut early, roads are falling

Reprinted by permission of the BUSINESS REVIEW, Federal Reserve Bank of Philadelphia.

into disrepair, and capital spending plans are shelved. Philadelphia, like other large cities, has had its problems compounded by uphill efforts to meet its chronic social ills. And, while demands on the City government have increased, soaring costs have heightened pressures on the budget. The major source of Philadelphia's increased costs in recent years can be attributed to the City's constantly expanding payroll.[1]

Rapid payroll growth is not peculiar to Philadelphia. City halls throughout the country as well as higher levels of government also have experienced large increases in payrolls as their workers have chalked up sizeable wage gains. Many commentators blame rising government wages on such forces as the spiraling costs of living, unionization, and "catch-up" increases. Yet, the underlying problem may be inherent in government itself rather than in these popular notions. If this is the case, taxpayers are in for some tough decisions.

WAGE PRESSURES ON CITY BUDGETS

Philadelphia's Growing Payroll.   During the past twenty years, the total wage bill—the payroll the City pays its workers—has grown dramatically; in fact, it more than doubled in the period between 1952 and 1965 (see Chart 1).[2] Between 1965 and 1970 the City's monthly wage bill increased at even a greater rate—from about $12 million to just under $30 million.

One reason for the payroll increases is expansion in City employment. Since the early 1950s the City's work force has swelled from 22,000 to over 35,000. The burgeoning payroll can only partially be attributed to increases in employment, however. Increases in the wage rate of city workers also have put great upward pressure on the payroll. As shown in the lower frame of Chart 1, the average monthly salary of City workers has climbed continuously since the early 1950s. In 1952 the monthly salary of a City worker averaged abut $291; in 1970 it was up to $835—a jump of 187 percent.

Over three-fourths of this increase in monthly earnings occurred between 1965 and 1970. Chart 2 shows the estimated pay increases of all City workers for each of these years. The yearly rise in per worker wage cost for the City ranges from 5.4 percent (between October 1966 and October 1967) to well over 20 percent (between the same months in 1969 and 1970). Over the entire five-year span annual gains averaged 12.4 percent. While these increases in monthly earnings were affected by such things as

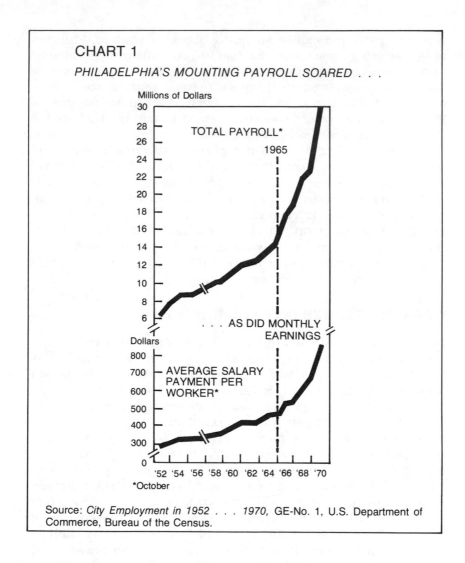

CHART 1

PHILADELPHIA'S MOUNTING PAYROLL SOARED . . .

Source: *City Employment in 1952 . . . 1970,* GE-No. 1, U.S. Department of Commerce, Bureau of the Census.

seniority gains, the types of employees hired during the period, and overtime payments, they have been caused primarily by frequent and substantial boosts in City workers' salaries.

Payroll figures do not represent the entire burden to the City of its employees, however. Nonwage benefits to City employees, the other part of the burden, have also risen substantially over the last five years. Consequently, the total increased cost to the City of Philadelphia over the period has been even greater than 12.4 percent annually.

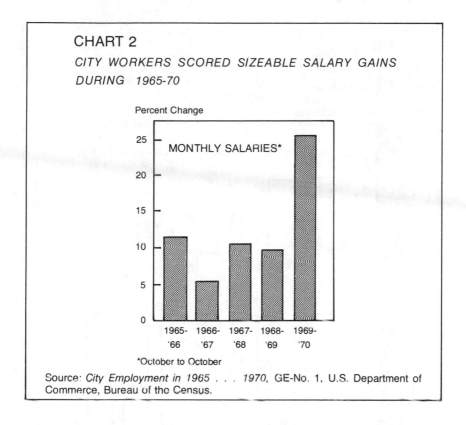

CHART 2

*CITY WORKERS SCORED SIZEABLE SALARY GAINS
DURING 1965-70*

Percent Change

MONTHLY SALARIES*

*October to October

Source: *City Employment in 1965 . . . 1970*, GE-No. 1, U.S. Department of
Commerce, Bureau of the Census.

Is Philadelphia Alone? While the gains of Philadelphia's workers have been large, those of workers in comparable cities have
also been substantial—some barely slower than the Quaker City's.
Of the nation's major cities, Philadelphia was one of four in which
monthly earnings increased more than 10 percent annually (see
Chart 3). At the other end of the scale, cities such as San Francisco, Detroit, and Cleveland posted rates of increase less than
half the size of Philadelphia's.

Part of the difference among cities may be attributed to
"catch-up" increases. As seen in Chart 4, City salaries were fairly
low when compared to those of some northern and western cities
in 1965. By 1970, however, Philadelphia's relatively large increases lifted it to a level more typical of these similar cities.[3]
Other cities—Houston, Dallas, and Atlanta—reporting annual increases almost as great, also ranked comparatively low on the pay
scale in 1965.

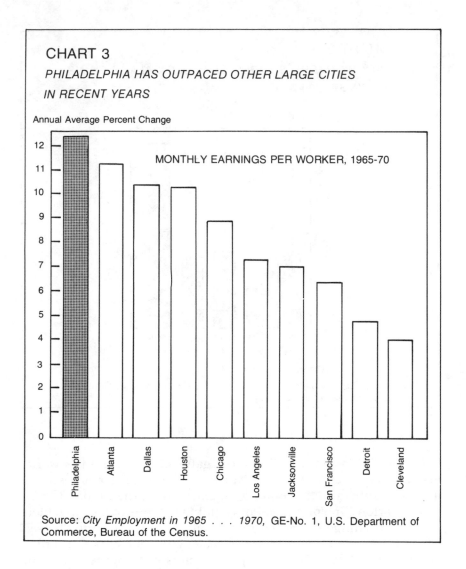

CHART 3

PHILADELPHIA HAS OUTPACED OTHER LARGE CITIES

IN RECENT YEARS

Annual Average Percent Change

MONTHLY EARNINGS PER WORKER, 1965-70

Source: *City Employment in 1965 . . . 1970*, GE-No. 1, U.S. Department of Commerce, Bureau of the Census.

WAGE PRESSURES ON CITY HALL: SOME POPULAR VIEWS

"Catch-up" increases only partially explain wage changes and only apply to a few cities. For Philadelphia and most other cities, additional forces influence earnings changes. Popular notions abound concerning these forces, but few have been verified. Some persons contend that skyrocketing wage costs are a consequence of the size of large cities. Others argue that the cost of living has

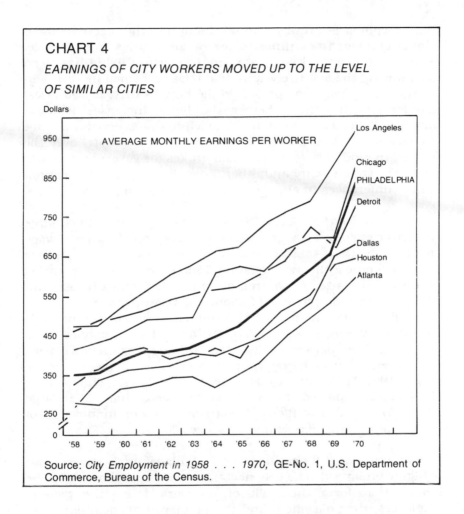

CHART 4

EARNINGS OF CITY WORKERS MOVED UP TO THE LEVEL
OF SIMILAR CITIES

Dollars

AVERAGE MONTHLY EARNINGS PER WORKER

Los Angeles
Chicago
PHILADELPHIA
Detroit
Dallas
Houston
Atlanta

950
850
750
650
550
450
350
250
0

'58 '59 '60 '61 '62 '63 '64 '65 '66 '67 '68 '69 '70

Source: *City Employment in 1958 . . . 1970,* GE-No. 1, U.S. Department of
Commerce, Bureau of the Census.

increased more in large cities and that government wages reflect
this. The most widely-held opinion, however, is that union activity caused the lion's share of recent wage boosts.

Cost of Living Pressures.   Since the cost of living has increased
substantially in recent years, wages could be expected to increase
accordingly. Between 1965 and 1970 Philadelphia's cost of living
rose at an average rate of about 4 percent per year. Obviously the
City's 12.4 percent average boost in earnings can be only partially
justified on these grounds.

Moreover, cities with the largest change in the cost of living
are not those where government earnings have risen the most.

Chart 5 compares average annual changes in the cost of living to similar changes in earnings in several large cities. For example, Detroit and New York—cities where the cost of living has risen most during the last five years—had relatively small increases in earnings over the same period. While Kansas City, Los Angeles, and Pittsburgh—cities where cost-of-living increases averaged only a half percent less than Philadelphia's—experienced wage changes a full 3 to 5 percent less per year. In short, over the five-year period, differences in salary hikes for government workers in the Quaker City and other large cities bore little relationship to differences in changes in the cost of living.

City Size and Labor Costs.   Contrary to popular notions, large city governments as a group do not have much higher wage growth rates than smaller areas. Chart 6 shows that, except for very small cities, the average annual increase in earnings varied little with city size. All groups of larger-sized cities (those over 50,000) averaged increases of about 7 percent per year.

Philadelphia's municipal government is one of the nation's largest. Only New York, Los Angeles, and Chicago employ more people. While employees in all of these urban governments experienced average annual wage gains greater than 7 percent over the period 1965-1970, only Chicago (8.9 percent) and Philadelphia (12.4 percent) posted much higher increases than other large cities. Thus, it is difficult to attribute a dominant part of Philadelphia's wage pressure to its size.

Unionization and Wage Increases.   Philadelphia's government is highly unionized. The City negotiates with spokesmen of three groups that form the bulk of its work force—the general employees, the policemen, and the firemen. Philadelphia is not alone in the degree of unionization of its workers, however. In recent years unions have organized workers at all levels of government, especially in large urban areas. Many persons blame the increasing wage pressures in the public sector on union activity.

Unions may affect wages by organizing employees so that they will not work unless wages are raised.[4] While studies of union influence have not been conclusive, they have shown that the effect of unions is strongest over short periods, especially in times when unionism is growing. The impact of public sector unions in Philadelphia and other cities in which unions have been aggressive has yet to be established. The influence of public sector unions should, however, be related to the same measures of

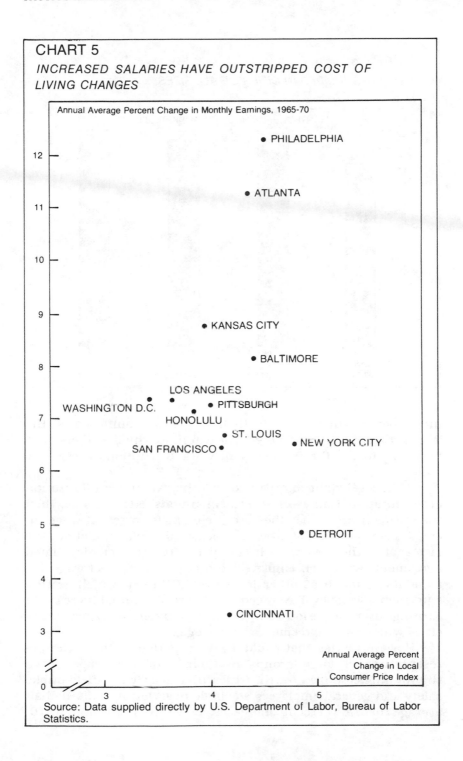

CHART 5

INCREASED SALARIES HAVE OUTSTRIPPED COST OF LIVING CHANGES

Annual Average Percent Change in Monthly Earnings, 1965-70

- PHILADELPHIA
- ATLANTA
- KANSAS CITY
- BALTIMORE
- LOS ANGELES
- WASHINGTON D.C.
- PITTSBURGH
- HONOLULU
- ST. LOUIS
- SAN FRANCISCO
- NEW YORK CITY
- DETROIT
- CINCINNATI

Annual Average Percent Change in Local Consumer Price Index

Source: Data supplied directly by U.S. Department of Labor, Bureau of Labor Statistics.

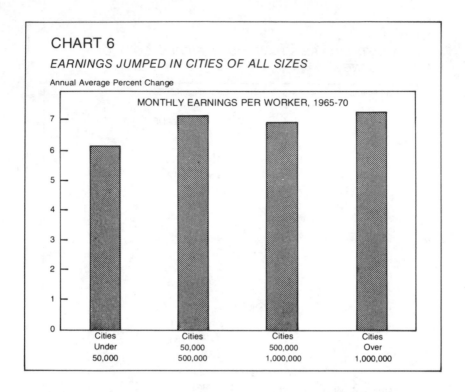

CHART 6

EARNINGS JUMPED IN CITIES OF ALL SIZES

Annual Average Percent Change

MONTHLY EARNINGS PER WORKER, 1965-70

| Cities Under 50,000 | Cities 50,000 500,000 | Cities 500,000 1,000,000 | Cities Over 1,000,000 |

union power which apply to their industrial counterparts: the legal status they have achieved, the extent to which workers have been organized, the frequency of work disruptions a city has suffered.[5]

If the legal right to organize and the extent of unionization are accurate measures of goverment unions' effectiveness, then the common belief that they are the culprits in recent wage increases is not valid. For cities of at least 250,000 population, the fact that authorities were legally permitted to sign negotiated agreements with their employees did not tend to affect wage settlements as much as other influences. Cities in which written agreements were legal averaged a 6.9 percent annual increase in earnings over the period 1965-1970, as opposed to 7.7 percent in cities where such agreements were illegal.

However, cities that could legally negotiate with single representatives of large groups of their employees experienced slightly higher wage growth. Cities that dealt with their public safety and general employees as single negotiating units had an average of 7.6 percent increases between 1965 and 1970.

DEGREE OF UNIONIZATION AND RECENT WAGE CHANGES IN
LARGE CITIES

Reported Degree of Unionization	Number of Cities Reporting	Average Annual Rate of Wage Change, 1965-1970
Completely Unionized	9	7.0
Highly Unionized	18	7.9
Moderately Unionized	25	7.3

Municipalities that could not legally negotiate with unions in this manner registered annual increases averaging 6.8 percent. Although other factors tend to obscure the exact relationships, it would appear that the ability to represent workers in a *large* unit may provide a more important avenue of union power than simply the ability to negotiate.

Perhaps the most commonly held belief about government employee unions is that the more organized they are, the more powerful they are, the higher the wage increases they can negotiate. There is no accurate yardstick of the strength of public unions in large cities. Available information does provide a general idea of union membership, however.

Among large cities there are no overwhelming wage effects associated with the extent of unionization (see Table). Cities reporting a completely unionized work force registered, as a group, the lowest average annual wage change. Highly unionized cities (above 50 percent but less than 100 percent of their work force unionized) posted the highest average annual increase– 7.9 percent. Moderately unionized cities (including only two cities that reported no union activity) also experienced large wage advances. In short, the degree of unionization alone did not have enough effect on the rate at which wages increased to overwhelm other forces which affect wages.

Because of their widespread impact on the public, work disruptions and other "labor troubles" have received much attention in recent years. If some public sector unions have been aggressive enough to disrupt government operations and successfully influence wages, cities that have experienced such problems should have registered the largest increases. Apparently, this has not been the case. Large cities that have been disrupted by strikes, slowdowns, or picketing do not appear to have had significantly higher wage increases than other large cities (see Chart 7). In cities where negotiations have broken down and work disruptions have occurred, earnings increases averaged 7.8 percent as opposed to 7.2 percent for those without strikes. If there were positive gains from striking aftr all other factors worked themselves out, then they were not very large ones. Furthermore, local governments facing recalcitrant unions that required binding arbitration in negotiations hadwage increases at the rate of 7.4 percent—almost the same as of those parties that did not have arbitration.

The averages cited in all these comparisons reflect more than just militancy. The salient point is that cities with strong and active unions do not as a class register higher wage increases than those with less aggressive unions. It is certainly possible that unions have caused wages in Philadelphia or other large cities to be higher than they would have been had workers never organized. It seems, however, that unions have hardly constituted the dominant force for wage increases in large city governments in recent years.

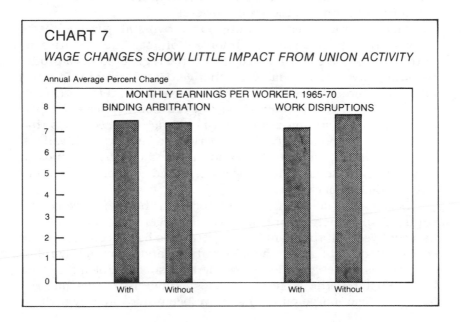

CHART 7

WAGE CHANGES SHOW LITTLE IMPACT FROM UNION ACTIVITY

Annual Average Percent Change

WAGES IN THE PUBLIC SECTOR:
A UNIVERSAL PROBLEM

Since popular notions about local governments do not fully explain why the wages they pay have risen, other possibilities must be considered. Wages in the public sector are determined differently than are those in the private sector, and the attitudes of government employees in part differ from those of other workers. Moreover, all levels of government are subject to interrelated demands and revenue sources. Consequently, growth in municipal wages may be subject to forces largely shaped by general characteristics of governments. Increasing wage burdens throughout the public sector indicate that the underlying reasons for budgetary pressures on local governments do pervade higher levels of government as well.

Public Sector Wage Determination. Although economists do not fully understand what causes wage changes in the public sector, there are several characteristics unique to wage determination in governments that may help explain recent wage increases. For example, unlike a private firm, a governmental unit does not operate under the profit motive. Therefore, the incentive for holding labor costs down may not be as strong as that in private firms where higher costs may be immediately translated into lower profits. Another aspect of public sector wage determination is that accountability for the outcome is often split. The executive branch of the government negotiates or decides upon wage settlements, while the legislative branch passes on the funding. For administrative and political reasons, the legislative branch is unlikely to reject or refuse to fund negotiated or promised wage boosts, thereby weakening resistance to such upward thrusts.[6]

Other economic forces may have generated additional pressure for spiraling government wages generally and those of city governments such as Philadelphia. Unlike most private sector jobs, a government position is viewed by most workers as a secure one because the chances of being fired or laid off are slim. This aspect of civil service has traditionally led government workers to accept low wages in return for security. In the 1960s the economy expanded steadily. Since most workers could find jobs easily, the security of a goverment position was not as attractive as before. Consequently, government workers at all levels may have received raises to compensate them for the loss of this advantage.[7] Finally, some wage gains in the public sector as a whole can be attributed to increased demand for government workers. In recent years employment in the public sector has been expanding faster than most other areas of the economy, and all governments have found that wage increases are necessary to attract capable personnel.

The Record. Philadelphia and other local governments were hardly alone in the late 1960s. Governments at all levels have experienced substantial earnings gains. While these increases fell somewhat short of Philadelphia's, they were in line with those of workers in most large municipalities (see Box).

Like Philadelphia's employees, other public workers have made real absolute progress. The wages paid by all levels of government have increased at a rate well above the average annual cost-of-living increase of 4.5 percent. Relative to workers in other industries, government employees have fared quite well. Only the "hard hats" of the construction industry have achieved wage gains in the same range as government workers. Except for the construction, mining, and service sectors, most other industries experienced wage increments at an average annual rate of 5 percent or less from 1965 to 1970 compared to the above 6 percent gains by government workers.

While the reasons behind the gains of public sector workers are unclear, it does seem that all levels of government have been suffering from wage pressures on their budgets. Everyday concepts about why cities are under wage pressures at best have explained the variations from the general trend among cities. Unless the underlying trend of economic forces affecting wages in the public sector is radically reversed, no city government should expect to be immune from rising wage demands.[8]

INCREASING WAGE BILLS AND THEIR CONSEQUENCES

Continuing Pressures. Although wage pressures will continue in Philadelphia, there are reasons to expect a partial easing. General movement in government wages may not create as strong an upward momentum as in the past. This is especially true in one area. Since recent gains by government workers have made earnings more comparable to those in the private sector, such adjustments should not be as important in the future. Likewise, local conditions indicate wage pressures on Philadelphia's City Hall may not be as great as before. If some of the past growth was, in fact, a "catch-up" gain, the future rate should be less than that of the past few years. Moreover, future wage settlements will certainly be affected by the City Administration's attitude at the bargaining table and by Phase II regulations. Still, there is little doubt that the problem of intensified budget pressure because of increases in the wage bill will be with Philadelphia and other cities for quite some time.[9]

Wage hikes are burdensome to all economic units that use labor, but they work a particular hardship on local governments. This results from the fact that local governments, such as Philadelphia, are what economists call "labor intensive." That is, their budgets are heavily weighted toward wage payments. In Philadelphia more than two-thirds of current general expenditures are for the money wage bill alone. Any increase in the wage rate, therefore, places a heavy burden on the budget.

The Choices Facing Local Taxpayers. Like any business firm experiencing increased wage costs, governments must adjust. One way is greater efficiency. If growing demands could be met by increased productivity from the City's labor force, the City could be relieved of the financial burden of new hiring and could more easily "afford" higher wages. Although gains can probably be made in this area, it is unlikely that they will offset the bulk of budgetary pressures. Thus, other adjustments will have to be made. One painful solution is cutting back on the use of the item—in this case labor—which is causing increased costs. An alternative course of action would be to pass the burden on to the consumer, either by higher taxes or reduced services.

The first alternative is a standard economic adjustment, but it may be of limited use to government. If wage costs are rising, a firm will attempt to use less labor and substitute more capital in the production process. It may be less expensive to buy a new machine than to hire several new workers. If wages keep rising in government, it may be cheaper to buy more street-cleaning machinery than to hire men to hand-sweep the streets. Or, alternatively, an expensive fire truck may take the place of several men and be more economical in the long run. Another possibility is that it may prove cheaper to farm out contracts for entire services such as recordkeeping or billing, rather than have government workers performing them. There is a limit to how much of this adjustment is possible, however. The policeman or the buildings inspector can probably never be replaced by a machine. Where this is the case, the burden must be borne by taxpayers.

When a firm's costs rise and internal economizing is unsuccessful, it must receive higher prices from consumers or accept lower profits. Since large city governments don't make profits, they must receive higher "prices" to continue operating at the same level. Governments "raise prices" by increasing taxes—the price of public services to citizens. This solution has fallen on hard times, however. Taxpayers across the land are "revolting" against increasd levies. Philadelphia's Mayor Rizzo has emphatically ruled out tax increases. If this adjustment cannot be made, another solution would be to have someone else—the State or the Federal Government—pick up the tab for increased wage payments in the form of government aid. However, this is often easier said than done and in the past has been only a temporary solution.

     If no other source of funds can be tapped, the only alternative for a government is to slash expenditures and services. If the price of theater tickets or dinners goes up, people generally go out less often. In sum, the taxpayers of large cities face a Hobson's choice. If wage changes raise the cost of police protection and city taxpayers refuse to fork over higher taxes, "somebody else"—the state house or even the White House—must foot the bill or there will be less protection. The same goes for schools, streets, and social welfare. The laws of economics apply just as clearly to governments as to firms. Public employees can not be paid more unless greater sacrifices are made.

NOTES

     1. Last year the Federal Reserve Bank of Philadelphia conducted an exhaustive study that projected a grim future of mounting costs and lagging revenues for both the City and the School District. The report singled out the City's ever-increasing payroll as the primary cause of the cost increases (see David Lyon, "The Financial Future of City and School Government in Philadelphia," Business Review, March 1971, pp. 3-71).
     2. The information in this study regarding payrolls and earnings in city governments was derived from data in City Employment in 1965 and City Employment in 1970. U.S. Department of Commerce, Bureau of the Census. GE-No. 1 and GE-70 No. 2. It is important to note that this study deals with only employees of the governments involved and not with teachers and other school-related employees. Data limitations made it impossible to include the latter group.
     3. It must be remembered, when comparing average monthly earnings across cities, that these figures reflect such factors as overtime, the number of part-time workers, and the composition of the work force. Therefore, Philadelphia could have been low in 1965 partly because it did

not employ as many relatively high-paid workers (such as policemen) as other cities. More important, these figures do not reflect nonwage benefits such as pensions, health plans, and holidays that could be much higher in Philadelphia.

4. Wage increases are only one facet of union activity. Unions may affect work rules and procedures, nonmonetary benefits, and even hiring and firing procedures. On the other hand, economic theory also tells us that if unions are effective in increasing wages, they will have an adverse effect on the number of jobs available. This study is concerned, however, only with the limited question of the union's effect on the size of wage increases in recent years.

5. The data in this study, upon which statements and conclusions about the effects of union activity are made, are based on a survey conducted by the International City Management Association. The survey, "Public Employee-Employer Relations in Local Governments," was sent to all major U.S. city governments in 1969. It asked for information on city background, number of organized employees, in addition to local laws, policies, and practices regarding local public sector unions. The results derived in this study from the survey are, naturally, limited by the usual problems of sampling. Statistical tests were applied to all comparisons made to determine whether the differences in question were significant.

6. The recent experience of the City of Philadelphia is illustrative. The previous Mayor's Administration negotiated a lowering of the pension age in August, and the City Council had little choice regarding the funding of it this past January. For Philadelphia and all local governments the issue of how public sector wage decisions are reached is even broader. Many commentators consider the union's political role in municipal decision processes as a serious factor in wage determination. For instance, see Harry H. Wellington and Ralph K. Winter, Jr., The Unions and the Cities (Washington: Brookings Institution, 1971).

7. Pressure from workers on this issue and the notion that government workers have been doing otherwise comparable work for less pay than other workers apparently has been held by many besides public sector union leaders. For instance, Congress evidently held this view. An increase of Federal salaries was mandated by Congress in 1962 in order to attain comparability between Federal workers and those in similar jobs in private industry. The average earnings increases of Federal workers over the last five years reflect this process. It is likely that many state and local governments have raised wages for this same reason. See Jerome Roskow, "Government Pay Trends," The Conference Board Record (New York: National Industrial Conference Board) 7 (July 1970): 15-22.

8. Generally one would expect that local governments in areas with depressed labor markets could escape upward wage adjustments by hiring locally. However, like most other employers in the economy, either union influence or feelings of "fairness" do not allow government units to use low-priced labor when it is available. Often governments give wage

increases to workers when there are many local workers who would be willing to work at the old wage.

9. The preliminary "demands" of Philadelphia's unions for next year have been made known through the press. Although a limit of 5.5 percent would be consistent with Phase II guidelines, it has been reported that the "demands" are for greater amounts, more in line with those of past years. Policemen are reported asking for about 23 percent, firemen want a 20 percent wage hike plus increased fringe benefits and representatives of the general city employees are said to be asking for about a 9 percent increase plus fringe benefits.

AN EXPERIENTIAL EXERCISE:
Police Begin Their Slowdown

The newspaper headline—POLICE BEGIN THEIR SLOWDOWN—signaled a major conflict between the county's police union and county officials. This encounter will affect the safety of the citizens and the traditional perspectives about strike or job action by these key public employees.

Question: What are the basis issues underlying this slowdown?

Question: What methods are available to bring this conflict under control?

Question: Should public safety personnel be allowed to strike?

DESCRIPTION OF THE CONFLICT

After working without a contract for nearly a year, the county police officers debated alternative actions. The question was: should they strike or stage a workdown? The answer came in the form of a slowdown.

BACKGROUND DATA

- Police officers sought retirement on full pension after twenty years instead of the current requirement of twenty-five years. Full pension benefits amount to 50 percent of a police officer's final salary.
- Officers asked general increase in salary of 20 percent inasmuch as there has been no general salary adjustment for two years.
- A police officer was fired for using excessive force—he shot and killed a shoplifter.

- The shooting deaths of two police officers had occurred in the line of duty.

The county's response has been:

- The only way to meet these demands is to raise taxes in the county—and the taxpaying citizen is unwilling to pay.
- Some lesser adjustment might be manageable if productivity can simultaneously be improved.
- The twenty year retirement rule will be considered provided the benefits are based on 46 percent of final salary.
- The public is to be educated on long-term liabilities of the pension benefits. Example: a police officer may retire at age 41 after twenty years service, with a lifetime pension of $10,000 based on 50 percent of final $20,000 salary.

The overall climate is reflected by:

- participation of 98 percent of police officers in slowdown,
- officers spotted honking and waving at speeding motorists,
- officers taking triple time to complete reports on accidents they are directed to cover,
- an eleven mile cortege of officers and friends attending the burial of two fellow officers, and
- 125 officers—with wives and children—protesting at the County Administration Building. They all wore T-shirts that said "Treat Us Right" and "No Tickey, No Laundry."

Some attempts at resolution:

- The County Council has recommended binding arbitration, but the County Executive opposes it on the basis that a third party cannot decide the disposition of tax revenues.
- A mediator has been working with both parties to reduce areas of disagreement.

But the slowdown goes on! What would you do?

ANALYSIS CHECKLIST

1. The basic issues are _____
2. The alternative solutions are _____ _____
3. The impact of each solution is _____

EXPERIENTIAL EXERCISE

1. Invite several police officers and an appropriate county official to class to review this encounter. Listen to their arguments, put yourself in the role of a mediator, and try to get the parties to agree. Or put yourself in the role of an arbitrator, render a decision, explain it to your guests, and analyze their reactions.
2. Design a questionnaire to be completed by police officers which raises the question: Should police officers be allowed to strike? Why? Present the same questionnaire to a sample of citizens in the community. Analyze and discuss the results.
3. Identify key roles in this situation and permit the students to assume the roles of:
   A. police officers
   B. county officials
   C. taxpaying citizens
   Present arguments for each position and let the professor be the arbitrator.

PART III

DISPUTE SETTLEMENT AND CONTRACT ADMINISTRATION

PART III
DISPUTE SETTLEMENT
AND CONTRACT
ADMINISTRATION

A final phase of the labor-management relationship involves the resolution of labor disputes which may arise when negotiations stall, resulting in a strike threat, or when grievances filed by employees, unions, or employers involve disagreements over the interpretation and/or application of contract language. Despite the fact that only eight states allow strikes by public employees and then only under specific circumstances, and in spite of statutory penalties and remedies such as injunctions, fines, suspension, dismissal, and loss of reemployment rights for involved public employees, the frequency and intensity of work stoppages has increased in recent years.

Dispute settlement approaches normally consist of intervention by impartial third parties via mediation, fact-finding or arbitration, with only the last technique resulting in a mandatory settlement of a controversy.

Grievances normally are handled through the contractual grievance-arbitration machinery. However, illegal "wildcat" walkouts do occur when grievances are not properly resolved. A labor agreement may seem to be a marvel of legal draftsmanship but if numerous grievances arise during its term, either the terminology is more ambiguous than it appears or the fundamental relationship between the parties is lacking in mutual trust and confidence.

Merton Bernstein argues that strike prohibitions in public employment are not effective and that legalizing public employee strikes is also not the correct approach. Rather, he contends that little-used alternatives such as the non-stoppage strike and the graduated strike would prove more effective in both preserving the bargaining function and protecting the public from the disruptions accompanying labor conflict.

In the second reading in Chapter 8, Paul Staudohar evaluates the efficacy of the court-ordered injunction as a dispute settlement technique. The injunction normally is issued when there is a showing of an imminent threat of irreparable harm to persons or property occasioned by a threatened or ongoing strike. He traces its use in the private sector and cautions against its over-use in the governmental arena.

Mediation involves the appearance of an impartial third party in a conflict situation, normally when negotiations have broken down or are on the verge of deadlock. The term is used inter-changeably with that of conciliation, although there is a slight difference. A mediator tends to be somewhat more aggressive than a conciliator in that the former not only attempts to restore communications between the parties but also offers solutions to disputed issues while the latter is more concerned with restoring communications between the disputants and getting them back to the bargaining table and usually will not proffer substantive suggestions. Jerome Ross informs us of the increasingly impor-tant role that the Federal Mediation and Conciliation Service is playing in settling public labor disputes and contrasts its techniques with those utilized in the private sector.

Another conflict resolution process is known as fact-finding. Here, an individual or panel reviews the position of the parties in a particular dispute in order to narrow the issues and clarify the facts. The fact-finder(s) report their findings, with or without recommendations for action, and hope that the disputants will iron out their differences peacefully, although compliance is vol-untary. William Simkin, former head of the FMCS, and a distin-guished neutral, enumerates the steps in the fact-finding process and tells us why he recommends the elimination of the term from the terminology of labor relations, a suggestion rarely encoun-tered.

The scope of legislated interest arbitration is the topic Charles Rehmus deals with in the next selection. There are two varieties of arbitration. One, mentioned earlier, is grievance or rights arbitration, where a contract clause calls for binding arbit-ration as the terminal step in the disposition of a grievance. Interest arbitration, on the other hand, concerns a binding set-tlement imposed on the parties when there is a bargaining im-passe involving economic benefits. The contract may include an arbitration clause where the arbitrator is voluntarily chosen by the parties who agree to adhere to the award or a state or local law may provide that governmentally chosen arbitrators will be em-powered to impose a settlement. Rehmus disagrees with the claim that arbitration may often lead to costly economic settlements.

Final offer or "either-or" arbitration is a type of binding arbitration being experimented with in a number of jurisdictions. Both sides submit their final bargaining offer to the arbitrator who then must accept the most reasonable package without room for compromise. Supposedly, the knowledge that the arbitrator will reject patently unreasonable last offers will act as a stimulus to the formulation of moderate bargaining positions since it is a win-lose situation. Nels Nelson calls our attention to this dispute settlement tactic and presents some of the difficulties inherent in its implementation as the final article in Chapter 9.

The day-to-day administration of a labor contract determines how workable the document really is and whether all the time and energy expended in its development has been worthwhile. In the conventional sense, management takes the initiative in administering the agreement since most of the managerial functions are covered in the contract. The union normally is content to challenge arbitrary or illegal management actions. However, employers are precluded from soliciting the views of employees relative to personnel policies and practices if a union has gained exclusive bargaining rights. Stephen Schumacher examines this dilemma facing Federal managers and defines the permissible limits of such employee input. The selection by James Craft features suggestions for improving the administration of agreements, assessing the transferability of contract administration principles utilized in the private sector.

The grievance arbitration machinery in the labor agreement is the quid pro quo normally sought by unions when they agree to no-strike clauses demanded by management. Paul Staudohar examines the prevalence of grievance arbitration and no-strike clauses in public employment and develops contrasts with the private sector experience. William Kilberg, Thomas Angelo, and Lawrence Lorber next outline the evolution of grievance arbitration machinery in the Federal government under several executive orders. They analyze contractual language in fifty agreements which were negotiated within the constraints of civil service law and regulations.

The final reading involves an innovative approach to grievance resolution in the federal sector described by Julius Draznin. It features a labor-management class at the Long Beach, California Naval Shipyard where union and management representatives explore their respective positions in grievance situations.

Case #5 has as its scenario the state of Hawaii and the use of a variety of impasse procedures in several strike situations by the

Hawaii State Teachers Association. Marvin Levine and Joy Luna describe this experience under the relevant statute, noting the uniqueness of the variables that influence public sector conflict resolution.

The sixth case is a recitation by Mary McCormick of the functional role played by interest arbitration during the period 1968-75 in New York City. She suggests that future costs may exceed the benefits gained because of the unsettled labor relations environment created by that city's financial crisis.

Jack Stieber and Benjamin Wolkinson follow with a case study involving the attitudes of Michigan fact-finders toward the fact-finding process. They describe the statutory fact-finding procedure in Michigan during the period 1966-73, indicating the disposition of fact-finding cases, the length of the process itself, and the manner in which issues were finally resolved.

The final case by James Stern evaluates the initial experience with final offer arbitration in Wisconsin under the 1972 statute. He concludes that definitive evidence as to its effectiveness is not yet available.

Our final experiential exercise is again drawn from a real-life situation. It describes the conflict that developed when a county school board ordered teachers to take reading classes and administrators to teach classes for one week every three years. A court challenge was initiated by the teachers' association to test whether this action came within the purview of non-negotiable educational policy or whether these issues were "working conditions" subject to bilateral determination.

CHAPTER 8.
STRIKES AND THE JUDICIAL RESPONSE

Alternatives to the Strike in Public Labor Relations
Merton C. Bernstein

Professor Bernstein analyzes the difficulties inherent in the regulation of collective bargaining in the public sector and examines the currently existing and proposed systems of regulation. He concludes that new arrangements are necessary and suggests use of the non-stoppage strike and the graduated strike.

For four decades collective bargaining has been the central feature of public regulation of private labor-management relations,[1] and the right to strike, while occasionally curtailed,[2] has been thought essential to making it work.[3] And it has worked reasonably well. Manhours lost in strikes constitute an infinitesimal fraction of all hours worked.[4] In the public sector, however, strikes have been prohibited. Strikes by public employees may cause intense disruption in community life, as when transit systems cease operation or schools close. Yet, there has been developed no other effective mechanism for resolving the inherent conflicts between public employers and their employees. This essay proposes, in the context of public employment at the local level,[5] two new methods of accomplishing the desirable functions of strikes without the illegality and disruption that are their present hallmarks.[6]

Merton C. Bernstein is a Professor of Law at Ohio State University.

I. PATTERNS OF PUBLIC LABOR RELATIONS

A. History

Until fairly recently unionization at all levels of government was slight. Public employees pursued their group interests through associations and leagues, and occasionally unions, whose typical operation was to lobby for favorable civil service laws, pay scales, fringe benefits, and administrative regulations. Before the surge of unionization in the private sector brought on by the New Deal and World War II, many public employees enjoyed job security, benefits, and status that few private employees could match. However, by the late 1940's unions represented a major segment of the privately employed and won protection and economic gains which appeared to outdistance the progress of nonunionized and public employees. Large numbers of semiskilled and skilled workers entered the ranks of the middle class, formerly the preserve of professionals and white collar workers. "Plumber" and "teamster" came to imply, not grubby and poorly paid work, but short hours and high pay, while "civil servant" came to be associated with drab routine and shabby gentility. For instance, to teach required a strong feeling of vocation and, some thought, a vow of poverty. In addition, in the 1960's the apparent success of the militant stands taken by civil rights groups emboldened government employees to use collective action and direct confrontation to obtain more security and better compensation. Consequently, in the last decade unionization grew more rapidly in the public sector than in the private.

Often in the early stage of union activity, public employers— especially the federal government—took the position that while employees' unions might be consulted about employee concerns, recognition of a union, let alone bargaining, could not be reconciled with the sovereignty of the state or the benign role of the nonprofit employer. Whatever its merits, that official posture began to break down soon after the election of President Kennedy, who had received heavy support from organized labor. A committee he appointed to study the role of employee organization, dominated by Secretary of Labor Goldberg, Undersecretary Willard Wirtz, and Theodore Sorenson, all firm believers in collective bargaining, could hardly have decided against recommending a representative role for public employee unions. The resulting executive order[7] provided for limited representative status to unions. President Nixon has continued this trend, making exclusive recognition even more central to the federal government's relations with its employees.[8]

Meanwhile, public employee unions at the state and local level grew, demanded to be recognized as bargaining agents, and agitated for significant pay raises, fringe benefits, and increased job security. Put to the test by illegal strikes and sometimes illegal "sanctions," and weakened by the example of the federal government, the "consultation without recognition" model was routed here, too, probably forever.[9] At the same time, public employees drew from their private counterparts' credo and habits. As a result, the pattern of at least the short term future will probably consist of union representation, where chosen by a majority of employees in appropriate units,[10] and negotiation of signed agreements covering at least some of the subjects traditionally bargained over in the private sector.

B. Recognition and Bargaining—Without Strikes

Modern public labor relations statutes provide machinery for unit determination, elections, certification of the successful contender (if there is one), and bargaining. However, all but two[11] ban strikes by public employees.

Various philosophical justifications have been offered for this ban: strikes against the sovereign state are intolerable; public employers are not motivated by profit;[12] public services are essential; and public employee unions with both political influence and coercive power through strikes would have an undue opportunity to distort the normal political process.[13] As a practical matter, the strike ban is the result of a different chain of reasoning. because the state now provides protection for union activities, machinery for union representation, and procedures for the promotion of bargaining such as mediation and factfinding with recommendations, unions and their members should count themselves lucky to receive the new dispensation and work within the system.[14]

Perhaps they should, but they have not; unions have resisted these arguments from the outset. There are a number of reasons for their attitude. Many leaders of public employee unions come from the ranks of organized labor in the private sector, where the strike is a legally protected, central tactic of bargaining and a means of enhancing organizational spirit and loyalty. Perhaps more important, strikes have been the weapon for transforming public employer intransigence into union reocgnition, better bargains, and even legislation for protecting union activities. Thus, while statutes have banned strikes as a matter of law, even those

with the most draconian sanctions have failed to prevent them as
a matter of fact when bargaining deadlocks occur. Indeed, the
imposition of sanctions may be counterproductive, for both
union and government officials may benefit from such occasions
for demonstrating personal intrepidity without dealing with the
hard problems of settling the underlying dispute. Russell Smith
observes that we perhaps accord

> a kind of de facto recognition to conduct officially declared illegal
> . . . [a] state of affairs scarcely desirable in any society which pur-
> ports to order its human relations according to the processes of
> law.[15]

His colleague, Professor St. Antoine, agrees:

> It is folly . . . [to outlaw] absolutely a form of conduct that is sure
> to be engaged in, under certain conditions, by respectable persons
> in the thousands.[16]

These observations have the ring of wisdom.

II. THE STRIKE WEAPON

Assessment of the strike weapon requires fresh recognition of its
differing settings, tactics, and impacts.[17] So many arguments for
and against allowing the strike in public labor relations derive
from its role in private labor relations that the analysis properly
begins with the private sector.

A. In the Private Sector

While potentially very destructive weapons, strikes are seldom
employed;[18] their salutary persuasive effect results from the mere
existence of the possibility of a strike. What damages strikes
cause are, arguably, the relatively small price paid to make collective bargaining work.

The classic model of the private strike is that of a group of
employees which withholds its labor from an employer in order to
gain recognition or bargaining concessions. The employees forego
their wages and the employer loses the revenue derived from the
sale of the goods or services they would otherwise produce. The
beauty of the strike is that while a potent weapon, it also inflicts
damage on the wielder, so that even the threat of its use induces
in both sides the degree of reasonableness essential to realistic
bargaining.[19] When the strike operates in this manner, it clearly
merits legal protection.

However, it must be recognized, especially by those who
counsel legalization of strikes in the public sector, that even in

the private sector strikes do not always perform their hoped-for function. In some private sector strikes, the contending parties suffer little or no loss while others bear the brunt of the stoppage. For example, in the extended New York City newspaper strike several years ago, the printers had full employment opportunities and the publishers actually saved money by not printing during low-advertising periods; it was the other newspaper employees, the retailers, and the retailers' employees who suffered serious loss. Moreover, economists have long been aware that some major strikes disrupt the economy so seriously as to put in doubt their classical justification.[20] In addition, employer mutual aid pacts and strike insurance[21]—and, probably to a lesser degree, union strike benefits[22]—operate to eliminate or reduce significantly the disciplining power of the strike weapon. In short, while often a salutary device, the private strike sometimes fails to operate as advertised.

B. In the Public Sector

So far as public employees are concerned, strikes have the same fairly direct effect that they have in the private sector: current income stops. However, when we compare private and public employers, we find differences that preclude reliance on the classical model of the private strike.

As noted above, the private employer is motivated by loss of sales—an occurrence which is direct, measurable, and predictable. However, in most public employee strikes, the government's revenues continue; only its wage payments stop. What creates pressure on the governmental employer to bargain are expressions by its citizens of their need for the public services.[23] Such expressions are rarely clear, however, for the citizenry is composed of many groups with overlapping interests in getting services, differing abilities to pay taxes, and varying degrees of political punch.[24] Moreover, citizens are rarely aware of the precise relation between costs and services. On innumerable occasions in the last decade rejections in referenda of taxes to support schools have led to subsequent school shutdowns; I suggest that the votes might well have been different had the shutdowns occurred before or during the time that the voters were registering their preferences. Unfortunately, the precision of citizen perception may not be significantly increased even by strikes, because the choice for citizens then seems to be, not how much of a public service to have, but whether or not to have it at all.

A second crucial difference between private and public

employers is that the former are, so far as labor relations are concerned, relatively closely knit organizations. Top management often participates in collective bargaining, and when it does not, the company negotiators generally report directly back to it. In addition, management has had, at least until Phases I and II of President Nixon's game plan, the ability to set prices and make similar policy decisions without interference. This concentration of power makes possible reasonably rapid and decisive resolution of disagreements with unions.

Government employers, however, are characterized by diffusion of responsibility. Typically, one set of officials is involved in the negotiation process and another in the appropriations process; and occasionally even the citizens may speak directly through referenda. For local governments this problem is exacerbated, for not only are thee executive and legislative officials at the local level, but also significant portions of local budgets are determined by the state legislature and the governor, and, indeed, by Congress and the President.[25] Therefore, those officials who participate in negotiations often cannot make binding decisions; at most they can pledge to seek requisite funds or legislation. And, as a corollary, those who allot funds have great difficulty in predicting how much each type of service will cost and thus in allocating resources among services. The result of all this is that the decisionmaking process takes much time.[26]

In order to perform their functions in collective bargaining, public officials usually need the citizen pressure generated by strikes, but they need it in a form that gives them more time than the traditional strike permits. In Pennsylvania, the early months under a statute allowing strikes[27] have been marked by numerous stoppages, possibly beyond the number anticipated.[28] This might be a temporary phase which will not be repeated as public employers and unions learn how to use the law.[29] I suspect, though, that the strike weapon is too drastic for the peculiarities of public labor relations. And in any event, the implacable opposition in most states to traditional strikes by public employees places the legalization of such strikes beyond debate for the foreseeable future.

III. COMPULSORY ARBITRATION—A DUBIOUS ALTERNATIVE

Compulsory arbitration is often proposed as a peaceful means of settling the differences between public employers and employees.[30] There are, however, serious objections to the use of this device in either the private or public sector. Successful bargaining requires that each side determine which issues it feels most strongly about, estimate the other side's priorities, determination, and strength, and then trade concessions with the other side in an effort to reach a mutually acceptable "deal." In arbitration, however, all arguments are supposedly based on logic—even though it has long been recognized that reasoned criteria, especially for setting wages, are illusory.[31] Consequently, compulsory arbitration undermines good faith bargaining, for the weaker party has little to gain from bargaining.[32] Furthermore, since arbitrators may treat the best disclosed offers as the permissible limits of the award, it pays for each side not to disclose how far it is really willing to go on each issue. As a result, the availability of arbitration saps the efficacy of factfinding; and, at the arbitration stage, the stated issues and arguments may so obscure the parties' true needs and desires that the resultant award may easily miss a satisfactory resolution of the dispute.

A further difficulty arises from use of compulsory arbitration of disputes in the public sector—the preemption of public officials from deciding policy issues. Viewed mechanically, the arbitration process does not seem to allocate public resources: arbitrators fix equitable salaries for employees, and officials determine, given these cost figures, how much public service should be purchased. As a practical matter, however, employers rarely contemplate and unions would rarely permit curtailment of services and employment. Thus, the wage decision and the resource allocation decision are inevitably linked. Also, professional employees often bargain over programs. For example, teachers' unions may demand certain kinds of educational offerings or limits on class size. Even if arbitrators were capable of dealing with the complexities of budgeting and choosing programs, elected officials should not delegate the duty they owe the electorate to settle these questions. Deciding policy issues is the vocation of officials, not of arbitrators. Furthermore, when decisions lack an adequate electoral base, they will be short-lived, as the drastic retrenchments of Medicaid demonstrate.

Compulsory arbitration in the public sector would also face a problem more mechanical, but no less important, than that of inappropriate delegation. Typically, the employment contracts of public employees are staggered, so that only one or a few groups will be negotiating new contracts at any one time. In such a context the frequent disputes over the relative pay scales of the various groups of public employees create nearly insoluble perplexities, with each group demanding higher pay scales than the previous group received. I suggest that the bargaining process offers a possible way off this treadmill: a compensation package can be negotiated with each group of employees which, while intrinsically satisfying to the group, defies comparison with those of other groups. It is dubious, however, that the traditional arbitration format can produce stable arrangements. Even if the arbitrators possess the abilities necessary to determination of the appropriate pay relationships—and they may not, since the basic problem requires policy resolution—they would not, in the course of arbitrating one group's contract dispute, have all the competing groups before them. Nor would some new scheme to allow all competing groups to present the merits of their claims be feasible, for it would incur the risk of a simultaneous strike by all those groups dissatisfied with the award.

I would also like to point out what would be a significant transitional problem were compulsory arbitration to be widely adopted in the public sector. Few potential neutrals now possess sophistication in public finance. While expertise might be developed, several years of factfinding in public labor disputes which involved budgeting issues seem to have produced little confidence among arbitrators that they are equipped to deal with such problems.

"Either-or" arbitration, having been specially proposed.[33] deserves special mention. Under this arrangement the arbitrators decide which side's final offer is more "reasonable" and take it as their award; they cannot choose any point between the parties' offers. While such a system is said to encourage reasonableness by both parties, it is actually gimmickry which encourages poker playing. Sweetly reasonable and unpalatably sour proposals may often be intermixed in each party's offer, but the arbitrators are powerless to select only the reasonable elements. Furthermore, even if under such a system it may be said that the parties deserve what they get, the ultimate award carries with it little promise of stability. Anyone with labor relations experience knows that whenever a winner and a loser may be identified, the leadership of the loser is likely, if only to regain face, to cause trouble.

In conclusion, since neither the union nor the local government may have agreed to the process of arbitration, to the selection of the arbitrator, or to the ultimate award, the resolution of disputes by this method is inherently unstable. Coercion is not only unattractive; it also works quite poorly.

IV. PROPOSED ALTERNATIVES: THE NONSTOPPAGE STRIKE AND THE GRADUATED STRIKE

It is reasonably clear that in public employment, the strike ban does not work; yet in most jurisdictions legalization of the strike is not a real possibility. And, I submit, the strike as it is known in the private sector would not function in the same way in the public sector and does not fit the peculiarities of public collective bargaining—diffuse responsibility and the consequent need for longer periods of time to reach settlements than in the private sector. Compulsory arbitration has serious drawbacks, not the least of which are its unacceptability to large segments of public management and unions and the likely instability of its results.

Therefore I suggest[34] that we explore the possibilities of two other arrangements which have neer been considered in the public sector[35] but which, I suggest, fit the needs of *all* the parties more adequately than either present practices or the currently proposed alternatives.

It will help to give a rough sketch of the functioning of these two arrangements before I go into them in detail. In a nonstoppage strike, operations would continue as usual, but both the employees and the employer would pay to a special fund an amount equal to a specified percentage of total cash wages. Thus, while both parties would be under pressure to settle, there would be no disruption of service. In a graduated strike, employees would stop working during portions of their usual workweek and would suffer comparable reductions of wages. Here, there would be pressure not only on employees and employer but also on the community; however, the decrease in public service would not be as sudden or complete as in the conventional strike. I believe that these two new types of strike substitutes would work best in tandem.

A. The Nonstoppage Strike

Under my proposal, a public employee union would be free to declare a nonstoppage strike after all other bargaining procedures failed to produce a settlement. Employees would be obliged to continue to work full time but would forego a portion of their take-home pay. I suggest that, initially, ten percent would suffice. This money would be paid by the public employer directly into a special fund (more fully discussed below). In addition to paying the equivalent of regular wages, the employer would also put into the fund an extra amount equal to what the emloyees have given up; this latter sum would constitute a loss to the employer. The union would have the option periodically to increase the amount of the foregone wages and employer payment, perhaps by increments of ten percent every two weeks. The public employer would have the option to require the union to switch to a graduated strike. If the employer did this, the employees would continue to lose the same rate of pay, but the employer would forego services rather than pay out additional funds.

I believe that exercise of the option to initiate the nonstoppage strike and increase the percentage can be limited to the union. The union has little other leverage, since the conventional strike would still be prohibited. Also, were the public employer able to initiate a procedure under which employees would work without pay, questions of involuntary servitude might arise. In any event, the employer would still have the strategic bargaining advantage of instituting, after a deadlock in negotiation, certain changes in pay or other terms of employment which have been offered to the union and rejected.

The nonstoppage strike would accommodate the peculiarities of public labor relations. It would attract the attention of and put pressure on both the public officials who deal directly with the union involved and other members of the executive branch whose own budgets might be affected, the local legislature, and state officials. And while a nonstoppage strike would not precipitate a crisis, its pressure would be steady and increasable. Thus, it may provide the necessary incentive for the various bodies of government to act, while allowing them the time they need to do so effectively. Moreover, it does not disturb consideration of the merits of the dispute with the hysteria and histrionics now typical of illegal strikes.

While nonstoppage strikes would create additional expense for public employers—many of whom are hard pressed as it is—they should also put an end to the present practice of paying the employees at overtime rates when a strike ends to reduce the backlog of work accumulated during the strike. Also, hopefully, the expense should be only temporary, and, as will be explained below, the money will not go to waste. In any event, the price does not seem too high to pay for a substantially improved process of bargaining.

Nonstoppage strikes offer significant advantages to employees, perhaps even more than would legalization of conventional strikes. In the first place, their rate of loss of pay would be lower at any given time than if there were an all-out strike. For employees with mortgage and other installment obligations to meet, this continuity of income is highly desirable. And, to the extent that the nonstoppage strike encourages more responsive bargaining without any stoppages, the total loss of pay may be less. In addition, in a full-scale strike, especially one of long duration, the employer is not liable for fringe benefit payments. Thus, life insurance policies may lapse or require payments by employees at a time when their income is interrupted, and group medical care insurance may have to be kept in force at the higher-cost individual rates. In a nonstoppage strike these benefits should continue.

Second, in actual strikes employees run the risk of losing their jobs. A common sanction in illegal strikes is to fire strikers. In the private strike, too, replacement of economic strikers has long been permitted, and while I have seen no data on public employer activity of this sort, I think it highly probable that permanent, nondiscriminatory replacement of strikers will become a feature of the legal public employee strike. In nonstoppage strikes, of course, jobs would be secure. Moreover, the absence of even temporary replacements would eliminate a traditionally potent source of violence, which everyone has a stake in averting.

Third, long-run employee and union interests are best served by a method that is legal and discomfits the community as little as possible. As union leadership knows from its post-World War II experience, unpopular strikes lead to distasteful legislation. And, by the same token, strikers, even if they feel their conduct justified, often must incur the disapproval of friends, neighbors, and others in the community. A peaceful method of pursuing demands seems clearly preferable.

The public employer would need some means of assuring union and employee compliance with the ground rules. Obviously, working full time for less than full pay might encourage some employees to slow down or "call in sick"—a favored device in strike-ban jurisdictions. Two procedures would minimize violations. First, the unions must see that it is to their advantage to persuade members that it is to *their* advantage to abide by the rules. That is, all must be made aware that the "struck" employer is indeed under strike-like pressure. Second, the statute should provide for an expedited (and I mean quick) unfair labor practice procedure to hear and determine charges of slowdown or improper absence. However, these areas are so sensitive and have such a potential for emotional overreaction that employer discipline of employees should be limited to those cases where impartial hearing officers make a finding that the improper action has taken place.

One serious problem with the nonstoppage strike is finding a suitable use for the special fund to which the public employer and employees have contributed. In order to insure that the loss will actually discipline the parties' conduct in bargaining, the fund would have to be placed effectively beyond their recapture.[36] I recommend that the fund be put at the disposal of a tripartite Public Purposes Committee in which respected community figures outnumber the total number of union and government members. This committee would be charged with the task of applying the money to publicly desirable, preferably short term projects that are not currently in the public budget—creation of scholarships or construction of public recreation facilities, for example. Certainly public employees would get little direct advantage from such a use of the money. Moreover, since these projects would not be currently funded, the committee's action would not discharge any of the government's present obligations; and since such contributions would occur irregularly, the government could not count on being relieved of any future burdens. Consequently, given public officialdom's abhorrence of losing control over money, this use of the funds should also provide an incentive for public employers to bargain.

Finally, I would like to dispel what may perhaps be a lingering doubt about nonstoppage strikes. Although they were initially proposed for use in the private sector more than two decades ago, they have had little acceptance by private parties. There are a number of reasons for this. First, although strikes have been the subject of some academic disapproval and periodic editorial dismay, they remain an acceptable device in the private sector. There has been, therefore, little real pressure for a substitute. Second, for a nonstoppage strike in the private sector to be as effective as the conventional strike, the contributions of the employer to the fund must be geared to the amount of profits it is spared from losing. Because of the obvious difficulty of calculating this figure, achieving a formula for employer contribution which is satisfactory to both parties could easily be more formidable an obstacle than resolving their basic economic differences. Third, any statutory imposition of a nonstoppage plan would, while solving in a crude way the complexities of computing the formula, raise the claim by employers of deprivation of property without due process and the analogous employee claim of involuntary servitude.

Clearly the first reason does not apply in the public sector, for strikes are not currently acceptable. Nor does the second carry much weight. There is no need in the public sector to base a formula on profits because there are no profits; what should be required by the employees is that there be sufficient pressure on the public employer, and I believe my proposal provides that. The third, too, is inapplicable. Government may of course impose conditions on itself; and since it is constitutional totally to deprive public employees of the right to strike,[37] it should be permissible to provide them with a halfway measure, especially when it is the union which voluntarily initiates its use. In short, no significant barriers to adoption of nonstoppage strikes exist in the public sector.

B. The Graduated Strike

A nonstoppage strike may be insufficient to induce responsive bargaining. More direct pressure may be required, and the graduated strike would provide it.

In a graduated strike the union would call work to a halt in stages. During the first week or two of the strike the employees would not work for half a day; during the next period, if the union so chose, they would not work for one full day per week; and so on, until they reached some floor short of total stoppage. Employees' take-home pay would be cut proportionately.

The effect of a graduated strike would be to give the public a taste of reduced service without the shock of immediate and total deprivation. This would start in motion the political machinery I described earlier,[38] but would not overload it. Citizens would make complaints about their inconvenience known to their elected representatives. Local officials, both executive and legislative, would thus be under pressure to *do* something, but would nevertheless be able to consult with each other and with the officials at higher levels of government. They would therefore be able to negotiate with the union in a reasonably coordinated and authoritative manner. Free of resentment and of posturing over illegality, the complicated political process of sorting out preferences between higher costs and fewer services and among competing demands could then work itself out.

To insure that employees really suffer proportionate loss of wages would require, first, that they be unable, after the strike, to reduce backlogs at overtime rates. This could probably be accomplished simply by a limitation on overtime pay for some period following the strike. It does not seem necessary to do more:

to the extent the employees ultimately recoup their lost wages, the public will have the lost service restored; and in any case it is unlikely that either side's losses will ever be totally recovered. Second, it would be necessary that the shutdown not exceed the announced level. While enforcement of this requirement would not be easy, it would probably be satisfactory for an impartial body with an expedited hearing procedure to determine the actual extent of the employee stoppage and to mete out appropriate penalties, including reduction of wages. In addition, there would be another strong inducement to proper observance of the ground rules: union and employee recognition that they have an effective, fair, and acceptable weapon to encourage good faith bargaining.

As I stated before, I think that the graduated strike and nonstoppage srike would work best in tandem. Because a nonstoppage strike would cause the public less disruption, we should perhaps require that unions try it for at least four weeks; they would then have the option of instituting a graduated strike. However, since both types of strikes are certain to put pressure on the public employer, I think we should give the employer some limited options. If it feels itself financially hard pressed, it can select the graduated strike, which would result in no additional expense. If it believed that the service performed by the employees was so essential to the public that cessation could not be tolerated—for example, fire and police protection—it should have the opportunity to persuade an impartial, preferably expert, tribunal that the services are in reality so indispensable. If successful, it could limit the union to the ever-more-expensive nonstoppage strike.

V. CONCLUSION

A blanket ban on strikes by public employees does not work. Illegal strikes are bad for labor relations and even worse for the rule of law. However, conventional strikes, if legalized, would be ill adapted to the complex procedures of public labor relations. Yet the public must accord its employees reasonable procedures that produce responsible bargaining. Under my proposals, bargaining could perform its salutary function, but without the disruption caused by the conventional strike and in ways adapted to the peculiarities of the public's needs and the government's intricate procedures for allocating resources.

Our federal system is complex and often awkward, but it enables us to experiment with various means of regulating public labor-management relations so that neither the public nor public employees are victimized. We should test the nonstoppage strike, the graduated strike, and indeed any other promising arrangement as we grope in this old field mined with so many new problems.

NOTES

1. Section 7 of the National Labor Relations Act [hereinafter cited as NLRA] declares:

Employees shall have the right to self-organization, to form, join, or assist labor organizations, to bargain collectively through representatives of their own choosing, and to engage in other concerted activities for the purpose of collective bargaining . . . .

29 U.S.C. Sec. 157 (1970) Several states have similar laws. See, e.g, State Labor Relations Law Sec. 3, MASS. GEN. LAWS ANN. ch. 150A, Sec. 3 (1971); N.Y. LABOR LAW Sec. 703 (McKinney 1965).

2. For example, secondary boycotts are illegal. NLRA Sec. 8(b) (4), 29 U.S.C. Sec. 158 (b)(4) (1970).

3. Section 13 of the NLRA supplements Section 7:

Nothing in this subchapter, except as specifically provided for herein, shall be construed so as either to interfere with or impede or diminish in any way the right to strike, or to affect the limitations or qualifications of that right.

29 U.S.C. Sec. 163 (1970).

4. In 1968 the 5,045 work stoppages accounted for .28% of total working time. U.S. BUREAU OF LABOR STATISTICS, DEP'T OF LABOR, BULL. NO. 1646, ANALYSIS OF WORK STOPPAGES, 1968, at 13 (1970).

5. In all but two of the eleven years 1958-1968, strikes by local government employees accounted for more than 90% of all government stoppages. TWENTIETH CENTURY FUND TASK FORCE ON LABOR DISPUTES, PICKETS AT CITY HALL 32 (1970). Consequently, while much of the analysis and all of the proposals here presented could be applied to higher levels of government, my focus is on local units.

6. The existing literature is massive, and no attempt will be made here to summarize it. For an excellent symposium on public employee labor relations, see Symposium: Labor Relations in the Public Sector, 67 MICH L. REV. 891 (1969).

7. Exec. Order No. 10,988, 3 C.F.R. [1959-1963 Comp.] 521 (1964).

8. Exec. Order No. 11,491, 3 C.F.R. 510 (1971).

9. The philosophy that public employees do not even have the right to join unions has finally become outmoded. See Smith, State and Local Advisory Reports on Public Employee Labor Legislation: A Comparative Analysis, 67 MICH. L. REV. 891, 892 (1969). A fine summary of the

transitional changes from ban to permission of union organization, bargaining, collective agreement execution, and arbitration is found in Smith & Clark, *Reappraisal of the Role of the States in Shaping Labor Relations Law,* 1965 WIS. L. REV. 411, 421-31.

10. The regularization of procedures for the selection of employee representatives is indispensable to public employee labor relations. Continued resistance to unionization may be expected for some time because so much unionization takes place at the local government level, particularly among teachers. Small community school boards, inexperienced in labor relations, frequently influenced by persons with an anti-union bias, and already beset by intractable problems, often seem incapable of dealing reasonably with unions. Stoppages caused by the combination of such reluctance with the absence of legally prescribed procedures for ascertaining bargaining units and determining employee desires are wasteful indulgences of attitudes whose time has passed. *See* GOVERNOR'S COMM'N TO REVISE THE PUBLIC EMPLOYEE LAW OF PENNSYLVANIA, REPORT AND RECOMMENDATIONS 6, 9 (1968).

Professor Charles Rehmus sets forth a useful catalogue of other measures to remove unnecessary sources of friction in *Constraints on Local Governments in Public Employee Bargaining,* 67 MICH. L. REV. 919 (1969).

11. HAWAII REV. STAT. Sec. 89-12 (Supp. 1970); PA. STAT. ANN. tit. 43, Sec. 1101.1003 (Supp. 1971). A Vermont statute prohibits strikes by local government employees if they "will endanger the health, safety or welfare of the public." VT. STAT. ANN. tit. 21, Sec. 1704 (Supp. 1971). The range of permissible strikes is unclear.

12. The logical consequence of this is hard to fathom. Presumably, nonprofit employers will act more fairly. However, employers motivated by profit may actively seek employee goodwill and bargain responsively because of the serious financial consequences of a stoppage; public employers, especially at the local level, have become motivated chiefly by a desire to make ends meet.

13. *See* Taylor, *Public Employment: Strikes or Procedures?,* 20 IND. & LAB. REL. REV. 617, 626-27 (1967); Wellington & Winter, *The Limits of Collective Bargaining in Public Employment,* 78 YALE L.J. 1107, 1123-25 (1969). However, unions in the private sector have long enjoyed such dual methods of influence. *See* International Ass'n of Machinists v. Street, 367 U.S. 740, 800 (1961) (Frankfurter, J., dissenting) ("It would be pedantic heavily to document this familiar truth of industrial history and commonplace of trade-union life.").

14. *See* Taylor, *supra* note 13, *passim.*

15. Smith, *State and Local Advisory Reports on Public Employment Labor Legislation: A Comparative Analysis,* 67 MICH. L. REV. 891, 917 (1969).

16. St. Antoine, *The Consent of the Governed–Public Employee Unions and the Law,* MICH. L. QUADRANGLE NOTES, Fall, 1970, at 9, 12.

17. John Dunlop discusses several, but not all, in *The Function of the*

Strike, in FRONTIERS OF COLLECTIVE BARGAINING 103 (J. Dunlop & N. Chamberlain eds., 1967).

18. *See* note 4 *supra.*

19. *See* D. CULLEN, NEGOTIATING LABOR-MANAGEMENT CONTRACTS 2-5 (1965).

20. *See, e.g.,* Marceau & Musgrave, *Strikes in Essential Industries: A Way Out,* 27 HARV. BUS. REV. 286 (1949).

Indeed, in 1947 Congress sought to curtail strikes capable of threatening the national health and safety by national emergency dispute provisions. *See* Labor-Management Relations Act (Taft-Hartley Act) Secs. 205-08, 29 U.S.C. Sections 175-78(1970).

21. *See. e.g.,* Comment, *Six Carrier Mutual Aid Pact: A New Concept of Management Strike Strategy in the Airline Industry,* 60 COLUM. L. REV. 205 (1960); Comment, *Strike Insurance: An Analysis of the Legality of Interemployer Economic Aid under Present Federal Legislation,* 38 N.Y.U.L. REV. 126, 127-34 (1963).

22. Strike benefits tend to be small. N. CHAMBERLAIN, THE LABOR SECTOR 620 (1965).

23. For many years I have suggested that the consumer-taxpayer-citizen be regarded as the real public employer. This characterization was independently espoused by Professor Clyde Summers at the 1960 Midwest Labor Conference. *See* 1969 LAB REL. YEARBOOK 305. An experienced nonacademic labor relations expert shares this analysis. Simons, *Discussion: The American City and Its Public Employee Unions,* in INDUSTRIAL RELATIONS RESEARCH ASS'N, COLLECTIVE BARGAINING IN THE PUBLIC SERVICE: PROCEEDINGS OF THE 1966 ANNUAL SPRING MEETING 104, 107 (G. Somers ed. 1966).

24. The rash of rejections of school bonds and levies indicates that the dominant instructions from citizens are to economize. *But see* Wellington & Winter, *Structuring Collective Bargaining in Public Employment,* 79 YALE L.J. 805, 849 (1970), which, remarkably, posits public pressure "for settlements without much regard for the costs . . . ."

25. In 1969 local government expenditures totalled about $80 billion, of which $48 billion came from their own sources. U.S. BUREAU OF THE CENSUS, 1971 STATISTICAL ABSTRACT OF THE UNITED STATES 400 (1971). The state governments contributed $22 billion. COUNCIL OF STATE GOVERNMENTS, THE BOOK OF THE STATES 1970-71, at 282 (1970). Together, local and state goverments derived $19 billion from the federal government, U.S. BUREAU OF THE CENSUS, 1971 STATISTICAL ABSTRACT OF THE UNITED STATES 403 (1971), much of it reaching the localities via the state governments.

26. "Frequently many months are needed to reach agreement . . . ." NEW YORK CITY OFFICE OF COLLECTIVE BARGAINING, 1969 ANNUAL REPORT 7 (1970).

27. PA. STAT. ANN. tit. 43, Sec. 1101.1003 (Supp. 1971).

28. I was so informed by one member of the Governor's Commission to Revise the Public Employee Law of Pennsylvania. Others with operating

responsibility, I am told, feel that strike activity has been slight and at the level generally expected.

29. On both sides, but especially on the employer's, one can expect lack of experience in labor relations frequently compounded by amateurism. The regular duties of district and county attornies do not equip them to deal with unions. Clearly, an important element of state labor relations policy is to supply education to public officials, preferably before they are confronted with a union challenge. And after the union is on the scene as bargaining representative, the state should furnish to local officials experienced lawyers and economists to familiarize them with the legal and practical intricacies of their unaccustomed situation and provide advice as to the peaceful alternatives available.

31. *See* I. BERNSTEIN, ARBITRATION OF WAGES 51-105 (1954); Taylor, *Criteria in the Wage Bargain,* in N.Y.U. 1st ANN. CONF. ON LABOR 65 (E. Stein ed. 1948).

32. *See* H. NORTHRUP, COMPULSORY ARBITRATION AND GOVERNMENT INTERVENTION IN LABOR DISPUTES: AN ANALYSIS OF EXPERIENCE 207 (1966); W. WIRTZ, LABOR AND THE PUBLIC INTEREST 52 (1964) ("Experience, particularly the War Labr Board experience during the forties, confirms that a statutory requirement . . . [for] arbitration has a narcotic effect on private bargainers . . . ."); Kheel, *Strikes and Public Employment,* 67 MICH L. REV. 931, 936-40 (1969). *But see* Finkelman, *When Bargaining Fails,* in COLLECTIVE BARGAINING IN THE PUBLIC SERVICE.

33. President Nixon has proposed such a plan for resolving emergency disputes in the railroads. *See* 1971 U.S. CODE CONG. & AD NEWS 42. Neil Chamberlain reports that this type of arbitration "was tried briefly and without much success under the German Weimar Republic . . . ." N. CHAMBERLAIN, THE LABOR SECTOR 640 (1965). For a seasoned observer's low opinion of "either-or" arbitration in public employment, consult Wildman, *Representing the Teachers' Interests,* in INDUSTRIAL RELATIONS RESEARCH ASS'N, *supra* note 23, at 113, 119.

34. I want to emphasize that the proposed procedures should be part of a comprehensive public labor relations scheme which provides protection of employees against reprisal for collective activity, procedures for ascertaining appropriate bargaining units, elections to determine employee preferences, recognition and mandatory bargaining, sanctions against improper union activity, mediation procedures for bargaining disputes, and factfinding with recommendations in the case of bargaining deadlock. Such procedures are necessary conditions to the proper functioning of the nonstoppage and graduated strikes. Happily, it is also the case that these procedures will work more effectively if the pressure devices I propose are available.

35. Several proposals for "nonstoppage" or "statutory" (because imposed by statute) strikes were made for the private sector starting in the late 1940's. They were, in chronological order, Marceau & Musgrave, *Strikes in Essential Industries: A Way Out,* 27 HARV. BUS. REV. 287 (1949);

Goble, *The Non-Stoppage Strike*, 2 LAB. L.J. 105 (1951); N. Chamberlain
& J. Schilling, *Social Responsibility and Strikes* 279-86 (1952); Gregory,
Injunctions, Seizure and Compulsory Arbitration, 26 TEMP L.Q. 397,
402 (1953). The major variations are summarized and assessed in
McCalmont, *The Semi-Strike*, 15 IND & LAB. REL. REV. 191 (1962);
Marshall & Marshall, *Nonstoppage Strike Proposals—A Critique*, 7 LAB.
L.J. 299 (1956).

All of these proposals envisioned that employees continue at work and
that the employer lose some income; and most involved a reduction of pay
between declaration of the nonstoppage and settlement. All were limited
to the private sector. The proposal I make here is the first to suggest
application to the public sector and differs in several respects from each
of the earlier versions.

The graduated strike is, to the best of my knowledge, original with me.
36. It might, however, be worthwhile to experiment with partial recapture as an incentive to rapid settlement. Thus, the amounts lost by the
parties in the week in which they reach a settlement might be returned to
them. *Cf.* Goble, *supra* note 35, at 106.
37. United Fed'n of Postal Clerks v. Blount, 325 F. Supp. 879 (D.D.C.
1971), *aff'd*, 92 S. Ct. 80 (1971).
38. *See* pp. 464-66 *supra*.

The Changing Role
of the Injunction
in the Public Sector

Paul D. Staudohar

*It is not wise to endorse blanket use of the injunction in any and
all instances involving ostensibly illegal, concerted action by
public employees. What may result, the author notes, is post-
settlement hard feelings on the part of employees as well as a
gradual diminution of the injunction's significance.*

One of the major weapons of the government as employer, which
is increasingly being used by the employee organization as well, is
the injunction. This device, particularly when utilized by the

Reproduced from the May, 1971 issue of the LABOR LAW JOURNAL published and
copyrighted (1971) by Commerce Clearing House, Inc., 4025 W. Peterson Avenue,
Chicago, Illinois, 60646. Reprinted by permission of Paul D. Staudohar, Professor
of Business Administration, California State University, Hayward, California and
Commerce Clearing House, Inc.

government to suppress demonstrative activity by employee organizations, is being deployed in a context not unlike that prevailing in the private sector some 40 years ago. This article will examine the injunctive process in public employment and the legal, political and social implications of its utilization. The main contention is that what is needed is a redefinition of the reasons for and circumstances under which injunctions are issued in the public sector.

A LOOK BACKWARD AT THE PRIVATE SECTOR

The history of the use of the injunction in private sector labor disputes prior to 1932 indicates a tendency for courts to use the injunctive order to shut off concerted action involving not only strikes but picketing as well and to do so even in situations where this activity was being exercised in an orderly and peaceful manner. Thus in the *Debs* case, the injunction issued by the United States Supreme Court restrained, among other things. "all other persons whomsoever, absolutely to desist and refrain from in any way of manner interfering with, hindering, obstructing, or stopping any of the business. . . ."[1] In the words of Summers and Wellington, these orders "enjoining 'whomsoever' from engaging in 'whatsoever' totally paralyzed the union from any concerted action."[2] So it was when the Supreme Judicial Court of Massachusetts issued an injunction against union picketing to establish wage increases and hours reductions, when this picketing was accompanied by a strike.[3] To no avail, Justice Holmes, then a member of the Massachusetts court, objected to this injunction in that he felt that when picketing was confined to persuasion and notification of the strike it should not be unlawful.

With some modification, the line of judicial reasoning indicated by the foregoing cases prevailed until 1932. In that year the Norris-LaGuardia Act markedly curtailed the use of the injunction in the private sector by permitting the issuance of injunctions only in cases where irreparable injury was threatened by unlawfu actions of either labor or management and where adequate protection could not be provided by the public law enforcement officers. This law, however, does not apply to public employees.

THE INJUNCTIVE PROCESS

In general, the nature of the injunctive complaint as initiated by the government employer might include a statement describing the governmental entity as to purposes and functions; an allegation of individual or collective action associated with a threat or actual occurrence of some unlawful undertaking; and a contention that the unlawful actual or threatened activities, unless restrained, will continue to violate the law or cause substantial disruption of the functions of government. Pursuant to such statement and allegations, a prayer for relief in the form of a cease and desist order is made. Once so ordered, if the activity does not stop, the person, persons or organization against whom the order was issued will be held in contempt of court and thereunder be subject to criminal sanctions.

There are three basic types of injunctive orders that courts are issuing concerning the public sector. An *ex parte* restraining order—which is essentially the same as a temporary restraining order—occurs where a court order to cease and desist is issued without affording the defendants any opportunity to present their side of the case. A preliminary injunction is then usually issued after a hearing on the contentions raised by the parties. Witnesses are sometimes called in this proceeding. Permanent injunctions are rarely issued in the public sector, in large part because the nature of the disputes is such that the strike is typically short in duration. The public employer ordinarily capitulates with wage and benefit concessions and grants amnesty to the striking employees. Any pending legal proceedings are then usually dismissed or withdrawn.

Criminal sanctions are infrequently invoked in the public sector despite the high incidence of injunctive violations. This also results from the nature of the disputes that arise. To enforce the penalties for violation of an injunction by imprisoning union officials tends to galvanize public reaction and labor organization support of the martyred officials. This is illustrated by the challenging of a court order in Newark by David Selden, American Federation of Teachers president, who served a 60-day prison sentence to dramatize his anti-injunction protest. Moreover, possibility of settlement is often made more difficult by having the leaders of one side incarcerated.

COURT TRENDS

The injunctive process has been resorted to by the government for two major reasons. First, issuance is requested against illegal activity such as a strike by public employees for reason of the illegality per se. Activities considered enjoinable are principally those considered by courts to be illegal in their object or method. Secondly, injunctions are sought to obtain quick relief from activities by public employees aimed at closing down governmental functions, the justification for the restraining order being the exigencies of government objectives.

The specific acts by public employees against which injunctions have almost exclusively been issued are strikes—including slowdowns, and picketing. Up to 1968, courts had in virtually all instances granted injunctions against strikes and picketing, although not necessarily in cases involving slowdowns, sanctions and other "quasi-legal" forms of collective action by public employees. Little, if any, consideration was given to the actual effects of the strike or picketing on the operation of the governmental entity. In 1968, however, cases were decided in Michigan and California which broke from the restraining of all strike and picketing activity, regardless of how innocuous, and began to examine the effects of the collective action on the operation of government functions and the exercise of constitutionally protected rights of public employees to free expression.

In the *Holland* case,[4] the Supreme Court of Michigan ruled that the fact that a concert of prohibited action had taken place and that schools would not open on time because of the teachers refusing to report to work was not *ipso facto* a sufficient reason to justify the court issuing an injunction. It was thought to be against public policy for the court to issue injunctions in labor disputes unless a showing of irreparable injury or breach of the peace occurs.[5] The *Holland* case represents a particularly important precedent because it spells out the conditions under which injunctions may be issued. The argument had been adduced in the case by the teachers' association that the school district had refused to bargain in good faith. The court, in remanding the case to a lower court, suggested that this issue be inquired into further. What the court thus implied is that the public employer should come to the court with "clean hands" by having bargained in good faith and that failing to do so may be additional ground for denying the request by the public employer for issuance of an injunction against demonstrative employee activity.

In two New York Supreme Court cases which involved a sanction, or directive to employee organization members not to apply for or take work in a jursidiction, and an attempt to compel a teachers' association to submit a dispute to a grievance procedure, the courts used *Holland* type reasoning in denying the injunctions. In the sanction case the court noted that injunctions should be issued "where the peril to the plaintiff is very substantial and imminent. . . ."[6] In the grievance procedure case, the court took the position that the situation was not "sufficiently extraordinary" to merit the issuance of a temporary injunction.[7]

In the other noteworthy breakthrough, the California Supreme Court in the *Berry* case[8] refused to issue a temporary restraining order against picketing county workers who were threatening to strike. The court's reasoning was that because the temporary restraining order was so broadly worded it restrained not only the strike but the peaceful exercise of the constitutional right of free speech guaranteed by the First and Fourteenth Amendments. This is not to say that the court in this case would not have issued an injunction against a public employee strike, but rather that in attempting to prevent the threatened strike through the injunctive order, other constitutionally protected rights could not be infringed upon where these rights were being peacefully exercised. The *Berry* decision is similar, in providing constitutional protection for picketing, to the *Thornhill* case[9]—a leading precedent in the private sector. The courts are drawing the line on picketing in the public sector when it is not peaceful or where it interferes with the routine operation of the governmental agency, such as by impeding ingress and egress to an area. These kinds of picketing are not thought by courts to be constitutionally protected and injunctions have been issued against them.[10]

The trend toward more restrained use of the injunction in public sector cases as indicated by *Holland* and *Berry* is materially reinforced by a recent Illinois decision. The case emanated from a strike and picketing by county nursing home employees against which a preliminary injunction was issued. The county was seeking to make the injunction permanent. The Supreme Court of Illinois held that the preliminary injunction was erroneously issued against the strike and picketing because the state's anti-injunction law provides that injunctions are not to be issued "in any case involving or growing out of a dispute concerning terms or conditions of employment. . . ."[11] Interestingly, despite its invalidation, the court still punished the violators of the injunction for contempt in that where the injunction is believed to be illegally issued, this must be proved by way of judicial determination and, in the meantime, the persons against whom the restraining order is issued must comply with it. This case would appear to be a most apposite precedent in the cases involving public employee strikes and picketing in other states which have anti-injunction or "little Norris-LaGuardia" laws.

Further illustration of the changing judicial attitude is a recent decision by a circuit court judge in Milwaukee, who refused to issue a temporary injunction against striking teachers. The judge's reasoning was that an injunction at that time would deny due process rights to the teachers inasmuch as they had not presented their side of the dispute to the court.[12]

What appears to be the reason behind these court decisions being less than dogmatic in issuing injunctions is that their issuance in cases where little evidence of harm is present has not been very effective in bringing an end to controversies involving public employees. Unless justified, injunctions can further exacerbate ill feeling between government and labor and tend to make labor-management relations more embittered than they might otherwise have been after the settlement. To a large extent, of course, the injunction issue is inextricably tied to the broader question of whether public employees should be granted the right to strike and to place similar pressures on the ability of government to operate in normal fashion in order to achive employee objectives of higher wages, improved working conditions and, in some cases, to influence government policy. Outlawing of public employee strikes and picketing in all instances, despite lack of essentiality of services, has been an increasingly untenable posture for government to take, and the changes in public opinion toward these issues is manifesting itself in a more relaxed judicial position toward injunctions in certain circumstances.

STATUTORY CHANGES

Besides some liberalization by courts, legislatures in two states have passed laws which would use the injunction more constructively in curbing public employee demonstrative activity and which are mainly aimed at the strike issue. The Vermont Teacher Bargaining Law which was effective as of September 1, 1969, permits the courts, following a hearing, to rule on whether teachers should be allowed to strike in a given situation. Emphasis by the court is to be placed on whether "commencement or continuance of the action poses a clear and present danger to a sound program of school education which [action]. . . it is in the best public interest to prevent."[13] In another Vermont enactment—which went into effect on July 1, 1970—municipal employees appear to have a right to strike absent an endangering of the "health, safety or welfare of the public"; redress against such action is to be sought in the courts.[14] Using similar language, the Pennsylvania Public Employee Relations Act, effective October 21, 1970, also leaves the question of relief from a strike up to the courts by way of a petition by the employer for an injunction.[15]

Such legislative enactments curtailing injunction issuance, especially the *ex parte* restraining order without a hearing, will likely continue to be passed in the several jurisdictions. Delaying of the injunction would permit most strikes to take place subject to the issuance of an injunction and should stimulate the use of mediation, fact-finding and arbitration of unresolved disputes. Indeed, the Pennsylvania law provides for dispute settlement devices prior to any strike as a condition precedent. Also, flexibility is an advantage of courts appraising the effects of actual or threatened action based on evidence submitted. For example, a sanitation workers' strike in a large city would presumably reach a danger level much sooner than in a smaller city, which may never reach that point.

In assessing the present overanxious use of the injunctive process in most jurisdictions, Kheel questions, "Would it not make better sense to save the awesome power of government for those few instances where its strength is really needed, instead of dissipating it in a complicated system of procedures and set of ambivalent penalties that may or may not work but do make a process we endorse as beneficial in the private sector subversive in the public sector?"[16] The Governor's Advisory Committee on Public Employee Relations in Michigan adds that "we reject . . . the views . . . that injunctions should always be issued, regardless of circumstances, upon a finding that a strike has occurred or is threatened. . . ."[17]

OTHER USES

Although the injunction has primarily been used against public employees and their organizations, the device is a two-edged sword. That is, in cases where government refuses to bargain or "meet and confer" pursuant to a statute, and assuming the employees do not take the law into their own hands by means of a strike, the injunction can be sought by the employee organization to compel bargaining under the law. Some cases have been filed successfully in this regard in lower courts by employee organizations in California.[18] In a situation where college trustees took unilateral action differing from contract provisions still in effect, the bargaining agent's rights were held to be infringed upon and an injunction was issued ordering the trustees to bargain in good faith over any contract changes.[19]

Also, as in the private sector, a collective bargaining agreement can be enforced by an injunction. It is even foreseeable that a no-strike clause and arbitration provision might be negotiated, the parties being constrained from violating these provisons by the use of an injunction.[20] The motivation to embody such provisions into the labor agreement would be promoted were these provisions to be enforced by court order.

CONCLUDING REMARKS

THe issuance of injunctions in all cases involving concerted action by public employees, regardless of the facts and equities involved, appears to be inconsistent with effective problem-solving in the changing framework of public sector labor relations. A more judicious use of the injunction is, of course, no elixir for the problems besetting public employment. Evolution and maturing of labor relations there, however, seem to merit experimentation with more flexible and equitable procedures in restraining concerted activity by taking greater cognizance of criteria such as public health and safety and the statutory obligations of the government employer.

NOTES

1. *In re Debs,* 15 S. Ct. 900, 158 U.S. 564 (1895).
2. CLyde W. Summers and Harry H. Wellington, *Cases and Materials on Labor Law* Mineola, New York, The Foundation Press, 1968, p. 167.
3. *Vegelahn v. Guntner,* 167 Mass. 92 (1896).
4. *School District for the City of Holland, Ottawa and Allegan Counties, Michigan v. Holland Education Association,* 157 N. W. 2d 206, 57 L C Sec. 51,874 (1968).
5. In a later case involving a substantially similar fact situation, the high court of Michigan reinforced its earlier holding in refusing to issue an injunction; see *Crestwood School District v. Crestwood Education Association,* 170 N.S. 2d 840, 61 L C Sec. 52,153 (1969).
6. *Board of Education of Union Free School District No. 3, Town of Brookhaven v. National Education Association of U. S.,* 311 N. Y. Supp. 2d 370, 62 L C Sec. 52,308 (N. Y. S. Ct., Suffolk Co. 1970). This case can be contrasted to *Board of Education, Borough of Union Beach v. New Jersey Education Association,* 247 A. 2d 867, 59 LC Sec. 51,989 (N. J. S. Ct. 1968), where the sanctions were effective in impeding entrance to the labor market and an injunction was issued restraining the action.
7. *Board of Education of Union Free School District No. 27, Town of*

Hempstead, West Hempstead v. West Hempstead Chapter Branch of New York State Teachers Association, 311 N.Y. Supp 2d 708 (1970).

8. *In re Colin, Scott, Berry,* 65 Cal. 273 (1968). See also, *Peters v. South Chicago Community Hospital.* 60 LC Sec. 52,075 (1969).

9. *Thornhill v. State of Alabama,* 310 U.S. 88, 99, 2 LC Sec. 17,059 (1940).

10. See: *Board of Education of Community Unit School District No. 2 v. Redding,* 207 N.E. 2d 427, 51 LC Sec. 51,231 (1965); *City of Rockford v. Local No. 413, International Association of Firefighters,* 240 N.E. 2d 705, 58 LC Sec. 51,959 (1968); and *Arizona Board of Regents v. Communication Workers,* 61 LC Sec. 52,159 (1969).

11. *County of Peoria v. Benedict,* 265 N. E. 2d 141, 64 LC Sec. 52,446 (1970).

12. *Government Employee Relations Report,* No. 387, February 8, 1971, p. B-18.

13. *Government Employee Relations Report,* No. 297, May 19, 1969, p. B-1.

14. *Vermont Labor Relations Act,* No. 198, L. 1967 as amended by P. A. 230, L. 1970.

15. *Government Employee Relations Report,* No. 359, July 27, 1970, p. E-1. The 1970 Hawaii law granting a limited right to strike to public employees in that state leaves the problem of terminating a strike to the newly created Public Employee Relations Board.

16. Theodore W. Kheel, "Resolving Deadlocks Without Banning Strikes," *Monthly Labor Review,* Vol. 92, No. 7, July, 1969, p. 63.

17. *Report of Governor's Advisory Committee on Public Employee Relatins,* Russell A. Smith, Chairman, Lansing, Michigan, February 15, 1967, p. 10.

18. Institute of Industrial Relations, University of California, Berkeley, *California Public Employee Relations,* No. 2, February, 1969, p. B1; and No. 7, November, 1970, p. 32.

19. *Seattle Community College Federation of Teachers (AFT) v. Arthur Siegal,* Superior Court for the State of Washington for King County, No. 727 875, November 4, 1970; cited in *Government Employee Relations Report,* No. 376, November 23, 1970, pp. B-1 to B-3.

20. An example of a negotiated agreement involving policemen where the employee organization agreed not to strike and the city to submit grievances to binding arbitration was cited in *Tremblay v. Berlin Police Union,* 237 A. 2d 668, 57 LC Sec. 51,833 (N. H. S. Ct. 1968).

CHAPTER 9.
TYPES OF THIRD-PARTY INTERVENTION

Federal Mediation in the Public Sector

Jerome H. Ross

Initially, the Federal Mediation and Conciliation Service approached disputes in public sector bargaining rather reluctantly, somewhat unsure of how to function in this relatively new environment that differed in many respects from its private sector counterpart. In early 1971, however, the newly appointd FMCS director, W. J. Usery, Jr., instituted sweeping changes in the Service's public sector policies and procedures which have enabled it to make significant contributions to the resolution of such disputes.

This article is concerned with the evolution of the FMCS' functioning in the new field. Inasmuch as the Service has developed separate policies and procedures for the mediation of disputes in bargaining of Federal employees and of State and local government employees, the article treats these jurisdictions separately.

FEDERAL SERVICE

Executive Order 211491 provided for FMCS assistance in settling collective bargaining disputes in Federal service, beginning January 1, 1970. Prior to that date, although FMCS had not been written into the procedures governing Federal service bargaining,

Reprinted by permission of the MONTHLY LABOR REVIEW.

Jerome H. Ross is Assistant Director of Mediation Services, Federal Mediation and Conciliation Service.

it had been requested to assist in the resolution of 22 negotiation disputes.

The first 2 years under Executive Order 11491 saw a dramatic turn to the bargaining table by Federal employee unions. Previously, these unions had been content to organize employees and to represent them in agency grievance procedures or under statutory appeals procedures; during fiscal years 1971-72, the Service monitored or mediated 524 Federal service bargaining cases.

The Service's policy as regards settlement of Federal employee disputes during these 2 years was essentially one of restrained assistance. When the paries requested FMCS assistance, a mediator was provided if private sector disputes would not be adversely affected by a lack of FMCS attention.

In most instances, mediators in Federal service negotiations confronted factors not usually present in private sector disputes. The parties were usually inexperienced in contract negotiation. Many issues involved questions of negotiability under the management's rights clauses in the executive order, and many other concerned complex problems dealing with civil service personnel relations not found in private sector labor relations. Further, several levels of management not represented at the bargaining table were involved in decisions which directly affected the negotiations, and the bureaucracy often was not responsive to the bargainers' needs for timely answers, nor were there any strong pressures on the parties to reach agreement as quickly as possible.

Because of these factors, mediators often determined that mediation could be of no service to the parties and withdrew from the negotiations. Union and agency bargainers usually remained at the negotiating table for many, many months before agreements were reached.

In 1973, Director Usery issued a new policy and procedures for mediators to follow in Federal bargaining disputes. In part, the new policy states:

> . . . Our Service will become an *active advocate* of collective bargaining in the Federal Government in units where unions have been appropriately recognized as certified bargaining agents. This new activist role requires that each of us give that extra effort we have so often extended in private sector bargaining. I recognize that we are dealing with a collective bargaining system that is in an early stage of . . . evolution toward producing effective results through mature, knowledgeable parties at the bargaining table. This is all

the more reason for every mediator to be prepared to work with representatives who are new to the process and with organization structures which have not yet developed to efficiently deal with agency-union problems.

Accordingly, we must recognize two important differences in the way mediators must work in Federal Government negotiations: (1) During negotiations more time must be devoted to patiently educating the parties to their roles and responsibilities, and (2) more time must be devoted to ascertaining, and dealing with, the real decisionmakers, especially within agencies. Of course, these two considerations must be coupled with the same aggressive mediation style which contributes to producing hundreds of settlements yearly in the private sector.

The Service's new policy, coupled with several organizational changes within FMCS, resulted in more effective mediation assistance to Federal agencies and unions. During fiscal years 1973-75, the Service monitored or mediated 959 disputes, and provided technical assistance to the parties during the term of their agreements on 76 occasions. (Technical assistance, previously called preventive mediation, involves services which mediators render to labor and management during the term of their agreement, to improve the parties' continuing relationship.) The size of the bargaining units ranged from 8 to more than 18,000 employees, with 25 percent of the disputes involving units of between 100 to 250 employees. Over 50 different unions were parties to bargaining, with the American Federation of Government Employees and the National Federation of Federal Employees representing employees in the greatest number of cases. Forty Federal agencies were involved in bargaining, with the employees of the Army, Air Force, Navy, Veterans Administration, and Department of Health, Education, and Welfare involved in a significant majority of cases. FMCS handled Federal service negotiation dispues in 47 States, the District of Columbia, and Puerto Rico. The jurisdictions with the most activity were California, the District of Columbia, Texas, and Virginia.

Mediators' experiences in Federal service bargaining over the past 6 years have shown they must adjust their approaches and techniques to successfully assist agencies and unions. Some of the factors which mediators must consider are:

1. Because the pressures usually attendant to a strike threat in the private sector are not present in the Federal service, mediators need to be more resourceful in intensifying other pressures for settlement by establishing artificial deadlines and time frames for bargaining. Mediators have recognized that more time

may be necessary to resolve Federal service disputes than is required in private sector cases, and often the time may be spent on seemingly minor issues. In cases where FMCS has been requested to assist in the resolution of disputes over ground rules for bargaining, the mediator usually withdraws from the negotiations when agreement on such procedures is reached. However, several months later the mediator is often requested to reenter the negotiations when settlement of the unresolved substantive issues has not been attained.

2. Mediators must thoroughly understand the operation of the Federal Service Impasses Panel. Under the executive order, the Panel is responsible for performing factfinding and arbitration when mediation has not been successful. Although separate and distinct agencies, the Panel and FMCS have closely coordinated their activities to insure that all possible attempts to resolve a dispute have been exhausted before the Panel consents to hear a case. On several occasions a staff factfinder from the Panel, after initially inquiring into a case or convening the parties in a factfinding forum, has recommended that the parties return to the bargaining table for further negotiation and mediation. In one case, the staff factfinder requested an FMCS mediator to join the factfinding hearing, which resulted in joint mediation of the dispute. In many cases, the staff factfinders working independently have successfully mediated disputes, thus obviating the need for a binding decision by the Panel.

3. Mediators must understand questions of negotiability, and they must possess the resourcefulness to assist in devising solutions to problems seemingly nonnegotiable under the executive order. Some bargaining proposals may merely require redrafting to provide for negotiable language that will retain the substance of the original wording in dealing with a problem. In other instances, the words contained in a nonnegotiable proposal may not address the specific problem with which the proposal is concerned. A mediator probing to discover the underlying problem can assist in defining it and in drafting negotiable language which effectively deals with the problem.

4. Mediators should recognize that a major portion of their efforts may entail a form of on-the-job training provided to many representatives of both sides at the bargaining table. Because of the parties' lack of experience, mediators can often be more candid and forceful with them than with the parties in most private sector disputes. Mediators have had to explain and illustrate basic aspects of negotiations, such as the desirability of written

proposals and the importance of retaining complete files on all issues. They often have had to prod the parties to make counter-proposals and to concentrate on the unresolved issues.

5. Because FMCS mediators are knowledgeable in many aspects of labor-management relations, their services may be requested on an informal basis in situations other than negotiation disputes, as in questions of "grievability," arbitrability, and unfair labor practices. The Service realizes that inherent in such questions are compromises with neutrality and acceptability of its mediators, and, as a rule, it has generally limited its assistance in such situations. Nonetheless, the FMCS's Office of Arbitration Services has worked closely with Federal agencies and unions by providing assistance for a variety of special problems, such as developing regional permanent panels of arbitrators and expediting arbitration services pursuant to grievance and arbitration procedures contained in negotiated agreements. FMCS assistance may be requested under a grievance procedure provision in a negotiated agreement which provides for mediation of grievance disputes prior to submission to arbitration. (In the private sector, under the National Labor Relations Act, as amended, the Service is precluded from mediating grievances except "as a last resort and in exceptional cases.")

STATE AND LOCAL GOVERNMENTS

The FMCS's involvement in the settlements of bargaining disputes in State and local goverments paralleled the Service's expanded role in Federal service collective bargaining. Growing organization of employees at all levels of government was most apparent in the late 1960's, and the number of government employee unions turning to the bargaining table to voice their demands increased in the early 1970's. As the bargaining table became a primary vehicle of communication to set economic and noneconomic standards of employment in many public sector jurisdictions, the use of mediation became more widespread.

The Service's role in the settlement of bargaining disputes in State and local governments also underwent far-reaching changes in early 1973. For purposes of FMCS's involvement, the new policies and procedures required that State and local government disputes be treated in a manner similar to private sector cases. That is, one party could request mediation or FMCS on its own motion could proffer its services. Requests for mediation would be processed by the various regional offices of the Service, rather than by the FMCS's national office. All restrictions on the amount of time which could be devoted to public sector disputes were removed.

The new policy statement, similar in tone and substance to the statement on Federal service mediation cited above, provided the framework for the Service's role in State and local government bargaining disputes. In part the policy stated:

(a) The Service shall encourage the development of dispute resolution capability by State, county, and municipal governments. To promote effective local resolution of public employee labor disputes, the Service shall provide technical assistance to such jurisdictions in the creation and development of dispute resolution capabilities.

(b) In those jurisdictions where adequate dispute resolution structures are not available, the Service shall, in the public interest, participate in the resolution of public employee labor disputes. Effective immediately, public sector disputes will be assigned by regional directors upon the request of one or both parties to the dispute.

(c) In those jurisdictions with adequate dispute resolution capability, the Service shall participate in the resolution of actual or potential public employee labor disputes of special importance upon the request of the mediation service of the State, county, or municipal government.

In accordance with section (a) of the policy, the Service has assisted many States during the past 2 1/2 years in developing State and local dispute resolution capability. Its most comprehensive efforts occurred in Florida and Iowa, pursuant to newly enacted public sector bargaining laws in those States. The Service provided a mediator to the Florida Public Employees Relations Commission for 6 months to assist in developing administrative procedures for the commission under the new law. The Office of Arbitration Services, working with the Florida body, established a special master system for arbitrating disputes if the parties do not reach agreement in mediation. Most important, the Service has provided mediators on a continuing basis to assist in the resolution of negotiation disputes. Extensive assistance was also rendered to Iowa Public Employee Relations Board officials, including the training of 30 ad hoc mediators to supplement FMCS efforts under the new Iowa law.

Because there are no procedures providing for formal notification to FMCS of potential or actual labor disputes involving employees of State or local governments, the Service placed great responsibility on its mediators, as members of the labor-management relations communities in which they function, to closely follow public sector bargaining developments.

The new policy and corollary procedures resulted in the Service becoming highly visible and accessible to the parties involved in State and local public sector bargaining. During fiscal years 1965-72, FMCS's services were requested in 193 State and local disputes; during fiscal years 1973-75, the number of cases in which the Service was involved rose to 501 and technical assistance during the term of labor agreements was provided in that period to the parties in 277 cases. The size of the bargaining units ranged from 5 to more than 6,000 employees. More than 50 unions were parties to the bargaining, with the National Education Association and the American Federation of State, County and Municipal Employees representing employees in the greatest number of cases. Public schools and higher education disputes constituted the greatest number of State and local cases, and, accordingly, teaching was the occupation most frequently involved. During 1973-75, FMCS handled State and local government negotiation disputes in 34 States and the District of Columbia, with Illinois and Ohio accounting for over half of the FMCS's State and local caseload. The increasing number of jurisdictions utilizing the collective bargaining process in States without dispute resolution forums indicates that the Service's non-Federal public sector caseload will continue to rise rapidly.

As with Federal service mediation, the experiences gained in State and local cases revealed the need for approaches in dispute settlement different from those used in the private sector.

First of all, because many States lack procedures for dealing with public employee collective bargaining, recognition of the union is a central problem in negotiations. Management may view its consent to participate in the mediation process as an implied acceptance of the union and a willingness to bargain. Therefore, mediators may be required to devote a great deal of effort to explaining their roles to management representatives in separate sessions prior to convening a joint conference. In one potential strike situation, a mediator discussed FMCS assistance with the mayor and appeared before the city council so that a formal resolution could be adopted allowing him to enter into the dispute. Settlement through mediation soon resulted. In some jurisdictions where no machinery exists for determining appropriate units or conducting elections, after discussions with a mediator, the parties have agreed to use an FMCS representative to assist them in establishing and conducting such procedures.

Further, because final decisions on economic benefits may have to be made by a legislative body of State or local government, it may be necessary for mediators to develop lines of communication with people other than those representing the parties at the bargaining table. Mediators report the need for contacting mayors, city council members, State legislators, school board members, judges, city managers, and various other influential persons in a community to bring significant pressures to the bargaining table so that settlements may result.

In many disputes involving State and local government employees, public interest and concern are intense because of possible or actual interruption of services which might accompany the bargaining. When mediators are involved in such cases, they are often required to make public statements. They must deal with news reporters who are intent on observing negotiations and receiving specific answers to questions concerning the status of negotiations. As a result of such contacts, many mediators have developed working relationships with reporters, which often produce a more accurate understanding of the status of a dispute by the press and the public.

The diversity of procedures used to resolve impasses in State and local government bargaining requires Federal mediators to bear in mind that factfinding and arbitration may be invoked subsequent to their mediation. As public sector bargaining laws continue to be enacted, most States will probably opt for a dispute resolution procedure calling for factfinding or arbitration—or both—to follow mediation, as opposed to granting public employees the right to strike. The result will be an increasing need for mediators conversant with various dispute resolution techniques.

The question of the public interest in public employee bargaining settlements is a factor which mediators may consider. Do mediators have an obligation to be concerned with the public interest at the bargaining table? Most mediators agree that little or no such obligation exists in the private sector, but there has been considerable debate concerning mediators' responsibility in public sector disputes. It is anticipated that mediators will continue to emphasize their responsibility to work for settlements. However, they may become increasingly concerned with the degree to which the public interest is reflected in collective bargaining agreements in the public sector.

FUTURE REQUIREMENTS

Public employee unions will continue to grow, and collective bargaining will be increasingly utilized by these unions and public management. So far, however, only 18 States have enacted laws to provide comprehensive collective bargaining procedures. Federal Government labor relations under the executive order system have also been under some criticism for failure to provide a neutral independent agency to administer the system and to establish it under statute.

The likelihood of enactment of Federal legislation governing Federal or State and local government collective bargaining, or both, is uncertain. Some believe such laws may be passed within the next 2 years, especially for Federal service. Others are of the opinion that a Federal law for State and local bargaining will never become a reality.

The Service will continue to assist the parties in public employees' bargaining to the fullest extent possible. All of the Federal service collective bargaining bills which have been introduced in Congress provided for FMCS assistance in the resolution of negotiation disputes. Most of the proposed Federal legislation for State and local public collective bargaining also has written the Service into the impasse resolution procedures. And the Service's record of assistance to public employee unions and government managements during 1973-75 has set a pattern for its future functioning.

Fact-Finding:
Its Values
and Limitations

William E. Simkin

As one of that now vast horde of ex-presidents, I receive copies of the minutes of board meetings. Some years ago, in a schismatic role as member of this Academy and head of an appointive agency, I delivered a luncheon speech. A revealing line in the minutes read substantially as follows: "One member of the board suggested that we instruct the incoming Program Committee not to invite speakers who castigate us."

At the outset, I want to assure you that I have no intention or desire to castigate anybody. However, we are not just a mutual admiration society, rewarding as that exercise may be. Moreover, my principal role here today is to stimulate discussion. For that reason, some of the statements that I intend to make will be deliberately provocative—probably stronger than I really believe. To this extent, I will undoubtedly be misunderstood—and misquoted if anybody considers it worthwhile to quote. If that be risky, so be it.

The principal theme of this paper is that the words *fact-finding* should be substantially eliminated from the labor relations vocabulary or, more accurately, that they should be relegated to more limited usefulness. This has happened already in the private sector. Some day, but not soon, I predict it will also occur in the public sector.

The words fact-finding conjure up notions of preciseness, of objectivity, of virtue. They even have a godlike quality. Who can disagree with facts? In contrast, the word *mediation,* that I do espouse, tends to have an aura of compromise, of slipperiness, of

Reprinted by permission from ARBITRATION AND THE EXPANDING ROLE OF NEUTRALS, copyrighted (©) by The Bureau of National Affairs, Inc., Washington, D.C. 20037.

William E. Simkin is a member and Past President, National Academy of Arbitrators, Lexington, Mass.

connivance, and of furtiveness. Since these are frequent impressions, why prefer the vulgar to the sublime?

There is a problem of semantics. Close examination of the actual functioning of fact-finding boards and of mediators or of mediation boards shows that the labels are quite secondary. The abilities and proclivities of the individuals named to those boards and, more important, the reactions of the parties to the process, determine what really happens. Fact-finders do or do not mediate. Some fact-finders who mediate find no facts. Persons appointed as mediators frequently do not mediate in any meaningful way but may announce some real or alleged facts and conclusions.

In view of this ambidextrous situation, I will attempt to set up a fact-finding straw man for purposes of this discussion—a procedure that is not a caricature. It will be an all-too-typical arrangement that needs no elaboration to arbitrators. It is the procedure we know so well.

It begins with formal or semiformal hearings. The parties produce the facts as they see them, or, more accurately, as they select and slant them for partisan purposes. Little or no opportunity is provided for private discussion. It may even be considered improper for the fact-finder to converse with representatives of the parties in the absence of persons from the other side. After all the evidence and testimony is in the record, the fact-finder withdraws to his sanctuary and prepares a report.

A first step in appraisal of this process is to compare it with the realities of collective bargaining of a new contract if the process is successful without any third-party intervention. When demands or requests are made by bargainers at the outset of negotiations, there is great variance both in the degree to which those demands are based on facts and in the types of facts presented. At one extreme, a demand can be made on a very simple basis: "We want it, and who cares about the facts." Raw power is the most significant fact. At the other extreme, the parties may do a tremendous amount of prenegotiation research. Positions on each issue are supported by an elaborate array of real or alleged facts. Most negotiations fall somewhere between these two extremes.

What happens to these real or alleged facts as negotiations proceed? Some facts are agreed to directly or tacitly. Some are irrelevant. Some are soft-pedaled or quietly ignored. Some remain in dispute.

The objective of bargaining is agreement. If settlement of an issue is accomplished, the residual status of the factual discussion is of minor consequence. The facts may be means to an end, but the end may be consummated in spite of the facts.

We are talking here only about a dispute. A stalemate exists on one or more issues. The fact-finder is brought into a negotiation where the residual status of the facts may be quite variable. Important facts may still be in dispute, or there may be no great factual differences but the argument is whether the facts are relevant and, in any event, what if anything to do about them.

The two principal types of fact-finding, (1) without recommendations and (2) with recommendations, will be considered in sequence.

FACT-FINDING WITHOUT RECOMMENDATIONS

The basic notion about this type of fact-finding is that somebody does not know the real facts and that establishment and proclamation of the facts will somehow assist in settlement. Who is that somebody who is ignorant of the facts? Is it the parties, the general public, or the public-opinion makers?

Experienced negotiators will seldom be surprised or influenced very much by the results of such fact-finding. In a limited number of situations, publication of unpleasant facts may bring pressure on the negotiators by their constituencies. Facts that are damaging to a union, published during a long strike, may result in diminished strike morale and more willingness of employees to compromise. Publicized facts detrimental to a company position may bring pressure on the company negotiators from the board of directors. However, these results are infrequent for a simple reason: Most labor disputes are so complicated that a mere portrayal of facts does not provide a "handle" for action or even suggest clear directional signals toward a likely settlement area.

Publication of facts will be of some minor interest to the general public but will not usually provide an adequate basis for translation into an informed opinion about the total dispute. The opinion makers (columnists, editorial writers, and the like) may welcome such a report. They will make fewer goofs of factual content and have a new reason for writing something. But the facts will seldom change any preconceived ideas they may have already expressed.

On a few occasions, fact-finders not empowered to make recommendations on the issues have indulged in assessing blame on one of the parties. This device seldom accomplishes anything. It is much more likely to exacerbate the dispute. In short, fact-finding without recommendations is likely to be an exercise in futility.

These observations may require modification in some current public employee disputes. Bargainers in the public sector sometimes lack some of the sophistication that is more typical in the private sector. Moreover, since the taxpayers are the employers, however far removed from the bargaining table, their appraisal of facts can assume more significance than is the case in a private dispute.

There is a potential and sometimes utilized variety of this general type of fact-finding that is seldom discussed. It is the use of impartial technicians, long in advace of negotiations, to work with the parties to develop pertinent background facts on such issues as pensions and insurance.

FACT-FINDING WITH RECOMMENDATIONS

When fact-finders are given the responsibility to make specific recommendations on the issues in dispute, the process becomes very familiar to an arbitrator, assuming the fact-finding strawman model noted earlier. It is arbitration with two major points to distinguish it from grievance arbitration. (1) Recommendations are not final and binding decisions. Either or both parties can reject. (2) The recommendations do not develop out of a contractual framework. They are legislative value judgments. Recommendations are not facts, nor are they based exclusively or even primarily on facts.

Many of you will disagree honestly with the last statement. One concept of this type of fact-finding is that the recommendations flow almost automatically out of the facts. In my considered opinion, this notion has little or no validity. I will try to amplify the point by a couple of illustrations.

Let us assume that a union in a manufacturing plant is requesting pension rights after 20 years of service, regardless of age. It is reasonably certain that the company could show beyond any doubt that such a benefit is virtually nonexistent in manufacturing. That is an important fact but it does not dispose of the issue. Collective bargaining is an innovative process. Many agreement provisions, now commonplace, started somewhere. If the fact-finder recommends against the union, as he probably will, additional considerations are involved. He may conclude that the benefit is not advisable on its merits, that the cost would be excessive, or that the request cannot take high priority among other matters. A number of other reasons could be utilized, all of which are value judgments. If he should conclude that such an obvious innovation should not be obtained by assistance of a third party, that is itself a value judgment.

This is not just a hypothetical situation. Substitute 30 years for 20 years of service and you have an important issue in the 1965 steel negotiations. It is almost inconceivable that a fact-finding procedure of the type under discussion here would have resulted in a recommendation favorable to the union on that issue. But it happened to be a top-priority demand, and the 1965 negotiations simply would not have been concluded peacefully without that item in the package.

During the guidepost period, it was an announced executive policy of the Council of Economic Advisers, supported by the President, that labor cost increases of new agreements should be held to an average of 3.2 percent per year. In the absence of statutory authority for that policy, it was a value judgment if a fact-finder decided to apply it in his recommendations in a specific case. In the face of a large number of departures, plus and minus, from that policy even during its most acceptable period of time, no fact-finder could take automatic refuge in it. Moreover, even if he did adopt the basic policy as an exercise of judgment, its application never was a precise matter of arithmetic. Some benefits could not be costed with accuracy. Some exceptions were stated in the policy. Did the facts of a specific case qualify for an exemption and, if so, how much? How should costs and benefits be distributed, with respect to time, throughout a long-term agreement? In short, even a mathematical formula required exercise of value judgments, not just arithmetic.

When noneconomic but highly emotional issues are also involved, when there is an imbalance of economic power, or when serious personality conflicts exist at the bargaining table—all too frequent ingredients in collective bargaining—who can say honestly that recommendations are or can be based solely and solidly on facts?

In arm's length fact-finding, where is the fact-finder to find a basis for his value judgments? In the last analysis, all he can do is to exercise his best intellectual powers and search his own soul. He has no adequate opportunity to gauge acceptability by the parties. No hearings can ever meet that need adequately.

This is especially true because the parties have known that recommendations will be forthcoming. During the interval between the appointment of the fact-finder and the issuance of his report, any bargaining that may have occurred is almost certain to stop. All efforts of the parties have been directed to getting the best possible set of recommendations. Nor is it an adequate refuge to conclude, as is sometimes the case, that the exposure of the parties to the fact-finder so frightens them that they will reach agreement to avoid recommendations.

We come now to the receipt of the recommendations. Either or both parties can say no. If that is not the situation, it is de facto arbitration and should be so labeled.

If a no is voiced, the dispute has not been settled. The fact-finder has been rebuffed and usually he has no place to go. If he reacts defensively, as he is likely to do, the dispute may be exacerbated. What has been a two-way dispute up to that point may become a three-way controversy.

Am I exaggerating the problems inherent in this type of fact-finding? The answer is yes. Despite the hazards, a surprising number of such operations have been successful. But if time permitted and restrictions of confidential information could be relaxed, I could cite chapter and verse of proceedings that were disasters. Some of the gory details were worse than anything I have outlined here.

Where fact-finding has been successful, I would suggest, but cannot prove, that the fact-finder has mediated—deliberately, instinctively, or surreptitiously. When fact-finding without mediation has succeeded in the public sector, I would suspect that it is a transitory phenomenon. Until recently, and even now in some jurisdictions, public employees have been so far behind that fact-finders have a broad target range. I would predict that the range will narrow in the years immediately ahead of us.

MEDIATION

What do I mean by mediation? Time does not permit analysis of the remarkably wide spectrum of mediation activity—things that a mediator can or cannot do. At one end, the spectrum begins by a decision not to intervene at all, to provide no third-party assistance. At the other end of the band, the mediator can issue public recommendations. A major principle is to maximize bargaining and minimize the role of the mediator, to exercise enough patience to let bargaining work. But the mediator must also be able and willing to "grasp the nettle," to recognize when patience is not a virtue and to act accordingly. Most mediation decisions are decisions as to strategy and timing, not decisions on the specific issues.

In the hands of a skilled mediator, facts are potent tools. It is seldom that publication of facts is either necessary or desirable, but facts can be most useful in hard-hitting deflation of extreme positions. This is accomplished in separate head-to-head conferences or meetings, absent the embarrassment of the other side's presence and certainly not in the press. Public reference to the facts, if required at all, comes after a settlement to help save face.

The mediator has unusual opportunities to explore a wide variety of solutions—to "try them on for size." Thus he acquires a strong intuitive sense, if not the certainty, of the vital element of acceptabiliy.

Package recommendations are a last-resort device, to be utilized only if all else fails and maybe not issued even then. The mediator is never committed to use of that device, and he will steadfastly refuse to take such action unless he is convinced or has a strong hunch that it may be productive.

Procedurally, there is little resemblance between mediation and an arbitration hearing except for the opening formalities.

In difficult cases, it may be necessary to employ successive stages of mediation. Escalation may be an appropriate word. The original mediator may be supplemented by a panel, or replaced if he "breaks his pick." In my judgment, successive stages of mediation are preferable to the mediation, then fact-finding sequence. It is especially important that the mediators, at whatever stage, retain control of the determination as to whether package recommendations should be made, and when. It is recognized that recommendations will be needed more often in the public sector than in the private sector.

It should be obvious by now that it is my considered opinion that the exercise of mediation skills is the prime requirement for effective dispute settlement involving new or renewed labor agreements. That is the basis for my recommendation that the words fact-finding be relegated to obscurity. If a fancier word than mediation is desired, there is nothing wrong with the *impasse panel* label.

Let me try to illustrate the fact-finding-mediation comparison by a crude analogy. In common with many in this room, I once played football. You will recall the coach's diagrams on the blackboard. Every play was a touchdown, except a punt. But the game wasn't played that way. Try to imagine the mediation team on one side of the line and the dispute on the other. The mediation team tries one play, to be thrown for a five-yard loss. Somebody may be bloody, but if the quarterback is half smart, he has learned something. The next play makes a little yardage. With adequate tenacity and ability, some play will succeed. I will confess, however, that there have been occasions when I have resorted to the "punt and pray" strategy, hoping that some management or labor guy will fumble the ball. They frequently do.

Fact-finding, of the prototype noted earlier, is a one-play ball game.

ARBITRATORS AS MEDIATORS

The concluding phase of this talk is approached with some reluctance because it can be most readily misunderstood. Moreover, it necessarily involves some self-analysis and can almost be interpreted as a public confessional.

Can arbitrators mediate?

It should be made clear that I am not attempting here to reopen the great debate of some years ago about mediation of grievances. We will be considering only those activities associated with new labor agreements or the renewal of such agreements.

Arbitrators start off with significant assets. We are or should be fully familiar with labor agreement language and intent. We know a great deal about motivation and personality characteristics that influence behavior at the bargaining table. But we also possess disqualifying attributes.

A successful arbitrator makes his living by making decisions. Because this is so, the arbitrator-mediator instinctively develops quite quickly his own concepts of good solutions. But decision-making on the issues is not a basic mediation function. It is the parties who make the decisions. Any too-ready propensity by a neutral to make tentative decisions in his own mind or recommendations on the issues to the parties can be fatal.

A closely related problem is that arbitration is not a process favorable to development of humility. The authority to make final and binding decisions immunizes us from the notion that we can be wrong. If we are fired as permanent arbitrators or never used again after an ad hoc decision, what are the reasons? Our likely reaction is that somebody was a poor loser. How often do we admit, even to ourselves, that we goofed? Mediators have egos too. This must be so if they are to survive. But the food for ego comes not from decisions on the issues; it comes from a belief that the mediator somehow assisted in a solution reached by others. And if a mediator does the very best job, he does not even get adequate recognition for a good idea. The parties grab it and claim it as their own.

Another frequent disqualification is that we tend to be thin-skinned. Defensive reactions to criticism are probable rather than possible. In contrast, a mediator is thoroughly accustomed to being rebuffed. Parties say no directly and positively, with picturesque embellishments and with great frequency. When a mediator hears the word no, he is not gleeful, but his instant reaction is the necessity to do something different. There can be no personal stake in an idea.

Without overemphasizing the point, let us examine the typical arbitrator's aversion to tripartite grievance arbitration boards. There are legitimate objections to such boards. Additional cost and additional time requirements are illustrative. But do we honestly answer the hard question: Is such aversion due to the fact that we shrink from the necessity of face-to-face justification of a decision? Believe me, that is an infinitely easier exercise than trying to make some tough cookie change his own mind.

These observations about the arbitrator's problems when he acts as a mediator do not develop out of any lack of high regard for members of this Academy. They come from reflection on my own experience and performance. I had to fight the disadvantages that have been noted. In every case of personal mediation involvement over an eight-year period, other mediators working with me taught me valuable lessons—prevented me from goofing. In some instances when I did not heed their advice, I learned my error the hard way. In self-defense, I will say that this was not a one-way street. Some actions, taken against my colleagues' advice, did work out. The hard fact remains that adaptation of an arbitrator to the mediation function is not an easy transition.

That it can be done is proven by the many excellent arbitrators in this Academy who are very skilled mediators. That it needs to be done cannot be questioned. The rising flood of public employee disputes is requiring an ever-increasing number of persons who can act as skilled mediators in an ad hoc capacity. Even in the absence of these new developments, there were never enough competent and available men to meet the needs of national-emergency or near-emergency situations in the private sector. On numerous occasions in the eight years I was in Washington, we were almost desperately searching for the right men who could be available at the time of need.

This is why I was and am in such wholehearted support of the special program of the past two days. We have started a long-needed endeavor. It is a significant beginning. Let us see to it that this effort will be expanded and pursued.

Binding Arbitration
in the Public Sector
Charles M. Rehmus

The important changes that public sector collective bargaining
has brought to our society have been achieved for the most part
under laws that expressly prohibit or do not confer the right to
strike on public employees. Yet the continuing increase in the
membership and strength of public sector unions has been paralleled by a rise in the number of job actions and strikes undertaken
by public employees when collective bargaining negotiations fail.
Our legislative bodies have increasingly turned to legislated interest arbitration as the alternative to the strike. As of this time,
at least 12 of the United States, the Canadian statute for Federal
employees, and the U.S. Postal Corporation Act provide for binding interest arbitration to resolve public employment labor disputes. In addition, a significant number of cities have also opted
for such an alternative.[1]

BINDING ARBITRATION AND DEMOCRATIC GOVERNMENT

Some critics have maintained that imposition of contract terms
upon an unwilling party represents a fundamental derogation of
our democratic system, which is dedicated to freedom of choice.
Others have challenged the delegation of governmental authorities' powers to appropriate funds to arbitration panels as

Reproduced from the Proceedings of the Twenty-Seventh Annual Winter Meeting,
IRRA Series, pp. 307-314, 1975. © Copyright 1975 by the Industrial Relations
Research Association. Reprinted by permission of Charles M. Rehmus, Director,
Institute of Labor and Industrial Relations, The University of Michigan and the
Industrial Relations Research Association.

Charles M. Rehmus is codirector of the Institute of Labor and Industrial Relations,
the University of Michigan—Wayne State University. His full IRRA paper is entitled, "Legislated Interest Arbitration."

unsound in principle because it strikes at the foundation of representative government. They contend that legislative responsibility and accountability cannot be transferred in its entirety to a *pro tem* appointed board. This view is perhaps epitomized in the dissenting opinion of the city's member of an arbitration panel appointed in one of the earliest arbitration awards rendered in Michigan. He asked, "Who elected the arbitration panel of which I am a part? To whom is this panel responsible or responsive? What pressures can the citizens. . . bring to bear on the panel? How do they express their satisfaction or dissatisfaction with the decision?"[2]

Answers to such questions must be in part philosophical and in part practical. Rampant disregard of anti-strike laws also erodes the foundations of government. If binding arbitration is necessary and sufficient to forestall illegal strikes it too strengthens our democratic system. Moreover, it is not at all clear that arbitration is any more corrosive of free decisionmaking than collective bargaining itself can sometimes be. A voluntary settlement accepted by one party only because the other has beaten it into submission may in truth be no less imposed than a decision rendered by a neutral, particularly if that neutral is indeed responsive to the needs and interests of both parties.

Secondly, it is not at all clear that binding arbitration awards invariably represent an imposition of terms to which the parties themselves are unalterably opposed. Nearly two-thirds of the arbitration awards rendered by tripartite panels thus far in Michigan have been unanimous, and a national survey of American Arbitration Association cases shows the same. Even where dissents have been written, we know of many cases where these are purely "for the record" rather than a manifestation of genuine opposition. Although some fear that arbitrators will impose unworkable or unreasonable contract terms on bargaining parties, experience to date is proving that arbitration has not resulted in a large number of third-party determinations imposed without regard to the needs or wishes of the parties.[3]

Labor leaders, although traditional opponents of binding arbitration as an improper interference with free collective bargaining, may be beginning to lend qualified support to interest arbitration experiments in the public sector. Police and firefighter representatives have lobbied for the establishment and continuation of many of our State arbitration statutes. State, county and municipal employees, President Jerry Wurf, Steelworkers President I. W. Abel, and AFL-CIO President George Meany have all suggested that their traditional concern about interest arbitration may be outweighed by the risks of insisting upon an inviolable right to engage in economic warfare under any and all circumstances. Finally, and most significantly, the municipal leagues in those States which have the greatest experience with arbitration are not at present mounting campaigns to repeal or amend these statutes.

INCIDENCE OF STRIKES

A second aspect of the conventional wisdom regarding binding interest arbitration is that it is ineffective because it will not eliminate strikes. This position is generally supported by reference to the fact that Australia has continued to publish strike statistics throughout the 50 years of its compulsory arbitration system. Opponents also cite the bitter strike of police and other employees in Montreal in 1969 against a binding arbitration award to bolster this view. The only reasonable answer to this challenge is to admit that binding arbitration may not eliminate all strikes but the data clearly show that it substantially reduces their frequency.

Five strikes by firefighters took place in Michigan prior to our arbitration statute. None have occurred since. One or two police strikes occurred after the enactment of compulsory arbitration, at least one of these because of a city's refusal to implement an award, but none have taken place in the last 3 years. No strikes have occurred by police and firefighters in Pennsylvania since it began its experiment with arbitration in 1968. The experience in Minnesota, Nevada, and Wisconsin is similar. While no one can be sure that this contemporary favorable record will continue into the indefinite future, it does seem clear that the attack on binding arbitration as being ineffective in its basic purpose is wholly unfounded, at least up to the present time.

THE EFFECT ON COLLECTIVE BARGAINING

The major attack made on binding arbitration by its critics is that it will have a "chilling" effect upon the bargaining process. The argument has been that binding arbitration will undermine collective bargaining whenever either party anticipates that it might gain more from arbitration than from negotiations. Moreover, it is alleged that the parties will evade responsibility for a hard decision and will maintain unrealitic positions hoping and anticipating that the arbitrator will draw a line somewhere in the middle. Arbitration, it is said, will inevitably be attractive to small unions or those unfavorably situated and without the muscle to force concessions from an employer. All of these arguments appear plausible; none appear to be strongly supported by the available data.

The experience in Pennsylvania seems to support these forebodings. Thirty percent of bargaining parties in public safety negotiations there go to arbitration and receive awards. The recent experience has been somewhat better than the earlier period, however, as the parties have gained in experience and sophistication. Moreover, it has been suggested that Pennsylvania's failure to provide mediation to parties who have arbitration available has had a major impact upon the unusually high incidence of arbitration in that State. In Wisconsin, on the other hand, the experience over the last several years has been that the parties will request arbitration in only about 15 percent of the situations when it is available to them. Admittedly, this rate is considerabl higher than the number of strikes that presumaby would have occurred if they were legal or a reasonable alternative for the unins.[4] But this 15 percent figure must further be tempered by another fact; because of settlements during the proceedings, number of awards rendered, even after arbitration has been instituted, is only 70 percent of the number of requests. In Michigan, the rate of petitions is higher than in Wisconsin, but because nearly two-thirds of the disputes in which arbitration has been petitioned for are settled without the need for an award, the ultimate rate of awards in Michigan is about the same as in Wisconsin—about 10 percent of all negotiations. In two such widely separated jurisdictions as New York City and Nevada, the number of arbitration awards rendered approximates seven and a half percent of the number of negotiations in which it is available.[5]

Several factors have been suggested as to why the rate of requests for arbitration and the number of awards rendered have not been nearly so great as was originally feared. In part, the answer may lie in the costs of the arbitration process. It has been estimated that the costs to a party for its share of the neutral's charges, to pay its own delegates and representatives, and perhaps to pay an attorney to prepare and present its case, range from $2,500 to $10,000 per case.[6] In large cities the cost to the parties may well exceed these amnounts by a factor of two or three. In such circumstances, a small union can rarely afford to go to arbitration. But these are the same unions which lack muscle and therefore could not effectively strike. In theory, disagreement should have some costs; it appears that these costs exist whether the ultimate dispute resolution mechanism is a strike or arbitration.

Probably the more fundamental reason why the incidence of arbitration awards in most jurisdictions is a small fraction of the exposure rate is that the interest arbitration process is evolving as less and less a judicial proceeding and more and more a search for accommodation. Adjustment and acceptability rather than win-lose adjudication is increasingly being emphasized in most contract rights disputes. Adjustment, accommodation, and acceptability are, of course, synonymous with compromise. Arbitrators are all too often criticized for compromising their awards. But compromise is the essence of collective bargaining and may therefore be exactly what is called for in the arbitration of contract terms. Experience has demonstrated that responsible neutrals through a process of interaction with their panel members and with the parties' representatives do actually achieve a genuinely close understanding of the legitimate interests and expectations of both parties to the dispute. Hence, they often are able to mediate or to set a framework in which the parties negotiate their own settlement. Even if not, the process is considerably more than a judgment from what has been characterized as that of an "itinerant phiosopher." It appears that in the hands of skilled individuals the interest arbitration process is a continuation of, rather than a replacement for, the negotiation process.[7]

THE IMPACT UPON SETTLEMENTS

A last charge against mandated interest arbitration is that it will inevitably distort market factors and will impose settlements far different from those which would be generated in pure collective bargaining, with or without strikes. The economic impact of interest arbitration is a subject of considerable interest to practioners and scholars of industrial relations alike. Measuring it is immensely difficult, however. Wage levels are not a true indicator of economic affect because they do not measure levels of employment or productivity changes. Local labor markets have many ingredients and the availability of arbitration is but one of those which can change wages. To what extent the threat of arbitration affects wages in a particular negotiation, as opposed to the actuality of arbitration, is almost impossible for any but the most sophisticated "insider" to evaluate. Finally, though there is undoubtedly a relationship between settlements in geographically related areas, the interrelation between negotiated and arbitrated settlements depends upon the timing of negotiations and who are the pattern-setters and pattern-followers in given years. Untangling this skein of variables is almost impossible.

Such data as are available suggest, however, that the resort to arbitration does not pay off in terms of unusually high wages. In one as yet unpublished study, Joseph Loewenberg compared policemen's wages in New York, Ohio, and Pennsylvania for a recent 6-year period. Of the three States, only Pennsylvania makes arbitration available to resolve negotiation impasses. Despite this fact, the level of police wages in Pennsylvania several years after the introduction of compulsory arbitration remained generally lower than the salaries of police in municipalities of comparable demographic characteristics in the neighboring States. A recent study in part concerning police and firefighter wages in Wisconsin during their period of arbitration shows that of many independent variables tested, the only statistically significant predictors of public safety wages were private sector wages and median family incomes in the same community.[8] This result is only what one would expect under "free" collective bargaining and in no way suggests that the availability of arbitration tends to skew resultant wage rates.

These and other research results tending to show that the regression coefficient for the use of arbitration is not significant raises the question of why the parties bother with it. Several possibilities suggest themselves, but are yet untested by research. One is that dependency upon, or resort to, arbitration is essentially political rather than economic. Another possibility is that arbitration is used primarily by parties where the wage is already relatively high and management is attempting to restrain further upward movement, or the wage is relatively low and the union is attempting to catch up. Assuming rational arbitration awards, one would think that management would be more likely to win in the first case and the union in the second. Certainly wage dispersion among cities has decreased in both Michigan and Wisconsin since arbitration was instituted. In short, some may be winning in arbitration and some may not, but statewide aggregated data show no overall payoff from the resort to arbitration. Both of these possibilities warrant further research and investigation. Neither hypothesis lends support to the gross allegation that arbitration tends significantly to distort economic settlements.

NOTES

1. A complete listing and analysis of these statutes and ordinances through late 1972 may be found in Joan Zeldon McAvoy, "Binding Arbitration of Contract Terms: A New Approach to the Resolution of Disputes in the Public Sector," *Columbia Law Review*, November 1972, pp. 1192-213.

2. Dissenting opinion of Arbitrator Jenner in *City of Marquette v. Marquette Police Local*, Mar. 26, 1970.

3. Arvid Anderson, "Interest Arbitration in the Public Sector: An Idea Whose Time Has Come" (Pace University Conference, May 15, 1974), p. 13.

4. In the Canadian federal sector, unions that have opted for the arbitration alternative required an award in 18 percent of negotiations. Those unions that opted for the strike alternative actually struck in a little over 8 percent of negotiations. Jacob Finkelman, "What's New in Dispute Settlement Techniques" (Convention of the Society of Professionals in Dispute Resolution, Nov. 12, 1974), p. 5.

5. Anderson, "Interest Arbitration," p. 8; Joseph R. Grodin, "Arbitration of Public Sector Labor Disputes: The Nevada Experiment," *Industrial and Labor Relations Review*, October 1974, pp. 89-102.

6. Robert G. Howlett, "Experience with Last Offer Arbitration in Michigan" (Annual Meeting of the Association of Labor Mediation Agencies, July 21, 1974), pp. 6-7.

7. Charles M. Rehmus, "Final Offer Arbitration in Practice: The U.S. Experience" (Canadian Federation of Engineering and Scientific Associations, National Seminar on Dispute Resolution, Nov. 4, 1974); Anderson, "Interest Arbitration," p. 14.

8. James L. Stern and others, *Final Offer Arbitration* (Lexington, Mass., D.C. Heath and Co., 1975). This study was sponsored by the Labor-Management Services Administration, U.S. Department of Labor.

Final-Offer Arbitration:
Some Problems

Nels E. Nelson

In simple outline, the idea of "final-offer arbitration" is appeal-
ing, especially in public employment: after the parties narrow
the gap as much as they can, let an arbitrator decide upon one
or the other of the two final proposed settlements. According to
proponents, the risk that the other side will be found more
reasonable will force both to adopt a realistic posture. The idea
has merit, and there has already been some satisfactory experi-
ence with it. But final-offer arbitration is not without its difficul-
ties. It works better, the author says, when single issues stand
in the way of agreement, than when the whole contract, includ-
ing a variety of economic and noneconomic benefits are at
stake. But with more experimentation, "it may prove to be the
most satisfactory alternative to the strike in the public sector."

There are a variety of statutory alternatives to the strike in the public sector. Some jurisdictions provide for mediation, factfind-ing, legislative determination or some combination of these. A small but growing number of jurisdictions have established com-pulsory arbitration for the settlement of unresolved contract dis-putes, especially for disputes involving policemen or firemen.[1] Despite the fact that only a few jurisdictions now have compulsory arbitration, the list of advocates is quite impressive.[2] Many au-thorities feel that it is the only acceptable alternative to the strike in the public sector. In fact, compulsory arbitration has been hailed by one expert as "the wave of the future" in public employee disputes.[3]

The most serious problem associated with compulsory arbit-ration is that it may damage or destroy negotiations preceding arbitration. In compulsory arbitration the award incorporates

Reprinted by permission of the ARBITRATION JOURNAL 30 (March, 1975).

The author is Assistant Professor of Economics at the State University College at Brockport, State University of New York.

parts of both parties' proposals so that it appears to the parties that the dispute is settled by compromise of the positions they present to the arbitrator. As a result, the parties may hold back in negotiations if they believe that the dispute will eventually be settled by arbitration. This is the so-called "chilling effect" of compulsory arbitration on negotiations.[4]

A new solution to the impasse problem in the public sector has been suggested which is designed to meet this objection to compulsory arbitration. This procedure is called final-offer arbitration. In final-offer arbitration, both parties submit final-offers to the arbitrator who simply selects the most reasonable final offer without modification.

At present, there are a few states and municipalities that have statutes or ordinances establishing final-offer arbitration.[5] This paper will look at a number of the most important problems in final-offer arbitration in light of the limited experience in final-offer arbitration.

EFFECT ON NEGOTIATIONS

One of the most damaging criticisms of conventional arbitration is the adverse effect that compulsory arbitration may have on negotiations. When the parties to a dispute believe that the dispute will eventually be settled by arbitration, the incentive to compromise may be weakened. In final-offer arbitration, however, both parties should be anxious to compromise in order to avoid the possibility that an arbitrator will find the other party's final offer more reasonable. When the opponent's final offer is selected, the first party loses on *every* point. Final-offer arbitration, therefore, should encourage compromise by both parties.

Actual final-offer arbitration experience can shed some light on this point. In Eugene, Oregon, where final-offer arbitration was established by local ordinance, no adverse effect on negotiations was apparent in the first six contracts negotiated under this procedure. In fact, in only one of six cases did a complete contract go to arbitration and, although arbitration was involved in four of the remaining five cases, two of these disputes were settled by the parties during the arbitration proceedings after receiving feedback from the chairman of the arbitration panel. The authors of a recent article describing the Eugene final-offer arbitration experience conclude that "the Eugene experience suggests . . . that final-offer arbitration, as compared to conventional arbitration, can increase the probability of negotiated settlements."[6]

In a number of additional final-offer arbitration cases reported in the *Government Employment Relations Report*, arbitrators indicated that the parties bargained effectively and, in most cases, reached agreement on all but a few issues before arbitration. In one of the first cases decided under Michigan's Policemen's and Firemen's Arbitration Act as amended in 1972 to provide for final-offer arbitration in impasse proceedings initiated after January 1, 1973, the arbitrators observed that the parties had made highly responsible efforts to reach agreement.[7] In an earlier Michigan case arising before the final-offer procedure was mandated but where the parties opted for final-offer arbitration, the arbitration panel stated that the contract "represents not so much the imposition of outside authority, but rather the good faith efforts of the participants."[8]

However, final-offer arbitration was judged more harshly in Indianapolis, where the city and the American Federation of State, County, and Municipal Employees agreed to settle a contract dispute using final-offer arbitration. One of the members of the arbitration panel felt that the Indianapolis case did not indicate that final-offer arbitration was conducive to effective negotiation. "Advocates of final-offer arbitration argue that a party will bargain more realistically and refrain from making unreasonable proposals if it fears that its final offer may not be selected by the panel. There is, of course, no empirical evidence that the threat of final-offer arbitration will produce such behavior at the bargaining table."[9]

In most cases, however, effective bargaining took place prior to arbitration and often continued after arbitration was invoked. In any event, the argument that arbitration of any kind has a "chilling" effect on negotiations seems ironic when strikes by public employees are almost always prohibited. According to one arbitrator, "if the strike threat is effectively eliminated, so that the public employer need not worry about its employees striking, that fact in itself is likely to chill the bargaining process, and it is arguable that the addition of arbitration in whatever form can do no worse."[10]

ELIMINATION OF ARBITRATORS' DISCRETION

Another frequently voiced objection to final-offer arbitration is that it eliminates discretion of the arbitrator to design a workable agreement. The arbitrator may feel that when he is limited to choosing between final-offers, he may have to select an offer which he is confident he could improve upon if he were allowed some flexibility.

The arbitrators in the Indianapolis case objected strenuously to their lack of discretion. They felt that they were forced to choose the city's offer but had they had the authority, they would have selected the union's wage offer along with some of the city's other proposals. The Board stated that "some degree of flexibility [should] be granted arbitrators in future cases so that they may appraise the merits of respective proposals, and make a determination on the basis of reasonableness of terms and conditions 'individually,' as well as the total impact of the package."[11]

In some jurisdictions the arbitrator's selection of final-offers is on an issue-by-issue basis.[12] The arbitrator doesn't pick one entire package or the other but may select one party's proposal on one issue and the other party's proposal on another issue. This procedure certainly allows the arbitrator more discretion but it may reduce the incentive to compromise during negotiations by reducing the probability that the other party's entire proposal will be selected. In addition, each party would realize that the arbitrator would to some extent compromise, i.e., select part of each party's proposal; as in conventional arbitration, it would not pay to give up too much before reaching arbitration.

The criticism that final-offer arbitration limits the discretion of the arbitrator involves a misconception of the final-offer procedure. The goal of final-offer arbitration is to make arbitration unnecessary. The compromises are supposed to be made by the parties in negotiations prior to arbitration not by the arbitrator. The function of the arbitrator is simply to penalize the least reasonable party by selecting the other party's offer.

SOPHISTICATION IN BARGAINING

Some experts feel that final-offer arbitration is best suited for parties with sophistication in the bargaining process.[13] The argument is that without experience in bargaining, the parties will be unable to judge the reasonableness of their own offer. Even where specific criteria are provided, parties inexperienced in bargaining might not be able to interpret or apply the criteria as an arbitrator would. As a result, "a serious misjudgement by either or both of the parties could produce gaps so extreme that any result will destroy the general acceptability of the arrangement."[14]

This is an important criticism since final-offer arbitration is being considered as an alternative to the strike or other impasse procedures for the public sector where both parties are likely to have limited experience with collective bargaining. This is not to say that there are not long standing bargaining relationships in the public sector but the fact is that public sector bargaining to a large extent is a relatively recent development. If a procedure is adopted for the public sector which requires too high a degree of bargaining sophistication, serious problems will be created.

Fortunately, experience under final-offer arbitration indicates that inexperience in collective bargaining will not create serious difficulties in final-offer arbitration. In Eugene, where final-offer arbitration appears to be successful, the parties had little collective bargaining experience. In fact, two initial contracts were included in the first six contracts negotiated under the final-offer ordinance.[15]

The success in Eugene can be credited to the nature of the arbitration panel provided by the city ordinance.[16] The arbitration panel consists of three members—one representing each party and a neutral chairman. The fact both parties are represented, facilitates the flow of communications between the parties and, more importantly, between the parties and the chairman. As a result, two disputes were settled by the parties during arbitration after receiving feedback from the chairman concerning his view of their proposals. In effect, the arbitrator by indicating to the parties his opinion of their proposals, served in a med-arb capacity. In Eugene it appears that final-offer arbitration may have facilitated rather than impeded the negotiations between parties with little bargaining experience.

Arbitrators reported similar experiences in Michigan. In a dispute involving the city of Mt. Clemens and Teamster Local 214 (police officers) five issues went to arbitration, but all but wages were settled during arbitration.[17] At Oakland University in Rochester, Michigan, an agreement between the American Association of University Professors chapter and the University provided for final-offer arbitration on an issue-by-issue basis.[18] In this case, the suggestions provided by the chairman during arbitration led to agreement on all but four issues.

The role played by the arbitration panel in Indianapolis was different. The arbitrators chided the parties for changing their proposals during the arbitration proceedings rather than encouraging them to be flexible so that a negotiated agreement could be reached or so that the scope of disagreement could be narrowed. The arbitrators felt that "a party should not alter the character of its proposals once arbitration is underway otherwise the collective bargaining process would be less meaningful, and whatever value there may be in final-offer arbitration would be considerably reduced."[19]

MULTI-ISSUE DISPUTES

When final-offer arbitration involves a single issue, the process is relatively simple, especially if the issue is wages. In the well-publicized baseball salary arbitration, all items except a player's salary were covered by a master agreement between the major league baseball clubs and the players' association so that the arbitrator simply picked the player's or club's salary offer.[20] In deciding between alternative wage offers, the criteria are relatively unambiguous, but when there are noneconomic issues involved, the criteria are less clear and more difficult to apply.

In the case of a multi-issue dispute involving a number of noneconomic as well as economic issues, the job of the arbitrator is much more difficult. Not only are the criteria for noneconomic items like the grievance procedure, seniority, and union security less clear, but each final-offer involves trade-offs between the various issues with each party trying to present the most reasonable combination of proposals. In such a situation, it becomes difficult for the arbitrator to justify his final-offer selection. Yet, in final-offer arbitration, where compromise by the arbitrator is not possible, justifying or rationalizing the arbitration decision is especially important. Unless the arbitrator is able to rationalize his selection, acceptance of final-offer awards by the public and the parties may be in jeopardy.

One possible solution to the problem presented by multi-issue disputes, is issue-by-issue selection. Michigan's Policemen's and Firemen's Arbitration Act provides that the arbitration panel will select the most reasonable last offer on each economic issue (the panel is not required to choose one or the other on economic matters).[21] The final-offer arbitration agreed upon by Oakland University and the Oakland chapter of the American Association of University Professors was also on an issue-by-issue basis.[22]

Although the reports of final-offer arbitration on an issue-by-issue basis referred to above did not discuss any particular problems associated with selecting final-offers on an issue-by-issue basis, an important problem can arise. Issue-by-issue arbitration would lead each party to make demands on every front, knowing it had nothing to lose and might gain a bit here and there. This variety of final-offer arbitration ignores the trade-offs and compromises within a contract. It might therefore make negotiations prior to arbitration less likely to lead to agreement.

The final-offer arbitration procedure in Eugene allows each party to submit two final-offers.[23] This may be useful in a multi-issue dispute. Not only will two offers by each party give the arbitrator more flexibility but it may make agreement between the two parties more likely, since the employer's "high" offer and the union's "low" offer might be quite close. After considering the possibility of multiple offers and issue-by-issue selection, one expert still concludes that "considering the complexities of multi-issue bargaining, the prospects for structuring positions to enable rational choice by the arbitrator do not seem bright."[24]

NEW FRINGE BENEFITS

One important problem in final-offer arbitration which has been overlooked is the difficulty which employee organizations may face in establishing new fringe benefits. If an organization's demand is refused by an employer and an impasse is reached, an arbitrator under final-offer arbitration chooses between the final-offers of the parties on the basis of specific criteria. The criteria involve comparisons of each of the parties' offers with what other workers performing similar work receive.

The specific criteria established by the various final-offer statutes are similar. The Eugene ordinance directs the arbitrator to select the most reasonable offer based on past collective bargaining agreements between the parties, comparisons of wages, hours, and conditions of employment with employees doing comparable work, similar comparisons with other municipalities, the public interest, and the ability of the city to finance economic adjustments.[25] The Michigan and Wisconsin statutes add to these criteria the cost-of-living, overall compensation including the stability of employment and "other factors . . . normally or traditionally taken into consideration in the determination of wages, hours and conditions of employment through voluntary collective bargaining."[26]

If the most important criterion for final-offer selection becomes what other public employees currently receive, the introduction of a new fringe benefit in the face of employer opposition may be impossible, since arbitrators prefer to leave the introduction of new fringe benefits to negotiations between the two parties. An arbitrator may not be confident that he can understand all the ramifications of a new fringe benefit or he may not want his decision to serve as a precedent for the other arbitrators' decisions. In any case, the employee organization would have to present a very convincing argument for an arbitrator to establish a new fringe benefit.

This situation arose in one of the first cases decided under the Michigan final-offer statute.[27] The Police Officers Association of Dearborn, in negotiations with the city, proposed a dental health plan, a recent innovation in fringe benefits which only a few cities had adopted for police officers. In denying the request, the arbitrators' opinion stated that although "this should not be conclusive in ruling it out as part of an arbitration award . . . it does seem to place a special burden of persuasion on the proponents."[28] The opinion added that the chairman of the Panel "would ordinarily prefer to leave most of the pioneering in labor agreements to voluntary bargaining, rather than impose new provisions through compulsory arbitration."[29]

CONCLUSION

The adoption of final-offer arbitration on a trial basis by additional states and municipalities seems desirable. The final-offer procedure not only protects the public from the damage and inconvenience caused by public employee strikes but it minimizes the adverse effect of arbitration on contract negotiations. In addition, limited experience indicates that the procedure can be used successfully by parties with little collective bargaining experience.

The procedure will present substantial new challenges to arbitrators. Multi-issue disputes, in particular, may present very difficult problems. The experience of arbitrators in grievance cases, however, should prove valuable; furthermore, the success of grievance arbitration demonstrates the capability and resourcefulness of arbitrators and the adaptability of the parties to collective bargaining. As public employers and unions become more familiar with final-offer arbitration procedures, it may prove to be the most satisfactory alternative to the strike in the public sector.

NOTES

1. Among the states with compulsory arbitration for at least some public employees are Alaska, Pennsylvania, Rhode Island, Massachusetts, New York, Wisconsin, Wyoming and Oregon.

2. Thomas P. Gilroy and Anthony V. Sinicropi, "Impasse Resolution in Public Employment: A Current Assessment,"*Industrial and Labor Relations review,* Vol. 25, No. 4, (July 1972), pp. 502-503.

3. Arvid Anderson, "A Survey of Statutes with Compulsory Arbitration Provisions for Fire and Police," *Arbitration of Police and Firefighters Disputes* (New York: American Arbitration Association, 1971), p. 9.

4. Carl M. Stevens, "Is Compulsory Arbitration Compatible with Bargaining?"*Industrial Relations,* Vol. 5, No. 2 (February 1966), pp. 44-45.

5. States with final-offer arbitration legislation include Massachusetts, Michigan, Minnesota, and Wisconsin.

6. Gary Long and Peter Feuille, "Final-Offer Arbitration: 'Sudden Death' in Eugene."*Industrial and Labor Relations Review,* Vol. 27, No. 2 (January 1974), p. 203.

7. *Government Employee Relations Report,* No. 545 (Washington: Bureau of Natinal Affairs, Inc. 1974), p. E-1.

8. *Government Employee Relations Report,* No. 501, p. B-10.

9. Fred Witney, "Final-Offer Arbitration: The Indianapolis Experience," *Monthly Labor Review,* Vol. 96, No. 5 (May 1973), p. 25.

10. Joseph R. Grodin, "Either-Or Arbitration for Public Employee Disputes,"*Industrial Relations,* Vol. II, No. 2 (May 1972), p. 263.

11. Witney, "Final-Offer arbitration: The Indianapolis Experience," p. 23.

12. *Government Empoloyee Relations Report,* Reference File-81, 51:3114-3116.

13. Grodin, "Either-Or Arbitration for Public Employee Disputes," p. 264.

14. *Ibid.*

15. Long and Feuille, "Final-Offer Arbitration: 'Sudden Death' in Eugene," pop. 193-195.

16. *Government Employee Relations Report,* Reference File-81, 51:4618-4620.

17. *Government Employee Relations Report,* No. 501, pp. B-9-B-10.

18. *Government Employee Relations Report,* No.526, pp. B-15-B-18.

19. Witney, "Final-Offer Arbitration: The Indianapolis Experience," p. 22.

20. See Peter Seitz, "Footnote to Baseball Arbitration," *The Arbitration Journal,* Vol. 29, No. 2 (June 1974), pp. 98-103.

21. See footnote 12.

22. See footnote 18.

23. See footnote 19 and Long and Feuille, "Final-Offer Arbitration: 'Sudden Death' in Eugene." p. 198.

24. Grodin, "Either-Or Arbitration for Public Employee Disputes," p. 265.

25. *Government Employee Relations Report,* Reference File-81, 51:4620.

26. *Government Employee Relations Report,* Reference File-78, 51:5821 and Reference File 69, 51:3115.

27. *Government Employee Relations Report*, No. 545, pp. E-1-E-6.
28. *Ibid.*, p. E-2.
29. *Ibid.*

CHAPTER 10.
ADMINISTERING
THE CONTRACT

Participative Management:
Can It Work
in the Public Sector?
Stephen E. Schumacher

Participative management can be a very effective management tool. But for Federal managers working in situations where collective bargaining with an exclusively recognized union exists, participative management must be changed to accommodate to labor relations.

Participative management as it is generally practiced incorporates two important characteristics. First, it directly solicits employee input into decisions which affect them, their work and their organization. Second, management retains unilateral control over decision-making and is free either to accept or reject employee input.

In collective bargaining, employees, through their union, participate in determining certain terms and conditions of employment. In most of the Federal service those matters subject to bilateral determination are spelled out broadly in Section 11(a) of Executive Order 11491 as being "personnel policies and practices and matters affecting working conditions." Section 11(a) is limited by other sections of the Executive Order which remove from the scope of bargaining matters covered by law, Executive Order, higher agency regulations promulgated by outside agencies such as the Civil Service Commission. It is precisely those matters within the scope of bargaining that are most conducive to change through participative management.

Reprinted by permission of THE PERSONNEL ADMINISTRATOR, Berea, Ohio 44107

Stephen E. Shumacher is labor relations officer for the personnel division of the Bureau of the Public Debt in the US Department of the Treasury.

DOCTRINE OF EXCLUSIVITY

A necessary corollary of collective bargaining is the doctrine of exclusivity, which confers upon the duly elected and certified union the exclusive right and responsibility to represent, without discrimination, employees in the bargaining unit on all matters within the scope of bargaining. Concurrent with the exclusive right of the union to represent employees is the obligation of management to consult, confer or negotiate only with the exclusive union on matters within the scope of bargaining. This doctrine is sanctioned by Section 10(e) of Executive Order 11491 which provides that "when a labor organization has been accorded exclusive recognition, it is the exclusive representative of employees in the unit and is entitled to act for and to negotiate agreements covering all employees in the unit."

To fully appreciate the practical impact that collective bargaining and exclusivity have upon participative management, one must look to the emerging case law in the Federal labor-management relations program and the impact this case law has had upon the two basic traits of participative management. Specifically, one must understand the extent to which management is constrained from exercising unilateral control over decisions affecting matters within the scope of bargaining and soliciting views and suggestions directly from employees. Most of the case law in this regard has come from the Office of the Assistant Secretary of Labor for Labor-Management Relations, the office with the responsibility for ruling on unfair labor practice charges.

The Assistant Secretary has determined that Federal managers may not unilaterally change the provisions of a negotiated agreement—that which is established bilaterally may only be changed bilaterally. The parties to the contract are the institutions of union and management and management may not effect changes in negotiated terms and conditions of employment without union concurrence. Following from this, it stands that management may not alter the terms of a negotiated contract even when employees—through participative management—express a desire for the change. In short, management does not possess final and unilateral authority to make and implement those changes desired to effectuate employee wishes or to promote employee interests. This authority is shared with the union.

Therefore, management's ability to use participative management as a means of altering terms and conditions of employment set forth in a negotiated contract is limited. What about situations where a contract exists but is silent on those matters upon which management wishes to act? In this instance is management free to make changes on matters within the scope of bargaining without union concurrence? The Assistant Secretary has made it quite clear that absent a "clear and unmistakable waiver" by the union of its right to bargain on matters within the scope of bargaining, management is *not* free to unilaterally change existing terms and conditions of employment. And further, in the words of the Assistant Secretary, a "waiver will not be found merely from the fact that an agreement omits specific reference to a right granted by the Executive Order, or that a labor organization has failed in negotiations to obtain protection with respect to certain of its rights granted by the Order."

Exactly what constitutes a 'clear and unmistakable' waiver of the union's right to negotiate is subject to debate. Generally speaking, though, a union may waive its right to negotiate on matters within the scope of bargaining in the following manner:

- By agreeing to contractual language which specifically waives the union's right to bargain about a specific matter.
- By failing to respond within a "reasonable" time to a management initiative to negotiate on a matter (waiver by inaction).
- By discussing a subject during contract negotiations and then "consciously yielding" its position and not requiring the matter to be included in the agreement.
- By informing management that it has no desire to bargain on the matter.

Without one of these waivers by the union, management is not free to unilaterally effect changes to existing terms and conditions of employment, even when these terms and conditions of employment are *not* covered in an existing negotiated contract. A logical extension of this reasoning is that where a union has exclusive recognition but no contract has been negotiated, management still may not impose new or alter existing terms and conditions of employment without fulfilling its duty to bargain with the union. The consequence to participative management, of course, is that the desires of employees with regard to matters within the scope of bargaining may not be effectuated by management in the absence of a contract without union participation. Again, management does not possess the requisite authority to act on its own volition.

Executive Order 11491 provides—and decisions of the Assistant Secretary confirm—that where a union has been accorded exclusive recognition and has not waived its right to negotiate, management has a duty to bargain with the union before imposing new or altering existing terms and conditions of employment. It matters not that management's decision to initiate change is prompted by employee input through participative management. Management must still involve the union before implementing any decision that would result in change. To the extent that management does not retain final and unilateral authority to act, participative management is not compatible with collective bargaining.

What effect does collective bargaining have upon the second integral part of participative management, namely management's prerogative to deal *directly* with employees? As discussed, Section 10(e) of Executive Order 11491 states quite clearly that the union is the exclusive representative of all employees in the bargaining unit. The significant consequence of exclusivity in the Federal labor relations program is that once a union has been accorded exclusive recognition, management is not free to deal directly with employees on matters within the scope of bargaining. Rather, management may deal with employees on these matters only *through the union* — the exclusive representative.

This means, of course, that management may not, under the guise of participative management, solicit directly from employees their views on personnel policies, practices and matters affecting working conditions. To do so would undermine the status and role of the exclusive union and would, in all likelihood, constitute a management unfair labor practice under Section 19(a) (6) of Executive Order 11491: the denial of the duty to consult, confer or negotiate with the labor organization as required by the Order.

EXISTING CASE LAW

To see the practical consequence that exclusivity has upon management's ability to deal directly with employees we may again look to the existing case law. In perhaps the most significant case in this regard, management established a Youth Advisory Council to serve as a steering committee for the activities and functions of the younger employees of the agency. Representatives of the council were allowed to attend and participate on various management staff committees where personnel policies and practices were discussed. The Assistant Secretary found that management had dealt directly with council representatives with respect to matters concerinng safety, fire protection, training, hiring, transfers and leave. Such conduct, according to the Assistant Secretary, was inconsistent with management's obligation to deal with the exclusive union concerning personnel policies and practices and other matters affecting general working conditions. As a consequence, management was found to have committed an unfair labor practice for failing to consult, confer or negotiate with the union.

The establishment and functioning of the Youth Advisory Council was an attempt by management to institute a form of participative management as a means of obtaining information from younger employees on matters which affected them. In doing so, management committed an unfair labor practice for dealing with a group other than the exclusively recognized union.

Management's ability to deal directly with employees is limited by another part of Section 10(e) which further affirms the doctrine of exclusivity by stating that the union should be given the opportunity to be present at all "formal" discussions between management and employees concerning grievances, personnel policies and practices or other matters affecting general working conditions. The threshold question of what constitutes a formal discussion has been answered, in part, by the Assistant Secretary. A meeting may be considered "formal" if it is called to resolve a problem, management provides for a record to be made by one of the management representatives present and several management representatives attend the meeting.

Thus, when a formal meeting of management and employees is called to consider personnel policies or practices affecting bargaining unit employees generally, management must notify the union so that it has an opportunity to be represented. This requirement, of course, is imposed to permit the union to represent all employees in the unit with respect to matters within the scope of bargaining. It should also be noted that this requirement exists whether or not a contract has been negotiated and is an obligation assumed by management the moment the union is certified as the exclusive representative.

Thus, when participative management has the vestiges of a formal meeting and is used for the purpose of discussing matters within the scope of bargaining, management must involve the union. The union must be given the opportunity to be present and to make its views known.

The obligation to invite the union to be present at formal meetings has some interesting implications beyond its adverse impact upon management's right to deal directly with employees. Managers everywhere, and especially those in the Federal sector, are confronted constantly by any number of diverse groups seeking and/or demanding management's attention—equal employment opportunity groups, professional and recreation associations, veterans organizations, etc. How can management deal with any of these groups in a formal and structured manner on matters within the scope of bargaining without undermining the status of the exclusive union and the concept of bilateralism? The best advice that can be provided at this time is to try to involve the union in any meetings with other groups where matters within the scope of bargaining are discussed. When this is impossible, impractical or unwise, management should listen to—but not negotiate with—the outside groups and keep the union constantly informed as to what occurs at the meetings.

The practice of participatory management traditionally has been predicated upon the prerogative of management to obtain directly from employees their views on matters which affect them. The doctrine of exclusivity, which is a necessary adjunct to collective bargaining, precludes management from dealing with groups of employees except through the union. To bypass the union is to undermine the union's right to exclusively represent the employees in the bargaining unit. (This is not to imply, however, that management must deal through the union when counselling or disciplining employees on an *individual* basis.

If traditional participative management is not compatible with collective bargaining in the Federal sector, then is it necessary to conclude that management may not employ participative management in a collective bargaining environment? Participative management may be employed so long as it is *accommodated* to collective bargaining. Participative management, in short, may be practiced under the following circumstances:

• Where employees are not represented by an exclusive union, management is free to follow the traditional model of participative management.

• Where a union does hold exclusive recognition, management is free to follow the traditional model of participative management with respect to those employees *not* included in the bargaining unit. (In the Federal program, in employee categories, such as management officials, supervisors, personnelists, etc., are excluded from union representation. The value of participative management is acknowledged by the requirement of Section 7(e) of Executive Order 11491 that each agency "establish a system for intra-management communication and consultation with its supervisors ..."

* With respect to those employees who are represented by an exclusive union, management must employ participative management in a modified fashion. Essentially, management must first obtain union concurrence before taking matters up directly with employees and the union must be given the opportunity to be present at all formal meetings between management and employees concerning general personnel policies and practices. Furthermore, in the absence of a waiver by the union of its right to bargain, management must involve the union in any decision it takes to change existing or to impose new personnel policies, practices, and working conditions.

Notes on the Administration of Collective Bargaining Agreements
James A. Craft

More and more public employees are included under provisions of labor contracts. Thus, a knowledgeable approach to contract administration is more and more important to public management.

With the very rapid growth in collective bargaining at all levels of government, increasing numbers of public sector employees are included under the provisions of bilaterally negotiated labor agreements. A recent study estimated that about 38 percent of executive branch federal employees and approximately 21 percent of state and local government employees were covered by collective bargaining contracts.

Reprinted by permission of PUBLIC PERSONNEL MANAGEMENT from PERSONNEL ADMINISTRATION/PUBLIC PERSONNEL REVIEW, 1(July-August 1972), pp. 30-33.

James A. Craft is associate professor in the Graduate School of Business, University of Pittsburgh. He received the Ph.D. at the University of California at Berkeley.

Generally, these agreements seek to define, in varying degrees of precision, the payment of wages, the hours and the conditions of work for public employees. In addition, many of these contracts include negotiated grievance procedures terminating in arbitration that can be used by the parties to challenge actions that are perceived to be inequitable or inappropriate interpretations, violations, or abrogations of the contract. With the currently large and continually growing number of public employees covered by labor contracts and the accompanying appeal procedures, a knowledgeable approach to contract administration becomes increasingly important to successful public management.

CONSTRAINTS OF CONTRACT

Most public administrators will probably never negotiate a labor agreement. However, a large percentage of them, at some point in their career, will have to carry out their management activities working under the constraints of a contract when allocating or utilizing human resources. They will be responsible for meeting the requirements of the agreement in their behavior and decisions, and will expect their subordinates to live up to their responsibilities. In short, they will have to administer the agreement.

The objective here is to provide some insights and guidelines that will be useful to the public official who must administer a labor contract. First, we will briefly discuss selected aspects of the labor agreement to obtain some insights into the nature of the document to be administered. Next, we will present some guidelines for effective contract administration that public administrators will want to consider in their daily relationship with the union and the employees covered by an agreement. Finally, some concluding comments will be made with regard to the importance of contract administration.

NATURE OF THE AGREEMENT

The collective bargaining agreement, as it emerges from the negotiating process, is a mutually agreed upon set of rules that have been jointly developed to guide an employer-employee relationship for a fixed period of time. Since collective bargaining is an adversary relationship involving the representatives of two groups with divergent goals, the emergent rules are likely to represent numerous compromises by both parties.

The rules embodied in the agreement will provide the framework to govern the day-to-day relationship between the parties. In particular, they will place limitations and constraints on managerial authority and they will define the rights, responsibilities, and duties of each of the participants in the relationship.

Generally, collective bargaining contracts will vary in their length and specificity. Some agreements are very simple documents. They consist of a few mimeographed or printed pages and deal with a limited number of basic items on which the parties wish to establish guidelines for decisions and behavior. Other contracts, generally where there has been a longer and/or a more conflict-oriented relationship, may be highly complex and lengthy documents with rules that attempt to define the responsibilities of the parties very specifically in a variety of situations.

While the length, subject matter, and detail of an agreement will be in some respects unique to each collective bargaining relationship, the substance of most contracts can be divided into three basic categories. Following an analysis by Leo Kotin, most contract provisions can be classed into one of the following groupings: (1) "fixed" provisions, (2) "contingent" provisions, or (3) dispute resolution provisions. The "fixed" provisions include clauses

> ...where it is anticipated, and where in practice, little change or no change will be proposed by the parties. Typical of these clauses are (1) wage rates ..., (2) union security, (3) duration and reopening provisions.

The "contingent" provisions of the contract are the clauses that

> ... govern the action of the union or the management to be undertaken contingent upon conditions arising which are not present at the time of agreement. Among these clauses are (1) lay-off regulations, (2) promotions, (3) severance, (4) discharge, (5) transfer, (6) significant change in schedule or manner of production.

RESOLUTION PROCEDURE

Finally, and perhaps most important from the point of view of contract administration, are the provisions defining a dispute resolution procedure. Generally, this will be the multi-step grievance procedure terminating in arbitration. The grievance procedure is established to resolve disputes that arise in the interpretation and application of the contract—particularly in the application of the "contingent" clauses. The significance of a dispute resolution procedure, such as the grievance procedure, for contract administration cannot be over-emphasized. It is essentially a mechanism to institutionalize conflict that arises during the term of the agreement.

Disputes over the meaning or application of the rules are placed in a jointly established and accepted channel to be resolved in an organized manner rather than breaking out in overt and disruptive direct action. The employees continue to work and earn their salaries and the agency provides its services and carries out its functions while the problem is being worked out by the parties.

In the early history of collective bargaining in the private sector, when there were few dispute resolution procedures incorporated in agreements, little distinction was made between negotiating an agreement and adjusting disagreements under an existing contract. Overt power was used by the parties to resolve their differences in both cases. This obviously had a highly disruptive potential effect on the continuity of operations of an employer, even though he had agreed to a contract.

Now that we have an idea of the nature of a labor agreement, let us turn our attention to some guidelines that may be helpful to the public manager as he administers the contract.

CONTRACT ADMINISTRATION

The negotiation of a labor contract receives the most extensive news coverage and stimulates high public interest, but the administration of the contract, while less spectacular and more mundane in process, is an equally important part of the collective bargaining relationship. The significance of contract administration is manifested in the statement by Harold Davey, a noted labor arbitrator, that a "contract is no better than its administraton." If what has been negotiated is disregarded, not enforced, or not used, then for all purposes the agreement is meaningless and ineffective as a framework for the relationship.

Since managers in most public organizations have the responsibility for supervising personnel, organizing, and directing the operations of the agency, they will have the primary responsibility for contract administration. If the union or an employee believes that management has violated the contract or is interpreting or applying the contract incorrectly or inequitably, then he has recourse to the grievance procedure to force the observance of the contract provisions. Given the lion's share of responsibility and the fact that problems will inevitably arise under the contract due to ambiguous language and new unexpected situations, it is important that management develop guidelines for its behavior in administering the contract.

GUIDELINES AND POLICIES

The following ideas and suggestions developed from the study of labor relations in the private sector may be useful to public officials in developing policies for their contract adiministration activity.

1. Management should have a systematic approach for dealing with the employment and personnel problems (potential grievances) that will arise in the routine daily operations of the organization. For example, management should establish a uniform well defined procedure for disciplining employees who violate contract provisions or agency rules (e.g., smoking in unauthorized areas, unauthorized absence, etc.).

Such a procedure might include three or four steps in which progressively severe, but well formulated and understood, disciplinary actions would be taken. The policy should be applied consistently, uniformly, and impartially in all of the agency departments. When such an approach is used, management has a much stronger position in any grievance protest that may result over the action it has taken.

Agency administrators should be particularly cautious in making exceptions and modifications in the procedure on an ad hoc basis ("just this once") due to expediency or the immediate needs of the agency. Such action may cause problems later in grievance negotiations when the union uses these exceptions in its arguments for further exceptions.

COMMUNICATION AND SUPPORT

2. Top management should be certain that its policies on contract enforcement and the intent of important clauses in the agreement are communicated to and understood by all levels of management. In addition, it is important that top management be willing actively to support lower levels of supervision in following the specified interpretations and policies that have been communicated—even though a short-run cost may be involved.

While lower management may be aware of the designated policies to guide contract administration, if they feel that they will receive only limited or inconsistent support, or if they will be reprimanded for short-run problems resulting from actions consistent with top management policy (e.g., short illegal work stoppages, slowdowns, excess grievances), they will most likely not follow them.

Given the pressures on first and second line supervisors by upper management and the public for the uninterrupted provision of the organization's services or product, there is a tendency for them to make informal agreements with strategically placed work groups or union representatives in order to get the work out. Such informal agreements can essentially undermine a negotiated agreement and establish a plethora of non-uniform sub-agreements in the various units or departments of an agency. These, in turn, can lead to disputes and grievances later as new supervisors replace those who made the informal agreements, management tries to tighten up work practices, or other forms of change affect the organization.

RESOLVING GRIEVANCES

3. In any employer-employee relationship covered by a labor agreement that specifies the rights and responsibilities of the parties, there are bound to be some grievances over the interpretation and application of the contract. When formal grievances are presented, management should take prompt action and try to resolve them equitably as quickly as possible.

Expeditious attention to grievances has a number of advantages: (1) it demonstrates to employees that management is interested in them and in the problems they face; (2) it prevents a feeling that the grievance system does not work and that direct action is needed to get results; (3) it prevents animosity and the smoldering resentment on the part of an aggrieved employee who sees little, or delayed, action on a problem he has experienced; and (4) it allows the parties the opportunity to solve the problem while it is still possible to obtain the facts of the situation and the problem can be clearly defined.

4. Management must insist that all parties live up to the requirements and responsibilities designated in the contract provisions. This includes the union and the employees as well as management. While most contract provisions are focused on defining employee rights, placing limitations on management dis-

cretion, and defining procedures for management to follow, there may be certain duties and requirements specified for the union and its representatives. For example, contract provisions can limit the amount of time union representatives may spend on specific union activities during work hours. They may require that the employees not strike during the period of the agreement, or that the union has responsibilities for maintaining facilities it is permitted to use on the agency premises.

It is obvious that the union will challenge management through the grievance procedure if there is any question that management is not living up to the contract. However, the grievance procedure should be used by both parties. Indeed, the contract should specify that management can submit grievances and management should do so in order to insure that the union carries out its responsibilities under the contract. As Harold W. Davey points out in *Contemporary Collective Bargaining,* management's use of the grievance procedure may be a useful "means of securing corrective action on undesirable union practices . . . without the necessity of disciplining individual workers."

BEFORE ARBITRATION

5. Since a substantial number of labor agreements covering employees at all levels of government include a grievance procedure that ends in some form of arbitration, management should have a definite policy on reviewing and screening all grievances before the final arbitration step. The objective of such activity is twofold.

First, by carefully reviewing a grievance in terms of the intent of the contract language, the circumstances and persons involved in the dispute, and considering any new information that might have emerged, management may find grounds for resolution of the dispute with the union without incurring the costs of hiring an arbitrator.

Second, by a careful final review of the grievance and the positions of the parties on the dispute, management can evaluate the merits of its case to determine the strength of its position and the probability of receiving a favorable award from the arbitrator. Such a review and evaluation by management can help avoid embarrassing unexpected losses and the establishment of undesirable precedent cases.

CHAPTER 11.
GRIEVANCE AND ARBITRATION MACHINERY

The Grievance Arbitration and No-Strike Model in Public Employment
Paul D. Staudohar

Whether public employees should have the right to strike is a controversial issue. But almost everyone agrees that effective grievance procedure and arbitration is essential, if a ban on work stoppages is to be enforced, and that such machinery for resolving problems is advisable, whether strikes are forbidden or not. In this study, the author shows the extent to which the private sector model has been carried over in the public sector.

A distinctive feature of labor-management relations in U.S. private industry under the National Labor Relations Act is the establishment of grievance arbitration and no-strike provisions in collective bargaining agreements. In this arrangement management agrees to arbitrate grievances arising under the contract, which ensures that disputes over the interpretation and application of its terms can be submitted to a neutral third party for a final, binding decision. Labor, for its part, agrees not to strike during the time the contract is in effect, doing so because it has an equitable procedure for resolving disputes under the contract and therefore does not need to strike to achieve fair enforcement of terms. Contractual obligation to arbitrate thus provides an alternative to use of the strike weapon as a contract enforcement mechanism. When the agreement expires the union's strike right

Reprinted by permission of the ARBITRATION JOURNAL, June, 1976.

Paul D. Staudohar is Professor of Business Administration at California State University, Hayward.

is re-effectuated, giving it necessary power to achieve a favorable replacement contract through negotiation.

Arbitration and no-strike agreements have worked out well over many years in the private sector by reducing strikes and providing an equitable system of industrial jurisprudence. Given this success, it is worth considering whether and to what extent they have relevance to public employment. This article examines the use of the grievance arbitration and no-strike model in the public sector.

Most public jurisdictions in the U.S. are still in the formative years of bilateral labor relations systems. Experimentation is proceeding under a variety of laws that establish joint determination of the terms and conditions of employment. Eight states provide a right to strike, as an adjunct to negotiation, to some or all of their public employees, limited by considerations such as a threat to public health or safety. The public sector is moving closer to the private industry system of labor relations, although there are important differences between the two that may suggest alternative ways of facilitating bilateralism.

One such difference should be emphasized here. A key feature of these few laws which grant the right to strike on a limited basis to public employees is that this right is not allowed during the time the contract is in effect. It is permitted only in situations involving negotiation of a new or replacement contract. This is in contrast to the private sector where the right to strike exists during the contract over issues within the scope of bargaining unless the right is given up in a no-strike clause.[1] Also, notably, most jurisdictions prohibit all public employee strikes. The question arising from this distinction is why might a no-strike provision be included in a public employment collective bargaining agreement when the employees do not have the right to strike *de jure* over contractual terms in any event?

One justification is that data on public employee strikes indicate that a large majority of these strikes have taken place in the presence of laws barring their use. Public employees strike when they feel it is necessary, preventative laws often notwithstnnding. Several strikes have resulted from failure by management to live up to its contractual commitments. Assuming the existence of a statute which mandates collective (and *a fortiori* when the strike right is extended on a limited basis to give greater equalization of bargaining power), the need to strike for enforcement of contract provisions is mostly eliminated when binding arbitration is available for disputes arising under the contract and when both sides implement the grievance procedure in accordance with their obligation. By formally denying the use of the strike weapon, and perhaps other pressure tactics as well, during the contract, the employee organization affirmatively commits itself to living within the terms of the agreement and its built-in mechanism for conflict resolution. Having the commitment of the employee organization not to strike, the government agency is given incentive to pledge arbitration of disputed interpretation or application of contract terms, with the joint promises having a greater likelihood of being mutually reinforcing in practice by virtue of their existence. Behest to comply becomes psychological as well as legal.[2]

Another justification for no-strike clauses in public employment is the web of legal entanglements that often confront agencies seeking to enforce anti-strike statutes or common law court decisions. This law may contain procedural conditions precedent to determining illegality, and in some states quasi-strike actions by public employees, such as slowdowns and sickouts, may be held to circumvent application of the strike ban to a particular job action.[3] A broad no strike clause in the negotiated agreement, prohibiting various job actions, thus serves as an additional or alternative mechanism that can be pursued to find illegality through breach of contract, strengthening the agency's case against these violations.[4]

THE PRIVATE SECTOR

It is useful to place the development of the model of no-strike and arbitration agreements in the context of Slichter et al's identification of three overlapping stages of maturation of labor-management relations—the 1) organizing stage, 2) contract development stage, and 3) adjustment and accommodation stage.[5] The first two stages are much more characterized by the use of pressure tactics than the third. Prior to the development of grievance procedures featuring a sequence of appeals to higher levels of authority of labor and management with binding arbitration as the final step, grievances were a frequent cause of work stoppages in private industry. Among the techniques for achieving resolution of disagreement over existing contract terms, however, the strike became relatively undesirable. Mutual respect, confidence, and cooperation were often found to be more difficult to cultivate when jeopardized by strike action and the coercion it represents. With the maturing of labor relations, and movement toward adjustment and accommodation, practitioners turned to alternative means of resolving their grievances.

Substitutes for the grievance strike were first established in the needle trades, where economic power substantially fluctuated on the basis of seasonal operations.[6] By the 1920's the ladies' garment, men's clothing, fur, and headgear industries had well-established permanent arbitration systems.[7] Encouraging development of arbitration as a substitute for the strike was the War Labor Board which, from 1942-45, ordered the inclusion of grievance arbitration in contracts and gave training and experience to a cadre of arbitrators. The Taft-Hartley Act of 1947 in Section 203(d) declared final adjustments by a method agreed upon by the parties to be a desirable method for settlement of grievance disputes arising over the application or interpretation of an existing collective bargaining agreement. Section 301(a) of the Act helped provide a legal framework under which arbitration could take place by making agreements to arbitrate and the awards themselves enforceable in the courts. Also important were state statutes providing for enforcement by the courts of arbitrators' decisions. By 1948 the no-strike clause was made a mandatory subject for bargaining.[8] As grievances were worked out and arbitration decisions handed down, procedures, rights and obligations were established, and meaning given to contract provisions. Greater acceptance of the other party's viewpoints and routinization of labor relations followed, reducing the need for pressure tactics in contract administration. Today, over 90 percent of collective bargaining contracts in the private sector provide for binding arbitration of grievances, and most of these have an accompanying no-strike clause.[9]

Court decisions have also been important in shaping the arbitration no-strike model in private industry. The "Trilogy," three U.S. Supreme Court decisions in 1960,[10] limited the intervention of courts in the arbitration process to situations in which the arbitrator exceeds his authority. These decisions greatly enhanced the status of arbitration and power of arbitrators. Moreover, court interpretations of Taft-Hartley have held that enforcement of agreements to arbitrate and not strike can be obtained in the courts. In the *Lincoln Mills* case,[11] the U.S. Supreme Court required management to arbitrate in accordance with its agreement to do so in the collective bargaining contract, where a part of the contract was a no-strike clause. In *Boys Market*[12] an injunction was allowed against a union which had struck in violation of a no-strike clause in the contract instead of engaging in arbitration which was contractually available for resolving the dispute.[13]

It should be noted that the arbitration no-strike arrangement may not apply to all of the issues dealt with in the collective bargaining agreement. Management may wish to exclude certain provisions of the contract from arbitration, not wanting to give up any decision-making prerogatives to an arbitrator who might construe the provisions unfavorably to the firm.[14] When items are excluded from the arbitration clause, the union in private employment may be allowed to strike concerning them during the time the contract is in effect, despite a no-strike clause covering arbitrable items. The language of the contract is crucial in these cases, since a general no-strike clause may bar all strikes, including those over matters not dealt with in the contract.

Strikes in violation of the contract, though relatively uncommon, may occur where there is growing dissatisfaction among employees with the contract and its implementation. Also, union leaders might call a strike to gain favorable interpretation of the contract, preferring direct action to a grievance procedure perceived as inadequate. There may be a dissident group within the union that is trying to get control by demonstrating militancy, or perhaps a rival union seeking a new election will pressure the certified union into striking in order to retain solidarity among its members.[15]

PUBLIC SECTOR GRIEVANCE ARBITRATION

Grievance procedures have become an important feature of collective bargaining agreements in public employment, and binding arbitration is often the final step in the grievance procedure. A national survey taken in 1970 of municipal collective bargaining agreements, including those involving teachers, shows that 87 percent of the agreements provided for negotiated grievance procedures.[16] Binding arbitration as a final step in the grievance procedure was specified in about half of the agreements.[17] Use of grievance arbitration in a jurisdiction largely depends on whether a law mandating collective bargaining with public employees exists, and whether it allows or requires inclusion of binding grievance arbitration. This is illustrated by experience in federal government employment. Executive Order 11491, effective on January 1, 1970, provided for negotiation of binding grievance arbitration on federal employee contracts. Prior to 1970, only nonbinding or advisory arbitration was legally authorized, and 70 percent of the grievance procedures provided for this means of final resolution.[18] By late 1971, however, nearly half of the grievance procedures included final and binding arbitration.[19]

More recent research on state and local government indicates that growth in negotiated grievance procedures with binding arbitration is continuing.[20] Fifty-six percent of the agreements studied specified binding arbitration of grievances. (See Table I.)

NO-STRIKE AGREEMENTS

While not as common as in the private sector, no-strike clauses are increasingly being negotiated in collective bargaining agreements in public employment. Some state laws require that a prohibition on strikes and other job actions be included in negotiated agreements. Examples are found in the laws in Florida (teachers), Georgia (fire fighters), New Hampshire (state employees), New Mexico (state employees), and Oklahoma (municipal employees). A typical requirement is found in Section 12 of the Georgia law, which states in part: "Any collective bargaining agreement negotiated under the terms and provisions of this Act shall specifically provide that the fire fighters who are subject to its terms shall have no right to engage in any work stoppage,

TABLE I
Grievance Arbitration Procedures in State and Local Government as of January 1, 1974

Grievance Arbitration Procedure	State	County	Municipal	Special District
All Agreements	400	85	137	164	14
Total With Reference to Arbitration	303	70	99	123	11
Advisory	55	3	45	6	1
Binding	224	63	47	104	10
Advisory and Binding	11	1	3	7	—
Reference to Arbitration,					
No Details Given	13	3	4	6	—
No Reference to Arbitration	97	15	38	41	3

SOURCE: U.S. Department of Labor, *Characteristics of Agreements in State and Local Governments, January 1, 1974,* Bureau of Labor Statistics, Bulletin No. 1861 (Washington, D.C.: Government Printing Office, 1975), p.41.

slowdown or strike, the consideration for such provision being the right to a resolution of disputed questions."

Out of 400 state and local agreements in heavily populated areas, only 139 made no reference to prohibition of work stoppages. (See Table II.) These data indicate a substantial use of no-strike clauses, at least as concerns the larger jurisdictions, which are typically more vulnerable to strikes than sparsely populated areas.

CONCLUDING REMARKS

The data show grievance arbitration and no-strike provisions being developed extensively in the public sector. These features provide equitable outlet for contractual disagreement and minimize strikes over grievances. Because in most jurisdictions public employees do not have a legal right to strike during an agreement's existence, they may not be giving up that much by agreement to forbear. However, the contractual obligation, with its attendant psychological and legal constraints, constitutes an additional barrier to strike activity, and in this sense appears to be in the public interest.

TABLE II
Work Stoppage Provisions in State and Local Government
as of January 1, 1974

Work Stoppage Provision	State	County	Municipal	Special District
All Agreements	400	85	137	164	14
Total With Reference to Work Stoppage or Slowdown	261	70	56	123	12
Prohibited	119	33	26	56	4
Prohibited; Union Must Work to End Stoppage	131	35	29	60	7
Permitted Under Selected* Conditions	11	2	1	7	1
No Reference to Work Stoppage	139	15	81	41	2

* Work stoppages would be permitted, for example, when the employer refuses to take a dispute to binding arbitration, when the employer rejects an arbitrator's award, or when a contract reopens.

SOURCE: U.S. Department of Labor, *Characteristics of Agreements in State and Local Governments, January 1, 1974,* Bureau of Labor Statistics, Bulletin No. 1861 (Washington, D.C.: Government Printing Office, 1975), p. 42. See footnote number 20 regarding coverage of the agreements.

NOTES

1. It should be further noted that the U.S.Supreme Court has held that a no-strike obligation is implied concerning those issues under the contract which are subject to binding arbitration. Strikes over these issues violate the agreement, despite absence of an express no-strike clause. See *Local 174, Teamsters v. Lucas Flour Co.*, 369 U.S. 95 (1962).

2. Collective bargaining agreements contain other provisions setting forth rights or restrictions which are regulated by statutory or common law. Examples are clauses on safety, nondiscrimination in employment, and management prerogatives. The management prerogatives clause has been referred to as serving a "psychological purpose," that can be thought of as reinforcing the legal protections of management rights. See Paul Prasow and others, *Scope of Bargaining in the Public Sector— Concepts and Problems*, Report Submitted to U.S. Division of Public Employee Labor Relations, Office of Labor Relations, Office of Labor Management Relations Services, U.S. Department of Labor (Washington, D.C.: Government Printing Office, 1972), p. 15.

3. See Paul D. Staudohar, "Quasi-Strikes by Public Employees," *Journal of Collective Negotiations in the Public Sector*, Vol. 3, No. 4, Fall, 1974, pp. 363-371.

4. For example, see *City of Dover v. International Association of Fire Fighters Local 1312, et al.*, New Hampshire Supreme Court, Strafford, No. 6885, July 19, 1974, reported in *Government Employee Relations Report*, No. 574, September 30, 1974, pp. B-8 to B-10.

5. Summer H. Slichter, James J. Healy and E. Robert Livernash, *The Impact of Collective Bargaining on Management*, (Washington, D.C.: The Brookings Institution, 1960), p. 665.

6. "Few discharges could be made in the weeks before Easter. Lost production would then be too serious to management. The tables were turned in the slow summer months when disciplinary layoffs and discharges could be made by an employer with relative impunity. For such reasons, both parties were under strong compulsion to work out a substitute for the grievance strike." George W. Taylor, "Collective Bargaining in the Public Sector," in *The Next Twenty-Five Years of Industrial Relations*, ed by Gerald G. Somers, (Madison: Industrial Relations Research Association, 1973), p. 35.

7. Irving Bernstein, *The Lean Years: A History of the American Worker 1920-1933* (Baltimore: Penguin Books, Inc., 1966), p. 74.

8. *Shell Oil Co.*, 22 LRRM 1158 (1948).

9. A 1966 report indicated that 94 percent of the collective bargaining agreements studied provided for arbitration as the final step in the grievance procedure, and 89 percent limited strikes and lockouts. While many of the contracts banned strikes and lockouts entirely, others limited the ban to issues covered in the contract. See U.S. Department of Labor, *Major Collective Bargaining Agreements: Arbitration Procedures*, Bureau of Labor Statistics Bulletin No. 1425-6, (Washington, D.C.: Gov-

ernment Printing Office, 1966), pp. 5, 83. A 1970 study showed that 90 percent of the contracts had no-strike clauses. See Bureau of National Affairs, "Basic Contract Patterns: No-Strike, No-Lockout Pledges," *Labor Relations Reporter*, News and Background Information, Vol. 75, No. 19, p. 199.

10. *United Steelworkers of America v. American Manufacturing Co.*, 363 U.S. 564 (1960); *United Steelworkers of America v. Warrior & Gulf Navigation Co.*, 363 U.S. 574 (l960); and *United Steelworkers of America v. Enterprise Wheel & Car Corp.*, 363 U.S. 593 (1960).

11. *Textile Workers Union v. Lincoln Mills of Alabama*, 353 U.S. 448 (1957).

12. *Boys Market v. Retail Clerks Union, Local 770*, 398 U.S. 235 (1970).

13. However, the Supreme Court has also held that violation of a no-strike clause by engaging in a strike is permissible activity when the strike itself is provoked by unfair labor practices committed by the employer. See *Mastro Plastics Corp. v. NLRB*, 350 U.S. 270 (1956).

14. For example, disputes over pension benefits, concerning which a "bad" decision could prove prohibitively costly to either party, may be resolved through a mechanism other than the grievance and arbitration procedures.

15. For discussion of wildcat strikes and estimates of their incidence, see Jack Stieber, "Unauthorized Strikes Under the American and British Industrial Relations Systems," *British Journal of Industrial Relations*, Vol. 6, No. 2, July, 1968, pp. 232-235. See also, Morrison and Marjorie L. Handsaker, "Remedies and Penalties for Wildcat Strikes: How Arbitrators and Federal Courts Have Rules," *Catholic University of America Law Review*, Vol. 22, No. 2, Winter, 1973, pp. 279-323.

16. The study was of cities with populations of 250,000 or over. U.S. Department of Labor, *Municipal Collective Bargaining Agreements in Large Cities*, Bureau of Labor Statistics, Bulletin No. 1759 (Washington, D.C.: Government Printing Office, 1972), p. 52.

17. *Ibid.*, p. 52. Of the total of 286 agreements, 147 provided for binding arbitration of grievances.

18. U.S. Department of Labor, *Negotiation Impasse, Grievance, and Arbitration in Federal Agreements*, Bureau of Labor Statistics, Bulletin No. 1661 (Washington, D.C.: Government Printing Office, 1970), p. 25.

19. U.S. Department of Labor, *Collective Bargaining Agreements in the Federal Service, Late 1971*, Bureau of Labor Statistics, Bulletin No. 1789 (Washington, D.C.: Government Printing Office, 1973), p. 74. Of the federal agreements studied, 549 out of 671 had grievance procedures, 45 percent of which provided for final and binding arbitration alone or in combination with advisory arbitration.

20. U.S. Department of Labor, *Characteristics of Agreements in State and Local Governments, January 1, 1974*, Bureau of Labor Statistics, Bulletin No. 1861 (Washington, D.C.: Government Printing Office, 1975), p. 41. The 400 agreements, all in effect after January 1, 1974,

covered states, counties with populations of 500,000 and over, cities of 250,000 and over, and special districts. Public education was excluded.

Grievance and Arbitration Patterns in the Federal Service

William J. Kilberg,

Thomas Angelo,

and Lawrence Lorber

The growth of grievance arbitration in the private sector has been traced to the need to maintain labor peace during World War II.[1] The National War Labor Board and the Wage Stabilization structure used during the Korean War produced a cadre of labor arbitrators sophisticated in dispute resolution procedures. Private dispute settlement has therefore evolved into a mature set of mechanisms by which the parties to an agreement are provided an expeditious, equitable and relatively inexpensive avenue of settlement although there are current complaints about rising costs and delays.

Unionization and collective bargaining in public employment are relatively recent phenomena, untested by the turmoil of wartime concerns. Thus when compared with the current state of the art in the private sector, public sector procedures may seem insufficient. It must be remembered, however, that these agreements were developed in an atmosphere significantly different from that in the private sector. Moreover, unlike the National Labor Relations Act, the Executive orders have provided restrictive guidance as to what may and may not be included within a negotiated grievance procedure.

In addition, the availability of alternate statutory procedures for dispute resolution provided by Civil Service regulation has

Reprinted by permission of the MONTHLY LABOR REVIEW.

William J. Kilberg is Associate Solicitor for Labor Relations and Civil Rights, U.S. Department of Labor. Thomas Angelo and Lawrence Lorber are attorneys in the Division of Labor Relations and Civil Rights, U.S. Department of Labor.

lessened both the need for and the impact of negotiated grievance mechanisms. It is only in the past year since the most recent Executive order has been issued that arbitration in the Federal sector has had an opportunity to come into its own.

The authors have reviewed approximately 50 agreements entered into since the issuance of the latest Executive order in an effort to discern present and evolving patterns of grievance arbitration in the Federal sector.

EXECUTIVE ORDERS PERMIT BARGAINING

In January 1962, the first of three Executive orders pertaining to labor-management relations in the Federal sector was signed by President Kennedy. Embodying the recommendations of the President's Task Force on Employee-Management Relations in the Federal Sector, Executive Order 10988 contained provisions in regard to grievance and arbitration procedures.[2]

Section 8 of that order permitted negotiation of grievance procedures if they conformed to Civil Service standards and did not "diminish or impair" any rights the employee already had. Arbitration provisions could also be negotiated so long as the arbitration award was only "advisory" rather than binding, dealt only with the interpretation or application of agreements or agency policy, and the employee or employees concerned approved of its use.

Thus, the Federal employee was presented with a bifurcated system for resolving his grievance, either through the applicable agency procedure or through the grievance procedure negotiated by his union. Furthermore, because the arbitral decision was advisory only, it left the ultimate resolution of the grievance in the hands of the appropriate agency head, essentially the situation predating the Executive order. After 5 years of operation under Executive Order 10988, only 19 percent of Federal employees were covered by any type of negotiated grievance procedure, and both management and labor found the dual systems for grievance resolution confusing.

As one consequence of this, in 1967 a second Task Force on Labor Relations in the Federal sector began analyzing the system. Its report, issued in 1969, commented that "so long as negotiated grievance procedures provided employees all rights prescribed by Civil Service Commission standards, they might properly be adopted by the agency and labor organization as the exclusive procedure available to employees." The report went on to state that "arbitration of grievances has worked well and has benefited both employees and agencies ...." They felt that arbitrators' decisions "should be accepted by the parties" and should be set aside only on "grounds similar to those applied by the courts in private sector labor-management relations...."

In October 1969, President Nixon issued Executive Order 11491 which codified these recommendations in its sections 13 and 14. While permitting the negotiated procedure to be the "exclusive procedure available to employees in the unit when the agreement so provides," the new order barred extension of arbitration to "changes or proposed changes in agreements or agency policy."[3]

In contrast to Executive Order 10988 which allowed both negotiated and agency-imposed grievance procedures to exist side-by-side, Executive Order 11491 permitted the negotiated grievance procedure to be the exclusive method for resolving disputes during the life of the contract. It was soon discovered, however, that the conflict between employee rights established by law or regulation and rights created by the collective agreement was not resolved by allowing the negotiated grievance procedure to be the sole route open to employees.

In August 1971, the President issued Executive Order 11616, which amended Executive Order 11491 substantively in the areas of grievance and arbitration procedures. The new order provides that negotiated grievance procedures and arbitration can deal only with the interpretation or application of a negotiated agreement, and cannot deal with matters outside the agreement, including those for which statutory appeals procedures exist. These changes are codified as section 13 of the amended order, and are applicable to all agreements established, extended, or renewed beginning November 24, 1971.[4]

DEFINING GRIEVANCES

Under Executive Order 11616, an agreement must contain a grievance procedure (this differs from Executive Orders 10988 and 11491), although no similar requirement is placed on arbitration provisions. The order limits coverage of negotiated grievance procedures to grievances which involve the interpretation or application of provisions in the agreement. Other types of grievances must be resolved through agency systems developed under Civil Service Commission regulations or other available agency procedures. Moreover, negotiated grievance procedures are not permitted to cover matters already dealt with by statutory appeals procedures. This prevents duplication or overlap in avenues of redress which could occur, for example, if a matter subject to a statutory appeals procedure also touches on provisions of the agreement.

Because the order makes specific reference to the right of "any employee or group of employees [to] present . . . grievances to the agency and have them adjusted," so long as the union (the exclusive representative) has the "opportunity to be present at the adjustment," a number of agreements reflect this injunction. Thus, in the agreement negotiated between the Germantown District of the Social Security Administration and Local 2327, American Federation of Government Employees, is the following:

> A grievance is an employee's or group of employees', expressed (oral or written) feeling of dissatisfaction with Management's interpretation or application of this agreement. It is initiated by the employee(s) himself (themselves), not by the union.

This clause clearly precludes the union from bringing the grievance in its own name, thus channeling the grievance procedure into resolving disputes between individual employees and management.[5]

In the multiunit agreement negotiated by the National Weather Service and the National Association of Government Employees (NAGE), grievance is defined in the following manner:

> A grievance, for purposes of this agreement, is any cause for dissatisfaction over the interpretation or application of this agreement, if the matter grows out of employment in the Agency and the remedy sought is within the authority of the Director of the Agency or other official to whom such authority has been delegated.

This clause contains the basic definition of a grievance without stating whether the grievance may be brought solely by the affected employee or employees. It also adds the important qualification that the remedy sought must be within the power of the agency head to grant.

However, in the agreement between Local 2486, American Federation of Government Employees, and the Baltimore District of the Food and Drug Administration, power to initiate grievances was expanded to include the union:

> The negotiated grievance procedure contained herein is applicable only to members of the unit and shall apply only to the consideration of grievances over the interpretation or application of this General Agreement. This procedure will be the only procedure for the con-

sideration of such grievances. Grievances under this procedure may be submitted by an employee, a group of employees, or by the Union.

This alternate definition of a grievance by allowing the union to be the instigating party gives it an added incentive to monitor the application of the agreement and permits the collective bargaining grievance procedure to be used to clarify contract disputes without recourse to any particular aggrieved employee. This provision therefore allows the dispute settlement procedure of the grievance mechanism to be applied in a preventive manner and opens the door to the possible use of arbitration for declaratory judgments.

An interesting variation on both these approaches can be found in the agreement between the U.S. Department of Labor and the National Council of Field Labor Lodges, American Federation of Government Employees:

> . . . Grievances initiated by individual employees or groups of employees in their own behalf, personally or through the union, are denominated as "Type A." Disputes initiated by the Union or affiliated lodges are denominated "Type B." Matters brought by the Union under this definition are not grievances within the meaning of the Civil Service Commission standards, and such standards do not apply to type B disputes.
>
> A Type A grievance is a statement of dissatisfaction and request for adjustment of a management decision or some aspect of employment status or working conditions which is beyond the control of the aggrieved employee but within the control of the Department. This may include disputes over interpretation or application of this agreement or any law, rule, or regulation governing personnel practices or working conditions.[6]
>
> A Type B grievance is a dispute initiated by the Union or an affiliated lodge concerning interpretation or application of this agreement. This procedure shall not be used in the adjustment of individual cases; however, arbitration decisions which are accepted by the Secretary shall be applied to appropriate individual cases.

Several of the agreements studied contain provisions allowing the public employer to file a grievance. In such instances, the grievance procedure often commences in one of the last steps of the process. An example of this can be found in the agreement negotiated between the Commissary Store at Quonset Point, Rhode Island, and Local 767, American Federation of Government Employees:

> Grievances initiated by the Union or the Employer will be submitted to the Officer-in-Charge or the President of the Union as approp-

riate. Grievances must concern interpretation or application of the specific provisions of this agreement.

ISSUES OUTSIDE THE GRIEVANCE PROCEDURE

Executive Order 11616 clearly excludes from coverage in the negotiated grievance procedure matters which are subject to statutory appeals procedures.

The phrase "statutory appeals procedures" is construed broadly to include appeals procedures established by Executive order or regulations of appropriate authorities outside the agency which implement responsibilities assigned by statute. "Statutory" is thus defined as relating to or conforming to statute as well as created, defined or required by statute. The negotiated grievance procedure, for example, may not include grievances based upon disciplinary actions because appeals from "adverse actions" are subject to Civil Service Commission regulations. Thus discharge, suspension for more than 30 days, furlough without pay, or reduction in rank or pay cannot be taken through a grievance procedure negotiated by labor and management.[7] If, on the other hand, an employee wishes to grieve over the interpretation or application of the agreement, he *must* use the negotiated procedure, the exclusive method available for this purpose under the Order.

Time Limits. While much has been written recently about the length of time it takes to process grievances in the private sector from initiation to binding arbitration, comparable studies of the length of time it takes to process grievances in the public sector are not available. Generally, however, civil service laws and regulations set firm limits on the time available for completing each step of the process. However, recognizing the realities of grievance processing, most regulations provide for some waiving of the rigid limits in particular circumstances or by mutual agreement of the parties. It is reasonable to assume that some difficult grievances may spill out of this loophole and consume considerably more time than that alloted for their completion.

This suggests that two particularly crucial areas in any grievance procedure are the time limits set for filing a grievance and those set on completing each step in the procedure.

Generally, in the contracts studied two approaches were taken on the question of how much time an aggrieved employee has to file his grievance. The strict-time-limit approach provides that the employee must take action within a fixed period after the date the act complained of occurred. An example of this type of clause can be found in the agreement between the Chicago District of the Food and Drug Administration and FDA Lodge 112, AFGE:

> Employee or group of employees having a grievance coming within the purview of this article should take it up first with his immediate supervisor within 15 calendar days after the occurrence of the act on which the grievance is based.

The other approach generally followed is to provide that the grievance must be filed within a set time after the grievance is *discovered*. This approach indicates awareness of the possibility that an employee or a union might not have immediate knowledge of a grievable act. An example of this approach can be found in the agreement negotiated between the Naval Amphibious Base and the Tidewater Virginia Federal Employees Metal Trades Council. The clause provides:

> It is agreed that an employee and the Council must file their grievance within 15 calendar days. The time is computed from the date of the occurrence of the incident which gives rise to the grievance or the date the employee becomes aware of the decision about which he is aggrieved.

A common variation on the latter approach is to provide for an extension on the original time limitation but to provide a final limitation after which the grievance cannot be brought. A representative example of this type of clause can be found in the agreement negotiated between the Washington Area Metal Trades Council and the Naval Research Laboratory:

> An alleged grievance, to be acceptable, shall be taken up by the employee or employees and the appropriate supervisor of employees involved within 15 days of the incident leading to the alleged grievance unless it is clearly evident that the employee had no opportunity to become informed of the action leading to the alleged grievance. In no event will an alleged grievance be accepted more than 3 months after the action or event leading to the alleged grievance.

Other contracts provide a specified initial time period but allow extensions upon showing of good cause or after mutual agreement between the parties.

The other area in which time limits may become an issue is when penalties are provided in the contract for failure by either party to follow the time limit set on each step in the grievance procedure. The penalty clause uses generally standard language and the only problems in this area occur when the contract fails to provide a procedure to follow when time limits are not met. In those instances, the limits are basically advisory and without force. The absence of such clauses can result in procedural grievances independent of the substantive matters which initiated the grievance. A standard example of the time limit clause including penalties can be found in the agreement negotiated between the Fleet Home Town News Center and Local 3229, American Federation of Government Employees, which provides an employee or union can move on to the next step in the grievance procedure if the employer fails to meet the time limits for any particular step. If the grievant or the union fail to meet time limits, the grievance is considered withdrawn and terminated.

STEPS IN THE PROCESS

Under Executive Order 11616, an agreement between an agency and a labor organization must provide a procedure for the consideration of grievances over the interpretation or application of the agreement. The form which this procedure is to take is not specified by the Order, nor is there any requirement that it culminate in any form of arbitration. However, a survey of contracts negotiated since the latest Executive order demonstrates that the most common procedure negotiated by the parties involves either a three- or four-step grievance procedure, with some form of third party determination at the end.

The First Step.   As a prerequisite to every formal grievance procedure, the employee bringing a grievance must exhaust his informal appeal rights. This usually consists of a discussion of the problem with his immediate supervisor. It may be an oral presentation, and the union representative need not be apprised of the situation.

In almost every contract, the immediate supervisor must make an oral decision within a set time limit. If the decision is unsatisfactory to the employee, or the supervisor fails to render a decision, the employee may then proceed to the next step.

A number of contracts take into account certain practicalities peculiar to their unit. For example, provision is sometimes made for the first-level supervisor to make an investigation within the scope of his authority before rendering his decision. (See, for example, the contract between the Coast Guard Aircraft Supply

Center and Coast Guard Air Base, Elizabeth City, N.C., and Local 2203, International Association of Machinists.)

Other contracts, while not requiring a supervisory investigation, do require that the first step of the grievance procedure be at a supervisory level at which a decision can be rendered. As a result, when the employee's grievance involves a question which can only be dealt with by a second-echelon supervisor, the contract requires that he be so notified and the grievance be referred at the appropriate step of the grievance procedure to the official having such authority. (See, for example, the contract between the American Federation of Government Employees and the Portsmouth, Va. Naval Shipyard.) A further refinement is found in those contracts which provide that if the employee feels that he cannot discuss his grievance with his immediate supervisor, he may go directly to the next level of supervision. (See, for example, the contract between the United States Information Agency and Local 1812, American Federation of Government Employees.)

The employee must utilize the informal procedures in the first step. If he fails to do so, it could result in dismissal of his grievance at a later stage, which could have the effect of precluding him from re-instituting his claim due to the time limits in the contract. By the same token, supervisory personnel at the first level must be aware of their responsibilities in providing the employee an opportunity to resolve the grievance at the first level. Failure to do so, particularly where some form of investigation is required, could prove to be a prejudicial error at some latter stage of the grievance.

The Second Step. While some contracts provide that a grievance may be submitted in writing in the first step, the overwhelming number of contracts examined in this study indicate that the formal grievance procedure is initiated in step two by the submission, in writing, of the grievance to the appropriate management official.

A most important consideration at this and succeeding grievance steps is the time requirements provided by contract. Equally as important is the requirement at this step that the written grievance conform to the requirements enumerated in the contract. While the agreements surveyed vary as to whether the name of the step one supervisor or the contract provision allegedly violated, and other such matters, should be included, those contracts requiring a written grievance be submitted provide that the following must be set out: (1) the basis of the grievance; (2) the facts out of which the grievance arose; and (3) corrective action requested. The person to whom the grievance should be sent is determined largely by contract, depending on the nature of the unit and the levels of supervisory contact. In one instance, provision is made for a "grievance control officer" whose duty it is to relay the written grievance to the appropriate management official. (See the contract between the U.S. Department of Labor and Labor Local 12, American Federation of Government Employees.)

Regardless of whether the employee has requested union representation, at this and at all succeeding grievance steps, the Executive order affords a union (if the exclusive representative) the right to attend all formal meetings between management and the aggrieved employee. It should be noted that some contracts have provided that an employee seeking to utilize this and subsequent grievance steps may do so only with the consent of the union. This language may well be in violation of the Executive order and deprives the employee of rights provided under it.

By requiring that a negotiated procedure be the only method available for the resolution of contract disputes, the Executive order requires an employee to rely on contractual methods of relief. Those contracts which prevent an employee from pursuing the contractual avenue of grievance resolution unless his union consents may perhaps extend too far beyond the language of the order.

In this step the appropriate management official is generally required to perform some factfinding or review based on the written allegation before him. The procedure requires generally that his analysis and decision be in writing, with a contractual time limit placed on his activities. The nature of the review required at this level varies. Some contracts provide only that the official "attempt to settle" the grievance (for example, the contract between the Germantown District Social Security Administration and Local 2327, American Federation of Government Employees), while others require an actual factfinding investigation (for example, the contract between Williams Air Force Base and Local 1776, AFGE). Regardless of the specific contract provision, the supervisor must be careful to perform required functions under the contract. Even more than under the informal phase, a prejudicial error here will be strong grounds for reversal at a later date.

The Third Step.   If the grievance is not resolved in a satisfactory manner during the second step, this allows invocation of the third and often final step of the grievance procedure. Depending

upon the size of the unit and the structure of supervisory authority within the agency, this may be the last opportunity for settlement before arbitration. However, in those agencies having more
than one tier of higher management authority, the formal grievance procedure may require a fourth step of managerial review,
in which case the same considerations that prevail in the third
step apply.

Most contracts require that the agency official meet with the
aggrieved employee in an effort to resolve the grievance. The
employee and his representative (if he has one) are given an
opportunity to present their case orally and informally under
most contracts. In any event, after a review of the grievance and
pertinent evidence, a written decision is required within a period
of time determined by the contract. Depending on the number of
steps included in the procedure, the union or agency may request
arbitration if it is provided for under the agreement.

UNFAIR LABOR PRACTICES

One of the significant changes implemented by Executive Order
11616 was in the area of alleged unfair labor practices.[8] Prior to
the adoption of the amending order, unfair labor practices were
dealt with in a variety of ways depending upon which party was
charged. Agency procedures and procedures under Executive
Order 11491 were both utilized. This dual process prevented a
uniform body of law respecting unfair labor practices from being
developed. The amendments proposed by the Federal Labor Relations Council and adopted in the Executive order provide for
alternate means of solving questions of unfair labor practice. The
aggrieved party now has the option of bringing an unfair labor
practice charge to the Assistant Secretary of Labor or of dealing
with the question under the negotiated grievance procedure. He
may not, however, utilize both procedures with regard to the
same allegation of unfair labor practices. If the contract course is
followed, any decision issued would not have value as a precedent
for other unfair labor practices charges. This follows the Council's
recommendation that "all Unfair Labor Practice complaints be
processed and decided only under the procedures provided by the
Assistant Secretary and the Council." Executive Order 11616
contains clauses dealing with Unfair Labor Practice charges
which reflect the view expressed by the Council and designate the
Assistant Secretary as the only recipient of unfair labor practice
charges. This Assistant Secretary's expanded role is also reflected

in his authority to determine questions of grievability and arbitrability.

ACCESS TO RECORDS

A question sometimes arises regarding the right of employees or
their representatives to have access to agency records in order to
facilitate the processing of grievances. Access to agency records,
for example, can be crucial in determining the exact date of the
grievable action. This is important when there is a strict time
limit in effect for instituting grievances. The obvious problem
here is potential conflict with the Freedom of Information Act and
Civil Service Commission regulations.[9]

Most contracts are silent on the question of records access.
Those that do contain clauses pertaining to the release of information provide for the release of all pertinent information subject
to any statutory or regulatory prohibition. (See the agreement
between Hill Air Force Base and Local 1592, American Federation
of Government Employees.)

IDENTICAL GRIEVANCES

Finally, many of the contracts examined attempt to deal with the
problem created by the submission of several identical grievances.
Joint submission of identical grievances assures greater prece-
dential consistency, binding all affected employees in the same
manner. Two approaches appear to have been followed in those
contracts which deal with the problem of identical grievances.
One is to utilize the class-action approach, with one employee
representing the class and the decision binding on all members of
the class. (See the agreement between Naval Support Activity,
Mare Island and the International Association of Fire Fighters,
Local F-48.) The other method is a joinder provision, joining all
the grievances into one action. (See the agreement between the
Naval Amphibious School, Norfolk and Local 1625, American
Federation of Government Employees.)

ARBITRATION UNDER THE ORDERS

While grievance machinery has been refined by each succeeding
Executive order, a similar impact has not occurred with regard to
grievance arbitration. Under Executive Order 10988, the only
type of grievance arbitration which could be utilized was advisory.

In the two Executive orders issued since that order, the only refinements made have been in allowing the parties the option of final or binding arbitration where arbitration is provided for and to allow appeal from binding arbitration to the Federal Labor Relations Council.

Binding or Advisory Arbitration. In those contracts which provide for advisory arbitration, the agency head reviews the arbitrator's decision and issues a final ruling. There is no appeal to the Federal Labor Relations Council. Where the parties have agreed to binding arbitration, the simplest and most concise method of providing for arbitration under the contract has been to include the following:

1. That the scope of the arbitrator's authority is limited (that is, he may not add to, delete, or modify the terms of the contract);

2. that the decision of the arbitrator shall be binding on the parties; and

3. that any exception to the arbitrator's decision may be filed with the Federal Labor Relations Council by any party under terms of Executive Order 11491 (as amended), and any regulations issued by the Council. (See 5 Code of Federal Regulations, part 2410.)

Whenever the parties attempt to go beyond these provisions, a danger exists that additional language may result in ambiguity and confusion. As an example of this, the following taken from the agreement between Defense Depot Tracy and Local 2029, American Federation of Government Employees, should be examined.

> Both parties will review the arbitrator's award and each will inform the other within 5 working days of their decision to accept or take exception to the award. If both parties accept the arbitrator's recommendation it will become the final decision in the matter. If either or both of the parties object to the award they have 10 days to notify the other party, the Director [Defense Supply Agency], and the National President of AFGE of the full nature of their objections to the decision. If the matter cannot be resolved within a reasonable period of time, either party may appeal to the Federal Labor Relations Council in accordance with its rules. The Council, after a review of the records, briefs and other information will then issue a final decision.

It is not clear whether the parties agreement calls for binding or advisory arbitration. That either party can resort to the Federal

Labor Relations Council would normally indicate binding arbitration was envisioned. However, an arbitrator's decision can hardly be considered binding where the parties have modification rights subsequent to the decision being rendered.

Picking an Arbitrator. The mechanics of picking an arbitrator are generally set down in the negotiated agreement. Generally, as in the private sector, when arbitration is requested in a timely manner under the contract, a request is forwarded to the Federal Mediation and Conciliation Service for a list of five arbitrators. Some contracts provide that the parties shall attempt to pick an arbitrator prior to the request to the FMCS. (See the agreement between the Naval Air Station at Norfolk and the International Association of Machinists, Local 39.) This process might enable the parties to choose an impartial arbitrator who is familiar with the contract and working conditions at the facility. One contract expressly states that the parties should attempt to acquire an arbitrator within the Federal Government Service. (See the agreement between the Public Health Service Hospital and the National Maritime Union—Government Employees Division.)

After the list of five arbitrators is received from the FMCS, the parties attempt to choose an arbitrator from the list. If agreement is not reached, the general approach is for the parties to strike one name in turn. The last person on the list is designated the arbitrator. This process is modified in several contracts. After the decision is made to go to arbitration, a list of five arbitrators is requested from the FMCS. The parties then meet to attempt to pick an arbitrator. If agreement is not reached, a second list is requested. The strike-off method is then used to select an arbitrator. (See the agreement between Federal Aviation Administration, Eastern Regional Headquarters and Local R2-72, National Association of Government Employees.)

Another clause appearing in several contracts provides that in the event of the refusal of either party to participate in the selection of an arbitrator, the FMCS would be empowered to make a direct designation of an arbitrator (agreement between Presidio Commissary and AFGE Local 1457). This provision serves to prevent a possible charge of an unfair labor practice for failure to participate in a negotiated grievance step by recognizing the right of either party not to participate at this step.

The problem of the phraseology of the questions put before the arbitrator is dealt with in several contracts by allowing the arbitrator to phrase the question himself based on suggested language provided by the parties and examination of the entire contract file.

Based upon the study of these contracts, we conclude that grievance arbitration procedures in the Federal sector have made many advances since their inception. The refinements in Federal labor relations made by Executive Order 11616 strongly indicate that Federal labor-management relations should continue to evolve into a fair and effective means of dispute resolution.

NOTES

1. A discussion of this (including a review of developments since 1940) in the automobile and steel industries can be found in Merton C. Bernstein, *Private Dispute Settlement* (New York, The Free Press, 1968, p. 285.

2. See sections 8(a) and (b) of Executive Order 10988.

3. See section 13 (grievance procedures) and section 14 (arbitration of grievances) of Executive Order 11491.

4. *Grievance and arbitration procedures.* An agreement with a labor organization which is the exclusive representative of employees in an appropriate unit may provide procedures, applicable only to employees in the unit, for the consideration of employee grievance and of disputes over the interpretation and application of agreements. The procedure for consideration of employee grievances shall meet the requirements for negotiated grievance procedures established by the Civil Service Commission. A negotiated employee grievance which conforms to this section, to applicable laws, and to regulations of the Civil Service Commission and the agency is the exclusive procedure available to employees in the unit when the agreement so provides.

(a) An agreement between an agency and a labor organization shall provide a procedure, applicable only to the unit, for the consideration of grievances over the interpretation or application of the agreement. A negotiated grievance procedure may not cover any other matters, including matters for which statutory appeals procedures exist, and shall be the exclusive procedure available to the parties and the employees in the unit for resolving such grievances. However, any employee or group of employees in the unit may present such grievances to the agency and have them adjusted, without the intervention of the exclusive representative, as long as the adjustment is not inconsistent with the terms of the agreement and the exclusive representative has been given opportunity to be present at the adjustment.

(b) A negotiated procedure may provide for the arbitration of grievances over the interpretation or application of the agreement, but not over any other matters. Arbitration may be invoked only by the agency or the exclusive representative. Either party may file exceptions to an arbit-

rator's award with the Council, under regulations prescribed by the
Council.

5. Merton C. Bernstein (*Private Dispute Settlement*) cites a U.S. Department of Labor (Bureau of Labor Statistics) study of 1,717 private
sector collective bargaining agreements, which found that in approximately 47 percent of them grievance definitions covered any dispute or
complaints; in 53 percent only disputes arising under or related to the
specific provisions of the agreement.

6. The scope of the grievance process, although broadly stated, may
not be interpreted to be broader than those matters raised specifically in
the agreement itself.

7. Examples of matters which are outside the grievance procedure are
reemployment priority rights (*Federal Personnel Manual*, Chapter 330;
5 United States Code 3502); reductions in force (FPM chap. 351, 5 USC
3502); reemployment or reinstatement rights (FPM chap. 352, 5 USC
2193(d), 2385(b); military restoration (FPM chap. 353,5 USC 3551);
performance ratings (FPM chap. 430,5 USC 4305); position classification
(FPM chap. 511, 5 USC 5112(b);; level of competence (pay) (FPM chap.
531, 5 USC 5304, 5338); salary retention (FPM chap. 531, 5 USC 5338);
job-grading (FPM chap. 532, 5 USC 5338); discrimination (FPM chap.
713, Executive Order 11478 (as amended)); national security (FPM chap.
732, 5 USC 7312, Executive Order 10430); political activity (FPM chap.
733, 5 USC 1504, 5, 6, 8); fitness-for-duty examinations (FPM chap, 831,
5 USC 8337); health benefits (FPM chap. 890, 5 USC 8912); injury
compensation (FPM chap. 890, 5 USC 8121, et seq.).

8. Section 19, Executive Order 11491, as amended.

9. See *Federal Personnel Manual* S-294-3, 294-4; FPM Supplement
950-1, Part 294, III-32.01.

A New Approach
to Grievance Handling
in the Federal Sector

Julius N. Draznin

*A labor/management class, thought to be unique in the area of
public sector labor relations and personnel work-study pro-*

Julius N. Draznin is Assistant to the Regional Director, 31st Region, National
Labor Relations Board, Los Angeles, California.

grams, has achieved at least in part its goal of having each side come to know the other side's position more clearly and with considerably more understanding.

Tension in labor relations is by no means a new phenomenon, but the methods for dealing with it should always be open to improvement, innovation, new approaches and new ideas. In April of 1973, one such innovation, which appears to have possibilities of defusing such tensions in a dramatic way, was put into effect at the Long Beach (California) Naval Shipyard.

At this shipyard, as in other such installations, a certain amount of tension can always be assumed, rising from a *situs* wherein 13 different union groups represent over 3,000 employees, with functioning contracts and grievance procedures to be administered. The purpose of the Yard is to refurbish, rebuild, modify, repair and otherwise affect naval vessels so that they are maintained as vital links in our defense posture. This purpose is paramount to all others at the Yard, as everyone there agrees. But experience has shown that in the Federal sector of labor relations, as in any other, general agreement on goals is not enough. Some give-and-take has to develop if carrying out this purpose is to succeed.

The number of grievances arising out of the Metal Trades Agreement with the Navy at Long Beach had been steadily growing during 1971 and 1972. Not only was the number on the increase, but hard feeling in some of the shops was developing to the flash point, and some quickie walk-outs and sick-outs were taking place in small work units at the base.

As this was building up in 1972, several of the Metal Trades Unions Council leaders were attending an unrelated class, under the auspices of the Institute of Industrial Relations, U.C.L.A., on the role and impact of government agencies on labor unions and their members. At this class, these Navy employees freely discussed their problems "off the record" with their instructor. From these discussions, the instructor determined that he might be able to make a contribution to the labor relations at the base by developing a joint labor-management class on grievance handling.

Encouraged by Russ Hatfield, president, Federal Employees Metal Trades Council and James Houston, industrial relations officer at the base, a proposal was submitted, and after intensive discussion, approved. A workshop class, jointly attended by representatives of labor unions on the base and by management-level personnel, general foremen and foremen-level employees, was devised.

At this writing, this course series is being given for the third time. The classes have been very popular and there are many more volunteers for enrollment that there are openings.

"Management-Labor Class in Grievance/Arbitration" is designed to give the students an intensive period of instruction. This is accomplished by having two Instructors and a Class Coordinator present at each three-hour class session, and by limiting the size of the class to 30 students.

Initial class sessions are generally introductory ones, acquainting the students with the history and theory of grievance handling and arbitration, as well as with the operation of Federal labor relations under the Executive Orders. After that, the class is divided into two groups, with a thorough mix of 15 labor and 15 management people in each group. This is done by numerical designations which remain with the students for the term of the class.

After dividing the class into two groups, the Instructor assigned to each group leads a short discussion regarding the principal factors involved in the grievance under consideration. (The Grievance Problem is presented at the start of each class for use that day, and is different for each class.)

After discussing major aspects of the problem, the group of 15 divides again, this time into a labor group and a management group, each side taking a stance and developing a position in support of the grievance. As each group of seven or eight works to develop its facts, witnesses and position, the Instructor spends his time explaining, directing, leading and discussing procedure, and observing the development of the students and their positions on the case at hand. The Coordinator, in turn, moves between the four groups, observing and listening, making suggestions and otherwise overseeing the operation of the class.

After sufficient time has been spent in preparing the pro and con positions, the two subgroups meet and present their positions to the Instructor, who then assumes the role of Group Superintendent, Base Commanding Officer, or the Arbitrator, as the case on hand may dictate. The presentation is kept informal, subject to interruptions to point out procedures, techniques, development of facts, investigation of events, interpretation of the contract language and discussion of any relevant matters that may have come up.

For the last half hour, the full class and all the Instructors meet to critique the issues and talk over what happened at the respective sessions. Discussion of the grievance problems and the source of the problem are invariably commented upon.

(An added touch was achieved early in the first series of classes when the Navy made available a crew with video-taping equipment who taped the joint session—of 15—when the two subgroups met and argued and presented their cases. These videotapes were later replayed to the whole class and further critiquing took place.)

The last of the eight sessions is a mock Arbitration of the full class before an Arbitrator, with each side of 15 students presenting either the management or the labor side, with the assistance of the Instructor assigned to them. Preparation for the final session begins the week before, when the students are given the problem for the last week and do their utmost to prepare witnesses and arguments.

The quality of the Instructors is a vital factor to the success of the class, and the Institute of Industrial Relations, U.C.L.A., has been very fortunate in securing the services of several attorneys, as well as practicing arbitrators, to give their time one night a week for this class.

The results have been noticeable on the base. Management men and women who previously had adamantly refused to consider any personnel problems that they felt were a danger to management's right to manage; and labor union representatives, who believed that all management spokesmen were cold and inhuman individuals, at the minimum, if not outright anti-union, have learned that the other side has something to say for itself that's worth hearing—and may be right, as well.

The *Federal Times*, a leading Federal employees' newspaper with worldwide distribution, recently ran an article about this course under the title, "Walk a Mile in My Shoes." This newshead is probably as fair a description of the class as any, since it exemplifies the aim of providing a means by which labor and management on the work site can find a common ground and come to know each other better, away from the pressure of the day-to-day problems.

The best evidence of the class achievement may be found in the comment made by one of the general foremen, a graduate of one of the early series of these classes, to his Base Commanding Officer, that he had learned to quit shooting from the hip whenever a grievance arose. As a result, his section has had less friction and greater productivity than ever before. Also he and many of his fellow students have made new friends on the other side of the table.

The democracy we espouse outside the plant gates is finding an outlet and having its impact inside the plant as well. This indicates that both labor and management *can* become more adept at fulfilling their own roles effectively and with greater understanding.

CASE #5
Comparison of Impasse Procedures in the Public and Private Sectors: The Hawaii State Teacher's Experience

Marvin J. Levine and Joy Jaeckle Luna

Academic debate over public sector collective bargaining impasse procedures generally includes references to the private sector experience of the 1930's.[1] The implication made is that there is no difference between labor-management relations in the public and private sectors; in fact, one author has asserted

> Governments who continue to assert the traditional aspects of sovereignty and resist collective bargaining efforts can expect a repeat of the private sector experiences which occurred during the 30's and 40's.[2]

Others, most notably Wellington and Winter,[3] argue that labor relations in the public and private sector are noticeably different. This study proposes to examine these differences in light of the experience of Hawaii teachers with impasse procedures promulgated under the Hawaii Public Employment Relations Act (HPERA). Since the Hawaii law comes close to what some have suggested as model legislation,[4] analysis of trends in implementation of the law may prove useful in other jurisdictions. An important caveat to any conclusions drawn from the study should be added, however. Few generalizations can be made about the

Reprinted by permission of PUBLIC PERSONNEL MANAGEMENT from PUBLIC PERSONNEL MANAGEMENT, 8 (March-April, 1978) pp. 108-118.

Hawaii experience, since its municipal governmental structure differs markedly from most states in the U.S.

THE DISSIMILARITIES

The major deterrent to good faith bargaining in the public sector is that a government cannot act as a third party arbiter of labor management relations as it does in the private sector; the government is also the managing entity. Some have argued that the key to successful collective bargaining in the public sector is enactment of a comprehensive federal law.[5] However, attempts to pass such legislation in Congress have proved unsuccessful, and a recent Supreme Court decision (National League of Cities v. Dunlop), which ruled that federal overtime pay requirements for state and local employees are unconstitutional, further lessens the probability that the federal government will assume the role of objective third party.

Imundo argues that this conflict results from the "sovereignty doctrine": "Any state that possesses and maintains supreme power can determine whether or not an individual or a group of individuals can initiate a claim against the state".[6] Imundo's argument applies even when a state government has passed a collective bargaining law: the power to repeal any law governing public sector labor negotiations still rests with management.

A second, and related problem, concerns the establishment of public agencies or boards to administer the impasse procedure. When such boards are appointed by the government/manager, there is bound to be some favoritism shown toward the appointer, especially in areas where the law is vague. Private sector management does not, in the final analysis, decide the entire membership of the National Labor Relations Board.

A third dissimilarity concerns the decentralization of authority; usually, the management negotiators in a collective bargaining agreement have no power to appropriate funds. Thus, an agreement bargained in good faith may be nullified by a legislature that refuses to appropriate the money needed to implement pay increases, duty-free lunch periods, and the like. In the private sector, the management negotiator represents the entire corporate board. This problem restricts nonmonetary areas as well. Groty notes:

> One agency, charged with the responsibility to administer this new legislation, decides certain subjects are bargainable, and yet

> another agency indicates the subject is restricted from public man-
> agement through earlier legislation . . . The lack of definition as to
> the powers to bargain causes as much unrest as what must be
> bargained.[7]

Gerhart presents an alternate view of the problem. Labeling this
concept "depth" (which he defines as the degree of influence on
particular issues held by the union) he points out that "Except in
a few instances where bargaining is well developed, . . . management officials are unwilling to admit that issues are 'jointly
determined' on an equal basis with the union representatives. In
their opinion joint determination would be equivalent to a delegation of their authority which they feel is not permitted by law."[8]

An associated problem has a negative influence on good faith
negotiations. Just as the bargaining agency can weaken good
faith discussions by arguing that certain issues are not bargainable by law, union officials can circumvent the negotiations process and use direct political pressure on the state legislature to
obtain the desired contract provisions by statute. However, the
same dispersion of authority can thwart union aims even in this
case; the governor may veto such legislation.

A fifth dissimilarity between public and private sector collective bargaining concerns the strike issue. Both Groty and Wellington, *et al.*, point out the differences. Wellington and Winter
state that

> The private sector strike is designed to exert economic pressure on
> the employer by depriving him of revenues. The public employee
> strike is fundamentally different: its sole purpose is to exert political
> pressure on municipal officials. They are deprived, not of revenues,
> but of political support of those who are inconvenienced by a disrup-
> tion of municipal services.[9]

Groty[10] views the problem from a slightly different angle: he terms
a teacher strike "psychological pressure" since it directly affects
children and parents. Because of this difference, these authorities view a public sector strike as an undesirable impasse
mechanism since it discourages joint determination of issues.

Finally, the courts have a much greater role in the resolution
of impasse in the public sector. It is not uncommon for a school
board to request a court ruling on an arbitrator's decision. Such
instances dilute the power of binding arbitration as an impasse
procedure.

Thus, dissimilarities between public and private sector collective bargaining create new and unique problems never encoun-

tered in private sector labor management relations. These dissimilarities have resulted in subtle changes in impasse procedures, as discussed below.

IMPASSE PROCEDURES

Lieberman and Moskow define an impasse as " . . . a persistent disagreement that continues after normal negotiation procedures have been exhausted."[11] Mechanisms developed to resolve an impasse in public sector negotiations include: mediation, conciliation, fact-finding, voluntary and binding arbitration, advisory arbitration, mediation-arbitration, compulsory arbitration, strikes, and court decisions. Much of the literature in this area argues the pros and cons of giving public employees the right to strike; since only three states (of which Hawaii is one) grant public employees a strike procedure, one can conclude that the strike procedure has not become institutionalized in public sector collective bargaining statutes. In fact, some authorities[12] feel that the dependency on third party neutrals to resolve disputes in the public sector is directly related to the prohibition of legal strikes in most jurisdictions. Whether such dependency restrains or expands good faith negotiations is open to debate. Since over 50 percent of third party interventions in states with a collective bargaining law concern teacher-school board negotiation impasses, the dependency question is especially relevant (HSTA brought 3 times more cases before HPERA in its first two years of negotiations than any other unit[13]).

Mediation has been called the most successful impasse resolution process and certainly has been employed more often than any other method.[14] Pennett remarks that

> Mediation in any form provides a process to define the scope of the dispute, pinpointing the key areas that must be settled and testing alternatives to the parties stated positions while protecting those positions as areas of agreement to be developed.[15]

The actual mediation procedure used depends upon the mediator. In certain situations, mediators will meet with the parties separately and endeavor to determine concessions which each party might make in order that an agreement may be reached. This procedure is most effective when the parties are afraid of showing any weakness in negotiating crucial issues.[16]An alternate procedure is for the mediator to meet with both parties in an attempt to assess the true status of negotiations and to resolve the phrasing of issues. Mediation is a voluntary process in most jurisdictions; either one or both parties may request this procedure to resolve an impasse. However, some state statutes grant the administrative board the right to demand mediation between labor and management under certain conditions. In any event, recommendations made by a mediator are not binding on either party unless mutual agreement is reached.

In the public sector, mediators sometimes play an additional role. Gilroy notes " . . . it has been found that the mediator plays a crucial role not only in bringing about a settlement but also in providing a resource to the parties in developing their appreciation of the subtleties of the bargaining process."[17] Because of this factor, and the widespread use of mediation in the public sector, authorities[18] caution against replacement of good faith bargaining with their party decision making and urge that only highly qualified neutrals be employed as mediators. Use of "professional labor relations experts" not trained as mediators can lead to more problems than it solves.[19]

Conciliation is usually lumped together with mediation in most public sector labor relations texts. Since conciliation is stipulated as a legal impasse procedure far fewer times than is mediation,[20] the subtle difference is not important in most cases (Hawaii's law authorizes mediation, rather than conciliation). However, for those parties using such mechanisms, the difference becomes important: "Conciliators only assist the parties in reaching agreement whereas mediators recommend terms for settlement."[21]

Factfinding is a more formal procedure than mediation, involving a third-party neutral or panel. Both parties to a dispute present their cases in a semi-judicial hearing. The factfinder or fact-finding panel then issues a report which explains the circumstances of the dispute and generally makes recommendations for settlement. The recommendations are not binding; however, in the public sector these hearings are generally made public (as is the fact-finding report) and this tactic serves as an additional inducement to settle. Other parties must usually be included in the fact-finder's deliberations. Gilroy and Sinicropi define this role succinctly:

> "The role of the factfinder neutral is situational and often he must direct his efforts not only to the interests of the parties but also to those of the public. The factfinder must often deal with the political

body in control of the particular public agency where the dispute is centered."[22]

Several types of arbitration are used in resolving public sector impasse disputes. Under binding arbitration, which can be either voluntary or compulsory depending on the collective bargaining statute, both parties to a dispute submit their cases to a neutral third party in a hearing. The arbitrator then reviews the evidence and issues an award which must be accepted by both parties. When the arbitration is voluntary, both parties must agree to submit their dispute to the third party neutral. Compulsory arbitration, required by law after an impasse exceeds a stipulated time period, must be submitted to by both parties.

Compulsory arbitration has become a popular mechanism for settlement of disputes in jurisdictions which prohibit the right to strike. Evidence is mixed, however, as to the effectiveness of either voluntary binding arbitration or compulsory arbitration. Reasons cited against the use of the arbitration mechanism include (1) knowledge that a third party neutral will make the final decision on disputed issues will deter both parties from bargaining in good faith; (2) third-party determinations on nonmonetary issues (when the enabling statute allows such determinations) may conflict with long-standing policy or law and can thus be overturned in court; (3) use of arbitration as a substitute for the strike is ineffective. Some empirical evidence exists, however, showing that arbitration is a viable means of resolving impasses in the public sector.[23] Bok and Dunlop point out areas where arbitration has been the most successful: "In contract matters, arbitration has been used where the precise question to be arbitrated and the standards to be applied by the arbitration have been agreed to already by the employee organization and the public management."[24]

Advisory arbitration is similar to binding arbitration with one important difference: recommendations made under advisory arbitration are not binding. However, advisory arbitration has been relatively successful, especially in the resolution of grievances. This type of arbitration is used on a large scale in public sector labor relations; it is rarely used in the private sector.

Mediation-arbitration combines aspects of the mediation procedure with binding arbitration. Generally both parties must agree to submit to the procedure. Mediation-arbitration is rarely used and typically occurs only when the dispute has become so complicated that the arbitrator must determine the status of negotiations before each party's case is presented.

Controversy over the use of the strike as an impasse proce-dure in the public sector has filled more pages in labor relations journals in the past ten years than most experts would like to admit. The argument against the right to strike rests upon the notion that public employees who provide essential services can-not be allowed to strike because it would endanger the health, safety, and welfare of the public. Since it would be difficult to formulate legislation allowing some but not all public employees to strike that would be upheld by the courts, critics of the right to strike issue argue that the only sensible alternative is to prohibit strikes completely. Proponents of the strike, however, argue that strikes

> . . . would put collective bargaining in the public sector on the same footing as private negotiations, reduce the time-consuming process of negotiation, and eliminate intransigence on the part of some public officials who use the authority of government to resist reasonable settlements in negotiation. In general, strikes of public employees do not burden the community more than stoppages in the private sector.[25]

Although there is little hope for resolving the controversy of whether public sector strikes are a legitimate means of resolving disputes, the most crucial argument for legalization of the strike mechanism is that ". . . even though public sector strikes are illegal and penalties often invoked, in fact the overall strike rate in the public sector is proportionately about that of the private sector."[26]

Court decisions have become an additional method of resolv-ing impasse disputes in the public sector. Such intervention appears to be unsatisfactory to both labor and management in most cases, however. A recent empirical study by Redenius[27] showed that union officials strongly opposed intrusion by the courts into collective bargaining disputes because they believed that such matters are not rightfully a concern of public policy. The study also showed that if the court assumes an activist role in mediating the resolution of a bargaining dispute, governmental officials perceived this intervention as favorable to unions and thus biased against their position.

Although Hawaii's statute does not specifically allow the use of all of the aforementioned impasse procedures, the law allows that additional impasse mechanisms may be used if agreed to in a collective bargaining contract. This law, as it pertains to the impasse procedure for Hawaii's teachers, is briefly described in the next section.

HAWAII PUBLIC EMPLOYEE RELATIONS ACT[28]

Hawaii's initial collective bargaining law (Act 171 SLH 1970) was promulgated in response to a state constitutional amendment (Article XII, Section 2) ratified in November of 1968, which states: "Persons in public employment shall have the right to organize for the purpose of collective bargaining as prescribed by law."

The ratification feature is significant, because the mandate of the law was supported by a broad representation of islanders rather than a consensus of opinion by state legislators. In fact, some feel that it was because of this support that such a progressive collective bargaining law evolved in 1970.

A brief detour into the history of Hawaii's labor relations and a skeletal explanation of its municipal government structure seems necessary at this point. As noted in the opening paragraphs of this study, Hawaii's experience is unique among the states.

A strong union orientation in the private sector, buttressed by a progressive state law which granted most of the rights of organization and collective bargaining contained in the National Labor Relations Act to intrastate employees as early as 1945, paved the way for public sector labor relations in the 50's, 60's, and 70's. In fact, the first Hawaii Constitution granted the right to organize and present grievances and proposals to management, to municipal employees as early as 1950, although the Constitution did not become effective until 1959, when Hawaii became the 50th state.[29] A "meet and confer" law for public employees was passed in 1967; the '68 Constitutional amendment noted above granted them the right to collectively bargain. Hawaii was one of the first states to allow public sector bargaining; in comparison with other state statutes, it still remains one of the most progressive.

The State's governmental structure and balance of political forces help to explain why the law contains certain provisions. Municipal functions are centralized in the state and four counties (Honolulu County, for example, includes the entire island of Oahu, which contains 80 percent of the population). Many of the functions performed by county governments in other states are carried out at the state level in Hawaii. The four counties thus perform most of the municipal functions (e.g. public works, sanitation, police and fire protection). City government is weak. With two thirds of total tax revenues being administered by the state, it follows that state domination of the entire spectrum of political forces is the rule, rather than the exception. The dominant party in the State is Democrat, and the legislature, viewed as a whole, is progressive.

The legislation adopted in 1970 incorporated provisions contained in earlier labor relations acts (NLRA, Executive Order 11491 and the state's own private sector relations act, among others) and thus some provisions outlined below will be familiar to those knowledgeable in labor relations law. Other provisions are less institutionalized.

Express public policy concerning public employee collective bargaining is contained in Section 89-1, Hawaii Revised Statutes. The relevant portion reads as follows:

> The legislature finds that joint decision-making is the modern way to administer government. Where public employees have been granted the right to share in the decision-making process affecting wages and working conditions, they have become more responsive and better able to exchange ideas and information on operations with their administrators. Accordingly, government is made more effective. The legislature further finds that the enactment of positive legislation establishing guidelines for public employment relations is the best way to harness and direct the energies of public employees eager to have a voice in determining their conditions of work, to provide a rational method for dealing with disputes and work stoppages, and to maintain a favorable political and social environment.

Thus, the legislative intent is to promote joint decision-making and cooperative labor-management relations.

A specific impasse procedure is spelled out in section 89-11(b), although the law encourages the parties to include dispute settlement mechanisms in their agreements. Since the Hawaii State Teachers Association (HSTA) and the Board of Education (BOE) did not include such a procedure in either of their contract agreements, impasse resolution follows the terms stipulated by law. The law requires that HPERB, at the request of either party or on its own motion, provide assistance at specific times after an impasse is reached. Appointment of a mediator or mediators, the first step in dispute settlement, must be accomplished by HPERB within three days of receipt of notification of impasse. Mediators have fifteen days after the date of impasse to settle the dispute. If an impasse still exists, HPERB must appoint a fact-finding board of not more than three members within three days. The fact-finding board is required to submit findings of fact and recommendations to both parties in the dispute within ten days after appointment. If the dispute is still unresolved five days after transmittal of the fact-finding board's recommendations, the board shall publish this information for public dissemination, unless both parties agree to final and binding arbitration.

At this point, three alternative mechanisms are available. The parties can submit to binding arbitration or take whatever lawful action either deems necessary to resolve the dispute as long as they submit to the legislature their recommendations for settlement of the dispute on all cost items along with the fact finder's report. HSTA, as exclusive representative, has the additional option of waiting sixty days after the fact finding board makes public its recommendations and going on strike, as long as a ten-day notice of intent to strike has been filed with HPERB and the BOE. If the arbitration procedure is chosen, an arbitration panel of three arbitrators—one chosen by each party to the dispute with the third chosen by the other two arbitrators—conducts hearings, investigations, and the like, with a binding decision required within fifty days after impasse.

HSTA'S EXPERIENCE WITH HPERA[30]

HSTA won the right to exclusively bargain for Hawaii's teachers in May of 1971. Bargaining with the Board of Education employer representatives began the end of that month. HSTA gave notice of an impasse in negotiations for the initial contract with the BOE to HPERB on October 22, 1971. HPERB appointed a mediator on October 27. The dispute revolved around many issues: class size, salaries, preparation periods, duty-free lunch, nonprofessional duties, personal leave, work year, and choice of department and grade level chairmen. (Salaries were listed sixth by teachers in order of priorities.) When mediation failed to resolve the impasse, HPERB appointed a fact-finding panel on November 16th. The panel's findings and recommendations were submitted on December 1, 1971. Since the BOE refused to accept the fact finders' recommendations or to submit to binding arbitration, HSTA called for a strike vote on January 30, 1972, and declared its intent to strike on February 17th. The BOE requested a ruling by HPERB on February 9th regarding the possible violation of section 89-9(d) of the collective bargaining law by including a provision in the contract agreement that would limit class size. The petition was subsequently dropped by the BOE and was regarded at the time as a delaying tactic.

The strike was averted narrowly by the personal intervention of the Governor. Agreement was reached between the BOE and HSTA at 5 AM on the 17th. Media coverage during this period shows evidence of a sharp negative public reaction as well as the use of lobbying tactics by the powerful Hawaii private sector unions to force a settlement. HSTA demands, in this first dispute, were not viewed by the public as unreasonable.

An agreement between HSTA and the BOE was signed on February 29th and subsequently ratified by the legislature.

This initial experience with the new collective bargaining law followed the procedures set forth to the letter, with one important exception: the Governor, rather than the HPERB appointed mediator or fact-finding panel, resolved the impasse. An objective assessment of the situation indicates that the strike mechanism (here the threat of a strike) was the deciding factor. The events seem to support Wellington and Winter's thesis—that the purpose of the strike is to exert political pressure on municipal officials—as well. Thus, the initial HSTA experience supports the notion that public employee strikes are an effective dispute settlement technique, though for reasons other than those involved in a private sector strike.

A second dispute between HSTA and the BOE began on May 24, 1972, when HSTA petitioned HPERB to find BOE guilty of prohibited practices for failing to implement provisions of the contract agreement regarding class size. Since this issue subsequently became the major dispute over when two teacher strikes occurred, the exact working in the agreement is given below (Class Size Committee):

> 2. Beginning with the 1972-73 school year, the Employer agrees to reduce the average class size ratio by approximately one student. Based on current Employer practices, this would require a minimum of 250 positions for the 1972-73 school year. These teaching positions shall be in addition to presently allocated positions, additional positions required by increased student enrollment and additional teaching positions created in the preparation time and duty-free lunch provisions of this Agreement.
>
> The current proportion (15 percent) of these positions shall be used to increase the number of counselor and bargaining unit supportive staff positions. The remainder shall be assigned to classroom teacher positions.
>
> 3. It is recognized in fulfilling the obligations set forth in the class size and preparation period articles that bargaining unit positions allocated for the school year 1972-73 shall not be reduced to implement said articles.
>
> 4. The committee established in Section A-1 above shall have the authority to recommend to the Superintendent specific changes to

be made to accomplish the objectives set forth in Sections A-2 and A-3. The superintendent shall implement the recommendations in each case as soon as possible.

5. In the event that a majority vote on a decision of the committee is not forth-coming within ten days after consideration of the issue, the Association may have the matter submitted to Ted T. Tsukiyama, who has been selected by the parties as the arbitrator. His decision shall be final and binding on both parties. The arbitration will be conducted in accordance with the rules pertaining to American Arbitration Association arbitration procedure and the sharing of arbitration fees by the parties as set forth in Article 7, Sections E-3 and E-4 of this Agreement.

6. The Employer will furnish all relevant information requested by the committee.

The Board's decision[31] was not made public until October 24th. A BOE petition on June 28th arguing that any provision in the contract agreement which would impose limitations on class size would violate section 89-9(d), Hawaii Revised Statute, was withdrawn with prejudice after the Hearings Examiner for HPERB stated that HPERB's disposition of the issue would be forthcoming from the HSTA petition.

Between the time that HPERB took the HSTA case under consideration and published its decision, HSTA management decided to call an illegal one-day strike to force implementation of contract provisions on October 5, 1972. The strike was illegal on two counts: (1) conditions precedent to striking under Section 89-12(b), HRS, were not fulfilled, and (2) it violated the no-strike provision of the contract agreement. The BOE petitioned the Circuit Court for an injunction against the strike on the grounds that the strike would "endanger the health, safety, and welfare" of the public. Circuit Court Judge Masato Doi issued a restraining order based upon this argument on October 3rd.

The reasons for the occurrence of these two events are unclear. Media coverage indicates that teachers were frustrated by the continued violation of the contract agreement, and much public resentment of HPERB's lengthy deliberations over the issue was voiced (however, HPERB did not violate Section 89-5, HRS, because no time limit is set on their decisions). The contract included a provision for reopeners by written notice in August, 1971, and provided that HSTA could invoke the impasse procedure allowed under Hawaii law. Why HSTA did not exhause the impasse mechanism before striking is open to debate. In addition, the rationale behind BOE's decision to file for an injunction against the HSTA action on the grounds that the strike would "endanger the health, safety, and selfare" of the public (the legality of which was unclear) when an injunction could have been issued for violations of Section 89-12(b), HRS, and the no-strike clause of the contract agreement, is even more baffling.

The failure of HPERB to make a speedy decision in this case is ostensibly a problem with implementation of the contract provisions. However, the use of the strike underlies HSTA's perception of the proceedings as an impasse. While a large portion of this problem probably emanated from each party's lack of experience with the collective bargaining process, some portion of the blame must be attached to the unwillingness of BOE to bargain in good faith, the impatience of HSTA, and the slowness of HPERB in rendering its decision.

A second strike was scheduled for October 19th. Binding arbitration on three issues—custodial chores, preparation periods, and duty-free lunch periods—was proposed by HSTA, but BOE refused the arbitration procedure. The subsequent events are summarized in HSTA: A Brief History:[32]

> The threat of a strike caused HPERB to move, and they ordered the issues of custodial chores, preparation periods, and duty-free lunch periods to binding arbitration. Arbitrators' decisions favored the Association on custodial duties and preparation periods. However, the lunch period arbitration was superseded by subsequent negotiations on a contract reopener.
>
> The Department of Education appealed the preparation period decision to HPERB and HPERB voided three of the arbitrator's awards. However, subsequently in May of 1974, Judge Doi upheld the remaining portions of the preparation case.

The HPERB decision on the HSTA petition on October 24th was made public (a) after HPERB ruled a strike authorized by teachers to take place on October 13, 1972, was illegal because HSTA was not in an impasse position[33] and (b) after contract reopener negotiations between BOE and HSTA began in early October. HPERB ruled that[34]: (1) It had jurisdiction over a prohibited practice charge involving an alleged breach of contract even if the contract contained a grievance arbitration provision; (2) The provision calling for reduction in class-size ratio was negotiable; (3) The contractual requirement that 15 percent of the 250 new positions be assigned counselor and supportive unit positions was not negotiable under Section 89-9(d), HRS; (4) The employer could transfer employees but should consult with the union before doing so; (5) The employer should restore benefits of preparation periods and duty-free lunch periods to any teacher who was receiving such benefits at the time of the execution of the agreement and who had since lost these benefits because of the transfer of 169.5 support positions back to the classroom; and (6) The class-size ratio was to be reduced was 26.4.

HSTA appealed this decision to the Circuit Court[35] which upheld HPERB's decision. The judge's opinion indicates that since the contract provision (see #3, above) was illegal, BOE could not be held in willful violation of the terms of the contract. Also, the court ruled that BOE was not stopped from challenging the legality of the contract provisions even after it is ratified by the legislature.

The difference between the operations of the NLRB and HPERB is evident from the foregoing. In the private sector, the courts are the proper authorities for adjudicating charges of contract violations. HPERB's administration of the Hawaii law expands management prerogatives and thus limits the scope of negotiations. The court's support of the HPERB ruling underlines the vagueness of the law concerning application of the managerial prerogative. The fact that HPERB decided that it had jurisdiction even though the contract clause made provision for binding arbitration in case of a dispute dilutes the authority of arbitrators in their decisions and lessens the effectiveness of the arbitration procedure. This analysis is supported by events leading up to another teacher's strike from April 2 to April 16, 1972.

Although reopening negotiations began in early October, BOE soon filed a petition before HPERB requesting that the opposing party be found guilty of refusing to bargain in good faith.[36] HSTA also filed a petition requesting declaration of an impasse on October 31st, which was consolidated with the BOE petition. The Board's decision on December 21, 1972, is a classic opinion. It declared the parties at impasse but found both parties guilty of not bargaining in good faith and exhibiting 'childlike' behavior. However, HPERB ruled that HSTA's "fault was greater":

> It was obvious that the HSTA was determined to delay on this issue indefinitely . . . There is an unyielding adamancy in the HSTA's attitude toward the whole question of getting together a large, representative group of employees to sit in on and report on negotiations. There is clear evidence of stubbornness in its behavior evincing a desire to create an impasse and thus position itself for a strike. For this desire to get into a strike position, the HSTA should not be too heavily faulted because under Sections 89-11 and 89-12, Hawaii Revised Statutes, pertaining to impasses and strikes, a union must

navigate through a rather rigid set of provisions to obtain the threat-of-a-strike clout which it may believe is necessary to get concessions from an employer.[37]

On the same day, HPERB, on its own motion, determined that the parties were at impasse. HPERB also handed down a declaratory ruling[38] that HSTA reopening demands on teacher workload and scheduling of preparation periods were not negotiable, even though the contract reopener clause specifically states bargainable issues would include "wages, fringe benefits, preparation periods, and workloads."[39] The impasse was referred to mediation and later to fact finding. DOE made its final offer on March 14, 1973, but refused to place cost items developed in the new contract before the 1973 legislature.

On March 29, 1973, the Circuit Court reversed HPERB's finding of impasse.[40] This BOE appeal was filed in January of 1973 to weaken HSTA's stance in the event a strike was called. Since no impasse was declared, the earlier Circuit Court injunction against strikes remained in effect. A strike began on April 3rd and lasted until April 18th, when a "joint trust statement" was signed between BOE and HSTA to submit disputed issues to mediation-arbitration. Arbitrator Sam Kagel made his award in early August granting teachers a 13 percent pay hike, a daily 40-minute preparation period, a 30-minute duty-free lunch period; extending the contract to February 28, 1975, and setting forth a complicated renewal bargaining procedure ending in final and binding arbitration. This decision was not disputed. However, HSTA paid heavily for its strike activity. After appealing a Circuit Court decision which fined teachers and the HSTA $190,000 for illegal strike activity, the HSTA was found in civil contempt of court. The Supreme Court decision, however, reduced the fine to $100,000.[41] Subsequent bargaining sessions in 1975 proceeded smoothly; however, bargaining dealt only with pay raises.

The lengthy and complicated negotiations undergone by HSTA to force compliance with a signed contract agreement were caused, to a great extent, by HPERB interpretations of Hawaii's collective bargaining law. Pendleton and Staudohar offer the following analysis:

. . . it may be that HPERB's role as defender of so broad a definition of managerial prerogatives (viewed in the Hawaii law as essential to protect public services and legislative budget control) will make the arbitration and no-strike procedures as commonly found in the private sector difficult if not impossible to effectuate in reasonable absence of conflict. In order for the procedures to operate and for labor relations to evolve and mature as they have in the private sector, less stringent interpretations by the Board of what is negotiable and arbitrable may be required.[42]

Certainly, much of the problem emanated from the sovereignty doctrine; however, as noted earlier, it is almost impossible to nullify the effects of this doctrine in public employee labor relations. A greater reliance on standard impasse procedures, as stipulated in arbitrator Kagel's award in 1973, might minimize conflict between the BOE and HSTA as long as HPERB or the court let arbitration awards stand.

CONCLUSION

An analysis of the experience of HSTA with the Hawaii Public Employee Relations Act from 1971 to 1975 documents problems that academics have noted in the literature as "unique" variables in the public sector collective bargaining experience. Problems with the sovereignty doctrine, establishment of a governmental agency as administrator of the law, union pressure on the legislature to further its own means, decentralization of governmental authority, the political pressures forced on municipal officials by the threat of a strike, and the role of the courts as the final authority on an arbitrator's decision have been documented in detail. The experience of Hawaii's teachers shows convincingly that public sector collective bargaining is vastly different from that of the private sector.

NOTES

1. Harold W. Davey, "The Use of Neutrals in the Public Sector" *Labor Law Journal* 20 (August, 1969) pp. 529-538; Louis Imundo, Jr., "Some Comparisons Between Public Sector and Private Sector Collective Bargaining", *Labor Law Journal*, Vol. 24 (December, 1973) pp. 810-817.

2. Louis Imundo, *op. cit.*, p. 819.

3. Harry H. Wellington, and Ralph K. Winter, Jr., *The Unions and the Cities*, The Brookings Institution (Washington, D.C., 1971) p. 20.

4. Robert Sebris, "The Right to Collective Bargaining for all Public Employees: An Idea Whose Time Has Come? *Journal of Collective Negotiations in the Public Sector*, Vol. 4:3 (1975); p. 298-306.

5. Harold W. Davey, *op. cit.*, p. 529-538.

6. Imundo, *op. cit.*, p. 811.

7. K. Groty, "Sources of Management Unrest Over Collective Bargaining in Schools". *Labor Law Journal* Vol. 20 (August, 1969) p. 540.

8. Paul Gerhart, "The Scope of Bargaining in Local Government Labor Negotiations" *Labor Law Journal* Vol. 20 (August, 2969), p. 547.

9. Wellington and Winter, *The Unions and the Cities*, p. 25-26.

10. K. Groty, *op. cit.*, p. 542.

11. Myron Lieberman, and Michael Moskow, *Collective Negotiations for Teachers: An Approach to School Administration*, (Chicago, IL, Rand McNally, 1966), p. 314.

12. George Bennett, "Tools to Resolve Disputes in the Public Sector", *Personnel* Vol. 50 (March-April, 1973) pp. 40-47; Gray and Dyson, "Impact of Strike Remedies in Public Sector Collective Bargaining", *Journal of Collective Negotiations in the Public Sector* Vol. 5(2)(1976) pp. 131.

13. Sonia Faust, *The Teachers, HPERB and the Courts*, Hawaii Public Relations Board (Honolulu, February 1, 1974) p. 1.

14. T. P. Gilroy, and A. V. Sinicropi, "Impasse Resolution in Public Employment: A Current Assessment", *Industrial and Labor Relations Review*, Vol. 25 (July, 1972) p. 498.

15. George Bennett, *op. cit.*, p. 43.

16. Lieberman and Moskow, *op. cit.*, p. 315.

17. Gilroy, *op. cit.*, p. 499.

18. *Ibid.*, p. 506.

19. *Ibid.*, p. 508.

20. S. A. Brooking, and Carl W. Curtis, "A Comparative Analysis of the States' Public Sector Labor Relations Statutes", *Journal of Collective Negotiations in the Public Sector*, Vol. 4(1), 1975, p. 120.

21. Lieberman and Moskow, *op. cit.*, p. 314.

22. Gilroy and Sinicropi, *op. cit.*, p. 500.

23. J. Joseph Loewenberg, "Compulsory Binding Arbitration in State and Local Governments in the U.S." *Proceedings of the International Symposium on Public Employment Labor Relations*, New York State Public Employment Relations Board, (New York, 1971) pp. 140-151; Gilroy and Sinicropi, *op. cit.*, p. 502-503.

24. Bok and Dunlop, *Labor and the American Community*, (New York, Simon and Schuster, 1970) p. 337.

25. *Ibid.*, p. 334.

26. Bennett, *op. cit.*, p. 40.

27. C. Redinius, "Participant Attitudes Toward a Judicial Role in Public Employee Collective Bargaining", *Labor Law Journal*, Vol. 25 (February, 1974).

28. Basic facts in this section were obtained from Paul Tinning's *A Guide to Hawaii Public Employee Collective Bargaining*, and the original statute, with amendments.

29. Paul Staudohar, "The Emergence of Hawaii's Public Employment Law" *Industrial Relations* Vol. 12 (October, 1973) p. 339.

30. Basic facts in this section were assimilated from a myriad of sources. Among them are: Sonia Faust, *The Teachers, HPERB, and the Courts*, and *Government Employee Relations Reports*, BHA (Washington, D.C.),

10-15-72;11-17-72; 1-22-73; 4-9-73; 4-30-73; 8-13-73; 10-15-73; 10-29-73; 12-17-73; 4-22-74; 8-19-74; 12-20-75.

31. *In the Matter of Hawaii State Teachers Association and the Department of Education,* HPERB Case No. CE-05-4, October 24, 1972.

32. Hawaii State Teachers Association, *HSTA: A Brief History,* (Honolulu, no date) p. 2.

33. *In the Matter of the Hawaii State Teachers Association and the Department of Education,* HPERB Case No. (S-05-1, S-05-2, October 11, 1972.

34. HPERB Case No. CE-50-4.

35. *Hawaii State Teachers Association v. Hawaii Public Employee Relations Borad;* and *Department of Education v. Hawaii Public Employee Relations Board;* Circuit Court of the First Circuit, State of Hawaii, March 30, 1973, Civil No. 38086 and 38097.

36. *In the Matter of Hawaii State Teachers Association and the Board of Education,* HPERB Case No. CU-05-9, December 21, 1972.

37. *Ibid.*

38. *Petition for Declaratory, Ruling by the Department of Education;* HPERB Case No. DR-05-5, Decision No. 26, December 21, 1972.

39. *Agreement Between State of Hawaii, Board of Education and Hawaii State Teachers Association,* State of Hawaii (Honolulu, 1972), p. 50.

40. *Department of Education v. Hawaii Public Employee Relations Board,* Civil No. 38416, Circuit Court of the First Circuit, State of Hawaii, March 29, 1973.

41. "HSTA Found in Civil Contempt of Court But Hawaii Supreme Court Reduces Strike Fine" *Government Employee Relations* Report, April 22, 1974, pp. 3-7.

42. Edwin Pendleton, and Paul Staudohar, "Arbitration and Strikes in Hawaii Public Employment", *Industrial Relations* Vol. 13 (October, 1974) p. 307.

CASE #6
A Functional Analysis of Interest Arbitration in New York City Municipal Government, 1968-1975
Mary McCormick

Increased public sector unionism coupled with legal prohibitions against public employee strikes have led to a proliferation of arbitration procedures designed to act as strike substitutes. This study offers a functional analysis of one of these procedures, interest arbitration, in New York City municipal government to determine who has used it and for what purposes.[1] New York City's experience is worthy of close analysis because interest arbitration has been available since 1968, and because, for the 1968-75 period under examination, 890 contract settlements were reached, with both uniformed and nonuniformed unions having access to interest arbitration.

The following major findings emerge from the analysis: First, interest arbitration was utilized primarily by a few bargaining units and unions; these tended overwhelming to be smaller units of "nonessential" employees. Second, interest arbitration served three functional roles that are important dimensions of collective bargaining and political processes, but that are only tangentially related to strike prevention.

COLLECTIVE BARGAINING STRUCTURE

New York City municipal government possesses a highly complex labor relations network and collective bargaining structure. This study examines the interest arbitration record of approximately 200,000 employees who were under the jurisdiction of the New

Reprinted by permission from PROCEEDINGS OF THE TWENTY-NINTH ANNUAL WINTER MEETING, INDUSTRIAL RELATIONS RESEARCH ASSOCIATION SERIES, 1976, copyright (c) 1977 by the Industrial Relations Research Association, Madison, Wis. 53706 and by the author.

Mary McCormick is a faculty member at Columbia University.

York City Office of Collective Bargaining.[2] These workers were employed in over 1300 job titles, belonged to 85 separate unions, and were represented in negotiations by as many as 405 bargaining units.

Membership in New York City public employee unions ranged from 120,000 employees in the City-wide Career and Salary Plan bargaining unit of District Council 37, American Federation of State, County, and Municipal Employees, AFL-CIO (DC 37), to 60 part-time employees represented by the Podiatry Society of the State of New York.[3] Some unions, such as the Uniformed Firefighters Association or the Patrolmen's Benevolent Association, were single-title unions with largely homogenous memberships all employed by one city department. Other unions were multioccupational, multititle, and multiagency with memberships that included heterogenous groupings of both white- and blue-collar workers. Moreover, a single union may have had several locals within it; DC 37 had over 60. With regard to collective bargaining units, the situation is even more complicated. Only in single-title unions were the union and the bargaining unit the same entity. In other unions, one local may have had several bargaining units and one bargaining unit also may have included several locals.

An important structural consideration influencing the functional role of interest arbitration in New York City is that little or no cost or uncertainty had been built into the arbitration process. The parties to bargaining did not have to exhaust the services of mediators or factfinders before an impasse could be declared. Impasse could be invoked by either party or by the Director of the Office of Collective Bargaining. Both labor and management had an effective veto over an arbitrator serving on an impasse panel if they deemed the specific neutral unacceptable. Moreover, even though arbitration panels' decisions presumably were made final and binding upon both parties in 1972, a decision could be appealed to the Board of Collective Bargaining.

IMPASSE UTILIZATION: NEW YORK CITY 1968-1975

During the 1968-75 period, bargaining impasses were declared in slightly more than 15 percent of all City of New York contract negotiations. The number of interest arbitration cases fluctuated in the first four years, but, as a percentage of settlements, stabilized after 1970. Since then, between 10 and 12 percent of all contract negotiations have resulted in a request for arbitration.

The utilization of interest arbitration appears to have been habitforming for some municipal employee unions.[4] Only 31 of the 85 unions ever declared impasse and 88 percent of the 124 arbitration requests came from unions that resorted to arbitration at least twice. Not unexpectedly, two of the largest multibargaining unit unions accounted for 50 percent of arbitration cases heard, but within these unions, arbitration usage was concentrated among a few bargaining units. For example, DC 37's Lifeguard local went to arbitration in 1968, 1970, and 1973, establishing a pattern similar to that of some single-title unions, such as the Licensed Practical Nurses who declared impasse in 1970, 1972, and 1974.

Not only was arbitration utilization concentrated among a few unions, but also it was used disproportionately by smaller bargaining units of "less essential" employees. Sixty-four percent of all bargaining units that went to arbitration had 500 or fewer workers. New York City employee unions have been willing to declare a negotiation impasse for the Director of Rent Research, a bargaining unit of one; the Supervisors of Menagerie, a bargaining unit of three; and Electroencephalographic Technicians, a bargaining unit of fifteen.

Twenty-eight percent of the arbitration cases involved units of 500 to 10,000 employees. Except for three cases brought by the Sanitationmen, none of these involved employees whose strike activity would seem to have jeopardized the city significantly. Nonessential employees who invoked arbitration during the period in this category included training probation officers, storekeepers, hospital security officers, off-track betting employees, licensed practical nurses, and administrative employees of the Board of Higher Education.

Seven of the arbitration cases involved bargaining units of 10,000 or more employees. Firefighters went to arbitration three times (including 1973 when arbitration was invoked after a strike); patrolmen twice; a DC 37 "aide" grouping once; and the DC 37 City-wide Career and Salary Plan unit once. In six of these seven cases a negotiation impasse was not declared by the parties at the bargaining table, but rather by the Director of the Office of Collective Bargaining or by a judge.

Though the purpose of this paper is not to measure the impact of interest arbitration on the level of strike activity of New York City municipal government employees, the record outlined above suggests that in as many as 94 percent of the cases, the bargaining units invoking arbitration procedures could not have mounted substantial or successful strikes because of their size and the nonessentiality of the services provided by the employees in the units. Following the hypothesis prompted by the general theory of government employee strikes outlined by Burton and Krider, if New York City's interest arbitration were a strike substitute then only moderate-sized unions would avail themselves of it.[5] The theory states, on the one hand, that weak unions have little reason to strike since their membership is better paid than their power and strength would justify, while on the other hand the largest unions do not need to strike because they can achieve their goals politically. The data presented here have demonstrated that relatively small units of New York City municipal workers were the heaviest users of interest arbitration procedures over the 1968-75 period and, thus, that those procedures were not so much strike substitutes as strike supplements.

Moreover, that small bargaining units resorted to arbitration so freely apparently supports, instead, the hypothesis generated by the work of Summers.[6] He argues that because public sector bargaining is a political process, powerful public employee unions will have access to that process and therefore do not require collective bargaining procedures. Summers notes further that, "Collective bargaining procedures most assist those groups which are least able to exert significant influence in the normal political process . . . ."

Additionally, these data tend to validate the hypothesis implicit in some collective bargaining theories that the functional role of most third-party procedures, including those of New York City, will not be one primarily of strike prevention because the procedures lack cost and uncertainty, the two key components of the strike decision.[7] This is not to say that interest arbitration does not sometimes play a role in strike decisions; rather, it is to suggest that its role as a strike deterrent may be a limited one and that interest arbitration performs other roles in the collective bargaining process, some of which may have important policy implications. These are examined below.

FUNCTIONAL USE OF INTEREST ARBITRATION

Interest arbitration assumed three key roles in the collective bargaining process in New York City, roles that are only tangentially related to the legislated function of strike prevention. First, interest arbitration played a large role in providing a forum to plead parity imbalances for certain less powerful occupational groups of city employees. Second, arbitration became an important element in the intraorganizational bargaining process for particular unions and city negotiators. Third, union leaders used the availability of arbitration to help them fulfill their leadership functions.

Parity Adjustment Role

The role played by interest arbitration in adjudicating perceived parity imbalances results from the pervasive significance of reference-group comparisons in the wage-determination process for New York City municipal workers. First identified by Ross as a determining variable in the wage-setting process in the private sector, reference-group comparisons are a key variable in New York City's public sector bargaining as well.[8] The complicating factor is that the extreme number of groups makes the process more complex for New York City than for most private sector employers.

For New York City's municipal workers, the overall percentage wage increase is established by the contract settlements of the large, politically potent unions in the public sector or by key wage settlements in the private sector. The wage base, however, for a bargaining unit is determined by narrower reference-group comparisons. For a bargaining unit to receive an increase larger than the basic wage pattern, it must improve its wages and benefits vis-à-vis another bargaining unit. In New York City the parity relationship is the measure of ranking among bargaining units.

Ninety-six percent of the interest arbitration requests between 1968 and 1975 presented claims for wage and benefit increases justified on the basis of a parity imbalance. Even more significant is the fact that the majority of parity arbitration cases involved employees in four occupational groups: health workers, court system employees, park and recreational workers, and law enforcement employees. Traditionally, these employees have occupied low-status jobs, and many were represented by small unions or were in small bargaining units. Moreover, these workers regarded other highly visible, better-paid employees, including some in the private sector, as providing comparable services. Lacking the clout to secure desired changes in parity relationships at the bargaining table, the unions went to impasse, hoping the arbitrator would recommend the adjustment they sought.

The arbitration cases involving workers in the law enforcement field offer a good example of the role arbitration played in parity adjustment. The large number of cases were stimulated primarily by the gains secured by New York City's police officers between 1960 and 1974. Hospital security guards wanted parity with city patrolmen; uniformed court officers sought parity with city police sergeants (as opposed to assistant court clerks with whom they had parity); detectives assigned to the District Attorney's office desired parity with city police department detectives; and court clerks wanted parity with housing patrolmen who themselves had full parity with city patrolmen. In one case, Senior Deputy Sheriffs attempted to reverse the parity gains made by Deputy Sheriffs by trying to have arbitrators reestablish the traditional 29 percent differential between themselves and the Deputy Sheriffs that had been eroded.

Further, it appears that New York City municipal workers did not distinguish between public and private sector workers when determining the appropriate reference group. The considerable number of impasse cases involving health workers underscores this point. Registered nurses, pharmacists, interns, and residents employed by the city all were oriented toward higher-paid reference groups in the private sector. These bargaining units went to impasse in order to achieve salaries more comparable to those in the private sector. Other health workers in the city, generally better compensated than their private sector counterparts, used references groups within the city system: practical nurses sought wages and benefits more similar to those paid to city registered nurses.

Intraorganizational Bargaining Role

Another important role played by interest arbitration procedures was to facilitate intraorganizational bargaining within the union's and city's management. The process of arriving at a consensus on the boundaries of a bargaining position was often difficult for both parties. The management of the city was highly fragmented, and the management actors in the negotiating process sometimes responded to different constituencies. With almost 100 contract settlements annually, many issues did not appear to be of sufficient importance to use scarce internal resources to create a consensus within the overall management ranks of the city or even between the city negotiator and his immediate superiors within the Office of Labor Relations, the agency that represents the city in negotiations. The top ranks of the municipal employee unions frequently were more unified behind a bargaining position, unless the leadership was being challenged by insurgent groups. The intraorganizational challenge for the top union leadership was to sell an already formulated negotiating position to bargaining unit representatives and members of the locals.

Often the negotiators for the two sides were in closer agreement with each other on a particular issue than with other individuals in their respective organizations. As constant actors in the labor relations process, having to work together in grievance proceedings, fact-findings, mediations and arbitration panels as well as contract negotiations, frequently both negotiators developed overlapping zones of acceptable outcomes. Rather than trying to secure agreement within their organization, the negotiators, instead, turned to arbitrators to hand down a decision that, for internal political reasons on one or both sides, the negotiators could not agree to publicly.[9]

The use of arbitration for intraorganizational bargaining purposes in New York City may explain the pattern of reliance on a few arbitrators to settle arbitration cases. If arbitrators were to fulfill the role expectations delineated for them by the city and the union negotiators, the arbitrators must be completely trustworthy. Ninety-four percent of the cases heard by arbitration panels over the 1968-75 period had at least one arbitrator who had sat on a panel at least twice. Only five cases were ever heard by an arbitrator, as a one-man panel, who had not previously served. When asked how their use of impasse procedures would change if they had no part in the selection of arbitrators, the union and city negotiators who invoked interest arbitration most frequently said that they would not use arbitration under those conditions.

Leadership Role
Closely related to the intraorganizational bargaining role is the leadership role that arbitration helps union leaders to fulfill. Arbitration provides a low-risk opportunity for union leaders to go "all the way" for their memberships in an environment with substantial interunion rivalry. Between 1968 and 1975, union leaders declaring impasse often acted as if going to arbitration was the equivalent of striking. Indeed, they wanted their memberships to believe that going to arbitration required the same qualities required of union leaders taking their memberships out on strike.

The leadership uses of interest arbitration were especially evident when union leaders were up for reelection or were newly elected. That going to arbitration could be a useful strategy for a union leader up for reelection was a fact not lost on city negotiators. The latter have aided union leaders they liked by appearing particularly intransigent at the bargaining table so the issue could be settled by an arbitration panel. A victory could then be announced by the union leader for an outcome the city would have been willing to accept in negotiations.

Newly elected union officials also found going to arbitration a valuable leadership tactic. They were able to assume tough postures publicly to help them secure and strengthen their positions within their unions, usually with minimal risk or cost. In 1974, Ken McFeeley, the newly elected president of the Patrolmen's Benevolent Association (PBA), made the optimal time to invoke arbitration the key strategy decision in the contract negotiations. He wanted to establish a solid position with his membership by showing his total commitment to an issue of importance to them, namely, that of breaking parity with the firefighters, without having to go out on a strike that the PBA had little, if any, chance of winning.

CONCLUSION

In the City of New York during the 1968-75 period, the functional role interest arbitration assumed was not its statutory role of providing a strike substitute. Rather, interest arbitration played three roles and performed these roles mainly for smaller, less powerful unions. While this study does not attempt to weigh the past benefits gained from these functional roles against costs, it is possible on the basis of what is now known to suggest that future costs may well outweigh future benefits because of three fundamental changes that are taking place in the collective bargaining structure in New York City. These changes will greatly reduce the need for the roles that impasse arbitration has so recently played.

First, the Office of Collective Bargaining and the municipal unions are engaged in a program of reducing substantially the number of bargaining units. The number of units already has declined by almost 300 since 1968, with 50 bargaining units eliminated by mergers in 1975.

Second, few new government programs that would employ thousands of new workers in new job titles are anticipated in the next several years. Thus, there will be few small bargaining units and few such units with inexperienced leadership and memberships requiring the types of support that have been provided by New York City's interest arbitration procedure.

Third, during the early stages of New York City's retrenchment process, city and union leaders have taken advantage of the availability of arbitration procedures and have relied upon arbitrators to decide basic questions concerning the legitimate functions of New York City government and the reallocation of its resources. These issues are primarily political issues, and they ought to be resolved by the political, not the third-party, process.

Changes in the current structure are necessary to strengthen the collective bargaining process and to insure that the benefits of collective bargaining mechanisms are not outweighed by costs. At the least, the present compulsory arbitration procedures should be changed to a type of final-offer arbitration. Because final-offer arbitration appears to incorporate more cost and uncertainty into the process, the functional role of final-offer arbitration is more closely related to its legislated role.

A more fundamental change would be to eliminate arbitration entirely or greatly reduce its scope. In order to eliminate arbitration, public employees must be given the right to strike, a position that is gaining wider acceptance as municipalities increasingly question the cost of labor peace. In these situations final-offer arbitration would be available to those relatively few employees whose services are deemed genuinely essential.

NOTES

1. Interest arbitration is also called impasse arbitration in New York City. The three basic types of interest arbitration are advisory, compulsory, and final-offer. These are procedures designed to resolve disputes arising from contract negotiation and should be distinguished from grievance arbitration procedures. References to arbitration in the text refer to interest arbitration.

2. All employees of New York City mayoral agencies fall under the aegis of the New York City Office of Collective Bargaining (OCB). Employees of quasi-mayoral agencies may elect to be covered by OCB or remain under the jurisdiction of the New York State Public Employment Relations Board (PERB). To date, employees of the New York City Housing Authority, Off-Track Betting Corporation, and Board of Higher Education have elected to be under the jurisdiction of OCB, while teachers and transit workers are covered by PERB.

3. The DC 37 City-wide Career and Salary Plan bargaining unit includes DC 37's membership of approximately 100,000 employees, plus all other nonuniformed employees, except prevailing wage workers and those in managerial and confidential job titles. For the Career and Salary Plan bargaining unit, DC 37 bargains on nonwage items such as health insurance, time and leave benefits, and pensions.

4. The "narcotic effect" of compulsory arbitration on collective bargain-

ing has been investigated by Wheeler. See Hoyt N. Wheeler, "Compulsory Arbitration: A 'Narcotic Effect'?" *Industrial Relations*, vol. 14 (February 1975), pp. 117-20.

5. John E. Burton, Jr., and Charles Krider, "The Incidence of Strikes in Public Employment," in *Labor in the Public Non-Profit Sectors*, ed. Daniel S. Hamermesh (Princeton, N.J.: Princeton University Press, 1975).

6. Clyde W. Summers, "Public Employee Bargaining: A Political Perspective," *Yale Law Journal*, Vol. 83 (May 1974), pp. 1199-2000.

7. See Richard E. Walton and Robert B. McKersie, *A Behavioral Theory of Labor Negotiations* (New York: McGraw-Hill, 1965) and Carl M. Stevens, *Strategy and Collective Bargaining Negotiations* (New York: McGraw-Hill, 1963).

8. Arthur M. Ross, *Trade Union Wage Policy* (Berkeley: University of California Press, 1948). See also Seymour Martin Lipset and Martin Trow, "Reference Group Theory and Trade Union Wage Policy," in *Common Frontiers of the Social Sciences*, ed. Mirra Komarovsky (Glencoe, Ill.: Free Press, 1957), pp. 391-411.

9. This information was obtained in confidential interviews with several New York City municipal union officials and Office of Labor relations negotiators.

For a different analysis, see Anderson *et al. Impasse Resolution, etc.*, 51 St. John's Law Review 1977.

CASE #7
Fact-Finding Viewed
by Fact-Finders:
The Michigan Experience

Jack Steiber and Benjamin W. Wolkinson

Michigan is one of three states that have had the most experience with fact-finding in public employee disputes. The other two are

---

Reproduced from the February 1977 issue of the LABOR LAW JOURNAL, published and copyrighted (1977) by Commerce Clearing House, Inc., 4025 W. Peterson Avenue, Chicago, Illinois 60646. Reprinted by permission of the authors and Commerce Clearing House, Inc.

Mr. Steiber is the Director and Mr. Wolkinson an Associate Professor at the School of Labor and Industrial Relations, Michigan State University. This paper is part of a larger study, sponsored by the American Arbitration Association, to assess Michigan's experience with fact-finding in public employee disputes. The authors wish to acknowledge the assistance of Ralph Polumbo, Janet Kreger, and Eric Chapman in collecting the data for this paper.

Wisconsin, whose experience has been longer, and New York, which has processed more cases.

This paper presents the historical record of fact-finding in Michigan for the period 1966 through 1973, and the views of fact-finders based on their experience with fact-finding for the two-year period 1972-73. The parties' perceptions of the fact-finding process were also included in the overall study and will be presented in another report.

Under the Michigan Act, fact-finding may be invoked only after collective bargaining and mediation have failed to produce a settlement. The process may be initiated by petition of either the Union or Management, the parties jointly, or by the Michigan Employment Relations Commission (MERC) on its own initiative. If the petition is accepted by the MERC, the Commission appoints a fact-finder who conducts hearings and issues a report with recommendations which are not binding on the parties.

The Michigan Public Employee Relations Act (PERA) was signed by Governor Romney on July 23, 1965. It took the form of an amendment to the 1947 Hutchinson Act which, while giving public employees the right to organize and bargain collectively, did not provide the administrative machinery to effectuate these provisions and assessed automatic and severe penalties for striking employees.

The Michigan Act is a comprehensive statute providing for employee organization, representation procedures, employee and union unfair labor practices, mediation and fact-finding. Strikes are prohibited but no penalties for striking employees are specified. Court decisions have blunted the significance of the strike prohibition by holding that injunctions should not be issued automatically and that the courts could exercise their traditional equity powers, including an evaluation of good faith bargaining and potential damage, before determining whether or not to issue an injunction. A separate statute, enacted in 1969 and amended in 1972, provides for compulsory arbitration for police and fire-fighter disputes, which were previously covered in PERA. Except for the period 1965-69, these disputes are not dealt with in this paper.

The first fact-finding reports under the Act were submitted in 1966 in four disputes. After that the pace quickened. Of the 368 reports filed through 1973, the busiest year was 1969, with 92 reports, and the least active year 1971, when only 28 reports were submitted. Unions initiated fact-finding petitions in 63 percent of all cases, employers in 7 percent, and the parties joined in peti-

TABLE I
Fact-Finding Reports by Petitioning Party
1966 – 1973

Party Petitioning for Fact-Finding	1966		1967		1968		1969		1970		1971		1972		1973		Total 1966-1973	
	No.	%	No.	%	No.	%	No.	%	No.	%	No.	%	No.	%	No.	%	No.	%
Union	1	25.0	23	46.0	40	61.5	62	67.4	32	69.6	17	60.7	29	70.7	26	61.9	230	62.5
Employer	1	25.0	5	10.0	3	4.6	5	5.4	2	4.0	4	14.3	3	7.3	1	2.4	24	6.5
Both	1	25.0	12	24.0	17	26.2	16	17.4	8	17.4	5	17.8	9	22.0	8	19.0	76	20.6
MERC	0	—	2	4.0	1	1.5	1	1.1	0	—	0	—	0	—	1	2.4	5	1.4
Not Available	1	25.0	8	16.0	4	6.2	8	8.7	4	8.7	2	7.2	0	—	6	14.3	33	9.0
TOTAL	4	100.0	50	100.0	65	100.0	92	100.0	46	100.0	28	100.0	41	100.0	42	100.0	368	100.0

TABLE II
Fact-Finding Reports by Employee Group
1966 – 1973

Employee Group	1966 No.	%	1967 No.	%	1968 No.	%	1969 No.	%	1970 No.	%	1971 No.	%	1972 No.	%	1973 No.	%	Total 1966-73 No.	%
Education																		
College teachers	0	—	2	4.0	3	4.6	0	—	2	4.3	0	—	2	4.9	1	2.4	10	2.7
Elementary & secondary teachers	1	25.0	41	82.0	40	61.5	65	70.6	34	73.9	12	42.9	24	58.5	19	45.2	236	64.1
Non-institutional education	0	—	0	—	7	10.8	6	6.5	1	2.2	3	10.7	4	9.8	6	14.3	27	7.3
Protective Services																		
Police	0	—	2	4.0	2	3.1	2	2.2	1	2.2	—	—	—	—	—	—	7	1.9
Fire	2	50.0	3	6.0	4	6.2	3	3.3	0	—	—	—	—	—	—	—	12	3.3
Health Services																		
Hospital & Health Care	—	—	1	2.0	5	7.7	1	1.1	1	2.2	3	10.7	1	2.4	1	2.4	13	3.5
Public Works	—	—	1	2.0	1	1.5	6	6.5	4	8.7	8	28.6	7	17.1	8	19.0	35	9.5
Administrative Services																		
Office and Clerical	—	—	—	—	—	—	—	—	—	—	1	3.6	3	7.3	1	2.4	5	1.4
Other Administrative	—	—	—	—	—	—	—	—	1	2.2	1	3.6	—	—	2	4.8	4	1.1
Social Services																		
Social Services	—	—	—	—	—	—	3	3.3	0	—	—	—	—	—	1	2.4	4	1.1
Other	1	25.0	—	—	3	4.6	6	6.5	2	4.4	—	—	—	—	3	7.1	15	4.1
TOTAL	4	100.0	50	100.0	65	100.0	92	100.0	46	100.0	28	100.0	41	100.0	42	100.0	368	100.0

tioning for fact-finding in 21 percent of the cases which ended with reports. The Board itself initiated only 5 fact-finding cases during the entire period. The distribution between petitioning parties varied little from year to year (Table I).

By far the largest number of reports was submitted in disputes involving teachers in elementary and secondary schools (K-12). Sixty-four percent of all reports dealt with such disputes; the next highest categories were public works (10 percent) and non-instructional school employees (7 percent). Teacher disputes declined during the three years 1971-73 to just under half of all reports as compared with over 70 percent during 1966-70, while public works and non-instructional school disputes showed the opposite trend (Table II). Fact-finding was little utilized in police and fire-fighter disputes, even during the early years and, in 1969, disputes in the protective services were made subject to compulsory arbitration, thus ending their experience with fact-finding.

REPORTS

Only somewhat more than half (57 percent) of all fact-finding petitions resulted in reports and recommendations. During the first seven years of the Michigan Act (1966-72),[1] 326 reports were issued from the 573 petitions filed with the MERC. The others were disposed of in the following ways: 3 were rejected by the Commission; 45 withdrawn by the parties; 69 settled after appointment of a fact-finder but before a hearing could be held; 91 were settled while hearings were in process, presumably with the assistance of the fact-finder; and 12 were settled after a hearing but before issuance of a report. There was no information on the disposition of 27 cases (Table III).

It is significant that some 20 percent of the cases which went to a hearing were settled while hearings were in process without a report being issued. Unlike New York, Wisconsin, and some other states where fact-finders are encouraged to engage in mediation as well as fact-finding, Michigan fact-finders are not supposed to try to mediate disputes. Mediation, according to the MERC, is the job of staff mediators who have already tried and failed in their efforts to assist the parties in reaching a settlement through collective bargaining. The next step is a hearing in which the parties submit evidence, call witnesses and present arguments on the issues in dispute. The fact-finder then prepares a report and recommendations which are designed to assist the parties in resolving the dispute with or without additional collective bar-

TABLE III
Disposition of Fact-Finding Cases
1966 – 1972

Year	Total Cases Closed	Accepted by MERC	Withdrawn Prior to Appointment of Fact-Finder	Fact-Finder Appointed	Settled Prior to Hearing	Settled During Hearing	Settled After Hearing	Disposition Unknown	Fact-finding Report Issued
1966	13	13	0	13	0	7	1	1	4
1967	99	99	1	98	15	30	2	1	50
1968	107	107	4	103	10	11	5	12	65
1969	135	133	5	128	13	16	2	5	92
1970	88	87	11	76	14	9	2	5	46
1971	51	51	10	41	5	8	0	0	28
1972	80	80	14	66	12	10	0	3	41
Total 1966-1972	573	570	45	525	69	91	12	27	326

gaining. The number of cases settled during hearings suggest that fact-finders are playing a more active mediation role than was contemplated by the MERC.[2] The MERC is aware of the predilection of some fact-finders to engage in mediation but has not tried to deter them in these efforts.[3]

Over the entire period under study, the average amount of time between the filing of a petition for fact-finding and the issuance of the fact-finder's report was about two months. However, there has been a significant increase in the time required for the fact-finding process to run its course. In 1967, it took only 36 days to process cases reported out as compared with 103 days in 1972.[4] There is a sharp break between the period 1967-70 and 1971-73 in time required for processing. During the first four-year period, the average number of days required was 46; during the last three years, time elapsed between filing of a petition and issuance of a report averaged 93 days (Table IV).

The increase in time required for processing cases may be attributable primarily to a change in procedure in the appointment of fact-finders. Until Spring 1971, the MERC appointed fact-finders without consulting with the parties. Starting in 1971, the MERC changed its procedure and submitted a panel of three names to the parties from which they were asked to select a mutually acceptable fact-finder. If the parties could not agree, a second panel of three was submitted.[5] If the parties were still unable to agree on a fact-finder, the MERC appointed one. In 1973, the MERC discontinued submission of a second panel.

The change in 1971 requires more time than the direct appointment process. In 1967-70, it took an average of about 12 days for the MERC to appoint a fact-finder after receiving a petition, as compared with 34 days during 1971-73.

While the change in appointment procedures accounts for a major part of the increase in elapsed time for a case to be processed from beginning to end, other elements of the process have also increased. In 1971-73, the average number of days between appointment of a fact-finder and the first hearing was 39 days as compared with about 17 days in 1967-70; and time elapsed between the final hearing and issuance of the fact-finder's report increased from 18 days in the earlier period to 30 days in 1971-73. The above data indicate that, even after appointment of a fact-finder, cases are taking longer to process than during the first few years of the Act. The first fact-finding session takes longer to arrange and fact-finders are taking more time to prepare their reports and recommendations.

TABLE IV

Number of Days Required for Fact-Finding Process
1966 – 1973

Average No. of Days Between	1966	1967	1968	1969	1970	1971	1972	1973	Total 1966-1973
Petition for and Appointment of Fact-Finder	53	9.6	16.9	10	9.3	31.7	39.9	29.5	19.5
N*	2	25	51	73	39	26	7	33	286
Appointment of Fact-Finder and First Fact-Finding Session	33	11.8	19.9	16.7	17.0	21.3	33.5	57.0	24.0
N*	3	35	52	80	45	25	38	37	315
First Fact-finding Session and Issuance of Report	112	27.4	24.5	19.9	32.4	34.2	43.0	38.0	30.3
N*	3	40	54	82	45	28	41	41	334
Final Fact-finding Session and Issuance of Report	71.3	23.3	19.1	13.9	20.9	25.3	29.3	32.7	22.5
N*	3	38	54	82	45	28	41	41	332
Request for Fact-Finder and Issuance of Report	161	36.4	56.2	43.3	48.2	77.0	103.0	93.9	61.6
N*	1	37	59	91	46	27	41	41	343
Average Number of Fact-finding days	2.0	2.1	1.8	1.7	1.5	1.8	1.6	1.4	1.7
N*	4	41	62	91	46	28	41	41	354

N*—denotes number of cases on which days were calculated. In other cases data were not available.

The increase in time taken by fact-finders to prepare their reports may be related to an increase in the average number of disputed issues presented by the parties. In 1967-70, there were usually about five issues in dispute as compared with almost seven during 1971-73 (Table V). Issues were rarely settled or withdrawn by the parties during the fact-finding process. As a result, fact-finders had to analyze and make recommendations on more issues in their reports, which understandably took more time. However, it is rather surprising that the number of fact-finding sessions per case declined somewhat at the same time that the number of issues increased: from 1.8 in 1967-70 to 1.6 in 1971-73. Most cases require only a single day of hearings. However, several cases have required more than five hearing days.

Nine out of ten cases involved the issue of wages, either as the sole issue in dispute (13%) or, more often, along with other issues (75%). Only eleven percent of fact-finding cases were concerned exclusively with issues other than wages. While there is some variation in issues from year to year, there is no significant deviation from the overall figures on issues involved in fact-finding cases.

After wages, issues most often in dispute were: medical and dental protection (44% of cases); contract duration (28%); calendar or work week (25%); life insurance (25%); union security and check off (21%); sick leave (18%) and class size (16%). Issues in dispute are closely related to the dominance of school disputes in fact-finding cases. Such issues as premium pay, shift differentials, subcontracting, pensions and others associated with private sector collective bargaining have rarely been submitted to fact-finding in Michigan.

FACT-FINDERS' VIEWS

The foregoing analysis of Michigan's experience with fact-finding raises several questions:

1. Why is fact-finding so much more acceptable to unions than to employers? Why has the MERC rarely used its authority to compel fact-finding in a state where strikes have frequently occurred without recourse to fact-finding?

2. What is the appropriate relationship between mediation and fact-finding? Should fact-finders mediate before, during or after issuance of their reports, or not at all?

3. Is time involved in processing fact-finding petitions related to the success or failure of fact-finding? If time is important,

TABLE V
Disposition of Issues in Fact-Finding Cases
1966 – 1973

	Submitted to Fact-Finding	Settled by Parties	Withdrawn by Parties	Remanded by Fact-finder to Parties	Recommendations Issued	Disposition Unknown
1966 Total	21.0	—	—	2.0	15.0	4.0
Average/Case	5.3	—	—	0.5	3.8	2.0
1967 Total	289.0	34.0	2.0	34.0	185.0	34.0
Average/Case	5.8	0.7	0.04	0.7	3.7	0.7
1968 Total	321.0	21.0	1.0	8.0	285.0	7.0
Average/Case	4.9	0.3	0.02	0.1	4.4	0.1
1969 Total	487.0	4.0	4.0	8.0	458.0	9.0
Average/Case	5.3	0.04	0.04	0.1	5.0	0.1
1970 Total	205.0	6.0	3.0	2.0	185.0	6.0
Average/Case	4.5	0.1	0.1	0.04	4.0	0.1
1971 Total	202.0	—	1.0	4.0	197.0	—
Average/Case	7.2	—	0.04	0.1	7.0	—
1972 Total	320.0	21.0	24.0	15.0	244.0	15.0
Average/Case	7.8	0.5	0.6	0.4	6.0	0.4
1973 Total	245.0	9.0	1.0	3.0	228.0	4.0
Average/Case	5.8	0.2	0.02	0.1	5.4	0.1
1966-73 Total	2090.0	95.0	36.0	76.0	1797.0	79.0
Average/Case	5.7	0.3	0.1	0.2	4.9	0.2

what can be done to speed up the process? Should efforts be made to appoint fact-finders acceptable to the parties by utilizing panel selection procedures as opposed to agency appointment?

4. What can be done to limit the number of issues submitted to fact-finding? Should fact-finders be required to make recommendations on every issue in dispute?

Some of these questions will be discussed in the next section dealing with fact-finders' views. Others will have to await analysis of the parties' questionnaire responses.

In order to determine the views of the parties and fact-finders, we conducted a questionnaire survey of union and management representatives and of fact-finders involved in all cases for which reports were issued in 1972 and 1973. Only the responses of fact-finders will be discussed in this article.

Of the 28 fact-finders appointed in 83 cases in which reports were rendered in 1972 and 1973, 26 returned useable questionnaires for 71 cases in which they were involved. Their responses were analyzed on two bases: on a case by case basis for questions dealing with specific aspects of individual disputes and on a fact-finder basis for questions pertaining to attitudes and general experience with the fact-finding process. Before discussing our findings, it may be useful to draw a thumbnail sketch of the "typical" Michigan fact-finder.

He (there were no women) is between 45 and 55 years of age, is a lawyer or has an earned Ph.D., has had experience in private sector grievance arbitration in addition to labor relations experience with management, labor and/or government. About one-third of the fact-finders have handled five or fewer cases, while some 20 percent have served in more than 20 cases. The others are fairly evenly distributed between these two extremes. Michigan has added new fact-finders almost every year since the PERA was enacted in 1965. Most fact-finders have also served as arbitrators under the Michigan Police-Fire Fighters Arbitration Act.

MEDIATION AND FACT-FINDING

More than two-thirds of the fact-finders consider it appropriate to combine mediation and fact-finding. However, only a few think that mediation is "always" in order (11.5%), while most (58%) regard mediation to be appropriate in some disputes but not in others. Somewhat less than one-third of the fact-finders think they should "never" try to mediate, presumably because mediation by MERC staff members has already been tried and has failed to resolve the dispute, or the parties do not expect them to mediate, or they see some inconsistency in combining the two functions.

Fact-finders actually engaged in mediation to a lesser extent than might be indicated by their widespread belief in the appropriateness of the process in conjunction with fact-finding. Of the 71 cases studies, fact-finders tried to mediate in only 21.[6] Almost invariably, mediation was undertaken at the initiative of the fact-finder (57.1%) or at the request of both parties (38.1%). Mediation succeeded in settling all disputed issues in a majority of the cases in which it was tried.

Nonetheless, reports were issued in these cases for a variety of reasons: one or both parties wanted a report for face-saving purposes; a school board wanted to use the report to try to get more state aid; the fact-finder was not sure that all issues in dispute had been resolved and issued a report for the record; some fact-finders believe a report should be issued even when the dispute has been resolved by mediation. In a few of the remaining cases, mediation succeeded in reducing the number of issues in dispute and/or in narrowing the gap between the parties.

Mediation by fact-finders was not extensive, usually lasting only one or two meetings and rarely exceeding eight hours. For the most part, fact-finders found the parties sincere in their efforts to reach agreement through mediation, though in a few cases they thought the union, the management or both took unrealistic positions or were hostile to their efforts.

THE FACT-FINDING HEARING

Fact-finding hearings usually last one day. Transcripts are not required and were taken in only a small minority of all cases (12.7%), at the request of either the employer or the fact-finder. The party requesting a transcript pays for it, with the MERC bearing the cost for the fact-finder. Unions did not insist on a transcript in any cases.

Most cases had five or fewer issues in dispute (52.3%). Three issues occurred most frequently (10 cases) and only a single issue was submitted to the fact-finder in 8 cases. Ten or more issues were found in 17 cases and three cases had over 20 issues. Fact-finders have usually made recommendations on all unresolved issues. The remaining issues were resolved by the parties during negotiations, withdrawn by mutual consent, referred back to the parties for negotiation, or resolved before fact-finding started. In only three cases were new issues, not previously discussed by the parties, introduced during fact-finding and, in two cases, parties reneged on issues previously resolved in negotiations and brought them to the fact-finding hearing.

Negotiations usually do not continue during fact-finding (74.1%),although this did happen in about one out of every four cases. Insofar as the fact-finders were aware, the parties rarely held back from good faith bargaining in anticipation of fact-finding. Nor was it common for either party to change its original position during the fact-finding hearings. For the most part, however, fact-finders professed ignorance of what had transpired before they entered the picture.

Though fact-finding hearings are open to the public, outsiders did not often avail themselves of the privilege of attending. Insofar as fact-finders were aware, members of the public were present in less than one-fifth of the cases and the news media were represented in one out of ten cases. Union members, on the other hand, attended three-fourths of the hearings, while government officials were present in almost half of the cases. It is difficult to gauge the impact of non-participant attendance, but fact-finders believed that they had "no effect" on 21 cases, "helped produce a settlement" in 9 cases, and were a hindrance to a settlement in 5 cases. In the remaining cases, only the party representatives were present or fact-finders did not respond to this question.

REPORTS AND RECOMMENDATIONS

Fact-finders found the parties "well prepared" or "adequately prepared" for the hearing in almost all cases. As a result, fact-finders received sufficient evidence in hearings to enable them to prepare their reports in 87% of the cases studied. In the remaining cases, fact-finders usually tried to obtain additional information by requesting it from the parties and resorting to other sources of information on such matters as cost of living increases, comparisons with other school districts, previous contracts, financial data, cost of the total package offered or demanded and confirmation of cited sources of data.

Fact-finders were asked to characterize their recommendations on the five most important issues submitted in each case in terms of the extent of their agreement with the parties' respective positions. On the most important issue in dispute (usually wages), fact-finders thought that they had taken a "middle position" between the parties in about 40 percent of the cases; in the remaining cases, they believed that their recommendations agreed "substantially" or "moderately" with the union position (33.4%) somewhat more frequently than with the employer position (27.8%). On the second and third most important issues, fact-finders also thought their recommendations were closer to the union than to the employer position. Only on issues rated fourth and fifth in importance did fact-finders believe that their recommendations tended to favor the employer's position more frequently than the union's. The number of non-respondents increased with each issue, reflecting the number of issues in dispute (i.e., all cases had at least one issue, somewhat fewer two, even less three, four, and five).

The objective to which fact-finders attached greatest importance in formulating their recommendations was "acceptability" to all the parties. Fourteen of the fact-finders considered "acceptability" to be the most important and five regarded it as second in importance. Five fact-finders attached greatest importance to recommendations which, in their judgment, "would approximate the settlement the parties would have achieved through collective bargaining" and an equal number considered "terms based solely on available facts and evidence without regard to acceptability to the parties" most important. None thought that "acceptability to the public" was a prime objective of their recommendations.

In view of the above responses, it is not surprising that fact-finders in less than one-fourth of the cases said that they had considered the public interest "very much" in formulating their recommendations, though in an additional 65 percent of the cases, they replied "somewhat" to the question regarding the extent to which they considered the public interest in their recommendations.

What criteria should fact-finders employ in reaching their recommendations? Greatest support is given to "comparisons with other units" and "ability to pay," which were regarded as "always proper" by more than 80 percent of the fact-finders, and "cost of living" was put in this category by 70 percent of the respondents. "Productivity effects" and "bargaining history" were also considered to be "always proper" criteria by a majority of fact-finders, while "acceptability" was supported by a sizable minority (42%). Almost all fact-finders who did not consider these criteria as "always proper" regarded them as "sometimes proper" and very few thought they were "improper" as criteria for recommendations.

On the other hand, "political power of the parties," "economic power of the parties" and what the parties "would have gained or lost if a strike were permissible" were generally regarded as "improper" or at best "sometimes proper" criteria to be employed in arriving as recommendations.

Actual use of these criteria in specific cases pretty much followed the fact-finders' views on the propriety of their use. Thus, major use was accorded comparisons with similar units in 83 percent of all cases, followed by cost of living (78%), ability to pay (61%), acceptability (58%), bargaining history (30%), and productivity (27%). Political and economic power, and potential gains and losses from strikes were "not at all used" in more than half of all cases, though "minor use" was made of these and "other" criteria in some cases. In practice, ability to pay, bargaining history and productivity effects were used less often in specific cases than might have been expected judging from fact-finders' philosophical inclinations, while "acceptability" turned out to be less important in practice than in theory.

Fact-finders expressed great confidence that their recommendations would be acceptable to both unions and employers. They expected the union to accept all their recommendations in over 80 percent of the cases and thought their recommendations would be acceptable to employers in three-fourths of the cases. In other cases, they expected at least part of their recommendations would be acceptable to the union (5.6%) and to the employer (9.9%). There were no cases in which fact-finders thought that "none" of their recommendations would be acceptable to either labor or management.

Most fact-finders write their reports "only for the parties," about one-third write "mostly for the parties but also for the community," and a relatively small minority consider the parties and the community "equally" in preparing their reports. None gave priority to the community over the parties. This view of their clientele is consistent with responses to earlier questions in which fact-finders indicated that "acceptability to the public" and "the public interest" were only minor considerations in formulating their recommendations.

CONCLUSIONS

Based on their responses to our questionnaire survey, the following conclusions may be drawn regarding the attitudes of Michigan fact-finders towards fact-finding and their behavior in handling cases assigned to them:

1. Fact-finders see nothing wrong with combining mediation and fact-finding and will not hesitate to mediate either at the request of both parties or on their own initiative. Furthermore, Michigan fact-finders have been quite successful in mediation when they have engaged in the process.

2. Fact-finding and negotiations appear to be separate procedures; negotiations usually stop when fact-finding begins. (Negotiations will of course resume after fact-finding, but, in Michigan, fact-finders do not participate in post-fact-finding negotiations.)

3. Members of the public rarely attend fact-finding hearings and appear to exercise little or no influence in either expediting or hindering a settlement in disputes going to fact-finding.

4. By 1972-73, both union and management representatives were competent in the preparation and presentation of their cases to fact-finders.

5. Fact-finders regard their recommendations as verging more often towards the union position than to the employer position.

6. The most important single objective guiding fact-finders in formulating their recommendations is "acceptability to all parties." The "public interest" as such is not a primary consideration. (Recommendations acceptable to the parties may of course also be in the public interest.)

7. "Comparisons with other units," "cost of living" and "ability to pay" are considered the most appropriate criteria and are most frequently used in arriving at recommendations. Political and economic power are regarded as inappropriate criteria and are accorded little importance in practice.

8. Fact-finders are a self-confident lot. They expect their recommendations to be acceptable to both parties in a substantial majority of cases. (Preliminary analysis of parties' responses in our questionnaire survey indicates that the fact-finders are overly optimistic in their expectations.)

9. Fact-finders, like arbitrators, regard their primary obligation to be to the parties rather than to the public in the preparation and dissemination of their reports and recommendations.

These findings are preliminary and tentative. More definitive conclusions must await analysis and comparison of union and management responses with those of fact-finders. We also intend to compare our findings for Michigan with studies in other states with a view to arriving at some general conclusions regarding fact-finding in public employee disputes.

NOTES

1. Information was not available for calendar year 1973.
2. Fact-finders have also issued reports in some cases where mediation has succeeded in resolving all or some issues.
3. The MERC attitude towards mediation by fact-finders has changed over the years. In the early years of the Act, fact-finders were cautioned not to attempt mediation. In recent years, the MERC has left it to the fact-finder to decide whether or not mediation would be appropriate.
4. 1966 is omitted because data were available for only one case which took 161 days to process.
5. In cases where rapid action is called for, the MERC has appointed fact-finders without prior submission of panels.
6. These figures do not include cases mediated by fact-finders in which reports were not issued.

CASE #8
Final Offer Arbitration—
Initial Experience
in Wisconsin

James L. Stern

In 1972 the State of Wisconsin amended its public sector labor relations statute[1] to provide for the resolution of interest disputes between local governments and policemen, firefighters, and county law enforcement officers by final-offer arbitration. During the previous 10 years, factfinding had been the terminal step. The amendments, including the binding arbitration provision, came as a result of a drive by the coalition of public sector unions for a major revision of the law.

THE FINAL-OFFER ARBITRATION STATUTE

The Wisconsin statute provides that either party may petition the Wisconsin Employment Relations Commission to order arbitra-

Reprinted by permission of the MONTHLY LABOR REVIEW.

James L. Stern is a professor of economics at the University of Wisconsin.

tion. The Commission investigates the dispute to determine whether an impasse has been reached. This is not a pro forma certification to arbitration, because the Commission conducts an intensive mediation effort during the investigation and orders arbitration only after it is convinced that there is a bona fide impasse. At that point, unless the parties have agreed upon an arbitrator or board of arbitration, the Commission orders the parties to submit their final offers and furnishes a panel of five names from which the parties select the arbitrator. The cost of arbitration is borne by the parties.

If both parties desire to use conventional arbitration rather than final-offer arbitration, the statute specifically authorizes this option. In the absence of such an agreement, however, the parties are bound by what is referred to in the Wisconsin statute as "form 2 arbitration," under which "[t]he arbitrator shall select the final offer of one of the parties and shall issue an award incorporating that offer without modification."[2] In only one of the first 24 cases in which awards have been issued did the parties agree on conventional arbitration.

The statute provides guidelines for the arbitrator in reaching his decision, identical with those specified in the Michigan arbitration statute. They state that the arbitrator shall give weight to the lawful authority of the employer, stipulations of the parties, ability to pay, cost of living, comparisons with other employees in the public and private sectors doing similar work, comparisons with other employees generally in comparable communities, and other factors which normally or traditionally are taken into consideration in determining wages, hours, and conditions of employment in the private and public sectors. Although the statute does not provide specifically that arbitrators may mediate issues, several of the more experienced arbitrators have occasionally attempted to do so.

Eligibility for use of arbitration is restricted to county and city law enforcement and firefighting personnel, and is further restricted to cities with a population of at least 2,500 and no more than 500,000. This last restriction exempts the City of Milwaukee from this portion of the statute.[3] Of the 143 cities that are eligible for final-offer arbitration, 101 bargain with either policemen or firefighters or both groups. One hundred cities have negotiated agreements with policemen and 51 have reached agreement with firefighters. (Fewer cities bargain with firefighters than with policemen because in many small cities there is a heavy reliance on volunteer firefighters rather than on full-time paid employees.)

Of the 72 Wisconsin counties, 41 have negotiated agreements with law enforcement officers. (Counties employ no firefighters.)

Responses from 71 percent of the bargaining units have shown that the average population of the cities that bargain is 20,000, the average number of all types of municipal employees is 190, and the average size of the policeman and firefighter units is 30 and 45, respectively. The 41 counties which bargain have an average population of 90,000, employ an average of 900 public employees, and have an average of 50 people in the law enforcement units. Bargaining is relatively new to a majority of these units as approximately 55 percent of the 192 units negotiated their first agreements less than 6 years ago.

ABSENCE OF NARCOTIC EFFECT

The Wisconsin record tends to refute the statement, made by Willard Wirtz at the 1963 meeting of the National Academy of Arbitrators in Chicago, that:

> Experience—particularly the War Labor Board experience during the '40's—shows that a statutory requirement that labor disputes be submitted to arbitration has a narcotic effect on private bargainers, that they turn to it as an easy—and habit forming—release from the obligation of hard, responsible bargaining.[4]

The data summarized in Table 1 indicate that the parties have tended to settle disputes by themselves, rather than abdicate this responsibility to arbitrators. In about two-thirds of the 173 negotiations in 1973, the parties reached agreements without any third-party assistance. Mediation took place in the remaining one-third of negotiations, either upon direct request of the parties or—as a result of their petitions for arbitration—in the course of the Commission's investigation. About three-fourths of the mediated disputes were resolved, including the few that were settled by the parties themselves during the procedure leading to the arbitration hearing, or at the hearing with the aid of the arbitrator. *In only 9 percent of the 173 negotiations were arbitral awards issued.* In negotiations of the 1974 agreements, the experience was similar: as of April 1, the proportion of negotiations in which the parties sought third-party assistance was still about one-third.

A question of particular interest to policymakers is whether the proportion of third party awards under a system of final-offer arbitration is less than under conventional arbitration, final-offer

TABLE 1

Collective bargaining agreements of policemen, firefighters, and county law enforcement officers in Wisconsin, by method of settlement, 1968—first quarter 1974.

	1968-71		1972[1]		1973		1974	
Method of settlement	Num-ber	Per-cent	Num-ber	Per-cent	Num-ber	Per-cent	Num-ber	Per-cent
All settlements	427	100	143	100	173	100	147	100
Direct negotiations	300	70	103	72	117	68	98	67
Third-party assistance	127	30	40	28	56	32	49	33
Mediation	102	24	29	20	40	23	[2]25	([2])
Factfinding	24	6	4	3	—	—	—	—
Arbitration	—	—	7	5	16	9	[2]1	([2])

[1] The arbitration statue became effective Apr. 20, 1972. Therefore, the disputes over contracts for calendar year 1972 which had not been resolved by direct negotiations or by mediation or factfinding awards prior to that date were resolved by arbitration awards under the newly enacted law.

[2] It is estimated that most contracts for 1974 had been negotiated by Apr. 1, 1974, or had been referred to the Wisconsin Employment Relations Commission for third party assistance of one form or another, although a few unsettled disputes over new contracts may have been included in the category of direct settlements which, subsequent to that date, were referred to the Commission for assistance. Of the 49 negotiations referred to the Commission for third-party assistance by Apr. 1, 1974, 25 had been settled by mediation and 1 by arbitration, and 23 were still pending at some step of the procedure.

NOTE: The number of settlements was calculated from the questionaires and adjusted to reflect the response rate of 71 percent and the number of 2-year agreements. The number of mediations and of factfinding and arbitration awards was derived from State records. State figures were adjusted to cover calendar rather than fiscal years, as municipal agreements are negotiated on calendar-year basis.

by issue arbitration, or factfinding. As yet, no definitive answer can be given, but the available evidence indicates that the percent of negotiations settled by arbitration awards is higher in Pennsylvania than in Michigan or Wisconsin, although this may be attributable to the absence of mediation and other differences in the statutes rather than to differences in the type of arbitration.

Differences that may be found between Michigan and Wisconsin also may be attributable to differences in mediation and other aspects of the statutes, as well as to differences in the arbitration process. Detailed figures for Michigan are not yet available. Theoretically, however, one would expect a lower proportion of awards in Wisconsin because of the all-or-nothing aspect of the Wisconsin procedure, as opposed to the choice of offers on an issue-by-issue basis in Michigan. Offset against this, however, is the greater use of mediation-arbitration in Michigan. Regardless of which State turns out to have the lower proportion of awards, it is clear that in both States the parties are resolving most disputes by themselves and that no narcotic effect has as yet appeared.

When the Wisconsin experience under final-offer arbitration is compared with its previous experience under factfinding, the results run contrary to what one might expect and to what some mediators have suggested. Mediators have noted that they may have more clout when mediation is followed by a binding procedure instead of an advisory one. The data in table 1, however, show that both the percent of negotiations referred to factfinding during the last 4 complete years of factfinding—1968-71—and the percent of awards issued were slightly less than under final-offer arbitration.

This result may be attributable to a variety of factors other than the change in procedures. Although law enforcement personnel had access to factfinding under the old statute, they were not considered employees and, therefore, did not have full bargaining rights. When full bargaining rights came along with final-offer arbitration, collective bargaining spread to smaller cities and rural counties. Conservative managements in those areas may have been less prone to accept bargaining and may have forced unions to rely on arbitration more heavily than in large cities. Also, the various phases of the Federal Government wage control programs may have inhibited recourse to third-party procedures to varying degrees at different periods.

CHANGES IN THE PROCESS AND OUTCOME

The availability of arbitration at the request of either party clearly helps weak unions—and it is assumed that this holds true for conventional arbitration and final-offer by issue as well as for final-offer arbitration. In formulating its bargaining position, municipal management must now take into account the possibility that the union will seek arbitration if the offer seems unsatisfactory. Unions which formerly presented suggestions for improvements in wages and other conditions of employment to a finance committee of a city council or county board and then, possibly with some grumbling, accepted the offer determined unilaterally by management, now have forced management to take bargaining more seriously. They meet more often, they exchange proposals, and they modify their positions. Both parties appear eager to settle by themselves rather than have an outsider impose on them a binding decision. Threats of bringing in an outsider are sometimes used by the weaker party, however, in attempts to induce change in the position of the other party.

In some industrial communities where the unions are very strong, one finds management petitioning for arbitration. The threat of third-party judgments performs a valuable function in those situations where elected officials are loath to alienate a potent labor vote. Existence of an arbitration system may restrain the strong union from pushing as hard as otherwise would be the case. In a few instances, it appears, the stronger party—and this applies equally to unions and managements—is unwilling to compromise on a particular issue and, as a facesaving measure, prefers that it be resolved adversely to its interests by an arbitrator. Overall, it appears that, since the parties prefer to reach their own settlement in most situations, the existence of arbitration helps them to do so, although the terms may be different from those that would have prevailed in the absence of arbitration.

Management and union spokesmen state that the existence of arbitration is raising wages of policemen, firefighters, and deputy sheriffs in the low wage communities and reducing the dispersion within each occupation. There is no consensus yet, however, about the effect of arbitration on the pattern setters, with some management and union leaders stating that the statute has minimal influence on such negotiations. Statistical evidence to resolve this question is not yet available, and quite possibly would not be conclusive if it were available. It does seem likely, however, that arbitration is causing the wages of the uniformed services to increase more than they would have under factfinding.

Another question raised about arbitration is whether unions and managements will comply with the statute. In Wisconsin, compliance is almost complete. This may be caused by the fact that the arbitration statute was sought by the police and firefighter organizations. They see it as their statute, and this seems to place a responsibility on them to abide by it. Although city managements opposed enactment of the statute, they have gone along with its provisions in most instances. There have been several court suits or requests for administrative rulings by cities, however, which have had the effect of delaying resolution of disputes through arbitration.

One instance of union noncompliance which is of interest occurred in a strong-labor town where the unions wished to introduce cost-of-living clauses. The spokesman for the labor groups believed that an arbitrator would be unlikely to innovate and that comparisons with other communities in the area would cause him to reject the union demand for a cost-of-living clause. He chose, instead, to initiate an intensive economic pressure and public education program favoring such clauses. This included sick-ins and rallies and picketing of city hall by firefighters and policemen supported by other city employees, teachers, and private sector union workers. In addition the union insisted that all negotiations be public and included television and press representatives in union caucuses. Sufficient pressure was generated on labor-supported public officials to force them to yield to the union demand for cost-of-living protection.

It is too early to tell whether this tactic will spread. It is limited, however, by the need for an issue on which popular support can be mobilized—and a cost-of-living clause in an inflationary period seems to be one of the few such issues. Further, it must be a community in which labor is strong enough to mobilize sufficient support to make the granting of this demand tolerable to the majority of the electorate.

Another aspect of the effect of final-offer arbitration on the bargaining process is whether it brings the parties closer to settlement than does conventional arbitration. This involves an examination of such matters as whether the number of issues referred to arbitration in each case is smaller than under conventional arbitration. Also, of interest is whether the gap between the parties on the wage issue is less under final-offer than under conventional arbitration. Detailed statistics on these points are not yet at hand but preliminary analyses provide fuel for discussion.

Twenty-four arbitration awards had been published by April 1, 1974. In one case, the parties agreed to proceed by "Form 1" conventional arbitration, and presented 11 issues to the arbitrator for resolution. In the 23 final-offer arbitration cases, 7 involved only one issue (in 4 of these situations it was wages); and 1, 12 issues. Examinations of the awards suggests that final-offer arbitration persuades the parties to reduce the number of issues to be arbitrated. Interviews with the parties reinforce this impression. Most of the parties are aware that by holding out for some particular item, they may jeopardize their entire position.

In several of the multiple-issue disputes, arbitrators were faced with the dilemma to which Fred Whitney referred in his article about the Indianapolis final-offer arbitration experience.[5] The problem arises when an arbitrator is in agreement with one side on one major economic issue and with the other on an equally important noneconomic issue; or, alternatively, he believes that one issue is sufficiently important to deserve a ruling in favor of the party with the better position on this issue, despite its weaker position on several other issues. For example, one arbitrator stated that the union wage position was more equitable than that of management, but believed that the union demand for a maintenance of standards clause (the Wisconsin public sector euphemism for what is called a past-practice clause in the private sector) should not be granted. Economic considerations prevailed and he ruled in favor of the union, but made clear that he did not appreciate being forced to put a maintenance of standards clause into effect and wouldn't have done so if he had the power to modify final offers.

In another case, in which management was not offering full retroactivity, the arbitrator selected the management position because he believed that its position on contract duration should be upheld. In a third case, an arbitrator stated that management's position on economic issues was reasonable except for its refusal to grant retroactivity. Because the arbitrator thought that retroactivity was essential to the maintenance of a sound bargaining relationship, he ruled for the union. Despite these problems, however, most Wisconsin arbitrators have stated that they favor the continuance of final-offer arbitration in preference to a shift to conventional arbitration or final-offer on an issue by issue basis.

Several managements have expressed the fear, however, that they may lose important management rights in multiple issue cases which are decided on the basis of economic considerations. Several union winners in multiple-issue cases have claimed that in subsequent negotiations they have moderated their demands in order to improve relationships that may have been exacerbated by an award upholding their positions. In any event, this problem occurs only rarely. Of the 173 bargains for 1973 agreements concluded under the final-offer arbitration statute, only about three or four involved this multiple noncompatible issue dilemma. It seems, therefore, that any loss attributable to this aspect of the program may be far outweighed by this potentially greater deterrent from usage associated with final-offer arbitration compared to conventional arbitration.

Personal interviews with some parties indicate that most managements and unions continue to favor final-offer arbitration over conventional arbitration, although responses to written questionnaires suggest that there is a good deal of misunderstanding about the process on the part of individuals who have not yet been involved in it. As for any damage wrought by the winner-take-all aspects of the final-offer arbitration awards (and, by the way, the box score on this in Wisconsin stands 12 to 11 in favor of management) it has not caused either the winners or the losers to condemn the procedure on this ground, nor to suggest that it be replaced by conventional arbitration.

In conclusion, it is particularly important to note that there is some ambiguity in the Wisconsin statute and the parties are still jostling for position about such matters as when the final offer must be tendered and the latest time at which it can be amended. We have those who favor a relaxed interpretation of the statute in order to facilitate settlement by the parties or through mediation. Against this position, however, are aligned those who believe that the deterrent power of final-offer arbitration must be fully protected by a stricter interpretation which precludes amendments of offers subsequent to 5 days prior to the arbitration hearing.

NOTES

1. 1973 Wisconsin Stat. 111.70.
2. 1973 Wisconsin Stat. 111.77(4)(b).
3. Milwaukee policemen are covered by a separate provision under the statute providing for conventional arbitration of interest disputes, while the firefighters are covered by factfinding.
4. *Daily Labor Report* (Washington, Bureau of National Affairs), Feb. 1, 1963, p. F-2.
5. Fred Whitney, "Final-offer arbitration: The Indianapolis experience," *Monthly Labor Review*, May 1973, pp. 20-25.

AN EXPERIENTIAL EXERCISE:
Teachers' Fight Goes to Court

The County School Board adopted new policies in an effort to (1) improve the quality of reading instruction, and (2) provide a new exposure for school administrators to the problems teachers face every day. These policies were translated into two specific directives:

1. Order teachers to take reading courses.

2. Order administrators to teach classes for one week every three years.

The County Educators Association, which represents the county's 8500 school professionals, objected. They claimed that such directives were matters affecting working conditions that should be negotiated in the collective bargaining contract.

In an effort to block these directives, a series of grievances were filed in accordance with the established grievance procedure. The School Superintendent, Tom Crawford, turned down the grievances, and then the parties jointly hired an arbitrator to render a decision on the issues. However, before the arbitrator could render a decision, the County School Board obtained an injunction barring the arbitration process until there is a court ruling on the Board's right to issue such directives.

The School Board has asked the courts to determine which issues are educational policy matters that boards can rule on and which issues fall under the "working conditions" clause typically found in collective bargaining contracts.

THE ANALYSIS

This series of conflicts requires careful analysis, and these questions will assist you in framing some of the more critical aspects.

Question: Is this a grievance which should be handled routinely through the grievance procedure?

Question: What is the normal relationship of the courts to such matters?

Question: Are these working conditions?

THE CONSEQUENCE ANALYSIS

It is important to look at the possible consequences of decisions. And to utilize the customary "what if" questions:

1. What if the court rules that such educational policies can be differentiated from so-called working conditions? What are the consequences for:

> School board
> The union
> Teachers
> Administrators

2. What if the court rules that such issues are in fact working

conditions and must be handled within the framework of collective bargaining? What are the consequences for:

> School board
> The union
> Teachers
> Administrators

3. What if these issues polarize the parties and create a major conflict, i.e., a strike or slowdown? What are the consequences for:

> Students
> Parents
> School board
> The union
> Teachers
> Administrators

4. What if you were the judge? Write a decision and defend it in class.

EXPERIENTIAL EXERCISE

If you are interested in exploring these issues in greater depth in your community, invite a member of the school board, a school administrator, and a teachers' union representative to class. Discuss the issues.

Explore methods for appropriately resolving complex issues.

Examine the consequences if the conflict is not resolved.